TROPICAL RAINFOREST

TROPICAL RAINFOREST

Our Most Valuable and Endangered Habitat with a Blueprint for Its Survival into the Third Millennium

ARNOLD NEWMAN

Foreword by His Holiness the Dalai Lama
Introduction by Jane Goodall
Prologue by Robert Redford

Checkmark Books®
An imprint of Facts On File, Inc.

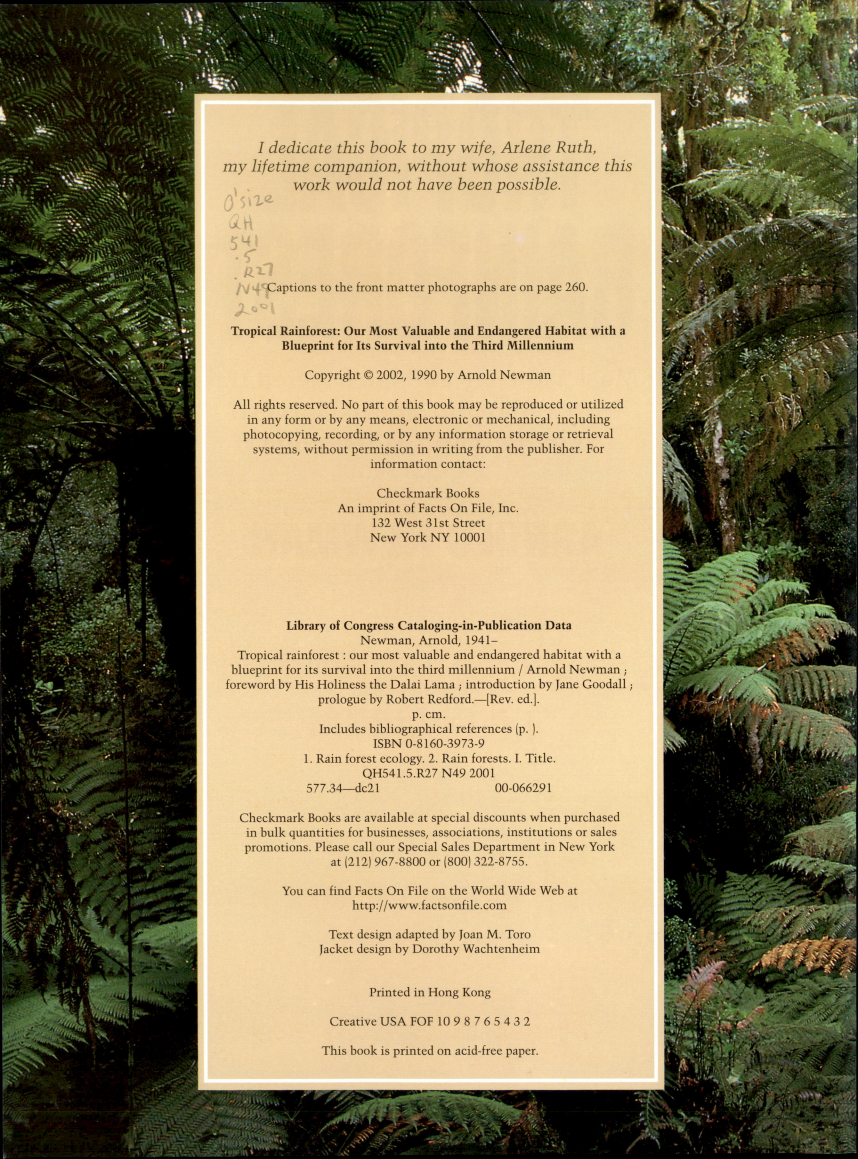

I dedicate this book to my wife, Arlene Ruth,
my lifetime companion, without whose assistance this
work would not have been possible.

O'size
QH
541
.5
.R27
N49
2001

Captions to the front matter photographs are on page 260.

Tropical Rainforest: Our Most Valuable and Endangered Habitat with a Blueprint for Its Survival into the Third Millennium

Checkmark Books
An imprint of Facts On File, Inc.
132 West 31st Street
New York NY 10001

Library of Congress Cataloging-in-Publication Data
Newman, Arnold, 1941–
Tropical rainforest : our most valuable and endangered habitat with a blueprint for its survival into the third millennium / Arnold Newman ; foreword by His Holiness the Dalai Lama ; introduction by Jane Goodall ; prologue by Robert Redford.—[Rev. ed.].
p. cm.
Includes bibliographical references (p.).
ISBN 0-8160-3973-9
1. Rain forest ecology. 2. Rain forests. I. Title.
QH541.5.R27 N49 2001
577.34—dc21   00-066291

Checkmark Books are available at special discounts when purchased in bulk quantities for businesses, associations, institutions or sales promotions. Please call our Special Sales Department in New York at (212) 967-8800 or (800) 322-8755.

You can find Facts On File on the World Wide Web at
http://www.factsonfile.com

Text design adapted by Joan M. Toro
Jacket design by Dorothy Wachtenheim

Printed in Hong Kong

Creative USA FOF 10 9 8 7 6 5 4 3 2

This book is printed on acid-free paper.

CONTENTS

FOREWORD

Nearly everywhere these days, our natural environment is degenerating. And yet it is the natural environment that sustains the life of all beings in the world. Therefore, it is more important than ever that we all make whatever effort we can, according to our own ability, to ensure the protection, restoration, and replenishment of our natural surroundings and their inhabitants.

A pure and unspoiled environment is beneficial for everyone. When the natural elements are in harmony, the quality and duration of life increase. For example, trees purify the air, providing oxygen for living beings to breathe. Their shade provides a refreshing place to rest. They contribute to timely rainfall, which nourishes crops and livestock, and balances the climate. They create an attractive landscape, pleasing to the eye and calming for the mind.

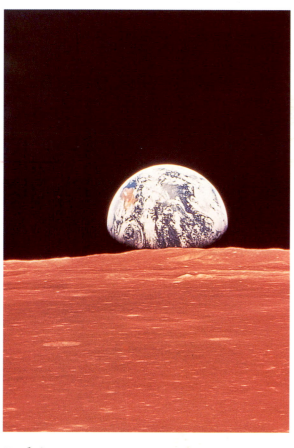

Earthrise

Many consider this the most transforming and compelling photographic image ever made. As seen by astronauts from the barren moonscape, the blue water planet, with its steady-state climate system, spawns storms to sustain the only life known in the lonely darkness of the cosmos. No other image or dialogue more eloquently transmits the crucial message: Spaceship Earth is the fertile, yet frail home of humanity and other diverse species; this complex, organized planet, integrated and interdependent, will maintain life, cost-free and in perpetuity—so long as we do not desecrate it by overriding or defiling its systems.

When the environment becomes damaged and polluted there are many negative consequences. Oceans and lakes lose their cool and soothing qualities so the creatures depending on them are disturbed. The decline of vegetation and forest cover causes the Earth's bounty to decline. Rain no longer falls when required, the soil dries and erodes, forest fires rage and unprecedented storms arise. We all suffer the consequences.

Resolving the present environmental crisis is not just a question of ethics but a question of our own survival. The natural environment is essential not only for those of us alive now, but also, and more so, for future generations. If we exploit it in extreme ways, even though we may get money or other benefits from it now, in the long run we ourselves and future generations will suffer. Such abuse arises out of shortsightedness and ignorance of the environment's importance. It is very important to help people understand this. We need to teach that the environment has a direct bearing on our own benefit.

It is in this context that Arnold Newman's beautiful book *Tropical Rainforest: Our Most Valuable and Endangered Habitat with a Blueprint for its Survival into the Third Millennium* is so valuable. The book not only allows the reader to appreciate the breathtaking beauty of the tropical rainforest and the rich variety of life within it, but also how it directly influences all our lives in many ways. I am reminded of the tragedy that has similarly overtaken my own homeland, Tibet, and the Himalayan region, where clear-cutting of forests has led to devastating consequences with soil erosion and flooding throughout South and East Asia.

I am confident that this book will inspire readers to contribute in many ways to preserving the tropical rainforest in order to help save our Earth. It is my hope and prayer that through understanding the interdependence of the environment and all the beings who live in it, people will adapt their behavior in ways that will allow the potential of our bounteous natural realm to be nurtured and preserved in order that all sentient beings may live out their lives in peace and happiness.

The Dalai Lama

INTRODUCTION

This is a beautiful book, grand in scope and gloriously illustrated. It is written from a vast fund of firsthand knowledge. It is truly a celebration of the magnificent and awe-inspiring variety of plant and animal life that exists in the rainforests of the world, much of it even now unknown to science.

I share with Arnold Newman his passionate love of the forest. I agonize over the terrifying rate at which the tropical moist forests of the world are vanishing—some 36 million acres a year. And I am only too well aware of the very real threat to the future well-being of our life on planet Earth if this destruction continues unabated.

There is one question that I am asked again and again as I travel around the globe: "Do you really believe there is any hope for the future?" I believe there is, despite the terrifying number of human beings, despite the shocking greed of the affluent societies around the world, despite the destruction and the pollution and the despair. My hope is derived from the problem-solving ability of the human brain; the resilience of nature when given a chance; the energy and dedication of those who understand problems and are empowered to act, especially youth; and the indomitable nature of the human spirit: the ability to persevere in the face of seemingly hopeless odds.

This book offers yet another ray of hope—for its author also has hope. Despite the daunting facts concerning human degradation of the forests, he still believes that dedicated, informed, and passionate individuals can halt, at least in some instances, the tide of destruction. And he shows, by example, that this can be done. This in turn will inspire others to join the groundswell of those forewarnings and take informed action.

Thank you, Arnold Newman, for giving us this beautiful volume, for enhancing our understanding, for increasing our sense of wonder, for encouraging us to become fervently committed and involved in saving the forests of the world for our children and grandchildren.

Jane Goodall, Ph.D.
Director of the Jane Goodall Institute
for Wildlife Research,
Education and Conservation
Author, *Reason for Hope*

The heart of the forest
Stunning aerial view of a mangrove forest on the island of New Caledonia. The heart formation is not humanmade but occurred naturally, as mangroves require brackish or saltwater contact at all times and the sandy, heart-shaped area rises above the water table—a botanical explanation which in no way diminishes the grandeur of this inspirational image.

Prologue

It is said that tropical rainforests could well be considered a womb of creation, and that there is more life per square inch of a rainforest than anywhere else on Earth, or surely beyond. When you think about the profundity of this it is almost overwhelming. To imagine losing any part of this is almost unthinkable.

However, the wholesale destruction of these places has had a tremendous impact on how Earth itself functions. And when you consider that we've lost more than half of these forests in the last 60 years, a call to action is clearly in order. By some estimates, tropical deforestation has contributed an alarming 27 percent to global warming and yet, it continues. Some 50 percent of all medicines are derived from the rainforest, yet humanity may be deprived of further discoveries and possible cures if we allow continued disruption and ruin.

Arnold Newman has done humanity a great service in his comprehensive documentation of the incomparable wonder and profound significance of the tropical forests and their place in the global life cycle. As we revel in both their magic and importance, it is almost inconceivable to imagine a world without them. This, I feel is one of the book's greatest contributions because with it may come the empowerment we, the people, will need to reverse the course we're on.

The book's blueprint for the survival of these necessary "organisms" gives me more than a cautious hope that the world citizenry will prevail for the generations that will follow us, and those that will follow them.

Robert Redford

AUTHOR'S ACKNOWLEDGMENTS

A book of global scope, encompassing many disciplines, evolves only through the assistance of a great many people, equally concerned with the issues addressed here.

Although it is impossible to note them all, my special thanks go to the late Professor Emeritus Mildred Mathias (1906–95), Department of Botany, University of California, Los Angeles, the very matriarch of the tropical forests; the late Charles Hogue (1935–92), a remarkable tropical entomologist and senior curator at the Los Angeles County Museum of Natural History; Andrew Starrett, Department of Botany, University of California, Northridge, and Robert Bailey, Department of Anthropology, University of California, Los Angeles, for their invaluable contributions in editing and expertise.

My appreciation goes to my wife, Arlene Ruth, for years of service toward this project's completion, and to our children, Gandhi and Shanti, for their assistance in the field in the tropical forests on many occasions and long hours of computer work on research and graphics; to the National Geographic Society for its support of me in the African and Asian forests and their generosity toward production aspects of this volume; to the many governments who have facilitated my work and travel in the tropics; to the splendid people of Facts On File, especially project editor Dorothy Cummings, for the meticulous expertise in the rebirth of this edition; for assistance in the prodigious research necessary for this second edition as well as editing and proofreading by the following stalwarts: Joan Larimore, Birgitte Rasine, Michael Regimbal, Karrie King, Beckie Jas, Pei-Hsuan Wu, Maggie Loo, Laurie Gates, Eileen Wedel, Erin Gorospe, and to Luba Ortoleva for her considerable talents; to the countless tribal people of the tropical forests who unselfishly assisted me, instructed me in their ways and the rhythms of the deep forest, and enabled me to see this awesome spectacle through their eyes.

This book is written in the memory of my mother, Johanna Helen (1915–85), and my father, Joseph (1906–89), who raised me to see all nature as a celebration of life.

Preface

*Never doubt that a small group of thoughtful
committed citizens can change the world; indeed,
it is the only thing that ever has.*
—Margaret Mead

From the very moment I first entered a tropical rainforest in the remote Sierra de la Macarena of Colombia in 1965, I was transformed as by an epiphany. Immersed in the womb of creation, I was overwhelmed by the magnificence of the experience. To this day that remarkable awakening continues to resonate and is renewed with every exploration since. It was a different world then, and the phrases *tropical deforestation* and *biodiversity* had not yet been coined. As I revisited the forest areas of my previous fieldwork, I became witness to the growing habitat holocaust and, by the close of the 1960s, I had resolved to write this book—how could I not have?

When the first edition was published in 1990, the issues of tropical deforestation were just becoming widely known. As the world tentatively takes its first baby step into the 21st century, there has been huge transformation in the tropical forest arena and much to report in this revised edition. The good news—and it is crystal clear—is that the tropical forests, their fate, and global effects of this destruction, have, at long glorious last, finally captivated the world's attention. This is an indelible prerequisite to solutions. A new rainforest action group is established every 10 days or so in the United States alone. The bad news is that the destruction has been amplified over the last three decades—more than tripling since the 1960s. As I write this, cataclysmic fires caused by slash-and-burn agribusiness activities and exacerbated by drought have resulted in the incineration of vast areas of virgin rainforests in Latin America and Asia—an insidious phenomenon visible from space and previously thought impossible.

As a result of these mixed fortunes, those of us who will play out the drama of our lives in the new millennium are presented with the rarest of opportunities to favorably effect the most compelling magnitude of change in the history of Earth—the chance to play a part in preserving the singularly most wondrous spectacle of life on our splendid planet! I invite those up to the challenge to step forward and be counted, for it will surely require a critical mass, nothing short of an *environmental revolution*, to overcome the growing momentum of exploitation at work in these forests.

Today, few lands remain unexplored. Yet we still know surprisingly little about the terra incognita of the vast equatorial rainforests, which broodingly retain their secrets. This exuberant pantheon contains almost half of Earth's forests and 65 percent of global forest vegetation, qualifying it as the largest terrestrial biomass. Inch for inch, it maintains more life than the productive oceanic kelp beds, coral reefs, or African savannas. Given that the tropical forests cover only 6 percent of Earth's land surface, yet shelter up to an estimated 100 million species—as much as 90 percent of our planet's total (Erwin, in Swerdlow 1999)—the reader will see how our lives are immensely enriched by these forests. There is a significant irony in the fact that we can measure the distance from Earth to the Moon to within 0.2 inches (0.5 cm) but have identified perhaps less than 2 percent of our species!

Yet even as we are discovering the mystique, lure, and value of this exotic habitat, this cornucopia of Eden is dying. Instead of viewing tropical forests as a sustainable font of products, medicines, and information, as well as a source of wonder, the insatiable and escalating demands of industrialized nations for raw materials, compounded by grossly wasteful agricultural practices in developing tropical countries, are resulting in the cutting of 69 acres (28 ha) of tropical moist forest globally every minute of every day. Outsized machines and armies of chain saws remove or degrade 56,462 square miles (146,225 sq km) of forest annually—an area larger than the kingdom of Nepal. It may be easier to comprehend this tragic reality if it is expressed in another way: In tropical moist forests globally, more than 16 million trees are felled daily! Some 54 percent of tropical forests have disappeared since 1945. With the destruction now proceeding at a faster rate than that of any other habitat, the tropical rainforest will be virtually extinct by the end of the first third of the 21st century! I do hope you find within these pages a source of wonder for these forests, one that would compel every reader to question, Doesn't it benefit us to protect what protects us?

The implications of tropical deforestation are so manifold and provocative that the global scientific and environmental community has variously described it as "the greatest natural calamity since the ice age," "the greatest biological disaster ever perpetuated by man," and "a threat to civilization second only to thermonuclear war." At present, a respected scientific consensus conservatively estimates six species per hour, 137 per day, and 50,000 per year fall to extinction in the tropical forests. With 20/20 hindsight we can extrapolate that we have lost millions of species to date, the very fabric of life. Unless concerted mitigative action is taken, it is expected that more than 1 million additional species, as well as the last of the primeval tribes, will disappear forever from the face of the Earth in the coming decade. It will be our action—or inaction—within this crucial time period that will dictate success or failure as *it is speculated that shortly thereafter, the future in these diverse issues will have been determined irrevocably.*

As we await an eloquently expressed appreciation for the "Temple of Flora" to fully germinate and come to bloom, tropical deforestation and the burning of fossil fuels have resulted in the now well-recognized "greenhouse effect," the cause of global warming. In 1990, when these concepts were reported in the first edition, the phenomenon was still considered controversial. Thankfully, that is, for the most part, no longer the case. The 2001 report from the 2,000 scientists of the Intergovernmental Panel on Climate Change has unequivocally stated the following: there has indeed been a discernible human influence on global climate contributing substantially to the observed warming over the last 50 years; temperatures are rising and over the next hundred years the change will be greater than any that has occurred in the last 10,000 years, the period over which civilization developed; the planet's ice caps are melting and sea level is rising—an increase of up to 37 inches (95 cm) is expected over the next century—all with "a risk of devastating consequences within this century," in the words of Michael Oppenheimer, atmospheric physicist and coauthor of the report.

We have now surpassed our 6 billionth soul. We can far too easily project the calamitous collision of orbits of projected global population increase, with falling agricultural production due to global warming and loss of fertility due to tropical deforestation to embrace the vivid concerns of these 2,000 respected scientists. Is there something here that reminds us of a 1950s science fiction movie? Well, every one of us now has a bit part in what is now a hovering reality. How is it going to play out? No issue has ever been a more global concern and responsibility, yet as it is one that involves virtually every nation, both developing and developed, it has defied a legally binding political response. As we come to learn that ours is not a disposable planet, and that our resources have quantifiable limits, a new global conservation ethic has never been more urgently essential.

Humanity has reached perhaps its most important crossroads. Which road will we choose to avoid the bleak futures prophesied by the scientists of so varied disciplines as meteorology, forestry, oceanography, glaciology, public health, and industry specialists in emissions, insurance, and more. All conclude in a consensus of more than 3,000 professionals that unless something meaningful is done to address tropical deforestation, which currently contributes a significant 27 percent to global warming, the road ahead will be as rough as our species has yet traveled in its brief history. Knowing that our world is far more than the sum of its potential commodities, let us work to meet the challenges and make the necessary sacrifices to rebuild the myriad frayed synapses between humankind and its original womb, the natural world.

This book, however, is not a doomsday oracle, but a blueprint of significant hope and opportunity. Viable solutions at our disposal are coalesced in this volume, many resulting from the cutting edge of research and current attention to the dire need to address sustainable development. The critical mass of broad, enthusiastic public response to the issues and their solutions will hopefully ensure that the appropriate technologies and mitigating factors are flown into the tropical developing world on the wings of sufficient global budgeting. Many question how we can afford the high price of stabilizing the tropical forest biome while ushering in a millennial enlightenment of sustained agriculture and timber extraction which will affect forest tribal people's survival as well as the species we share this planet with. I would ask, "How can we afford *not* to?" This book is addressed to that rarest of opportunities by clearly demonstrating that the potentially bleak and unacceptable consequences of humanity's current activities may yet be affordably avoided. If ever there was a time for humankind to cast away its daily trappings and adorn itself for battle, it is now! I urge you to read on and grasp this auspicious opportunity—nothing less than effecting the preservation of creation itself!

1

WHAT IS A TROPICAL RAINFOREST?

The land is one great, wild, untidy, luxuriant hothouse, made by Nature for herself. . . . How great would be the desire in every admirer of Nature to behold, if such were possible, the scenery of another planet! . . . Yet to every person . . it may truly be said, . . . that the glories of another world are opened to him.

CHARLES DARWIN
From *The Voyage of the Beagle,* when first he experienced the tropical rainforest a century and a half ago.

This panoramic view of the rainforest interior portrays the baffling array of species and forms that awaits the inquisitive visitor. [Puracé National Park, Colombian Andes.]

The most beautiful thing we can experience is the mysterious . . . the source of all true art and science.

ALBERT EINSTEIN

▲ *Exploration and discovery—parting the fronds of the Malaysian sealing wax palm* (Cyrtostachys lakka), *the author's son, Gandhi, beholds its blazing scarlet crown shaft.*

On October 28, 1492, Christopher Columbus gave the first known written description of a tropical rainforest when he reported to King Ferdinand and Queen Isabella, "Never [have I] beheld so fair a thing; trees beautiful and green, and different from ours, with flowers and fruits each according to their kind; many birds, and little birds which sing very sweetly." When he realized he had not found the Indies, the great navigator decided he must have discovered the Garden of Eden.

We commonly refer to tropical rainforest as "jungle," a name derived from the Sanskrit word *jangala*, which actually means "desert." This confusion has its history, in turn, in colonial India and Persia, where dry, impenetrable scrub brush and low trees were by this time called *djanghael*. British sportsmen of that era found the word jungle easier to pronounce, and more to their liking, and carried it over to include the tall tropical wet forest, which we will see is not a difficult tangle of vegetation at all. But the word *jungle*, with Rudyard Kipling's help, struck the imagination and stayed with us.

Scientific literature has generally preferred the more accurately defined term *tropical rainforest*, which derives from the German *tropische Regenwald*, after A. F. W. Schimper's early classical work *Plant Geography* (1898, 1903). Scientists of the day also used the word *Urwald*, meaning "original" or "primitive" forest, and this was the genesis of the graphic term "primeval rainforest." The heartthrob of the botanical kingdom is also variously referred to as "equatorial rainforest" and with precision, "tropical wet closed broad-leaved evergreen forest."

As you approach the forest from a road cut or riverbank, you face an impenetrable solid mass of towering vegetation. This outside barrier, known as the "wall effect," is approximately 20 feet (6.1 m) thick and is compacted with a tangle of light-hungry vines and climbers. Faced by this intimidating fortification, most people would assume that the interior is just as dense and would require the use of a chain saw to move in any direction. But the wall effect is deceptive. To pierce directly through this armor would require rigorous machete work, but the initiated can usually find an animal trail or stream to follow, and thus slip through the "curtain." We may now penetrate the interior of the "terrestrial sea," the very heart of darkness, and explore a realm of natural prehistory.

ENTER THE INTERIOR

Quite suddenly, you find yourself inside a majestic basilica, the height of a seventeen-story building. You are immediately dwarfed (perhaps relegated to proper size) by the sheer immensity of the biomass. Your senses are assailed by the thick, pungent scent of life, and its partner, decay. The aromas of this forest are so vibrant they seem audible—not malodorous but somehow intoxicating. You breathe cautiously at first, then inhale by the lungful.

Your eyes take a few moments to adjust to this world of perpetual twilight. The sun's rays pierce the verdant green leaves like the stained glass of a cathedral, generating a resplendent emerald green aura, a subdued fire whose tranquilizing effect lasts for some time even after leaving the forest. Against this background flash such brilliant phenomena as the huge *Morpho* butterfly, flapping its electric-blue wings in a mesmerizing strobe effect, and pendulous scarlet *Heliconia* flower chains 8 feet (2.4 m) long, ignited in a twilight world by swordlike shafts of light. The Sun creates mobile mosaics on the forest floor.

The tallest trees tower to a height of perhaps 200 feet (60 m), averaging around 120 feet (37 m), and below these giants are as many as five tiers of straight-trunked trees that refrain from branching until their umbrella heads finally find their own available space in the strata.

The upper layer, often difficult to see from the forest floor, consists of the scattered giant monoliths called emergent trees, that tower over the canopy. In Borneo, an outstanding specimen of tualang (*Koompassia excelsa*) has been recorded at a height of 282 feet (86 m), and a klinki pine (*Araucaria hunsteinii*) in New Guinea at 292 feet (89 m) (Richards 1996). It is not uncommon for the expansive umbrella crown of a massive emergent tree to spread over an entire acre (0.4 ha).

The bases of the medium- and larger-size trees very often send out immense flying, snake, or plank buttresses from a height of 20 to 30 feet

▼ *A formidable wall of light-loving photophytic vegetation seals the more spacious forest interior from view. This formation, typical of the lowland rainforest edge, fits the common idea of "jungle" and creates the intimidating illusion that the entire forest is of similar density. [Tortuguero, Costa Rica.]*

African Forest Strata

In the layered world of the forest, individual species find sustenance, safety, in some cases dominance, in their own specialized niches. Plants and animals often occupy specific strata, each with its own climate, while others are generalists, feeding wherever opportunities present themselves.

Yellow-casqued hornbill
Ceratogymna elata

Collared sunbird
Anthreptes collaris

African gray parrot
Psittacus erithacus

African giant swallowtail
Papilio antimachus

Blue fairy flycatcher
Erannornis longicauda

Golden cat
Felis aurata

Golden potto
Arctocebus calabarensis

Four-striped squirrel
Funisciurus lemniscatus

Chimpanzee
Pan troglodytes

Chequered elephant-shrew
Rhynchocyon cirnei

Leopard
Panthera pardus

Giant snail
Achatina sp.

Goliath frog
Rana goliath

Okapi
Okapia johnstoni

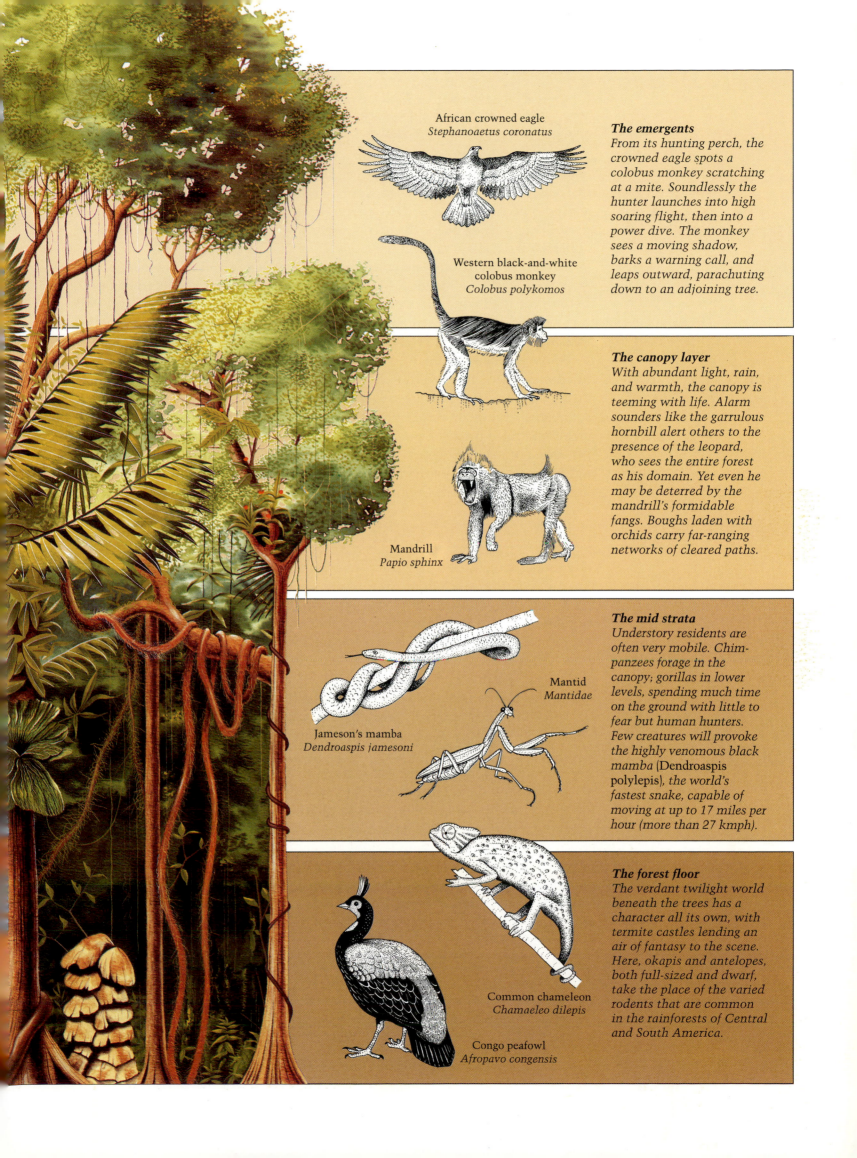

The emergents

African crowned eagle
Stephanoaetus coronatus

From its hunting perch, the crowned eagle spots a colobus monkey scratching at a mite. Soundlessly the hunter launches into high soaring flight, then into a power dive. The monkey sees a moving shadow, barks a warning call, and leaps outward, parachuting down to an adjoining tree.

Western black-and-white colobus monkey
Colobus polykomos

The canopy layer

With abundant light, rain, and warmth, the canopy is teeming with life. Alarm sounders like the garrulous hornbill alert others to the presence of the leopard, who sees the entire forest as his domain. Yet even he may be deterred by the mandrill's formidable fangs. Boughs laden with orchids carry far-ranging networks of cleared paths.

Mandrill
Papio sphinx

The mid strata

Understory residents are often very mobile. Chimpanzees forage in the canopy; gorillas in lower levels, spending much time on the ground with little to fear but human hunters. Few creatures will provoke the highly venomous black mamba (Dendroaspis polylepis), the world's fastest snake, capable of moving at up to 17 miles per hour (more than 27 kmph).

Jameson's mamba
Dendroaspis jamesoni

Mantid
Mantidae

The forest floor

The verdant twilight world beneath the trees has a character all its own, with termite castles lending an air of fantasy to the scene. Here, okapis and antelopes, both full-sized and dwarf, take the place of the varied rodents that are common in the rainforests of Central and South America.

Common chameleon
Chamaeleo dilepis

Congo peafowl
Afropavo congensis

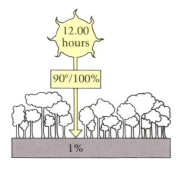

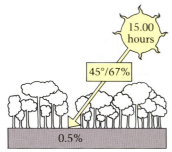

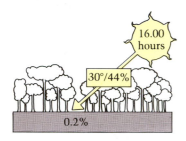

▲ *The multitiered closed canopy absorbs light with astonishing effectiveness. Using noon as a 100 percent value for light intensity above the canopy, by 4 P.M. on a cloudless day only 0.2 percent of the light will reach the forest floor. The light of a full moon is not even perceived here. Stepping from the interior into full sunlight can be a dazzling experience.*

(6.1–9.1 m) up the trunk. These sinuous, winglike flanges of high-tensile-strength wood help stabilize the top-heavy trees during the frequent gale-force winds and occasional hurricanes and tornadoes that lash the canopy. The characteristics of this extraordinary "tension wood" are not lost on certain indigenous forest peoples who press their bodies against a buttress wing then hit it with their fists or with a wooden club. The resulting percussions resonate through the body. Face to face with a monolithic wall of magnificently sculpted wood, I invariably take pause in a blissful artistic appraisal.

The heads of the trees are bound together by woody vines known as lianas, some approaching 800 feet (244 m) long, and this further serves to stabilize them in the high winds that sweep over the crowns. (Some species of vine coil to the left in the Northern Hemisphere and to the right in the Southern, to make best use of the Sun's rays.)

Below the canopy, visibility is usually good for 50 feet (15 m), and often much more. Due to the dim light, which averages less than 1 percent of that falling on the canopy above, vegetation is relatively sparse at ground level. Conceivably, you could ride a bicycle through the forest, although this is not a recommended mode of travel. In the interior of the rainforest, a machete is unnecessary for movement—but very useful for marking your trail. This is highly recommended as the forest interior is so bewitching that it can easily disorient even the most experienced forest explorer.

THE LAND OF THE GIANT LIFE-FORMS

The forest interior is a magical and mercurial place—an enchanted realm where anything is possible. Wandering an unknown planet full of strange life-forms could not be more stimulating; indeed, such an image is an apt metaphor for the tropical rainforest experience. Everything appears to grow out of proportion. Families and other taxa that in other habitats are small, grow here as if they were outsized mutants. Woodiness, a predominant feature of the vegetation, allows for part, but not all, of this gigantism. The parade of species reads like a catalog of the inconceivable. Grass in the form of bamboo grows 100 feet (30 m) high, at the rate of 47.6 inches (121 cm) in 24 hours. That's 0.00003 miles per hour (0.00005 kmph)! There are "roses" with 145-foot (44-m) trunks; daisies and violets as big as apple trees; 60-foot (18-m) tree ferns with some of the hardest wood to be found; 32 foot, 9 1/2 inch (10 m) constricting snakes, the goliath bird-eating spider with an 11-inch (28-cm) leg span, and lily pads 7 feet (2 m) in diameter which can support a child's weight. The parasite *Rafflesia* boasts the world's largest flower—38 inches (97 cm) across, weighing 38 pounds (17.2 kg), and holding several gallons of liquid in its nectaries. Here too are basilisk lizards that actually run on the surface of water; bats with 5.5-foot (1.7-m) wingspans; vining rattan palms with 785-foot (240-m) trunks; 18-foot (5.5-m) cobras; moths with 12-inch (30-cm) wingspans; frogs so big they eat rats, and rodents themselves weighing over 120 pounds (54 kg).

The rainforest is our planet's most astounding expression of life, the very womb of creation. Here, a single hectare (2.47 acres) may contain 42,000 different species of insect, up to 807 trees (more than 4 inches or 10 cm diameter at breast height) of 313 species and 1,500 species of higher plants (Richards 1996). Try to imagine, if you can, that a single tree was found to contain 54 species of ant, more than recorded in the entire British Isles. There is a greater diversity of plant and animal species in the rainforests of the small nation of Panama than exists in the entire continent of Europe. Two-thirds of all flowering plants are found in the tropical forests where climate and the numerous niches represented in the varied strata of the forest architecture are the key to this phenomenal diversity.

DEFINING A TROPICAL RAINFOREST

It may seem difficult to assign specific parameters to so unrestrained a habitat as tropical rainforest, especially since one forest type often merges gradually into another. Yet such a definition has evolved out of botanical consensus. Schimper's definition, largely unchallenged to this day, states that the lowland rainforest formation is "evergreen, hygrophilous in character [flourishing in perhumid dampness], at least 98 feet (30 m) high, but usually

▲◀ *The strangler fig* (Ficus sp.) *is a huge predatory hemiepiphyte which often begins life when a seed is deposited in a bird's droppings on the branch of a host tree. Germinating there, it drops numerous air roots until they make contact with the ground. Access to an abundant supply of water and nutrients then enables the fig to grow into a full-sized tree, which eventually consumes its host and sometimes neighboring trees as well. [Yala National Park, Sri Lanka.]*

◀ *Like the carnivores after which they are named, wolf spiders like this 4-inch (10-cm) leg-span species from Costa Rica run down their prey instead of spinning a web—so keen eyesight is an essential asset. Their nemesis, the hunting wasp, will pursue a spider, then paralyze it, and lay its eggs on the helpless animal, leaving them to hatch into larvae which will eat the spider alive.*

◀ *Shanti Newman with a huge rococo toad (Bufo paracnemis), protected from predators by toxins secreted by glands at the base of its head, and by its ability to inflate its body by gulping air. [Argentina.]*

▲ *Gandhi Newman has no fear of this mass of Lepidopterous caterpillars, but their colors and platoon behavior signal danger to potential predators. [Petén Forest, Guatemala.]*

▼ *Typifying gigantism, and dwarfing Shanti, the Amazon Basin's royal water lily (Victoria amazonica) spreads 7-feet (2-m) leaves on air-filled ribs that produce enough buoyancy to support a child's weight. Red spiny edges deter most herbivores. These quiet oxbow lakes on the Amazon are a favored habitat of piranhas (Pygocentrus spp.) whose predatory habits may provide a further measure of protection to this elegant Amazonian species.*

▶ *The dramatic buttresses
of rainforest trees serve as
supports—stabilizing the
tall, shallow-rooted trees
when tropical gales lash
the canopy. [Osa Peninsula,
Costa Rica.]*

▼ *Author and son examine
a thick woody vine rising
from the forest floor on
Peucang Is, Udjung Kulon
National Park, Indonesia.*

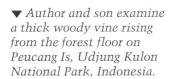

much taller, rich in thick-stemmed lianes [vines] and in woody as well as herbaceous epiphytes." (I would add to this the dominant characteristic of tree buttressing, which we will examine later.)

Lowland tropical rainforest is further characterized by its precipitation. Here, annual rainfall will never be less than 67 inches (170 cm) (Richards 1996) and may even exceed 300 inches (762 cm). Totals of 24 to 27 *feet* (732 to 823 cm) have been recorded in the Chocó of Colombia. The worldwide annual average for tropical rainforests is roughly 92 inches (234 cm). These forests are incredibly wet, but just as important, their rainfall is without long disruption throughout the year. So another criterion for a tropical rainforest is that it must receive at least 4 inches (10 cm) of rain each drought month (fewer than four consecutive months) for two out of three years.

Tropical rainforest requires a mean temperature of at least 64°F (18°C) and must be essentially frost free. Conditions are so constant inside the forest that it has been compared to a laboratory culture-growth room.

Where Are the Tropical Forests?

In historical times (postglacial) tropical moist forests, which include tropical rainforest and cloud forest (closed broadleaved evergreen) and tropical moist forest with short dry season (closed broadleaved semi-deciduous—i.e., monsoon forest), clothed some 9,653,000 square miles (25,000,000 sq km) (Terborgh 1993) of the humid equatorial belt lying between the Tropic of Cancer and the Tropic of Capricorn (23.5 degrees north and south of the equator). Since 1950, 54 percent have been removed at an accelerating pace. Today approximately 4,447,150 square miles (11,517,320 sq km) remain, still covering 6 percent of Earth's land surface in three major areas of the Americas, Africa, and Asia.

The largest of these areas are the American or neotropical forests of the Caribbean, Mexico, and Central and South America, which on the eastern side of the northern Andes begin Earth's largest tropical forest mass, the Amazon Hylaea. (*Hylaea*, an antiquated Greek term meaning "forest," was used by early explorer Alexander von Humboldt, and now refers specifically to this great, expansive forest.) Amazônia is bordered by the geological formation called the pre-Cambrian Shield, consisting of the Guiana Shield to the north and the Brazilian Shield to the south. In this botanical "heartland" of our planet, a man could descend the Andes foothills, enter the Amazon forest, and walk for 2,000 miles (3,218 km) before again seeing the sun directly as he reaches the Atlantic. Altogether, 1,678 million acres (679 million ha) remain of these American tropical forests.

The second most extensive block remains in Africa, Madagascar (Malagasy Republic) and environs. The largest expanse covers central and west Africa with the Congo River flowing through this "heart of darkness." Dominated by the Democratic Republic of the Congo (Zaire), it includes the Ituri Forest, and next to the Amazon is the world's largest contiguous tropical moist forest. Altogether the extant tropical moist forests in Africa total 591 million acres (239 million ha).

The now least extensive block of tropical moist forest is that comprising the Indo-Malayan Pacific forests, which include New Guinea. All told, these Asian forests total 576 million acres (233 million ha).

150 million years ago

105 million years ago

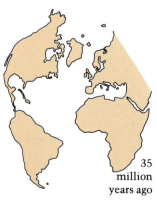

35 million years ago

▲ *Plate tectonics, the movement of huge "rafts" of Earth's crust by convection currents in the molten rock below, led to the breakup of the vast, ancient supercontinent of Pangaea; the process is still at work today.*

THE WOMB OF THE EARTH

These prolific wombs of life hold the largest biomass of any terrestrial habitat. By far the planet's richest environment, aside from regional climatic fluctuations they have remained basically unchanged since prehistoric times. We can move through them with awe and know what it was like to walk the Earth's lush wilderness of 70 million years ago. They have served as the planet's major gene pool, constantly evolving new microorganisms, insects, fish, birds, and mammals to fill gaps in an ever-changing world. It was here, only 136 million years ago during the early Cretaceous period, that the flowering plants evolved and spread over the surface of our planet (Richards 1996). One of Earth's most ancient ecosystems, the tropical rainforest has been our Garden of Eden—a veritable cornucopia of life. Far from stagnant in its creativity, one aspect of the forest's history has been constant, and that is its capacity for change.

The forest mass contracts and expands in response to glaciation, tectonic plate movements, and other long-term dynamic phenomena that we are only now beginning to understand. New species have evolved in response to changing conditions, phasing out less adaptive life-forms. Yet the tropical rainforests around the world conform so closely in their structure, and in their parallel evolution of species, that if a lay person were blindfolded and parachuted into one of the tropical rainforests of the world he would find it very difficult to determine on which continent he had landed. Even serious nature students might take time ferreting out clues to their location. General similarities include giant, smooth-barked buttressed trees with similar laurel-like leaves, complete with drip-tips; a profusion of palms, spiny and unarmed, with climbing, vining species on several continents, such as rattan (*Calamus*) in the Old World and *Desmoncus* in the New. *Philodendron* exists in tropical America and the perplexingly similar, though unrelated, *Epipremnum* in Eastern Hemisphere tropical forests. In the New World, boas (Boidae) dominate; in the Old World, it is the pythons (Pythonidae). Jaguars (*Panthera onca*) are king in the New World forests; while leopards (*Panthera pardus*) rule in the Old World. Tapirs occur in both hemispheres, and vipers of different species are distributed throughout. These convergences and coevolutionary adaptations penetrate so deeply into the biological fabric that although rattlesnakes occur only in the Americas, in both Old and New Worlds other snakes—both harmless and venomous—rapidly vibrate their tails in dry leaves to produce exactly the same alarming sound: similar niches filled by similar yet unrelated fauna and flora—a recurring theme in the natural world.

Ultimately, the botanist could determine his location, at least to the proper continent. He might recognize bromeliads as basically neotropical, with the unsettling exception of one West African species (*Pitcairnia feliciana*), or staghorn ferns as Old World, despite a similar problem with an inexplicable Peruvian species (*Platycerium andinum*). The zoologist might know the gharial (*Gavialis gangeticus*) as an Indian crocodilian, provided he could distinguish it from its look-alike, the false gavial (*Tomistoma schlegeli*) of Borneo. He might also know the hornbills (Bucerotidae) of Asia and Africa from the toucans (Ramphastidae) of South and Central America.

Although many regions, now separated, were once connected and thus exposed to exchanges of species, it is a matter of great fascination to science that similar niches on different continents have been filled by species quite

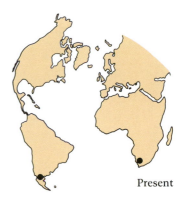

Present

▲ *We now have proof that continents that today are widely separated were joined in the geological past. Remains of the freshwater aquatic reptile* Mesosaurus brasiliensis *have been found in identical 250-million-year-old rocks (•) where southeast Brazil joined southwest Africa in the Pennsylvanian Period.*

DEFINING A TROPICAL RAINFOREST

The luxuriant and species-rich lowland equatorial rainforests are a product of unvarying warmth and moisture. Here, foliage is lush and often leathery, lianas and other typically herbaceous plants are commonly woody, and epiphytes abound in a truly magnificent "temple of flora."

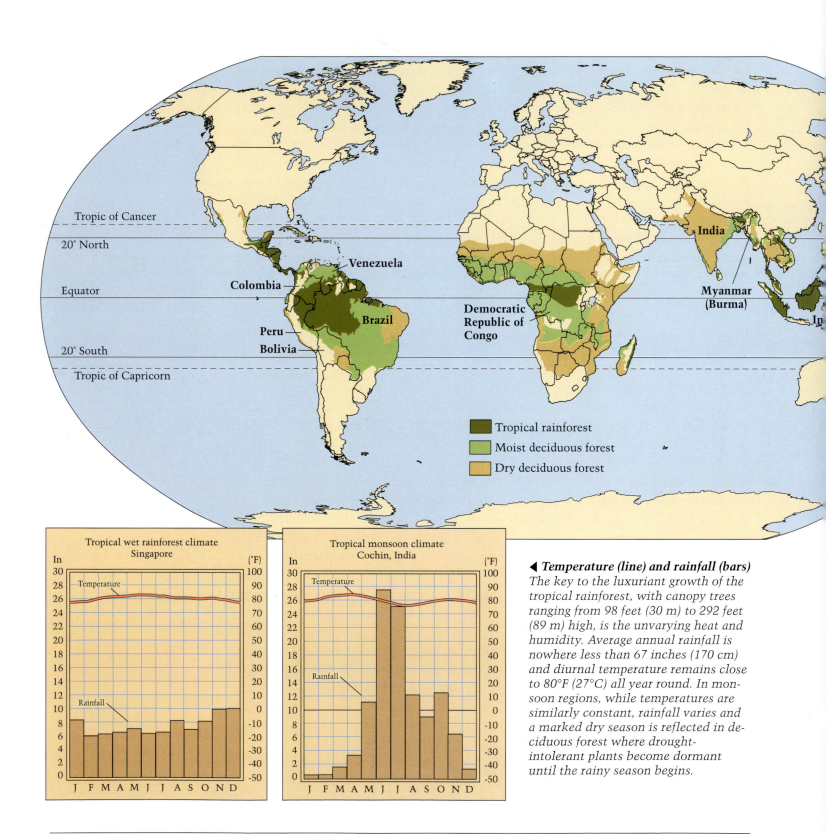

Tropical rainforest

Moist deciduous forest

Dry deciduous forest

Tropical wet rainforest climate
Singapore

Tropical monsoon climate
Cochin, India

◀ *Temperature (line) and rainfall (bars)* *The key to the luxuriant growth of the tropical rainforest, with canopy trees ranging from 98 feet (30 m) to 292 feet (89 m) high, is the unvarying heat and humidity. Average annual rainfall is nowhere less than 67 inches (170 cm) and diurnal temperature remains close to 80°F (27°C) all year round. In monsoon regions, while temperatures are similarly constant, rainfall varies and a marked dry season is reflected in deciduous forest where drought-intolerant plants become dormant until the rainy season begins.*

| Country | National area | | Tropical moist forests | | | | % world |
	Sq mi	Sq km	1980		1990		total
Brazil	3,286,727	8,511,965	1,725,550	4,468,830	1,632,910	4,228,910	36.72
Indonesia	735,057	1,903,650	467,418	1,210,520	421,029	1,090,380	9.47
Democratic Republic of Congo	905,633	2,345,409	443,876	1,149,550	418,044	1,082,650	9.40
Peru	496,260	1,285,215	269,994	669,230	260,055	673,490	5.85
Colombia	439,769	1,138,914	206,039	533,600	194,961	504,910	4.38
Papua New Guinea	183,528	475,300	140,976	365,100	136,682	353,980	3.07
Venezuela	352,170	912,050	138,655	359,090	127,238	329,520	2.86
Bolivia	424,195	1,098,580	120,554	312,210	107,317	277,930	2.41
Myanmar (Burma)	261,808	678,030	78,381	202,990	69,642	180,360	1.57
India	1,222,808	3,166,828	69,048	178,820	65,766	170,320	1.48
Total for the 10 principal nations			3,660,491	9,479,940	3,433,644	8,892,450	77.21
Remaining 80 nations			1,123,496	2,909,630	1,013,541	2,624,870	22.79
World total			4,783,987	12,389,570	4,447,185	11,517,320	100.00

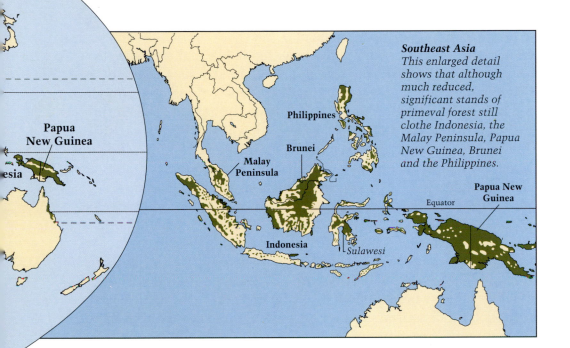

Southeast Asia
This enlarged detail shows that although much reduced, significant stands of primeval forest still clothe Indonesia, the Malay Peninsula, Papua New Guinea, Brunei and the Philippines.

◀▲ *Forest zones in the tropics*
But for the very specific climatic conditions required for its growth, and the effects of deforestation by man, a dense band of tropical forest would completely encircle Earth's equatorial zone. Primeval forests now clothe some 6 percent of the land surface—over 4.45 million square miles (11.5 million sq km), of which the largest blocks are the 2.3 million-sq-mi (6 million-sq-km) Amazonian hylaea, the Ituri Forest in the Democratic Republic of the Congo, and the now-rapidly disappearing forests of the Malay archipelago. The chart above shows the 10 countries within whose borders lie three-quarters of the world's remaining tropical forests.

▼ *Global annual rainfall*
The average yearly precipitation for the whole globe is an estimated 39 inches (100 cm). Over land, where continental air masses tend to be less humid, the average is about 26 inches (66 cm), while over the oceans it is 44 inches (112 cm). However, such averages conceal huge variations. While many parts of the world receive less than 5 inches (13 cm) of precipitation a year, there are some that receive over 400 inches (1,016 cm). The record is held by Cherrapunji in India, with 1,042 inches (2,647 cm).

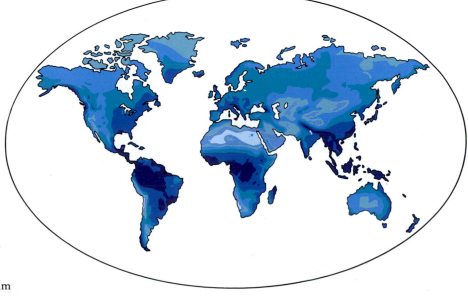

Mean annual rainfall
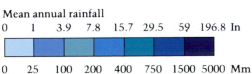

▲ *Even to an untrained eye, these intercontinental co-evolutionary adaptations are astoundingly apparent in these rainforest mammals from Africa (left) and Latin America (right). The similarities run deep, including behavior, niche preference, and food choice. From top to bottom, the pairs are: royal antelope* (Neotragus spp.) *and agouti* (Dasyprocta punctata); *water chevrotain* (Tragulus spp.) *and paca* (Agouti paca); *giant ground pangolin* (Manis gigantea) *and giant armadillo* (Priodontes maximus); *pygmy hippopotamus* (Choeropsis liberiensis) *and capybara* (Hydrochoerus hydrochaeris); *yellow-backed duiker* (Cephalophus silvicultor) *and red brocket deer* (Mazama americana).

unrelated yet with much in common. On the other hand, scientists explore and study the tropical rainforest with such zeal precisely because of the staggering differentiation that exists in this laboratory of infinite creativity.

The Unique Climate of the Tropical Forests

When people in the humid tropics refer to summer and winter, they talk of the dry and rainy seasons. Summer and winter are marked not so much by temperature, which is only somewhat cooler in the rainy season due to cloud cover, but by the amount of rain. Average temperature for the dry season is 82.2°F (27.9°C) and for the wet season 78.5°F (25.8°C) in the Amazon Basin.

It is clear that temperatures in temperate zone forests and other habitats may soar much higher and, of course, drop much lower than in rainforest areas. Under the forest canopy you are generally comfortable unless performing physical labors, at which time you may become oppressed by the humidity. Summers in New York and Florida, by contrast, are far hotter—and for the most part more uncomfortable.

As time periods are rarely punctuated by extended droughts, a neophyte visiting a tropical rainforest during the height of the dry season might assume he had experienced the rainy season. The dry season is not truly dry but sees rain intermittently, with dry spells perhaps lasting only two or three weeks. For the visitor, torrential rain is to the rainforest what unmitigated scorching sun is to the desert: enjoyed or just accepted; a fact of life. The rain is the major factor responsible for the unsurpassed biomass, and it takes approximately 40 gallons (152 l) of water to produce each pound of leaves.

Some areas of the tropics are remarkable for the amounts of water cycled. In a record year, between August 1, 1860 and July 31, 1861, Cherrapunji, in what was then called Meghalaya, in India, reached an all-time high of 1,042 inches (2,647 cm) or more than 86 feet—enough to cover a 10-story building! The record for 24 hours is 74 inches (187 cm) at Celaos on Réunion Island in the Indian Ocean. Perhaps not surprisingly, some parts of India are busy in the rainy season with Arab tourists, who come from their desert homelands where years frequently pass without an inch of rain, to see the grand spectacle of the monsoon.

In Cherri we have an example of one forest type—seasonal deciduous forest, also known as monsoon forest. In such areas, although voluminous rain falls during the monsoon, the year is punctuated clearly with a dry season which may last for four months or more, during which time rain is infrequent and light. During the drought, many monsoon forest trees drop their leaves so as to conserve water by preventing transpiration. Delicate leaves such as those of ferns and some orchids desiccate and wait for the rains to arrive. The canopy here is more open, and trees do not attain the height of forests in areas of more constant rainfall. Adding further to drying conditions in many seasonal forests are hard-driving wilting winds, such as the harmathan, blowing off the Sahara in Africa, which affects forests as far away as Asia. We employ the recently (1976) coined term *tropical moist forest* to include both tropical rainforest, cloud forest, and short-dry-season monsoon forest.

In the tropical rainforest proper, almost every afternoon during the rainy season there are torrential downpours lasting several hours, after which the

sun usually shines, although it is not uncommon for rain to continue for several days and nights without stopping. These rains are an experience on their own, with all the leaves dripping and gleaming. It is true you must "see the jungle when it's wet with rain."

In these forests, humidity is permanently high, oscillating between 88 percent in the rainy season and 77 percent in the dry season (Amazon Basin figures). Unlike the deciduous forests, the tropical rainforest never "dies back," even during its short droughts. To remain evergreen and support feathery vegetation like delicate ferns which would otherwise become desiccated, the tropical rainforest functions like a thermostatically controlled greenhouse. Summer or winter, wind seldom pierces this dense mass of vegetation. It is rare for a breeze to be felt on the ground, even, remarkably, as a tropical gale rages overhead. On the floor of the forest, far beneath the canopy, you are insulated from the occurrences of the outside world. Even during cataclysmic rain squalls you are not aware that it is raining until five minutes after the rain commences because of the adequacy of your living roof. These are truly green mansions. The main canopy under the giant emergent trees appears to roll on forever—the lush green carpet of the "closed forest."

▲ *Sierra palms* (Prestoea montana) *and heliconias* (Heliconia caribaea) *delight the eye on El Yunque Mountain in the Caribbean National Forest in Puerto Rico—one of the very few tropical rainforests on United States territory.*

THE RAINFOREST CANOPY—THE EIGHTH CONTINENT

The hub of life is a three-dimensional jigsaw puzzle, with every plant from the smallest fungus to the giant emergent trees and species in between filling its own selected (and hard-won) niche to perfection. An apt description might be "order out of chaos."

With innovative climbing equipment, pioneering canopy-exploring biologist Donald Perry discovered that wind in the rainforest roof generates a sawing action, pitting large limbs of neighboring trees against each other in a

▲ *The simultaneous blooming of these canopy trees* (Erythrina sp.) *is referred to as "Big Bang." [Brazilian Amazon.]*

▲ *"Crown shyness" is elegantly exhibited in this view from the forest floor. The jigsaw-puzzle structure of this umbrella canopy of kepong trees* (Dryobalanops aromatica) *in this Malaysian dipterocarp forest demonstrates a territoriality among trees.*

macabre "battle of the trees." Usually the softer wood is worn through first and the contest ends, sending Goliath limbs, together with their burden of clinging epiphytes and lianas, crashing to the ground. Such falls can be heard sporadically throughout the day and night, eerie and unnerving. The most common cause of tree mortality here is windthrow. In a study plot 37 percent of fallen trees had roots, an indication that they were alive when toppled. The annual mortality of trees greater than 12 inches (30 cm) diameter at breast height (dbh) from all causes is 1.6 percent (Richards 1996).

The sunlight-bathed canopy is rich in flowering trees, vines, orchids, bromeliads, and other photophytic plants. During the blooming season it is abuzz with bees, flies, bats, hummingbirds, and countless other pollinators. It is likened to an elevated flower field, and some of the insect residents never go to ground. To our surprise Perry has found some typical ground-dwellers up in the great height of the living roof. They include mice, centipedes, scorpions, cockroaches, and even earthworms burrowing in the build-up of humus in the forks of tree trunks. It is interesting to note that the largest tree canopy, the great banyon (*Ficus benghalensis*) of India, boasts a circumference of 1,350 feet (411 m), approximately 3 acres (1.2 ha).

Canopy trees are crowned by the jewels of the plant world, the epiphytes. Unlike parasites, which extract sustenance from the plants to which they attach themselves, epiphytes use trees, vines, other plants, and even rocks solely for support, and do not take nourishment from their hosts. Included in this uniquely adapted group of plants are orchids, ferns, bromeliads, and surprisingly, even cacti, among many other less familiar families. When you look up and see a cactus cascading from a tree, with a rainbow-colored flower the size of a man's head, you know you are in a very special place. There are epiphytes in 33 different families of flowering plants in the neotropical forests alone. A single tree has been found to contain 300 orchids and more than 2,000 epiphytic plants.

The combined weight of the epiphytic mass is often equal to one-third of the total weight of the tree, and contains approximately 45 percent of the nutrient total of the canopy. Limbs become so overburdened with the weight of epiphytes that they often collapse. As a result many tropical moist forest trees have evolved smooth bark, or even shed their barks to discourage over-colonization by epiphytes. Some rough-barked trees, however, contain toxins that may discourage epiphytes, which also harbor insects. Typical of these is the garlic tree, known in Costa Rica as arbol de ajo (*Carvocar costaricense*), whose cut bark precisely mimics the aroma of garlic.

In this competitive world, there are even epiphytes that grow on epiphytes, and on the leaves of other plants. Known as *epiphylls,* these include the mosses, algae, liverworts, and lichens. These primitive plants will also flourish on rocks and on any other surface they can pirate, including animals. Many a crocodile and mossy-backed turtle is adorned by these growths, which symbiotically offer the protection of camouflage. Lichen itself is a mutualistic relationship between an alga and a fungus. The alga produces sugar through photosynthesis, and the fungus provides nutrients captured from the environment. Together they can more effectively ply the available resources.

Plants may be categorized by the method they use to take up nutrients. Carnivorous plants trap and consume small animals; saprophytic plants such as most fungi digest decaying organic matter; parasitic plants tap nutrients directly from living plants, while autotrophs are the plants we are most familiar with. They take nutrients directly from the soil and manufacture food from carbon dioxide and water using the energy of sunlight to drive the process. Epiphytes, growing far out of reach of the soil, trap falling litter and nutrients in rainwater for nourishment.

The tropical rainforest has developed yet another, recently discovered, category: an auto-epiphyte . . . a plant that is epiphytic upon itself! A few varieties of trees rooted in the ground have rosettes of litter-trapping leaves which collect debris. Into this debris grow roots to absorb the nutrients. Such profound thrift and efficiency typifies the biological processes of the tropical forest.

MICROHABITATS AND AERIAL HIGHWAYS

In their search for light, the epiphytes have left the ground, but in the bargain they have also had to leave the soil behind. How some of these have adapted to their divorce from the earth is interesting. Ants make their home in the supporting root masses of some epiphytes, and in their constant foraging they bring back much leaf debris, fruit, and other vegetable and animal matter that is shared by the "air plants."

Found almost exclusively in the New World forests, many bromeliads have a water reservoir formed by closely fitting and overlapping leaf rosettes. Great amounts of nourishing leaf debris, as well as water, collect here, sustaining the plant during drought periods. Virtual arboreal marshes, these tanks—which may hold as much as 30 gallons (114 l) of water in the case of *Glomeropitcairnia* sp.—are the home of many and varied creatures, some of which never come to the ground. Microorganisms and insects feed on the algae that grow in the water. Tree frogs, tree snakes, and lizards make these bromeliads their permanent homes or temporary camps. There is even a crab

▲ *Nature's opportunism at its best. A seed from an upper-canopy tree, probably deposited in the droppings of a passing animal, has taken root and grown into a natural bonsai version of its species, perched on the broken bough of its host.*

Synusiae of the Tropical Rainforest

A. Autotrophic plants (with chlorophyll)
  1. Mechanically independent plants (arranged in a number of strata [layers])
    (a) Trees and "shrubs"
    (b) Herbs
  2. Mechanically dependent plants
    (a) Climbers
    (b) Stranglers
    (c) Epiphytes (including semiparasitic epiphytes)
B. Heterotrophic plants (without chlorophyll)
  1. Saprophytes
  2. Parasites

THE TROPICAL RAIN FOREST (1996) BY P. W. RICHARDS ET AL.

▲ *Synusiae—a group of plants of similar life-form that play a similar part in their community and occupy the same ecotope habitat as well as the role in the ecosystem—thusly, a plant as a niche.*

UNDER THE SOUTH AMERICAN CANOPY

The dense canopy of the equatorial rainforest is an all-enveloping umbrella which hides and protects a dimly lit world pungent with the scents of life and death. The visitor's first impressions are of the rapid recycling of living matter and the artful adaptation of each organism to its niche. Opulent and lush as the forest may be, a living is not easily made, even here. A coatimundi must paw off the irritating hairs of a tarantula in order to eat it, and the jaguar will hunt peccaries with tusks as sharp as knives. Venomous snakes must be grappled with before being consumed.

The lower canopy

The booming call of a troop-leading howler monkey shatters the still silence of the understory. Then, in an escalating call-and-response chorus, the rancorous cries of a macaw join in, building to a crescendo of noise that will draw the attention of a jaguar, who will finally home in on the troop's location by listening for the steady "plop" of discarded fruit cores. Intent on their own business, the understory animals fail to notice the silent Yanomamö hunter as he aims his poisoned arrows.

The understory and forest-floor domain

Setting the scene for the understory theater, the morpho butterfly's strobe-effect wingbeats send a blaze of electric-blue impulses direct to the observer's brain—a dazzling phenomenon that typifies the New World rainforest experience. A lone tapir or armadillo may bolt as you approach, sending a hidden ocelot streaking into the mid canopy. Inspection of logs at your feet reveals a host of beetles, many of them magnificent in size and iridescent color, but beware of testy bands of peccaries—more likely to charge than to flee like the tapir. The aquatic scene is no less dramatic, with pig-sized capybaras swimming unscathed among piranhas and arapaimas.

Scarlet macaw
Ara macao

Three-toed sloth
Bradypus tridactylus

Kinkajou
Potos flavus

Sulfur-breasted toucan
Rhamphastos sulfuratus

Tamandua
Tamandua tetradactyla

Iguana
Iguana iguana

Ring-tailed coati
Nasua nasua

Giant armadillo
Priodontes maximus

Capybara
Hydrochoerus hydrochaeris

Hercules beetle
Dynastes hercules

Morpho butterfly
Morpho sp.

Spider monkey
Ateles sp.

Howler monkey
Alouatta sp.

Prehensile-tailed
porcupine
Coendou prehensilis

Emerald tree boa
Corallus canina

Arrow
poison frog
Dendrobates sp.

Ocelot
Felis pardalis

Piranha
Pygocentrus nattereri

Yanomamö
Homo sapiens

Arapaima
Arapaima gigas

▲ Lianas are typified by the woody structure of their stems. Some, like these "monkey ladders" (Bauhinia spp.) in Costa Rica, are pierced with natural footholds, and grow to venerable stature.

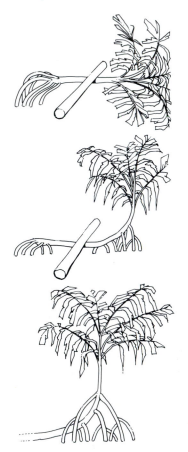

▲ Botanists working in Latin America have found that the palm Socratea exorrhiza can literally "walk out" on stilt roots from beneath a fallen tree that would have flattened and killed most species.

that lives only in the tanks of bromeliads. Birds and monkeys that rarely visit the ground drink from these benevolent fountains.

Other bromeliads of the genus *Tillandsia* are even more truly "air plants," in that many do not have a tank structure for food and water collection but instead their leaves contain hairlike scales known as trichome cells. These absorb airborne dust, nutrients, and humidity from the air and enable the plant to withstand long periods of drought. A species of *Tillandsia* familiar to many people is Spanish moss (*Tillandsia usneoides*). Not a moss at all, this epiphyte has a wider range than any other plant in the world. Chain colonies of this plant are seen gracefully cascading from tree branches and telephone lines, where seeds have been deposited in birds' droppings, all the way from Virginia to Argentina. Birds also propagate it when they use live cuttings to construct their nests.

Monkeys also benefit trees by ripping off epiphytes in their search for grubs and other edible insects or animals. The upper canopy, which contains most of the forest's wildlife, is laden with epiphytes, but a clean network of paths exists along the center of certain main limbs and branches. This is a treetop game trail kept clear by constant use. It has been speculated that before the recent cutting of the Transamazon Highway, a monkey could have traveled all the way from Colombia to Argentina without ever touching the ground, crossing even the Amazon River in the trees of floating islands that have broken away from the river's banks.

UNDER THE CLOSED CANOPY

In the understory, where you stand, is the grandest spectacle yet. Because of the constants of moisture and warmth at this level, the soft, delicate, and graceful plants make this their home. In most such forests, palms set the mood, and no single plant more typifies the experience. Their diversity is staggering, with over 2,500 species in 200 genera worldwide. The arching grace these treelets lend to the floral mosaic might be a definition of splendor; but be warned, their trunks are often viciously armed with whorls of stiletto-shaped spines—often coated with a defensive toxin. (Should one slip on the wet clay forest soil, these barbs invariably offer the nearest handhold.) Here also are many of the shade-tolerant species we have adopted as houseplants; they include ferns and aeroids, such as the philodendrons which climb up tree trunks in a spiral, dropping a cascade of air roots to the ground. You will recognize fleshy friends such as dieffenbachia or dumbcane; intricately veined and red-hued anthuriums with their familiar jack-in-the-pulpit spike and shield; sensuous dracaenas bending into vacant arenas, ancient cone-bearing cycads, and many more.

Huge flowering lianas, some thicker than a man's torso, weave along the ground and loop and spiral into the air to knit together the canopy above. Some vines, *Bauhinia* spp. called *monkey ladders,* have see-through windows and zigzag forms resembling staircases; others are perfectly square in cross-section. These climbers include the Asian rattan palms (*Calamus* spp.) and other closely related genera that have long whips, appropriately called flagella, hanging from their fronds. These are often viciously armed with sharp hooks, which serve to anchor the plant to its supports. Gorgeous flowers fall from these vines and trees, often carpeting large areas of the forest floor.

Life in the understory, however, has its hazards. Research indicates that on average, one tree with a diameter greater than 8 inches (20 cm) falls per acre (0.4 ha) per year, a common and mortal danger to seedlings, saplings, and pole trees, which may be flattened to the ground by such objects. Implausibly, it has been recently discovered that when knocked down, a species of palm, *Socratea exorrhiza*, actually forms new stilt roots, picks itself up on stilt legs over a period of time, and "walks out" from under fallen trees, limbs, and other obstructions and back into light and space.

CLOUD FORESTS AND ELFIN WOODLANDS

From the lowland rainforest, as elevation increases up mountain ranges and upland valleys, environmental conditions begin to change, and this gradually affects the stature, structure, and composition of the forest. Although the soils are different, the main regulator appears to be temperature. For every 1,000 feet (305 m) increase in elevation, average daily temperature drops by 3.6°F (2°C). This effect, known as the lapse rate, varies from place to place, and also with the time of day, the season, the size and positioning of mountains, and the water vapor content of the air. Biological reactions are retarded as temperature declines, and we find this translated into diminished tree height, reduction in animal and plant diversity, and a transition from the luxuriant five layers of trees to only a few or perhaps just one. Due to the reduction in canopy cover, we find more light reaching the ground and supporting a more profuse shrub growth.

As New Guinea has several peaks in excess of 13,000 feet (4,000 m), it can serve us here as a dynamic example, but because of the factors cited above, these altitudinal demarcations cannot be applied across the board to other areas. Zonations, generally gradual and ill-defined at any particular altitude,

▼ *Towering tree ferns of the genus* Dicksonia *are a prominent feature of the rapidly diminishing Atlantic rainforest of southeastern Brazil. These forests, quite distinct from the Amazon Basin biome, once covered more than 400,000 square miles (1,036,000 sq km): today they cover less than 20,000 square miles (52,000 sq km).*

LIFE ZONES OF THE MOUNTAINS

While lowland wet conditions and homogeneous soils produce more consistent forest formations, a surprising range of variation exists in forests at higher altitudes, as shown by the Costa Rican cloud forest pictured below. A key factor is decreased biological production due to lower temperatures.

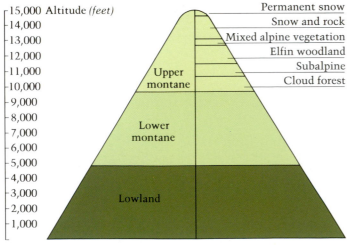

◄▲ Cloud forests and elfin woodlands

The warm, protected conditions in lowland wet rainforests produce floral empires of great luxuriance. But with increasing elevation the biomass is gradually exposed to more rigorous and demanding conditions, and these are directly reflected in the form and composition of the forest. As temperature falls, the cloud forest is blanketed in almost permanent mist, pro-ducing a thick layer of moss on nearly every surface. Higher still, in the elfin woodland (exemplified here by New Guinea's high montane forests), trees take on a stunted and twisted form, while the forest itself is poor in species compared with the rich species diversity of the lowland rainforests. Above the elfin woodland, a narrow band of mixed alpine vegetation quickly gives way to bare rock and snow.

▶ Equatorial highlands

Flanking the Great Rift Valley, Mt. Kilimanjaro, 19,340 feet (5,595 m), Mt. Kenya, 17,058 feet (5,200 m), and the fabled Mountains of the Moon—the Ruwenzori Range—16,794 feet (5,117 m), all share very similar vegetational successions. With increasing altitude the visitor climbs through plant communities that are quite distinctive, in some cases almost alien.

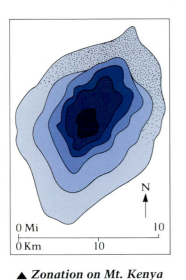

▲ Zonation on Mt. Kenya

A plan view of vegetation zones on Mt. Kenya shows a marked asymmetry between the scrub (stippled) of the relatively dry north-facing slopes and the more typical montane forest zones of the wetter southern slopes.

The nival zone

This montane zone is a bizarre world of tall arborescent (treelike) plants. It is the upper limit for animals, and one of the few animal sounds heard here is the ethereal, almost human scream of the hyrax (Dendrohyrax *spp.*).

Moorland/heath zone

Tree heaths dominate the moorland belt while spongy bogs of **Carex runssoroensis** *occupy the wetter valley floors. Wild dogs roam here, and leopards hunt small mammals such as duiker (*Sylvicapra*).*

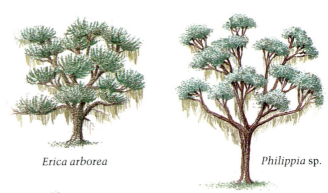

The bamboo zone

The upper limit of this zone is marked by virtually solid stands of bamboo, which provide a home for the mountain gorilla (Gorilla gorilla beringei), elephant (Loxodonta africana), buffalo (Syncerus caffer), and the giant forest hog (Hylochoerus meinertzhageni).

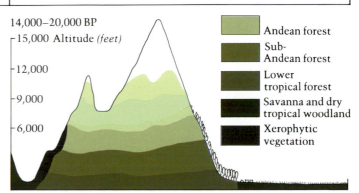

△ **The Andes today**
The upper zones are higher and broader than they were during the Ice Age. The lowland forests were less drastically affected and so have remained largely intact.

Legend (Andes today):
- Perennial snow
- Super-paramo
- Paramo
- Sub-paramo

△ **The effect of the Ice Age**
The vegetation zones became compressed, in some cases by several thousand feet. The lower zones were less affected and became vital refuges for many species.

Legend (Ice Age):
- Andean forest
- Sub-Andean forest
- Lower tropical forest
- Savanna and dry tropical woodland
- Xerophytic vegetation

▲ Montane forest
Within the cloud forest at 10,800 feet (3,300 m), woody, looping vines clamber up trees for support, while ferns and other epiphytes cling to them. Bryophytes (mosses and liverworts), in turn, attach to their leaf surfaces in the perennially most supersaturated environment on Earth. This biomass, in turn, cloud-strips water equivalent to 15–20 percent, but as much as 50–60 percent in more exposed conditions, of ordinary rainfall—a factor which plays critically in regulating water flow down the mountain into agricultural fields. [Cayanabe National Park, Ecuador.]

can also be abrupt due to, say, prevailing cloud level or sodden accumulations of *Sphagnum* moss. This ecotone, or zone of change, between lowland forest and lower montane forest occurs at about 4,900 feet (1,500 m). The canopy may still reach 98 to 118 feet (30–36 m) tall here, and the ferns, mosses, and herbaceous flowering plants are abundant.

Above 9,800 feet (3,000 m), upper montane forest takes over. This is divided into two rather distinct formations; the cloud forest between 9,800 and 10,800 feet (3,000–3,300 m) and the lower subalpine forest at 10,800 to 11,650 feet (3,300–3,550 m). As we know, clouds love to congregate and loiter over mountains. This drastically reduces the amount of sunlight available to plants below for photosynthesis. At this elevation, the arrow-straight giant tree boles of the lowlands, which reach toward the heavens, become more twisted and animated in forms reminiscent of oaks (*Quercus* spp.). Indeed, the higher elevated forests contain more and more temperate species, which include the oaks, and canopy height may reach 60 feet (18 m). Their limbs, however, are overloaded with a profusion of mosses and liverworts due to the supersaturated environment. While species diversity becomes more narrow, the components of the cloud forest are quite artfully assembled.

Here you walk through a forest in the clouds as in an ethereal dream, where the sun rarely shines. There are abundant flowers in the herb layer, countless epiphytes at eye level, and benevolent, wise old trees, twisted into frozen positions, standing silently all around.

Even if it is not raining here, the trees are always dripping. In a process called "cloud stripping," the leaves cause condensation of the moisture from the clouds, and water constantly drips off them. It is interesting that you can generally tell what climate a given plant is from by its manner of directing water, either shedding water away from itself, as in rainforest drip-tip leaves or the feather palm frond structure, or funneling water toward the roots as in agave, cactus, or certain fan palm structures typical of more arid lands.

On higher ranges, between 11,650 and 12,800 feet (3,550–3,900 m), the dwarfed 15-foot (4.5-m) tall and even more diminutive upper subalpine forest can be defined as a rare-air habitat of grotesquely twisted, wind-tortured bonsai specimens, often on exposed ridges. This forest is appropriately known also as elfin woodland. Above this tree line is a complex mosaic of dwarf shrub heath, short grassland, moss tundra, and fern meadow, classified as alpine vegetation. This gives way to a sparse lichen growth a little higher up. Above 13,120 feet (4,000 m) precipitation falls as snow, which collects permanently at slightly above 14,760 feet (4,500 m). There are even signs of glaciation on New Guinea's Mt. Wilhelm, which reaches 14,793 feet (4,510 m). Life is very sparse here. It seems strange indeed to encounter what amounts to a permanent ice age and glaciers right there on the equator.

It seems rather incongruous to find one mountain supporting lush vegetation on one side and desert scrub and cacti on the other, but this is not an uncommon feature and is due to a rain-shadow effect in which most of the precipitation is dumped on the lush upwind side. Diverse habitats in the Hawaiian Islands are a good case in point. There, rainfall on the windward slopes can average more than 400 inches (1,016 cm) annually while the leeward slopes are deserts averaging 15 inches (38 cm) at most.

▲ Cloud forests produce many bizarre tree forms which, seen through the drifting mist, often seem to be in lurching, near-human motion. [Monte Verde, Costa Rica.]

II Creatures of the Forest

The Domain of the Insect

Quickly apparent to the visitor who has breached the rainforest wall is that this is the domain of the insect; not necessarily bothersome, but myriad in form, color, size, and shape.

Their athletic prowess dwarfs the efforts of the world's Olympic champions. The commonest of fleas can jump 150 times its own length (the equivalent of a man jumping six city blocks from a standing start), go months without feeding, and after a year of being frozen solid, be revived. An ant can lift 50 times its own weight and carry it in its jaws proportionately farther than an average man can walk empty-handed, while to match a bee's strength, a man would have to pull a load equal to a 30-ton trailer truck.

Insects vary in size from 0.008-inch-long (0.02 cm) hairwing beetles (Ptiliidae) to the 12-inch (30-cm) wingspan of the atlas moth (*Attacus atlas*) and the 13-inch (33-cm) body length of the Borneo walking stick (*Palophus titan*). The Polyphemus moth larva in its first two days of existence eats 86,000 times its own birth weight in food. And so the catalog runs on.

In this damp, warm habitat, glorious beetles are everywhere, competing for center stage, clothed in brilliant colors, patterns, shapes, and blinding metallic iridescence. British biologist J. B. S. Haldane (1892–1964) was once asked what organic evolution had revealed about God's design. Because there are so many spectacular varieties, his answer was, "An inordinate fondness for beetles." Indeed, the recent exploration of the rainforest canopy has pushed the projected number of Earth's species from 10 million to 100 million—the majority will be beetles.

A species called the bombardier beetle (*Brachinus* sp.) stores hydrogen peroxide and chemicals called *hydroquinones* in its glands. At will, the insect mixes these chemicals in a "reaction chamber" containing enzymes, resulting in the formation of benzoquinones and gaseous oxygen as a propellant. The chemical reaction causes the mixture to boil in this species, adding scalding heat to an already unique and devastating defense mechanism. These creatures apparently have no need to bite or sting.

The Invasion of the Giant Penlights

Certain beetles assume preposterous proportions and powers. My wife, Arlene, and I, while investigating a lowland rainforest in the Veracruz state of Mexico, had camped, finished dinner, and were sitting around our campfire. Through the trees in the distance we noticed the flashing of fireflies. Being used to the splendid little three-quarter-inch (2-cm) fellows (Lampyridae) of northern latitudes, we watched in the black forest night as they wove in and out of the trees, growing larger and larger as they approached us. This presented no problem at all as fireflies are completely harmless, and this in any case was quite a spectacle. However, *these* "fireflies" continued to grow as they got closer. Without saying

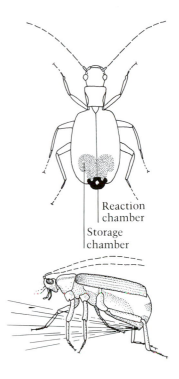

Reaction chamber
Storage chamber

▲ *With an explosive "pop" the bombardier beetle* (Brachinus sp.) *blasts its attacker with a scalding jet of irritant chemicals. Tiny though it may be, this 0.8-inches (2-cm) creature will deter adversaries as large and varied as mice, praying mantids, wolf spiders, and frogs—for as long as its ammunition supply lasts!*

a word, we looked at each other and then back at the advancing lights, which were now as big and prominent as a horde of penlights. I then recalled a story told during the building of the Panama Canal, in which surgeons successfully used a jar of only three luminescent click beetles (*Pyrophorus* sp.) to illuminate a patient for surgery during a power blackout.

The penlights kept coming, and finally reached us. What happened next staggered the imagination. They were 3 inches (7.6 cm) long; their green glowing abdomens fully 1.5 inches (3.8 cm). Blinded by our fire, these ponderous creatures bounced off trees, careened into our faces, and got caught in our hair, but still they kept coming. What a show. We had to smother the fire (the point of attraction) because some of them were landing in it. Then we were plunged into the pitch black of night, with scores of satellite full moons dispersing through the forest. Back home, identification proved them to be the same giant *Pyrophorus* click beetles that had illuminated the old Panama Canal operating room.

WHAT ARE THE DANGERS IN THE TROPICAL FOREST?

While such episodes as the giant click beetles are far more typical of the tropical forest experience, many visitors anticipate their travel there will abound with violent encounters with dangerous animals. Be assured that such a myth represents one of the world's great misconceptions. As plant defenses against animal depredation are so effective, the undisturbed forest is simply not overburgeoning with animals, and where animals are present they are not apt to be highly visible. One study estimates the animal biomass at 18 pounds (8.2 kg) per hectare (2.47 acres) for ground-dwelling mammals and 21 pounds per hectare (9.5 kg/ha) for arboreal mammals, the equivalent of approximately five domestic cats in weight.

Further, save for mosquitoes and odd parasites, most of the rest of the fauna, with rare exceptions, is shy and retiring and has no reason for contact with humans. Given that travel in the forest is never silent, most creatures are either in hiding or have vacated the area ahead of your arrival. Should you be fortunate enough to view one of the animals that enjoy a high public profile, there is still no reason why the incident should become perilous so long as certain basic rules are not violated. These include refraining from handling venomous snakes, and avoiding surprising a potentially dangerous animal by stalking it or by suddenly appearing and blocking its flight path or moving into its attack range.

But perhaps the abundance and complexity of tropical forest beauty cannot be fully appreciated without at least some measure of its antithesis for contrast. In an attempt to set the record straight, we will investigate some of the charismatic creatures of infamy that a traveler in Amazônia, for instance, might possibly, but not probably, encounter.

PIRANHAS AND OTHER DANGEROUS AQUATICS

Most everyone is familiar with the piranha (Serrasalminae), which early explorers called the scourge of the Amazon. Yet a person can swim unmolested in the Amazon and other waters they inhabit, as long as blood is not present and swimming strokes are calm and not panicked. To avoid cannibal fish, it is best to be cautious in the sluggish backwaters of oxbow lakes. Also be aware that more danger exists during low-water periods when the piranha schools are more concentrated. At these times competition for available food is at a peak, and humans are then more likely to become targets. Menstruating

▲ *On Komodo Island, Indonesia, I was treed and repeatedly attacked by this 11-ft (3.4-m) Komodo dragon which pressed home its attack despite all attempts to drive it away. It was a rare glimpse into the prehistoric past to be pursued as food by a ruling reptile more than three times my own weight.*

women should keep any essential swimming or bathing to faster-moving waters or clear streams at any time of the year. In the Venezuelan llanos, my guide showed me numerous bite scars from an attack by red-bellied piranha while he was fording a river with his cattle some years before. This remains the only attack on a human that I can personally document.

A catfish, the giant piraiba (*Brachyplatystoma filamentosum*), has an ignoble reputation for purportedly eating small children. This is certainly not its natural diet, and records would indicate that this behavior is extremely rare—if indeed it occurs at all. More deserving of infamy is the candiru, whose unique life cycle has resulted in its being viewed as rather diabolical. These spiny fish, of the family Vandelliinae, may reach 2 inches (5 cm) in length, are attracted to urine and are small enough to enter the human urethra via the genitals and lodge there or in the bladder, which may necessitate surgical removal to save the victim. The tightly woven fabrics of some underwear and bathing suits are a hindrance to this fish, and their use is strongly recommended! (The men of many Amazonian tribes customarily tie off the foreskin over the urethral opening [see photo page 151], but it is not yet known whether this is a purely social custom or whether it has originated as a protection against the candiru.)

The electric eel (*Electrophorus electricus*) is one of about 40 species that can knock a person senseless and in rare cases cause drowning, but a negative encounter is unusual without having first molested the eel. Similarly, the freshwater stingray (*Potamotrygon hystrix*), if stepped on, can incapacitate you for days, but can also be avoided by refraining from wading in sandy or muddy river shallows. Where such travel is necessary, shuffling, rather than stepping along, will generally encourage the ray to move out of the way without a painful confrontation.

Latin America is home to a number of species of crocodile and caiman. Unprovoked attacks are quite rare in these species, although certain Old World crocodiles, especially rogue individuals, pose a much more formidable threat.

Crocodilians are the last surviving Archosauria, or ruling reptiles, which included the dinosaurs dating from the Mesozoic era (245–65 million years ago). Of 23 surviving species, 17 are endangered.

Your chances of experiencing an attack by the last of the ruling reptiles increase in this species order: the aptly named mugger crocodile (*Crocodylus palustris*) from India, the nilotic crocodile (*Crocodylus niloticus*) from Africa, and the saltwater crocodile (*Crocodylus porosus*) of India, the East Indies, and Pacific regions. The saltwater croc, which has been measured at 23 feet (7 m), is possibly the most aggressive animal on Earth. Most are retiring, but individuals have been known to attack native canoes 100 miles (160 km) out to sea and even to have devoured the occupants. During World War II, on the night of February 19–20, 1945, during the Allied invasion of the Pacific island of Ramree, between 800 and 1,000 Japanese troops were trapped in a swamp. By morning only 20 men remained alive; the rest had been eaten by saltwater crocodiles. While they can outrun a horse for short distances, I have never been attacked by any but captive specimens—a harrowing and indelible experience in itself, nevertheless.

Our last compelling aquatic inhabitant is the anaconda (*Eunectes marinus*), the heaviest snake in the world, estimated at more than 500 pounds (227 kg) for a specimen almost 28 feet (8.6 m) with a girth of 44 inches (112 cm), as thick as an obese man's body. Although over the years this giant constrictor

▲*The Orinoco red-bellied piranha (*Pygocentrus cariba*) is also known as the Cappiburro, or donkey castrator, due to its disconcerting habit of biting off the genitalia of wading livestock. I have seen a school strip the flesh of an 8-foot (2.4-m) crocodile in 20 minutes while an Indian, confidently standing waist deep in the river, groping the piranha from the carcass, remained unbitten.*

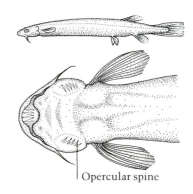

Opercular spine

▲ *The dreaded candiru, or carnero (*Vandellia cirrhosa*), inhabits Brazilian rivers. It is a parasite, normally living in the gill cavities of other fish, but will also penetrate the urethra of a human bather unless precautions are taken.*

may have devoured an unfortunate here or there, you may count confirmed incidents on one hand. To put this into perspective, an average of 51 people die every decade in the United States alone due to honeybee (*Apis mellifera*) stings. We now move to terra firma Amazônia.

SNAKES—THE MOST MISUNDERSTOOD OF THE FOREST INHABITANTS

Naturalist Henry Beston (1888–1968) remarked that "animals move finished and complete, gifted with extensions of the senses we have lost or never attained, living by voices we shall never hear."

As snakes are so prominent in many people's minds, and so closely associated with the tropical rainforest, we shall investigate what snakes are and what they are not. It will surprise most readers to know that you may walk for perhaps three days or more in the tropical rainforest without ever seeing a snake, although on another day you may observe several. In no way are snakes abundant, and if you take care when moving through the forest you have very little to fear. Nevertheless, travelers should always be conscious of snake safety.

Animals and plants that have dangerous or lethal defenses usually have a universal method of warning prey species, or incidental adversaries, of their potential prowess. Hornets are flighty, contrastingly colored, and have a paralyzing hum; the rhinoceros has one or more long horns, and snorts intimidatingly; orange, red, and black markings of certain insects warn of toxicity.

Snakes are no exception. To protect themselves from being trampled by American mastodons (*Mammut americanum*) and other large animals, rattlesnakes (*Crotalus* and *Sistrurus* spp.) evolved rattles, while others have adopted different fearsome gestures and appearances to avoid having to close with their enemies. Many snakes, as we will see, do not live up to all this posturing; when pressed, others do!

Poisonous snakes inject venom, which kills the prey and also helps to predigest its tissues. Other snakes are constrictors, suffocating their prey by prohibiting the rib cage's ability to expand, and so preventing the victim from inhaling. All must swallow their food whole, so they never attack animals too large for them to eat. Although there are a handful of recorded instances of human beings being killed and a few actually consumed by large constrictor snakes, no snake instinctively seeks humans as food.

Constrictors include not only large and small varieties of boas and pythons, but also the more typically diminutive species. A truly large snake, after consuming a heavy meal such as an antelope, can go for as long as two years, if necessary, without feeding. Unless molested, even these giant snakes are of no particular concern to people.

Most people are relieved to know that the snake's flickering tongue is a sensory organ used to pick up scent particles from the air and transfer them to sense organs in the roof of the mouth. It cannot inflict injury. Snakes, in short, are not malignant creatures spoiling for a fight, but superbly adapted (and beautiful) animals that fill a vital niche and are of much benefit to humankind. They prey mainly on rodents, and by consuming enormous quantities of these, significantly more food is left for us in the world's fields and granaries. As such, snakes should never be summarily killed when they are encountered. As well as being needlessly destructive, such an action presents a splendid opportunity to be bitten.

As virgin tropical rainforest floors are dimly lit and support moderately scant vegetation, you can easily see where you are walking. In thicker secondary growth, however, more caution is necessary. In any habitat, travelers should always be aware of snake safety. Step on, not over logs or other suitable snake microniches, and always look where you put your feet and hands. Following these rules, bites are an extreme improbability. Be assured, snakes do not drop from trees to attack people. In four decades of work in tropical forests around the world, neither I nor anyone in my party has ever come close to being bitten. Further, I have encountered in that time only one victim of venomous snakebite (illustrated by photo on page 31), excluding herpetologists bitten while handling specimens.

Very simply, wilderness areas do not abound with snakes. This is especially true in tropical rainforests. There is no abundance of perennially seeding

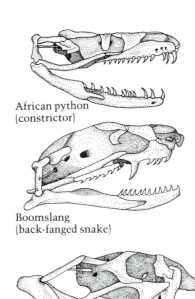

African python (constrictor)

Boomslang (back-fanged snake)

Boomslang (rear-fanged snake)

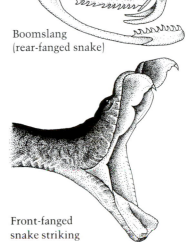

Front-fanged snake striking

▲ *Nonfanged snakes are rarely venomous. Rear-fanged snakes must use a chewing action to deliver their venom, but the front-fanged snakes inject the toxic dose through hypodermic-like fangs.*

▲ *A rare sight, witnessed on the Rio Claro, Costa Rica. Here, a 6-feet (1.8-m) cannibal indigo snake (Drymarchon corais) is swallowing—whole— another indigo snake, 8 feet (2.4 m) long.*

plants at ground level, and thus few rodents. Consequently the snake population is quite low. Many snakes are sedentary, patient, beautifully patterned, and a marvel to behold.

In the Amazon, what then of the much feared and "lethal" fer-de-lance (*Bothrops atrox*), alias *barba amarilla* (yellow beard) or *terciopelo* (velvety

▲ *The emerald tree boa (*Corallus canina*) has unusually long teeth which enable it to seize and hold the birds on which it preys. Thermoreceptors located in shallow pits on the snake's lips can detect temperature gradients of as little as 0.4°F (0.2°C) and are the main sense by which the snake finds its prey and directs its strike. While a compellingly beautiful snake, it is not known for its size. The world's longest snake is the Asian reticulated python (*Python reticulatus*) measured at 32 feet 9½ inches (10 m).*

▲ *The venomous rear-fanged mangrove snake (*Boiga dendrophila*) adopts such an effective aggression pose that it often repels its adversary without having to bite. This snake inhabits mangrove swamps in Asia.*

▲ *A 15-foot (4.5-m) Burmese python (*Python molurus bivittatus*) tracks its prey through giant bamboo.*

◄ *The blood python (*Python curtus*) of Malaysia and Sumatra blends with the leaf litter of the forest floor.*

one)? It is illuminating to note that although this species causes 80 to 85 percent of the snake bites reported in its Latin American range, only 2 to 3 percent of the bites are fatal. These stunningly beautiful snakes will not attack unprovoked. For the great majority of tropical forest travelers, their rare encounters with snakes are nothing more than an exotic memory to embrace. But what of other Amazonian zoologicals of sinister reputation?

ANT SOLDIERS AND ARMIES

Significantly, we have two ant groups on our list. The first, the giant tocandiras (*Dinoponera* and *Paraponera* spp.) are well respected by all who know them. Not all ants sting; these sting, and bite—and are terribly good at both! A nervous, aggressive, solitary hunter, the giant tocandiras flits about like a wasp on the forest floor, on trees, or on epiphytes, and while its sting is quite painful, at 1 inch (2.5 cm) long it is fortunately quite easy to see, so avoiding confrontation is simple (though I have been assaulted by them on two occasions while inspecting bromeliad interiors).

The second is the army ant (Dorylinae) and its Old World counterpart the driver ant (*Dorylus* spp.). A single ant will weigh not more than 0.000165345 of a pound, which means that a 200-pound (91-kg) man will weigh as much as 1,209,921 ants. It is surprising that creatures this small can be such a major concern for human beings.

Conquering hordes of army ants ride rampant over everything in their path and the sight is extremely impressive. Although a tethered donkey and a caged gorilla are recorded among the ants' unfortunate victims, most mammals this size, in good health, are able to flee in advance of the army as the ants can be heard approaching through the forest-floor debris. Opportunist ant-following birds pick off escaping victims, but the army of the ant marches patiently onward.

On a long trek in the Ituri Forest, Mbuti Pygmies who accompanied our expedition, but who were perhaps more accustomed to quieter travel, inadvertently led us into a swarm of driver ants. Our party was both stung (perhaps one-quarter bee-sting power) and bitten ruthlessly until we could make our way clear of the area under siege.

Drawing analogies between these ants and human armies is unavoidable: their nest is even called a bivouac. It is to this base camp that the army returns each day during half the month, pressing on in its "pillage-and-looting" march during the other half. Indian villages are usually abandoned in advance of an approaching ant army, and after the horde has passed through, the residents happily return to a village completely cleared of insects, rodents, and snakes.

NO-SEE-UMS

The subject of insects would not be complete without mention of the most infamous of all, the biting midges, alias piums and red pepper gnats (*Culicoides* spp.). Encountered most commonly on sandy river beaches, they can be relentless tormentors. So small they are difficult to see with the naked eye, they easily go through screening and any mosquito net coarser than cheesecloth. Female no-see-ums deliver a nasty little nip, suck blood, and may on occasion transmit filarial worms that infect humans, but the measure of audacity

▲ *This pregnant Bantu woman was bitten by a deadly black mamba (*Dendroaspis polylepis*) while working in the field. As our expedition was known to be in the region, and we had antivenin in our supplies, we were summoned from the forest by villagers to assist. In my absence, my son, Gandhi, then 12 years old, administered a dose of the life-saving serum, saving the woman. Two weeks later she gave birth to a healthy child. [Ituri Forest Region, Democratic Republic of Congo.]*

▲ *Individual army ants often sacrifice themselves to the good of the colony. Many perish by drowning when they instinctively form living bridges over water obstructions. The author observed this army ant "tunnel" as the insects emerged from a forest into sunlight. [Neivamyrmex sp., South America.]*

in this pestiferous fly is that one species will drain from a mosquito the blood that the mosquito has just withdrawn from a human. To be rid of them, use extra-fine netting, wait for a good breeze, or break camp on the run.

Vampires

Vampire bats (*Desmodus rotundus,* and two other species, each in its own genus) either concern or intrigue people as they have the dubious distinction of being the only true mammalian parasites.

The bat's first approach at night is to flutter in front of its host's face, and some believe in the myth that it releases a soporific or tranquilizing scent. It then lands on the ground and scuttles forward to pounce. With a downward stroke of the head it pierces the skin with razor-sharp triangular front teeth, either puncturing a neat hole or slicing off a tiny sliver of skin. The host, usually a cow, pig, goat, or similar-size animal, is unaware of the cut on its ear, nose, or foot since the bat's saliva contains an effective local anesthetic. But the adaptation is even more ingenious. The saliva also contains an effective anticoagulant which keeps the blood flowing freely while the bat feeds on this, its sole form of food.

Amerindian folklore claims that the vampire was responsible for the disappearance of the original American horse, a weak but interesting theory. It is true, however, that vampires are responsible for depletion of cattle throughout their range from Argentina to the southern border of the United States. There is some concern that with the progressive warming trend (due in part to tropical deforestation), vampires will move northward. They do occasionally prey on humans as well as their more usual hosts, and can transmit rabies, murrina, and other lethal infections which they can incubate in their bodies for long periods without mortality. In vampire country you do well to sleep under the adequate protection of a mosquito net, with toes and nose safely inside.

The Great Cats

The jaguar, alias *el tigre* (*Panthera onca*), figures in most people's anxiety on entering the South American rainforest. The third largest of the great cats, following lions (*Panthera leo*) and tigers (*Panthera tigris*), the jaguar is less aggressive than either, and unprovoked attacks are rare in the extreme. Count yourself as one of the truly blessed if you even manage to glimpse one in its natural setting.

A reclusive, solitary cat of the deep forest, the jaguar places its privacy in high regard. One resides within the borders of my own Cathedral Rain Forest Science Preserve in Costa Rica, and more than once I have interrupted it on a peccary kill. On two occasions it retired seconds before my arrival. When pressed, though, a jaguar proves a fierce and persistent adversary. In Venezuela, a jaguar approached a colleague of mine to within 20 feet (6 m) in a threatening manner. His guide was forced to throw half of the monkey he was preparing to the cat, which fortunately satisfied it.

Public Enemy Number 1

The mosquito has rightfully earned the position of public enemy number one, being a far greater menace than rats and lice combined. In tropical forests the mosquito can be *the* real hazard. "Wigglers" and "tumblers" (larvae and pupae) require water to complete their development, and depending on species preference, almost any water can qualify—salt, fresh, stagnant or clear, down at ground level, or caught in the tanks of epiphytic bromeliads high in the treetops.

It is the female that parasitizes (except for plant feeders and one species that drains out the contents of an ant's stomach) and she needs a blood meal before laying her eggs. Only a tuppence of blood (0.1 ml) is removed through the insect's hypodermic-like proboscis. However, it injects its saliva, containing anticoagulants and anesthetic, so as to assist in making the deed go unnoticed, to avoid being expunged by a swat. It is this saliva that causes the allergic reaction of itching and swelling which is of no more than transient consequence. Unfortunately, however, pathogens too are often introduced via the saliva. As biological vectors, mosquitoes directly transmit the microorganisms that cause malaria, dengue fever, yellow fever, and encephalitis, as well as many worm parasites (filariasis). The last category includes those that cause elephantiasis, an advanced condition that can swell limbs as well as genitalia to grotesque size (see page 141).

As well as the notorious *Anopheles* mosquito, the main carrier of malaria, and other members of the Culicinae family that carry dengue or breakbone fever, there are yet more species which enjoy a lower public profile but nevertheless cause untold human misery. To appreciate the scale of the damage they can do, consider that a single outbreak of yellow fever in southwest Ethiopia in the late 1950s killed 15,000 souls—almost 10 percent of the population. Malaria, also transmitted by *Anopheles,* is responsible for more fatalities than any transmissible disease, infecting 500 million people globally, killing 2.7 million annually, including 3,000 African children per day. In the Pacific campaign of World War II, malaria was responsible for five times as many casualties as were inflicted by the enemy.

There are, of course, a host of other diseases that must not be taken too lightly, although the chance of one becoming infected while visiting a tropical forest area for a short time is rather remote provided proper health precautions are taken. Research carried out by the various United Nations agencies (UNESCO, UNEP, and FAO) shows that within the African tropical forest zone there is a significantly lower incidence of disease, especially of malaria, in the deep forest tribes compared to the peoples living in progressively more disturbed forest habitats. Cities, towns, and villages in the tropics are far more likely places in which to become infected, and we will see in a later chapter that many tropical diseases are largely the product of deforestation.

Many tropical forest areas are actually fairly free of disease and mosquitoes for that matter. The basic rules are simple: travelers should always check the conditions of the area they plan to visit and, if necessary, take the appropriate prophylactic to prevent disease. Using common sense and a good mosquito net, most will enjoy what can be the most rewarding of life experiences.

THE AMAZON: SOUTH AMERICA'S GREEN MUSEUM

The Amazon forest, by combined facets of expanse, river volumes, species richness, and indigenous cultures, is the most compelling of the world's great forests which cover 2.3 million square miles (6 million sq km). The Amazon Basin, the world's largest hydrographic basin, is an expanse of 2.8 million square miles (7.3 million sq km) of mystery (Almanaque Abril 1996)—93 percent of the area of the contiguous United States. Through its heart runs the

▲ *The sheer enormity of the Amazon River can be truly appreciated only by drawing comparisons. In these maps, Marajo Island, located in the mouth of the river, is shown at the same scale as the New England coastal states and Switzerland.*

world's greatest river. One-sixth of all the freshwater that flows on Earth moves through its vast drainage system, and its flow is greater than the world's next eight largest rivers combined.

At its mouth the Amazon is more than 200 miles (320 km) wide. Marajo, a single island in its mouth, is as large as Switzerland. Even 1,000 miles (1,600 km) inland it is often impossible to see from one bank to the other. Averaging 100 feet (30 m) deep over much of its course, it is so enormous that an oceangoing vessel may navigate 2,300 miles (3,700 km) of its 4,195-mile (6,751-km) length counting its most distant mouth, the Para estuary. This would be like entering Chesapeake Bay and sailing all the way to Denver, Colorado. There are more than 1,000 tributaries, 17 of them more than 1,000 miles (1,600 km) long, and the average flow of this mightiest of rivers is 170 billion gallons (644 billion l) of water an hour: more than 4 trillion gallons (15.4 trillion l) a day pour into the Atlantic Ocean—enough to satisfy New York City's water needs for 12 years! So powerful is the Amazon's impact on the Atlantic Ocean, that adjacent to its mouth you can lean over the side of a boat 100 miles (160 km) out to sea and fill a glass with freshwater.

The Amazon is so immense and wild that it naturally inspired legend and myth. In 1542, Francisco de Orellana became the first European to travel the length of the "green tunnel." The river was named after a tribe of giant warrior women his expedition reportedly encountered there. Although such people have never been found, "Amazon" now seems more fluidly to refer to the river and to the region's almost incomprehensible immensity. The

▼ *The primordial soup of life itself, the black water of Rio Cuieiras, a tributary of the Rio Negro, is one of thousands of tributaries of the Amazon. The opulent forest, here in Brazilian Amazônia, is unbroken as far as the eye can see. Envision yourself in the center of this Eden.*

Amazon Basin is the size of the United States east of the Rockies, and by itself would be the ninth largest country in the world. Recently, vast mountain ranges have been found far from where they were thought to be, and several large rivers have become known only in the last few years due to satellite scanning.

So scant is our present state of exploration and knowledge here that since Bates first scratched the surface of scientific investigation of the Amazon in the 1850s, when he collected more than 8,000 new insects, it was not until the beginning of the 1970s that another large-scale effort was made to discover new fauna and flora in this vast biological frontier. On a recent collecting trip in the Amazon Basin, Oliver Flint of the Smithsonian Institution in Washington, D.C. gathered 55 caddis flies belonging to several different families: 53 of them were species completely new to science, offering a hint at the magnitude of future potential discoveries. The bird life of the great forest is no less rich. On one expedition, 76 different species were counted near the mouth of the river—in the branches of a single tree.

There are more species of fish (about 1,800) in the drainage basin of the Amazon River than exist in the entire Atlantic Ocean (about 1,700). Many of these creatures resemble marine species: electric eels, stingrays, shark-related sawfish, whales in the form of pink dolphins, and manatees—the origin of the mermaid myth. It is estimated that 45 percent of the Amazon Basin's fish species are yet to be discovered.

The Amazon comprises much more than one-half of Earth's tropical rainforests, and already roughly 12 percent of it has been removed. As we shall see, the global implications of this are enormous.

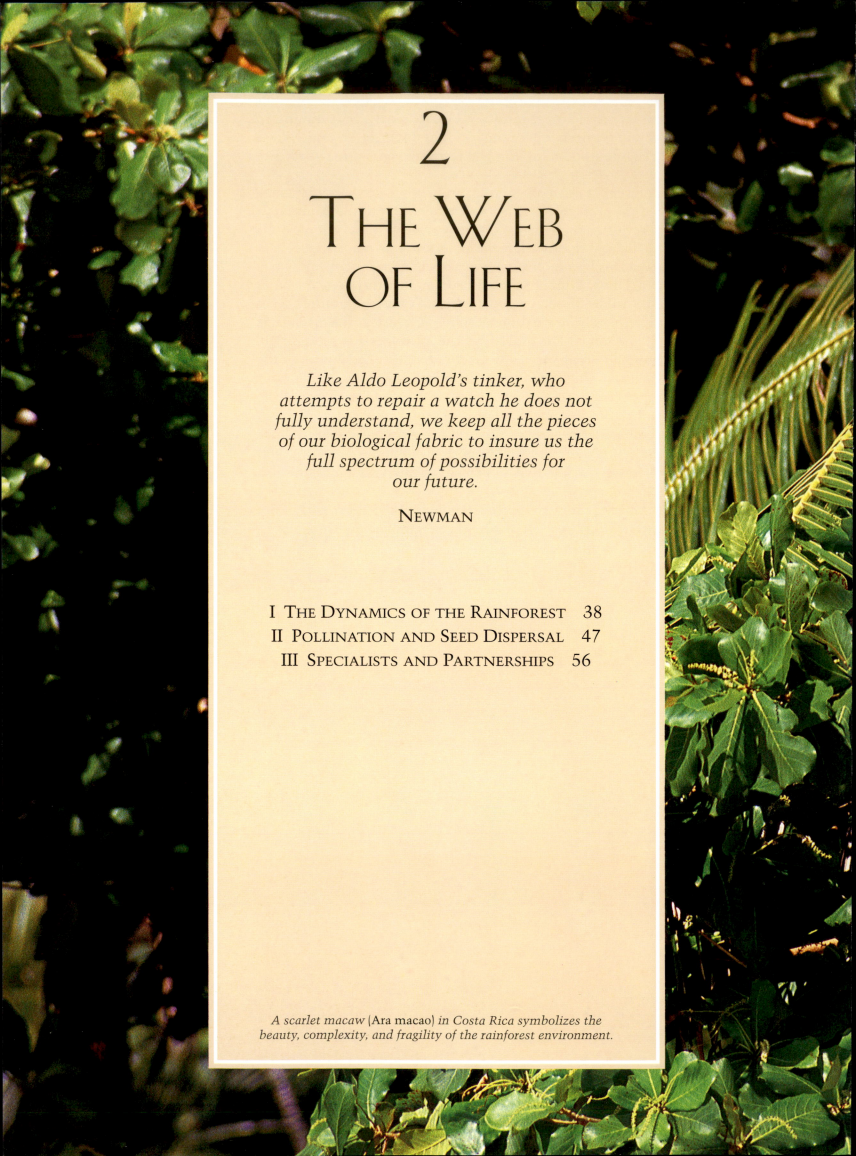

2
THE WEB OF LIFE

Like Aldo Leopold's tinker, who
attempts to repair a watch he does not
fully understand, we keep all the pieces
of our biological fabric to insure us the
full spectrum of possibilities for
our future.

NEWMAN

A scarlet macaw (Ara macao) in Costa Rica symbolizes the
beauty, complexity, and fragility of the rainforest environment.

1 THE DYNAMICS OF THE RAINFOREST

To understand nature is to gain one of the greatest resources of life.

JOHN BURROUGHS,
NATURALIST
PHILOSOPHER

Tropical rainforests differ from the forests of temperate regions in many crucial ways. We have seen the critical range of temperature and rainfall required to support the rainforest and other tropical forest formations, and how those essentially nonseasonal characteristics have conspired to produce such rich and varied plant and animal communities. Because abundant supplies of nutrients are not available to the tropical forest as reserves held in the soil, as is classically the case in the temperate forest, the rainforest depends for its nutrients on a constant recycling of its own enormous biomass.

A MYTH DEBUNKED

Temperate forests are nurtured by a rich topsoil which may be 7 feet (2.1 m) deep and more, while the leaf mulch itself may exceed a foot (31 cm) in thickness. It was long assumed that the massive and lush tropical forests stood on rich, deep soils as well. It was surprising, therefore, to find that tropical rainforest soils were, in fact, exceedingly thin and fragile. Leaf litter averages a scant 1 inch (2.5 cm) in depth or less, and topsoil will be a mere 2 inches (5 cm) on slopes and often not much more in level areas. Typically, below this soil horizon lies a red lateritic clay. Due to their composition, and given the high rainfall, most of these soils are poor retainers of nutrients. To a large extent, the forest makes a perpetual reservoir for these substances in the biomass itself. In certain areas of the Amazon Basin and Borneo, great forests are, surprisingly, supported on almost pure white sand. In fact the tropical rainforest has been aptly described as trees growing in a desert.

▲ *A fallen canopy tree reveals the shallow root mass and absence of a taproot so common in rainforest trees. The basic instability due to such root systems is mitigated by buttressing and by the lianas which bind the tree crowns together.*

DYNAMICS OF THE RAINFOREST ENGINE

If we can use an engine as analogous to the forest, its fuel is the nitrogen made available to the living plants by the fuel pump, decomposition. The multitude of soil fauna responsible for that ongoing year-round process are rife in the thin topsoil and humus, and as temperatures are so constant, release of nutrients proceeds continuously. We can now visualize how efficiently the biological powerhouse operates—and also how vulnerable it is to disturbance. Inside the forest, temperatures are constant at the optimum level for the teeming soil fauna. Temperatures outside the forest are generally 13–18°F (7–10°C) higher. As long as the forest remains intact, the fuel pump can operate.

To lubricate this engine, rainfall must be high—never less than 67 inches (170 cm) per year—and humidity must also remain high at around 95 percent so that evaporation does not exceed precipitation. Under these conditions the heat of the engine canopy catapults into the atmosphere some 200 gallons (760 l) of water per canopy tree—roughly 20,000 gallons (76,000 l) per acre per day—and as it is carried upward it condenses into clouds, which eventually release the water again as rain and so complete the cycle. So efficient is the rainforest's water budget that up to 75 percent of its evapotranspiration is returned to it.

The abundance of rainfall in the tropical rainforest, and its constant recycling, laden with nutrients, is the key to this biome's astonishing ability to support the earth's richest vegetation cover on some of the poorest soils imaginable. While the cycle remains unbroken, the forest flourishes; but if the forest is removed, or the water cycle is disrupted, the entire system collapses, the engine stalls.

RECYCLING THE NUTRIENT STOCK

As we shall see, even though rainfall is recycled back onto the forest that produced it, it is essential that the nutrients and scarce minerals carried in that water should also be harvested back by the forest. This is done, improbably, with hardly any loss to the system. Carbon, now recognized as a pivotal factor in atmospheric stability, is just one of the crucial elements cycled and stored by the forest.

In virgin forests, enormous quantities of nutrients circulate freely between vegetation and soil, and very little is lost to the ecosystem through drainage water. In one study near Manaus, Brazil, the litter raining down to the floor of a forest plot contained 41 pounds (18.6 kg) of calcium. When the area's stream water was analyzed, no calcium was detected. What little is lost is replaced by weathering of rock.

Aside from what weathers out of bedrock, the minerals and nutrients in the moist and wet tropical forest are, in significant part, locked up in the vegetation in an all but leakproof, closed system. Due to the uninterrupted warmth and humidity, falling leaves and other debris decompose at a very rapid pace. Leaves are most often partially decomposed by insects and fungi even before they fall from the tree. The nutrient budget here may be large, but it is in a constant state of motion; a mass equivalent to that of the entire forest biomass dies and is renewed every 40 to 100 years. This forest quite literally feeds on itself.

The tropical rainforest soil is alive and teeming with fungi and decomposing organisms which very quickly release the nutrients from vegetation debris, animal excretions, and corpses. Most of the giant trees do not have taproots but, along with much of the balance of the vegetation, are very shallow rooted. In fact, aside from support, one of the main functions of their spreading buttresses is to increase the tree's absorptive area. Around 50 percent of the tree's fibrous rootlets, which are the most active in nutrient intake, are found directly under the leaf litter and just below the soil surface. These do not desiccate in the constantly moist conditions and can rapidly absorb nutrients released back into the system.

THE BUSY DECOMPOSERS

A common feature of the forest understory is decomposition: all about you seems to decay and crumble. The facilitators in this endeavor are heat and moisture; the perpetrators—fungi. Once wet, articles never dry out again unless constant efforts are taken to move them into the elusive sun. Leather, especially, soon becomes covered with fuzzy green mildew. Attempts to keep yourself above the fungal morass, in a sense, become a way of life.

When I had a field research station and house constructed in the interior forest of my Cathedral Rain Forest Science Preserve in Costa Rica, I remarked

▲ *Black water rivers, such as the Rio Negro, are the result of highly concentrated tannins in the bark and leaves of regional vegetation. These toxins, strong enough to tan leather, evolved as an effective protection from the predation of its leaves in order to conserve mineral content, which is scarce here in the Guiana Shield region of the Amazon Basin due to the ancient weathering of its mineral base. This spectacular* quebrada, *or streambed, is composed of pink quartz sand, amplifying the highly concentrated tannins. The rare result: a luminous red aura revered by local tribals and visitors such as the author's wife, Arlene. [Tepui region, Venezuela.]*

▲ *The phenomenal rate of decomposition and the very rapid recycling of nutrients account for the rainforest's ability to support such a vast biomass on such poor soil. [Petén Forest, Guatemala.]*

DYNAMICS OF THE RAINFOREST

While temperate forests rely on a bank of resources and deep rooting structures to sustain their growth, tropical forests must combat extreme climatic pressures, nutrient-poor soils, and shallow rooting systems with strategies of remarkable thrift. They can truly be likened to forests growing in a desert.

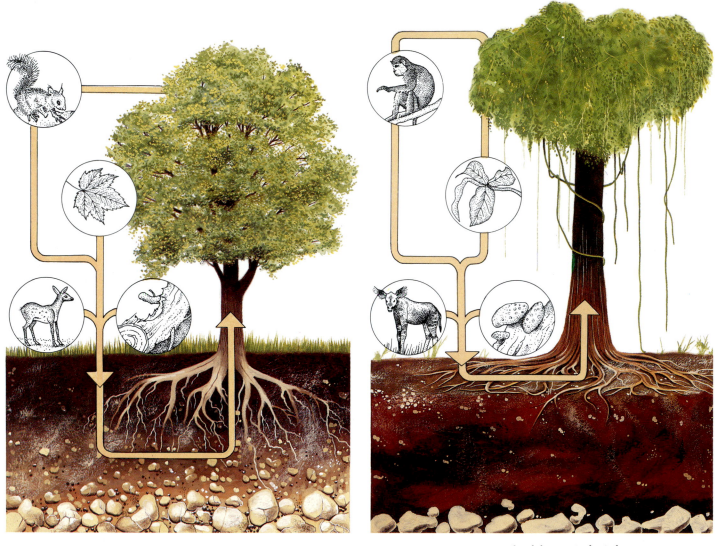

Nutrient cycle of the temperate forest

Nutrient cycle of the tropical rainforest

△▷ **Nutrient storage**
Tropical soils are so thin that nutrient stocks must be held in the biomass; in temperate forests a much higher proportion of the stock is held in the soil.

 Temperate forest

 Tropical rainforest

 Percentage in biomass

 Percentage in soil

Nitrogen   Phosphorus   Potassium   Calcium   Magnesium   Carbon

◀ Forest comparisons

Temperate and tropical forests process their resources very differently—this accounts for the vulnerability of the rainforest when its cycle is broken or disturbed.

◀◀ The temperate cycle

Here the primary nutrient reservoir is in the soil. Not exposed to intense leaching, it contains a high proportion of organic matter which in turn holds nutrients. Additional minerals are also available from weathered rocks accessible to deep roots. Recycling is slower than in warmer climes but there is always a reserve, and good farming practices can maintain the balance in agriculture.

◀ The tropical cycle

In marked contrast, the tropical forest nutrient reservoir is in the plants themselves. A fine network of surface roots retrieves the nutrients released from plant and animal remains by termites, fungi, and other decomposers.

Felling these forests and farming without careful conservation measures quickly results in loss of nutrients—and the topsoil itself—stripped away and lost in surface water runoff.

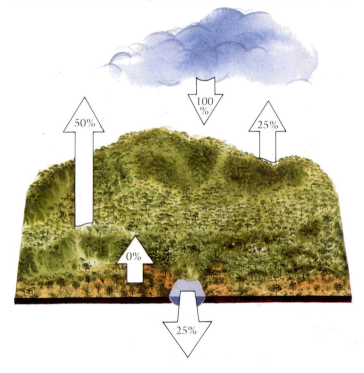

◀ The global water cycle

Water is the lifeblood of our planet. It is an essential compound in its own right; it transports dissolved nutrients, and it cleanses and refreshes the land by flushing away wastes.

The whole cycle is driven by the Sun. Of the water entering the atmosphere, 84 percent evaporates from the ocean surface, the rest from soil and inland waters and from evapotranspiration by plants. Of this water, 23 percent falls on land as rain and about 7 percent finds its way to the sea—balancing the roughly 7 percent carried inland on prevailing winds.

◀ The Amazon Basin cycle

Up to 75 percent of the water falling on the Amazon Basin as rain will be recycled into the atmosphere by the forest vegetation—50 percent by evapotranspiration and another 25 percent by direct evaporation of rainwater intercepted by the leaves. It is a virtually closed cycle quite unlike that of any other biome on Earth. There is now compelling evidence that a largely deforested Amazon *would reduce precipitation by 26 percent, evaporation by 30 percent, and, in a self-amplifying cycle, lower outside moisture entering the basin by 18 percent, a total of 74 percent reduction. Under those conditions, the forest would not return and forest remaining would be susceptible to destruction by dessication and fires.*

◀▶ The nitrogen cycle

The diagram here shows the broad global cycling of nitrogen—one of the key nutrients. In tropical forests this nutrient is scarce, and some plants have resolved the problem by utilizing the nitrogen held in animal tissues. The carnivorous pitcher plants of Southeast Asia (Nepenthes spp.) for example, digest insects lured into their pitfall traps by sweet nectar bait.

Atmospheric N₂

N_2 fixation

Addition

Nitrogen compounds in rainwater

Symbiotic

$N_2O_1N_2$

Plants → Animals   Legumes   Nonsymbiotic

Dead organic matter

Plant uptake

Ammonia → Nitrite → Nitrate

Ammonia released by weathering

Leaching

Ammonia in sedimentary rocks

◄ Yet another fascinating example of rainforest gigantism. Not a toadstool, but a giant "human stool" (Leucocoprinus gongylophorus) where researcher Robin Taylor takes pause at the Smithsonian Tropical Research Institute on Panama's Barro Colorado Island, where the fungus erupted from a fertile leafcutter ant (Atta sp.) mound.

▼ The otherworldly earthstar (Geastrum sp.) is a resident of the forest floor in northern Sumatra. The fungus is actually a puffball which, when the papery center is struck by a raindrop or falling twig, discharges a cloud of spores into the air.

▲ Carlyle said, "Nature alone is antique, and the oldest art a mushroom." Were it not for fungi like this Lentinus species from the forests of Sumatra, the Earth would long since have been buried beneath piles of organic debris.

to José, the builder and caretaker, that the structure was splendid—but how long would it last? José enthused that it was a *casa fantastica* and that it would last for *mucho tiempo*. I pressed José, saying, *bueno, pero cúantos años exactamente?* José proudly replied, *siete* (seven). In fact, the house lasted only five years, and then had to be completely rebuilt. Termites, dry rot, and wet rot had completely gutted the entire facility.

Other than powdery, troublesome fungi, other strange and elaborately hued species are commonly encountered. There are cup-shaped fungi so deeply orange as to startle the observer. Bracket fungi, some far larger than dinner plates, jut out in tiers on dead trees. Mystical puff balls, some 2 feet (0.6 m) in diameter emit huge clouds of spores at the prompting of a raindrop.

Encounters with some fungal forms can be an altogether otherworldly experience. At dusk in a Papua New Guinea lowland forest, I noticed an eerie green glow emanating from scattered pieces of rotten wood forming a perfect circle on the forest floor some 25 feet (7.6 m) in diameter. When total darkness enveloped the forest, this chartreuse gloaming became as prominent as the rings of Saturn must be as viewed from that planet. This is a variety of fungus that forms "fairy rings." Legend has it that in the night, elves dance around in a circle, their footprints leaving glowing traces. Actually, their "footprints" are luminescent fungi. Beginning as a spore, each consecutive "fruiting" forms ever-widening rings of this strange fungal colony, sometimes expanding for several hundred meters and age estimated at 1,000 years.

Colonies of such luminescent fungi are maintained in the astronauts' living compartments on NASA space missions. Supersensitive to any escape of fuel, chlorine, or other noxious fumes, the fungi cease to luminesce when exposed to only 0.02 parts per million. When all lights are turned off for a routine check, and the fungi are not glowing their eerie green, there is an immediate investigation as to what turned them off, rather like the death of the deep miner's canary serving as an indicator of lack of oxygen or presence of dangerous gases underground. Representatives of several aerospace industries were eager to obtain samples of the fungi that I had collected on that New Guinea expedition, and I found it pleasantly surprising and sobering to know that modern space science still relies on such primitive yet reliable technology.

TRANSITIONAL FUNGAL-ANIMAL ORGANISM

In Costa Rica, and only again in Peru, I was fortunate to observe unique examples of the potential for species diversity in tropical forests where even distinctions between plants and animals become veiled and finally disappear. A shimmering, simpering, translucent gray, jellylike mass of mucus the size of a football, it is singularly the most inexplicable life-form I have ever seen. It appeared transitional between plant and animal; indeed, current scientific thinking places it separate from either and is given its own phylum, Myxomycota, in the Protista kingdom. Be assured, no alien organism could be more otherworldly. From the fungal group Myxomycetes (whose derivation means "fungus-animal"), this blob is actually a traveling mass of protoplasm made of but a single cell, the largest cell known. While fruiting like a fungus it is motile like an animal. Somehow it seems such an organism would make an appealing pet.

Fungi are saprophytes, like bacteria. Simple nonflowering plants, they have no roots, seeds, leaves, or chlorophyll so they must use food produced by other plants and animals. They can be roughly divided into three ecologi-

▲ *Arguably the most perplexing of Earth's life-forms, the myxomycetes, while up to a foot (1.3 m) or more in diameter, are composed of but a single cell called plasmodia. These fascinating amoeboid protozoans come from so ancient a lineage that they date back even before the split between fungal and animal forms. Biologists cannot definitively classify them as either, so they are now being given their own phylum—Myxomycota. Oblivious to the spines of this palm the creature climbs, it consumes bacteria and other micro-organisms. In the Sucusari River region of the Peruvian Amazon where I led a rain-forest workshop, almost 200 ecotourists waded chest deep through the flooded forest—at night—to arrive with me at the location where they could observe this rare, otherworldly organism. The evanescence of their transformation from a traveling mass of jellylike protoplasm into a fragile, alluring, flowerlike mushroom form accounts, in part, for the beauty of this beast.*

cal categories: decomposers, parasites, and mycorrhizal fungi. The unheralded decomposers, of course, consume and digest dead plant and animal matter and create humus for other vegetation to utilize. Were it not for these, and their cohorts the bacteria and insects, our world would be buried beneath vast accumulations of organic debris—a garbage dump.

Parasitic fungi attack living plants and animals, and can be very destructive. Spores of these organisms are sometimes eaten by insects such as wasps and springtails. When the fungus matures, it kills the wasp and from its body emerges a macabre but delicate mushroom. Such corpses are frequently observed in the forest, frozen in their last activities as though their health was sustained until the terminal moment.

The third group, the mycorrhizal fungi, form an extremely beneficial relationship with many forest trees. They surround or penetrate the tree's roots with the threadlike mycelia which form the body of the fungus as distinguished from the aboveground mushroom which is only the temporary "fruit" responsible for producing spores to propagate the fungus. Through these microscopic threads they transfer nutrients directly to the tree.

Practical Nitrogen Fixers

Plants, we know, rely on nitrogen for their survival and growth. This commodity is rarely overabundant in soil, and most plants must acquire it from the sparse amounts released in soluble nitrate form by microbial decomposition of dead organisms and animal waste products. In the case of legume-producing plants (the bean and pea family, Leguminosae), a marvelous symbiosis exists between the plant's roots and *Rhizobium*, a soil bacterium. Nitrogen makes up 78 percent of our atmosphere, and *Rhizobium* has the rare talent of being able to trap this nitrogen from the air and use it to manufacture ammonium nitrates. In trade for sugar and safe housing in the root nodules of most of the Leguminosae, it passes these nitrates on directly for the plants' use in the production of protein.

The amount of nitrogen acquired ("fixed") by leguminous plants such as alfalfa, peas, and soybeans is so high that it is profitable to plow in these crops when market price is low or after the harvest has been gathered in. This, of course, releases the nitrates for use by another crop. Current research continues to establish this beneficial relationship of *Rhizobium* with other agricultural crops.

Investigation has revealed another similar mutualistic dependency. It has long been noted that certain soils including rainforest soils are alive with fungi, and it was suspected that they served some specific function. The discovery was made that at least some mycorrhizal fungi integrate with the roots of certain tropical forest trees. In some classes of this association, in exchange for sugars, they super-inject nitrogen they have gleaned from the soil directly into the trees' roots. In certain types of this association, insolubles such as phosphorous and zinc are also transferred to the trees. This is believed in part to account for the very rapid uptake of nutrients and certain minerals by tropical rainforest plants. The nutrients are delivered "door to door."

Pine trees did very poorly in Australia and Puerto Rico until mycorrhizal fungi from the pines' original territory was introduced into the soil, after which growth was swift. These discoveries are expected to have an even broader agricultural application for it appears that not only all lowland forest trees but almost all nongrain crops can develop this mutualistic relationship between fungi and their roots.

THE SCRAMBLE FOR LIGHT

The constant drama of the survival of the fittest is always quite overt in the rainforest. Plants compete aggressively for their share of light. A small tree sapling, the diameter of a finger, will remain dormant for many years, not growing at all until a large limb or tree falls, creating a gap in the canopy overhead. Some vines are known to use this "dormant" time to grow an energy-storing tuber underground in preparation for the moment of opportunity. When this happens, just as a starter's pistol begins a race, there is a mad scramble of growth among the plants to reach the light and spread their crowns, thus closing the door to unsuccessful competitors. Natural disturbances are very much a part of the forest cycle, and the forest biomass is always prepared to heal the wounds of violent weather, landslides, or simply the termination of senile canopy trees.

Contrasting with the complex equilibrium and order of the climax forest, the secondary vegetation which replaces it is a riotous community in intense competition, striving for dominance from the very instant light becomes available. The pioneer trees, shrubs, herbs, and climbers differ from the climax species they replace by being light-demanding and shade-intolerant so that they are not only suppressed by shade-tolerant species of the virgin forest but often will not germinate in their own shade. This ensures that their life span on the site is but one generation, so that they quickly yield to climax species after performing their function—which is protection of the soil from erosion.

This they accomplish with remarkable abilities. Recent research unravels some of the mystery of secondary-forest succession. Artificial clearings of 1,000, 2,000, and 3,000 square meters have been made in climax tropical moist forest, and whereas light gaps of up to 1,000 square meters were soon filled by regenerating climax species, the larger gaps became swamped by the aggressive pioneer (secondary) species. But from where, all at once, does this secondary species seed come, especially as these plants do not occur primarily as adults in mature forest in any numbers?

Trees grow in three ways: from shoots issuing out of roots, stumps, or fallen trunks; from established seedlings; or from seeds. You will not often find light-loving secondary species as seedlings in the dark climax forest. Climax species' seeds generally have a short germination period "window" after which they are no longer viable. It is found, however, that seeds of secondary species, opportunists that they are, can still germinate after many years. They arrive as a gradual but constant "seed rain," by both wind and animal transport. They accumulate steadily through the years and may become buried 8 inches (20 cm) below the soil surface—ready and waiting to sprout when light and temperature dictate. Such specialist species' talents hold a fascination for students of the forest, giving an order to life as we come to know it more intimately.

Further, in their function as forest healers, the pioneer species are quick to provide a protective cover over exposed soil. A wound is covered in only a few weeks' time, and in three years the trees may have attained a growth of some 40 feet (12 m). Such fast growth lends a soft and light quality to the wood, and balsa (*Ochroma* spp.), a typical secondary species of the Neotropics, is well recognized by model enthusiasts as one of the lightest woods

▲ *A nurse log sprouts what will one day develop into a puzzling, arrow-straight line of mature trees. The demise of the parent tree has created a small patch of light—sufficient only for the most competitive species. The plant's red leaves may signal danger to herbivorous insects, so giving the plant just the extra competitive edge it needs. [Osa Peninsula, Costa Rica.]*

known. Quite commonly a secondary forest stand is dominated by a single species, in high contrast to the diverse composition of the climax forest.

The study of forest succession is still too young to give hard figures to the time span allotted for forest disturbance, from light-gap colonization by pioneer species, through infusion of climax species and their inevitable eventual dominance over senile pioneer species, to the final return of climax forest. Certain hard facts are known, however, which lead us to believe that that period may be a lengthy one.

As the water content is too high to allow tropical wet or moist forests to burn, under natural conditions, areas of disturbance are generally restricted to sizes that allow the surrounding climax-forest species' seed to infiltrate. (We will see in the following chapter that that is not the case with vast man-made clearings.) Although the precise ages of mature climax trees are not known, due to the absence of tree rings (seasonal fluctuations being largely absent in the wet tropics), it is speculated that some at least reach 200 years and more, though certain species are thought to be far more ancient. Add to that the time period necessary for the full-climax community to out-compete secondary species and mature fully, and today a trained observer may walk through forests originally cleared by Mayans up to 2,000 years ago and still distinguish them from virgin formations. It is with this enormous time scale in mind that we must plan for future development in tropical forest areas.

II POLLINATION AND SEED DISPERSAL

Shelley wrote, "The forest is the perpetual work of Thy creation; finished, yet renewed forever."

As most rainforest trees are dependent on the services of animals for pollination or seed dispersal, especially the large-seeded species, the interrelationships between members of the plant and animal communities have evolved to such a finely tuned state that the functioning of the forest as an integrated and resilient system has evolved, in turn, a dependence on those very liaisons. By dissecting them we may put our finger on the pulse of the biome itself and better perceive its fragility.

THE MARVEL OF THE POLLINATION ARRANGEMENT

Many plant and animal interactions and mutual dependencies are bewildering in their implications for evolution. If we investigate pollination, for example, we find that flowers exhibit very definite constructions, shapes, colors, and scents, which in various cases are linked directly to specific animal pollinators. These well-devised and time-tested plans are referred to as flowering strategies.

Bat-pollinated flowers open at dusk, when the bats are active, and have a sour odor not unlike the smell of the bat itself. The nectar is sticky, and the flower color is usually pale to improve its visibility at night. Flowers are often pendulous and are held away from the foliage by long twigs. These features facilitate bat visitation while discouraging other animals. In their search for nectar the bats pick up pollen on the fur of the head and chest, and subsequently distribute it to other flowers, thus consummating fertilization. Bird-pollinated flowers, such as hibiscus (*Hibiscus* spp.) on the other hand, are scentless, display bright colors, and have a watery nectar.

QUESTION:
How many wasp species are needed to pollinate the world's 900 fig species?

ANSWER:
900

◀ *Predation ensures that species remain at peak efficiency, be they hunter or hunted. Here in a Trinidad forest, ants of the Ec-tatomma genus lie in wait to ambush the fungus gnats that will come to feed and lay their eggs on the fungi's fruiting body. This is natural selection at work.*

AMOROUS WASPS AND BEWILDERED BEETLES

Males of certain wasp species attempt to mate with specific species of orchids, whose flowers are near-perfect mimics of female wasps of the same species. Covered with pollen after an abysmal disappointment, the male wasp moves on to another flower for another amorous encounter and, incidentally, consummates pollination in the strategy of *pseudocopulation.* Orchid flowers also imitate a species the pollinator likes to kill, provoking an attack which coats its assailant with pollen, in the strategy of *pseudoantagonism.*

If life is full of frustrations, nature balances her cruel deceptions, in this case with a more pleasurable bout between an orchid (*Gongora maculata*) from South America and its bee pollinator. This orchid produces an intoxicating substance on the upper lip of its flower. The bee, attracted by this chemical, must crawl into the flower upside down where he becomes, frankly, quite drunk. In his stupor, he stumbles and falls bodily through the air. He is quite handily caught by the lower flower parts where he deposits the pollen he brought with him and picks up more before continuing on to his next double-martini encounter with life. Fortunately for our bee's "liver," temperance returns with the close of the orchid's flowering season.

Closely related plant species even flower at different times as a precautionary adaptation against hybridization. There is much wonder and speculation about the intricacies of these arrangements.

In many of our food crops we depend on quite specific pollinators. It was once thought more profitable to grow plantations of Brazil-nut trees (*Bertholletia excelsa*) instead of harvesting the nuts from scattered trees in the forest. The planted trees grew well enough, but yielded no nuts. It was subsequently found that the insect that pollinated the Brazil nut lived in other types of trees in the natural forest.

It becomes easy to see how a great many of these species obtain exalted positions as "keystone mutualists," integral and necessary links in the survival of species, both to those they serve directly as well as to those up and down the food chain.

On backwaters of the Amazon River grows the giant royal water lily (*Victoria amazonica*), with leaves big enough, at 7 feet (2 m) across, to support the weight of a human child. The lily actually imprisons its scarab-beetle pollinator (*Cyclocephala hardyi*) by closing its enormous flower after the 1-inch (2.5-cm)-long beetle has moved in to feed on the flower parts. The reasons for what then takes place are not presently understood, but during the night, the flower raises its temperature an incredible 20°F (11°C) higher than the ambient air temperature. A delicious fragrance similar to a mixture of butterscotch and pineapple fills areas of this river at night. The nocturnal jungle music mixed with this overpowering aroma is truly a memorable experience . . . Exactly 24 hours later, the flower opens to release its captive, now covered with pollen, to seek a new flower to fertilize.

THE WORLD'S LARGEST FLOWER

A journey through the tropical rainforest is clearly an intensely olfactory experience. The aromas, however, are not always the most pleasant: some will be the violent fragrance of decomposition itself.

PLANT POLLINATION STRATEGIES

Because the survival of many plant species depends on their success in attracting efficient animal pollinators, numerous complex and intriguing strategies have evolved. In many cases, the plant and its pollinator have evolved together in a close, often exclusive, mutually beneficial partnership. So intricate and specific are these arrangements that they are among the wonders of biological science.

Swordbill (*Ensifera ensifera*) and *Passiflora*

Sicklebill (*Eutoxeres aquila*) and *Heliconia*

◀ *Hummingbird partners*
The boundless energy of the hummingbird requires a staggering intake of high-calorie nectar. The same daily activity rate would require an average man to consume 155,000 calories—the equivalent of 370 pounds (168 kg) of potatoes or 130 loaves of bread. The swordbilled hummingbird is able to refuel in flight from the long tubular flowers of the Passiflora *plant, and just as the swordbill's hugely elongated bill is matched to the shape of its food-flower, so is that of the white-tipped sicklebill to the flowers of the* Heliconia *plant.*

▼ *Darwin's moth*
Seven decades passed before the discovery of the Madagascan hawk moth, with its 8-inch (20-cm) tongue, proved the accuracy of Darwin's prediction that only such an animal could pollinate this Angraecum *orchid.*

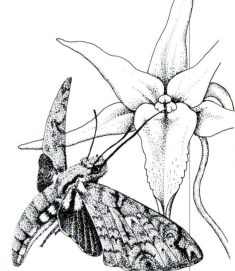

Darwin's moth (*Xanthopan morgani praedicta*) and *Angraecum sesquipedale*

Gongora maculata and its euglossine bee helper

▽▷ *Flies and bats*
Inquisitive observers have been known to faint from the overpowering stench of the giant arum lily, which is pollinated by carrion flies. Long-tongued night-flying bats perform the same function for the pendulous blooms of the Datura *tree.*

Giant arum lily *Amorphophallus titanum*

◁ *The drunken bee*
Intoxicating substances produced by the upper lip of the Gongora *orchid entice bees into the flower. Once inside, they become drunkenly unstable and fall into the lower lip, where pollen they are carrying is deposited on the plant's stigma.*

Bucket orchid (*Coryanthes* sp.) and euglossine bee

Datura sp. in flower

Giant water lily *Victoria amazonica*

◁▷ *Sweet entrapment*
Both the giant Amazon water lily and the bucket orchid trap their insect pollinators. The lily opens after 24 hours to release its beetle helper, but the bee that assists the orchid must force its way out through the side door while completing its pollination task.

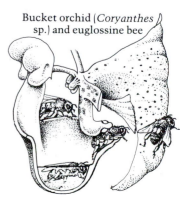

In the deep tropical forests of Indonesia grows the rafflesia (*Rafflesia* spp.), the world's largest flower. It spans 38 inches (97 cm) across and, holding a special fascination for me as a carrion flower, it both resembles a rotting carcass and smells exactly like one. Not surprisingly, its pollinators are carrion flies (*Calliphora*), always the first scavengers to arrive at the scene of death.

While on an expedition in 1983 to locate the rare *Rafflesia arnoldii*, my then 13-year-old son Gandhi and I penetrated a remote upland forest in Gunung Leuser, northern Sumatra, that had been only lightly studied by botanists in the past. The reason for such light scientific scrutiny, we soon found, was this particular forest's extremely heavy infestation with land leeches (Hirudinea). With each hour's travel within the leech forest, we acquired up to 25 of these parasites, some several inches in length.

The rafflesia flower we were searching for has a bud the size of a basketball, opens with the hiss of a cobra, and may take as long as two years to develop. The bud then opens to its 36-pound (16.3-kg) full-flower size, which varies within the species. In some, the central cup will hold 1.5 gallons (6 l) of water. The flower remains open for only three days, after which it quickly decomposes. Imagine our delight when we found one—among the very rarest of plants—and one of truly enormous size. To add to its natural scarcity, most of its habitats are heavily deforested. Upon returning home, it was also with considerable gratification that we discovered that this was not *R. arnoldii* after all, but a new species, and

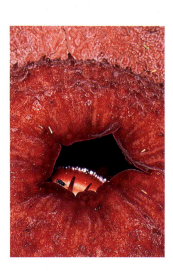

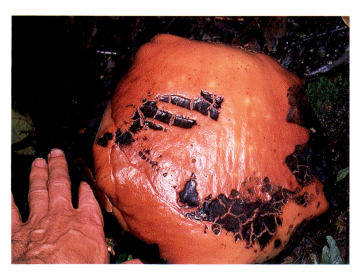

given its close approximation to the maximum size for the genus it is likely the largest of the world's flowers. It is named *R. micropylora*.

The flower's odor was putrid, but still utterly alluring, and it was abuzz with carrion flies. So rare is any species of *Rafflesia* that few who search for it will find it, and yet it manages its precarious pollination strategy on the apparently outrageous assumption that the same fly will seek out yet another flower, in such infrequent bloom, in the vastness of the forest.

To add to its macabre profile, the rafflesia is noted also as being one of the most complete parasites known. The entire plant lives within the root or stem tissues of only a few specific vines in the grape family (*Tetrastigma* spp.), existing entirely at the expense of the host. Only the flower shows itself to the world as this bizarre and exotic blossom thrusts itself briefly above the ground or from the stem of its host. From its center, an inexplicable incandescent fire seems to glow. We felt fortunate in finding this extraordinary flower and reflected that it was tragic that, though just discovered, it was already endangered. It was, I must say, the most extraordinary and compelling vision I have ever seen.

Darwin's Orchid

So as not to be outdone by exotic pollination schemes, the Darwin orchid (*Angraecum sesquipedale*) rests its case on the unimaginable. The legendary Charles Darwin, on his travels to Madagascar, noted that the flower of this orchid was so constructed that its nectary was at the end of an extremely long tubular spur. He concluded that the only plausible pollinator would be a moth with a tongue 8 inches (20 cm) long. At that time, no such moth was known to exist. The scientific establishment guffawed at his deduction. Sixty-five years later, the Madagascan sphinx moth (*Xanthopan morgani praedicta*), which possesses just such a tongue, was discovered. There are many examples of such coevolved adaptations by flower and pollinator. They ensure that flowers are available only to certain animals, who visit these flowers, sometimes dispersed over great distances, and so ensure their pollination.

How did this plant exist before the specific pollinator developed? In mutual dependencies, did both plant and animal rely on the incredible odds of a simultaneous coevolution? Although this is doubtful, the remarkable degree of adaptation expressed by both species begs inquiry. If the explanation of a tropical rainforest is the sum of its functions, these are predominantly orchestrated under biological controls where temperate forests fall under physical control. Where far fewer species, for example, make up the latter forest structure, wind will be an effective pollinator or seed disperser. In the tropical forest, the enormous diversity of plant life demands the attentions of species-specific facilitators.

The Forest in Bloom

For virtually every situation, we find a solution in unique adaptation. Where rarely a breeze penetrates into the rainforest understory, progeneration has been answered in some plants by a strategy called *cauliflory*. Instead of flowers and fruits being borne on terminating parts of branches, as we are used to in temperate climate trees, many tropical understory trees carry them right on the trunk, near the ground. This makes a strange and startling display for the jungle traveler, whether human or other animal, and this is precisely its purpose. This strategy ensures that flowers and fruits are boldly

▲ *Many rainforest plants exhibit cauliflory. Their flowers and fruits sprout direct from the stem where they are openly exposed to the animals that will pollinate and disperse them. This species,* Urera elata, *is from Costa Rica.*

▲ *Canopy trees in full flower provide a breath-taking sight in the highly endangered Atlantic forest of southeastern Brazil. This eye-catching "Big Bang" display is no accident: it is a compelling invitation to the trees' pollinators.*

advertised, and so prove tempting to passing animal pollinators and seed distributors. They are much too easily missed if hidden among the leaves. Many forest tree-dwelling animals are specially equipped with prehensile tails, suction cups, or digits of great dexterity so that they may ply this fruit source.

As an alternative, many upper-canopy trees shed their leaves when flowering, and so offer a magnificent bouquet that is hard to ignore. As most trees of the same species are synchronized, the spectacle from a hilltop or from an aircraft, of purple, pink, yellow, or red eruptions of color scattered over the canopy is magnificent.

To add to the already miraculous story of coadaptations, certain pollinating bees have their life cycles timed to coincide with this massive "Big Bang" type of flowering, and set out from their underground or otherwise secluded catacombs after a dormant stage just before the trees explode into bloom.

While this spectacular flowering is taking place, usually during the dry season, some plants such as certain species of lianas, whose flowers contain no nectar, solve the problem of pollination in a cleverly devised deception. They have been blessed with flowers that mimic the nectar-filled blossoms of "Big Bang" and cornucopia-style flowering trees, and they time their flowering to begin at the waning of these trees' display. By doing so, their smaller displays are pounced on eagerly by the pollinators of tree bouquets, who realize too late that the liana's flower gives no nectar reward. Yet another of life's little disappointments, but one which is more than amply balanced by the advantage to another life-form.

An Infinite Talent for Seed Dispersal

Plant species must be sure to distribute themselves over wide areas of their range in order to ensure against extinction. Growing only in localized clusters, individual species would easily fall victim to plagues of insects or other blights. Of course, many plants with featherweight seeds or gliding apparatus very adequately travel by air if they have access to regular breezes, such as occur high in the canopy. Indeed, certain fern sporangia explode when ripe, and high-level winds may carry their spores completely around the world. But what solution is built in for the many plants with large and often ponderous seeds and seed pods? The plant's good friend and courier—the animal. Many seeds with spurs will hitch a ride on an animal's coat. Birds and bats, of course, eat fruits and later, often at great distances, disperse the seeds in their droppings.

Some plants such as the beke tree (*Irvingia* spp.) of Africa rely not on birds but on the African elephant (*Loxodonta africana*) to eat their seeds and digest away the durable outer shell to effect germination. Horses (*Equus caballos*) and, we can assume, other wild Equidae are also found to retain certain large, tough seeds in their digestive system for almost a year before passing the still viable seed. During the critical beginning then, the seed has a most nutritious and protective medium in which to grow . . . a large, moist, and steaming warm pile of animal dung.

Many fruit-eating carnivores are attracted by a rich odor rather than color, since many of these prowlers are nocturnal. Even though basically a meat eater, the tiger (*Panthera tigris*) has a passion for durian fruit that is legendary.

Of course, fruit is tasty in order to encourage animals to consume it, the seed subsequently to be softened in the animals' digestive tract to facilitate germination, and then dispersed. There are seeds which actually require animals' digestive enzymes in order to germinate. Many such dependencies are acute, and are dramatized by noting that the ranges of some of these animal-dependent plants are abruptly marked by rivers—which also form impassible barriers for their animal partners. Such is the case for the eastern lowland gorilla (*Gorilla gorilla graueri*) and certain plants that make up its diet.

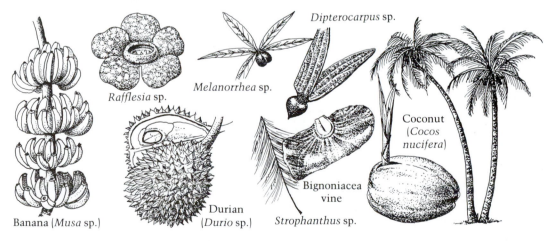

Dipterocarpus sp.

Melanorrhea sp.

Rafflesia sp.

Coconut (*Cocos nucifera*)

Bignoniacea vine

Durian (*Durio* sp.)

Strophanthus sp.

Banana (*Musa* sp.)

▲ **Animal dispersal**
To encourage animals to spread their seeds, many plants have attractive fruits, or burrs which cling to the feathers or fur of passing birds and mammals.

▲ **Wind dispersal**
In the high, wind-exposed canopy, a prime dispersal strategy of trees is to produce winged seeds that will be carried well clear of the parent tree's shadow.

▲ **Water dispersal**
The coconut, rare in its ability to tolerate long exposure to salt water, avoids mass germination in one place by drifting far on ocean currents.

The heliconias or "wild plantains" (Heliconia spp.) are the New World representatives of the Old World banana family. Water collects in the upturned bracts of this perennial herb, providing a watering place for birds and a breeding pool for a myriad tiny freshwater organisms. [Isla de Cano, Costa Rica.]

▼ The heliconias are among the most stunning of the rainforest flowers. This specimen, H. mutisiana from Colombia, is adorned with a newly hatched boa. It is an upland plant, which evolution has equipped with a dense hair coat to insulate it against the cool night air and making the inflorescence unpalatable to browsers.

◀ Many orchids, like this Cattleya forbesii, a member of the genus from which the corsage orchid was hybridized, are epiphytes. To ensure its survival without contact with the soil, the plant possesses a pseudobulb which stores reserves of food to nourish it through periods of nutrient shortage. [Atlantic rainforest, southeastern Brazil.]

▶ In the fierce competition for space and light, few forest niches remain unoccupied. These epiphytic bromeliads (Vriesea heterostachys), and several unnamed ferns, growing on the moss-covered trunk of a tree, are nourished by the swirling mist and the organic debris raining down from above. [Atlantic rainforest, southeastern Brazil.]

III SPECIALISTS AND PARTNERSHIPS

The tropical rainforest, even more so than other tropical forest formations, is a surprising synthesis of harmony and competition; an overt rhythm radiating out from the Sun itself, the source of the very energy that drives the biome's dynamo. Plants, the primary producers, are the basis for the food chain as they alone are able to capture the Sun's energy and incorporate it into their tissues. We have seen how the faunal community is directly and craftfully enlisted by the plants as pollinators, seed dispersers, propagators, decomposers of litter, feeders, and even defenders. That the creatures who perform these services most often benefit themselves, only makes the arrangements so much more ingenious and flawless—the foundation of evolutionary adaptation.

HIGHER ANIMAL FOOD-CHAIN DYNAMICS

By examining the behavioral patterns, methods of locomotion, and food gathering of the higher animals, we will see how their abilities are finely tuned as primary consumers in their quest for plant material, and as secondary consumers as they prey on the plant-eating species.

Animals are not allowed the dubious luxury of senility. If the law of the jungle is the survival of the fittest, the carnivore is the ruling enforcer. Just as soon

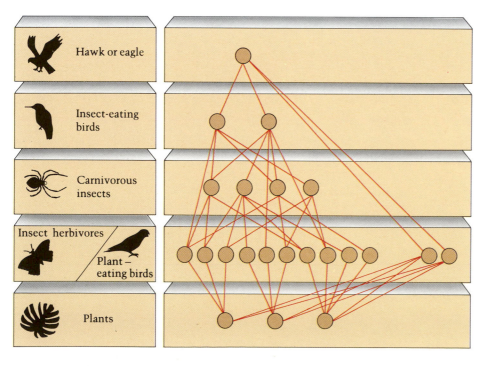

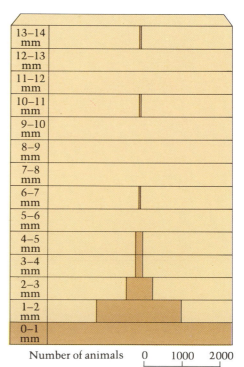

▲ **The rainforest food web**
This simplified, hypothetical food web pictures a habitat with three plant species, 10 plant-eating insects and two seed-eating birds, four predatory insects, two insect-eating birds, and one top predator (which has no enemy but man).

It becomes abundantly clear that overall species diversity is dependent on the basic plant resource, and on the great variety of animals at the first feeding level. There can be no clearer proof of the vital role of tropical vegetation in maintaining our planet's species diversity.

▲ **The pyramid of numbers**
In this sample of leaf-litter life, the most numerous animals are mites and springtails, all herbivores and scavengers. Carnivorous beetles and spiders are far less abundant.

as the flying lemur or colugo (*Cynocephalus variegatus*) becomes enfeebled enough to drop its guard in scanning the sky as it forages in the treetops, it will be carried away by the Philippine eagle (*Pithecophaga jefferyi*), its particular nemesis. In South America the harpy eagle (*Harpia harpyja*) will similarly pursue, at 50 miles per hour (80 kmph) through the trees, a capuchin monkey (*Cebus* spp.) caught up in a noisy squabble with his mates. A creative adaptation of a light sensor atop the green iguana's (*Iguana iguana*) head will detect the shadow cast by the great bird causing him to dive to safety into the river below.

The ruling mammals at the top of the food chain are the canopy cats of medium size, such as the ocelot (*Felis pardalis*) of Latin America, the golden cat (*F. aurata*) of West Africa, and the clouded leopard (*Neofelis nebulosa*) of Southeast Asia, as well as the great cats which range across all the continents. Most have adapted a spotted or striped coat to imitate the broken pattern of the sun-dappled forest background. As secondary consumers they ambush or pursue their chosen prey species, culling infirm individuals by the most natural selection, and thus serving to keep the animal population at optimum level and in good condition, a much tidier method than the alternatives, which are famine and its lethal silent partner—disease.

While many of the predators at the top of the food chain have no apparent natural enemies, they are themselves controlled in part by injuries sustained while dispatching prey, by intersexual aggression, and by territorial competition within their own species. As anyone knows who has acquired an injury in the moist tropical forest, wounds fester quickly and soon become flyblown. The predator is then exposed to the patient pathogens of bacteria, viruses, fungi, and other parasites that await us all. It is sometimes the case that incapacitated large cats, unable to run down their customary prey, will finally resort to killing and eating relatively defenseless humans.

SELECTIVE ADAPTATION

Many prey species have themselves evolved intriguing defensive adaptations, thus ensuring that they are not merely so much hapless meat in the

▼ The fulguroid's fierce appearance convinces many in its Latin American range that it has a bite to match. Such is not the case. The species on the left (Fulgora servillei) *flashes its eye markings to deter predators. The one on the right* (F. laternaria) *shows the savage toothed, but quite empty false head that earns it the name "lantern," "peanut," or "alligator" bug.*

▶ *Protective adaptation is so perfected in this "walking stick" (Pseudophasmatidae) that, unless moving, it remains quite invisible against the decayed palm frond that is one of its most common niches. [Venezuelan rainforest.]*

▲ *The casque-headed mantis (*Choeradodis rhombicollis*) is a perfect mimic of the forest orchid* Epidendrum ciliare. *Its camouflage is complete, even to the false fungus holes on the casque.*

treetops—as indeed humankind would be without the benefit of our most highly developed attribute—intelligence. Instead, the flying lemur (*Cynocephalus variegatus*), flying dragon (*Draco volans*), flying squirrel (*Petaurista,* and others), flying or paradise tree snake (*Chrysopelea pelias*), and Wallace's flying frog (*Rhacophorus nigropalmatus*), to name but a few, have taken to quite efficient gliding, if not true flight, by the development of expandable membranes on feet, flanks, and tails. The snake can cover 160 feet (50 m), and the lemur's flight has been measured at 443 feet (135 m) with an altitude loss of only 40 feet (12 m). Through this miraculous flight we can see the designs of evolutionary adaptation at work. It is probable that more of these flying species are found in Asian tropical forests than, say, Africa, as trees are taller in Asian forests on average and less well connected by a network of lianas which would afford transport. Bats (Chiroptera) we know have taken this option to full fruition as the only mammal to consummate full flight. The giant fruit bat or flying fox (*Pteropus giganteus*), whose wingspan can reach 69 inches (1.75 m), can cover 155 miles (250 km) in a single evening's flight, feeding and dispersing fruit seed in its journey.

The males of many forest birds, such as the birds of paradise (Paradisaeidae), resplendent quetzal (*Pharomachrus mocinno*), cock-of-the-rock (*Rupicola rupicola*), and peacock pheasant (*Polyplectron emphanum*) display incomparably stunning plumage in their bizarre courtship rituals. While these would appear initially to have negative implications for survival value by attracting predators, such bright colors and aggressive movements often serve to signal danger and may even momentarily stun a potential attacker. (It is equally significant that the females of most species have inconspicuous brown, olive-drab, or mottled plumage. What use would bright colors be to a hen bird, tied to the nest, static and vulnerable, while incubating her eggs?)

The cassowaries (*Casuarius* spp.), standing as tall as 6 feet (1.8 m), have evolved such formidable size that most adversaries, including New Guinea tribal people, treat them with great respect, acknowledging that this giant ground bird could gut them with a flash of its massively clawed foot. The aye-aye (*Daubentonia madagascariensis*) from the island whose name it bears (and where profound evolutionary adaptations seem almost the rule) has developed an enormously long third digit on its front paw, which far from being a defensive weapon is used instead as a tool to extract grubs from decaying wood, for which it listens with its exaggeratedly large ears. A great many nocturnal animals, including the bush babies (Galagidae) and tarsiers (*Tarsius* spp.), have faces dominated by colossal eyes, quite circular in outline, which enhance their night vision immensely.

CANOPY AND MIDSTRATA RESIDENTS

Looking more closely at the forest's residents we see how they are adapted to their own specific strata in the forest, and then to specific niches in those strata. Through these traits we can see an infinitely efficient design in what appears at first to be reckless chaos. Even more so than the chimpanzee (*Pan troglodytes*) which will move readily from arboreal to terrestrial activities, the appearance of the Asian gibbon (*Hylobates* spp.) reveals it at once as a canopy specialist and premier seed disperser. Its gangly arms are twice as long as those of a human, compared to body length, almost reaching the ground when the animal stands upright. These long limbs and long, strong-fingered hands, facilitate the flowing, rowing, brachiating movement by which the gibbon moves through the trees, sometimes leaping 20 feet (6 m) from one tree to the next. The elegantly plumed tail of the African colobus monkey (*Colobus polykomos*) serves as a rudder and even as a parachute to control (or recoup from) its extended leaps.

▲ *The tamandua or lesser anteater* (Tamandua tetradactyla) *has a prehensile tail to aid its foraging high in the tree canopy. This one is clawing at a termite-filled branch.*

◀ *No one who has visited the Latin American rainforest could ever forget the booming calls of the howler* (Alouatta fusca) *proclaiming his territorial rights.*

◀ ▼ *Toucans such as Costa Rica's Swainson's toucan (Ramphastos swainsonii) are New World counterparts of the Old World hornbills, such as the rhinoceros hornbill (Buceros rhinoceros) of the Sumatran forest. Both are known for their personality and inquisitiveness, often checking up on travelers in the forest.*

▲ *Spectacular adult male cotingas like this Guianan cock-of-the-rock (Rupicola rupicola) often gather in large numbers in forest clearings to perform their elaborate courtship displays in front of audiences of drably colored females.*

▶ *Runaway evolution has given the birds of paradise the most elegant plumage in the avian world. Because the rate of predation in New Guinea is low, the dangers of sporting such extravagant plumes are minimized. [Lesser bird of paradise (Paradisaea minor).]*

▶ *Complex adaptations are woven into the nesting habits of caciques like the Amazonian yellow-rumped cacique* (Cacicus cela). *To deter nest parasites their pendulous nests are hung from slender twigs, often in trees infested with wasps. Nevertheless, they are often parasitized by the giant cowbird* (Psomocolax oryzivorus), *whose eggs they sometimes eject.*

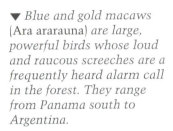

▼ *Blue and gold macaws* (Ara ararauna) *are large, powerful birds whose loud and raucous screeches are a frequently heard alarm call in the forest. They range from Panama south to Argentina.*

In the New World forests, many primates, typified by the woolly monkeys (*Lagothrix* spp.) and spider monkeys (*Ateles* spp.) have answered the need for canopy-top stability by evolving the prehensile tail. This fifth limb also identifies the tamandua (*Tamandua tetradactyla*), kinkajou or honey bear (*Potos flavus*), and tree porcupine (*Coendou* spp.) as arboreal. Through these examples we can clearly recognize convergent evolution at work, yet it is perplexing that prehensile tails are largely absent in the Old World.

As large size is a limiting factor in the trees, some of these occupants, such as the dwarf anteater (*Cyclopes didactylus*) and the mouse opossums (*Marmosa* spp.), are diminutive in the extreme. The favorite nesting place of one species of the latter is in hollowed-out cocoa pods (*Theobroma cacao*).

Middle-canopy specialists, such as civets (Viverridae), martens (Mustelidae), and marmosets (Callithricidae), are commonly typified by sharp claws to facilitate constant vertical climbing. This stratum is not without its own drama. Of these residents, none is more otherworldly than the tree hyrax (*Dendrohyrax*). Not much larger than a rabbit, this most feisty mammal is obtusely one of the elephant's closest relatives. Its call is a bone-chilling agonized screeching sound, mimicking hysterical human lamentations. In the Virunga Mountain range in Rwanda, at 10,000 feet (3,050 m) in the middle of the night, we were, to our horror, unable to distinguish it from the latter.

The food resources in midlevel consist of chicks, eggs, the young and tender liana shoots and leaves, and a heavy palm flora whose buds, seeds, and fruits are particularly rich nutritionally. As one would expect, the maneuverable owls

▼ *All forest animals live by the law of the jungle— and this animal is the enforcer. The jaguar (*Panthera onca*) rules from forest floor to canopy, and even the tribal people of the rainforest acknowledge its supreme position at the top of the food chain. [Brazilian Pantanal.]*

(Strigidae) and hawks (Accipitridae) patrol the midcanopy by night and day respectively.

In no way are all forest creatures rigidly relegated to a distinct strata. It is estimated that in order to match the high intensity and energy output of hummingbirds (Trochilidae), and their Old World counterparts the sun birds (Nectariniidae), in their flitting from forest floor to canopy tops in search of flowers, the average-size man would require a daily caloric intake of 155,000 calories—the equivalent of 370 pounds (168 kg) of potatoes or 130 loaves of bread. The margay (*Felis tigrina*) and the coatimundi (*Nasua* spp.), or zorro as it is known in Latin America due to its face-mask markings, ply the full range of forest levels. As a generalist, the zorro's elongated rubbery nose is particularly suited to probing into holes in search of small mammals, bird's eggs, and the like. With a stretch of its traditional definition as a forest-floor dweller, as well as a stretch of its elongated neck and hind legs, the okapi (*Okapia johnstoni*), a deep-forest dweller and only other member of the giraffe family (Giraffinae), predominantly browses on the leaves of sapling and pole-size trees which extend into the midcanopy levels.

Forest-Floor Specialists

Ground faunas fill a surprising latitude of form and function. As the soil and litter seldom desiccate in tropical rainforest proper, many life-forms in contact with this microhabitat are rarely seen elsewhere outside of strictly aquatic or cave habitats. Polychaete worms and the centipede-like *Peripatus* owe their paleontological antiquity, in part, to the extreme, steady state of forest-floor conditions.

In illuminating how no resource goes unexploited, we note that in certain forests that are inundated periodically, making them unsuitable for terrestrial termites and ants, the niche of litter disposer is filled instead by a variety of often colorful land crabs (Decapoda), whose constant scuttling is a common sight. Where insects dominate the forest floor, specialist insectivores as well as generally larger mammals, such as the giant pangolin of Africa (*Manis gigantea*), ply the resource. The pangolin's long, sticky tongue is tailor-made to consume enormous amounts of ants and such (while intriguingly excluding soil and litter). Its New World counterpart is the giant armadillo (*Priodontes maximus*). Both are heroically armored and clawed.

As one might expect, many forest-floor species are large—the Asiatic and African elephants (Elephantidae), pygmy hippopotamus (*Choeropsis liberiensis*), tapir (*Tapirus* spp.), and Javan one-horned rhino (*Rhinoceros sondaicus*) being prime examples—but also adapted for amphibious life or at least aquatic performance when necessary. The key to these animals' ease in water is the trunks or semitrunks of elephants and tapir and the nostril arrangements of the rhino and hippo. Full aquatic adaptation by mammals is seen in both the freshwater river dolphin, typified by the pink boto (*Inia geoffrensis*) of the Amazon and Orinoco basins, and the manatee (*Trichechus senegalensis*) of Africa. (The latter is another relative of the elephant, offering possible clues to its liking for aquatic habitats.)

Many of the smaller rodents and insectivores, such as bamboo rats (Rodentia) and the foul-smelling moon rats (*Echinosorex gymnurus*), forage in the litter for edibles and new shoots and in turn provide an excellent food resource for the snakes. It is interesting that while New World forest floors are popu-

▲ *The bright red color of this wasp moth (*Dinia subapicalis*) proclaims an aggressiveness and a matching armory that this cunning mimic does not possess. [Mexico.]*

▲ *The female ichneumon wasp lays her eggs in a host insect. Later, the larvae consume the nonvital parts first, so prolonging the life of the host. [Venezuela.]*

▲ *The offspring of this large wolf spider (*Lycosidae*) cling to their mother's body for several weeks as they continue to feed on their yolk sacs. [High Andes of Peru.]*

◀ The skin of the arrow-poison frog (Dendrobates pumilio) contains a powerful toxin, used by forest hunters to tip their arrows and blowgun darts. [Costa Rica.]

▼ The rudely pugnacious Bell's frog (Ceratophrys ornata) is capable of taking prey as large as young rats in its damp rainforest floor domain. [Argentina.]

◀ Delicately transparent green skin camouflages this Costa Rican glass frog (Centrolenella sp.) against the leafy backdrop of the canopy.

▼ Internal organs are clearly visible through the thin translucent skin of this red-eyed tree frog (Agalychnis callidryas).

lated with large rodents, such as pacas (*Agouti paca*) and agoutis (*Dasyprocta* spp.), that niche is largely filled in the Old World by miniature ungulates typified by chevrotains (Tragulines), royal antelopes (*Neotragus pygmaeus*), and barking deer or muntjac (*Muntiacus muntjak*), the last of which is equipped with prominently exposed canine teeth, probably of importance as a secondary sexual characteristic.

These, together with ground birds such as the ground hornbill (*Bucorvus leadbeateri*) and tinamous (*Tinamus* spp.), ply the forest floor to feed on the constant rain of fruits, flowers, seeds, and leaves that cascades from the canopy. More general forest-floor feeders include the Malay sun bear (*Helarctos malayanus*), Asian sloth bear (*Melursus ursinus*), and the South American spectacled bear (*Tremarctos ornatus*)—all are omnivorous opportunists not adverse to taking insects and reptiles, eggs and young, and small mammals as they appear.

Certain mangrove-swamp specialists, typified by the scarlet ibis (*Eudocimus ruber*) and the boat-billed heron (*Cochlearius cochlearius*) have bills with obvious adaptations to the food resource of their muddy habitat. No such understanding yet exists for the strangely exaggerated tubular nose of the mangrove-dwelling proboscis monkey (*Nasalis larvalus*), which in the male may exceed 3 inches (7.6 cm) in length.

PEOPLE AS FOREST ANIMALS

How then do humans (*Homo sapiens*) fit into this intricately balanced collage of species? There is no reason to assume that archaic human cultures, especially nomadic hunter-gatherers such as still exist in the tropical forest biome, should be considered a disturbance of the natural order. Even when primal

▲ *Heliconius melpomene caterpillars absorb the toxins in passion flower leaves (Passiflora spp.) and retain them even after transformation into butterflies. This makes them highly distasteful to predators. Other Latin American butterflies, many of them nontoxic, mimic the Heliconius coloration and patterning and share in its deterrent effect. The exceptionally long (nine-month) life span of the insect is due to feeding on pollen rich in amino acids, and high-protein food from members of the melon family.*

cultures extend their activities to cultivation, which has quite widely been the case at least in the past 10,000 years, natural and regenerative rhythms appear to have dominated those processes—tribes moving on when the return on hunting efforts fell below acceptable limits; fauna and flora repopulating the area during healthy fallow periods. Inherently low population numbers in the past, of course, now contrast with the current invasion of swidden (migrant) agriculturists. Moreover, the original indigenous population produced almost exclusively for their own sustenance (save for limited trade with other in-forest, as well as out-of-forest tribes). This, too, is in marked contrast to modern cultivators, and to the increasing concentration of cash and export crops which have stressed the land beyond anything resembling healthful capacities.

In what is not at all a rancorous relationship, the forest offers the hunter-gatherer everything he needs. Local materials provide his blow gun, spear, and bow and arrows, while native plants such as *Strychnos* are used in preparing curare for hunting, and timbo vine (*Lonchocarpus* spp.) provides the source of rotenone, widely used for stunning fish. The forest furnishes building and roofing materials, serviceable string, wild cotton (*Gossypium* spp.) with which to weave clothing, pharmaceuticals, cosmetics, and more. In fact, *all* needs are met from the forest cornucopia. As food in the forest is generally scarce, the resources are never abused. Actually, one of the principal responsibilities of village headmen in Latin American forest tribes is the imposition of seasonal restrictions on such resources as *Dioscorea* for birth control, or *Euterpe* palm for its growing leaf buds, the hearts of which are eaten as a vegetable, thus culturally guaranteeing the regeneration of these natural crops.

Humans can clearly be seen in exactly the same context as other forest creatures as efficient dispersers of seed over the most extensive ranges. This is borne out by the fact that today's botanists have no way of identifying the source habitat of many useful cultivated species, such as betel nut palm (*Areca cathecu*) and peach palm (*Bactris gasipaes*) or even the original continent of the coconut palm (*Cocos nucifera*), which was always carried by migrating tribes, even from ancient times, and has been replanted wherever they settled.

Human physical adaptations to the hot, perhumid environment have included relatively small size (perhaps as a result of lower protein intake), and lower basal metabolic rate (BMR), both of which serve to produce less heat and to enhance the body's ability to lose heat faster. In addition, under conditions of 95 percent humidity, evaporation of moisture is impaired. As such, sweating is not an efficient means of cooling, and so human forest residents sweat less, this being immediately apparent to any wringing-wet, outside-forest person following an undaunted, comfortably dry, in-forest person on a trek. Also noticeable is an almost uniform sparsity of body hair which would provide insulation.

Furthermore, medical investigations have revealed that certain tribes have a degree of immunity to malaria due to high concentrations of gamma globulin (Pygmies), and sickle cells (Congo tribespeople) in the blood. The advantages of the latter far outweigh the disadvantage of the anemia it produces, at least in the forest. Once removed from the forest, however, we can only see sickle-cell anemia as problematical. This is evidenced in West African descendants, now residents of temperate countries, who still carry the anemia, even many generations removed from the forest.

Over the years I have noted, and speculated about, both the remarkably wide, splayed feet of certain Papua New Guinean tribespeople and the

Amazonian deep-forest Yąnomamö, and the concurrent astounding tree-climbing ability of these forest people. Without the advantage of the ankle wraps used by certain other primal tribes, these indigenes literally run up wide-boled vertical emergent trees to the top, then explore the limbs, quite effortlessly and fearlessly. Such plantigrade feet also have advantages in traversing the muddy forest floors typical of the rainforest habitat.

The specializations we have reviewed in forest species variously include genetic dispositions such as aversion to light, extreme heat, and low humidity; strict adherence to routine as dictated by forest rhythms; often very narrow diet options; and a psychological need for pack, herd, flock, or tribal security. In the case of forest people we might add a marked vulnerability to alcohol, and a well-developed religion centering on the forest and its components. Such prerequisites will work to enhance survival in forest conditions; ironically, they also prove the undoing of the majority of species if they are removed from the insulation of the forest womb.

The Partnership of Honeyguide and Pygmy

Mutualistic relations exist between forest people and a number of other species. The Pygmies' caloric intake is highly dependent on their success in foraging for honey, and in that pursuit the Pygmy relies almost exclusively on the greater honeyguide (*Indicator indicator*) to direct him to a hive. Although not a manifestation of rational behavior on the part of the bird, it is even more difficult to comprehend it for what it is—instinctive habit.

UCLA anthropologist Robert Bailey, a leading authority on the Pygmy culture, followed the forest people to 72 beehives over a one-and-a-half-year period. On all but three of these episodes, the honeyguide led them to the hives with its rasping, churring chatter, its white outer tail feathers flagging the men to the proper tree. This guiding will often end in success within a half hour, though it can last through a 5-mile (8-km) meander.

It was found only a few decades ago that the bird's insatiable hunger for beeswax derives from its all but unique ability to digest the substance, due to the presence of a hitherto unknown organism (*Micrococcus cerolyticus*) in its stomach. (A 16th-century Dominican missionary in Mozambique reported little birds entering his church and pilfering wax from altar candles.)

Once the bird leads the Pygmy to the nest, he climbs the tree with a bundle of smoking leaves to sedate the bees, and then hacks his way into the tree to emerge with baskets full of honey. The waxy remains of the hive are left for the bird as a reward. The honey badger or ratel (*Mellivora capensis*), which is assumed to be the prehuman benefactor of the honeyguide's behavior, would invariably offer the bird this same service.

It is known that the bird, with its short, ineffective beak, could not ply this resource without the aid of its willing helpers. The bird's assistance is rewarded additionally by the deep-seated protection afforded it by tribal groups. In some regions, anyone found killing a honeyguide might have their ears removed as a punishment.

▲ *So unlikely is the relationship between the Pygmy and the greater honeyguide* (Indicator indicator) *that for many years naturalists refused to credit it. Here, a Pygmy climbs a tree to reach a wild bees' nest, having been led to it by the flitting flight and chattering calls of this remarkable bird. Smoke from a bundle of smoldering leaves will tranquilize the bees and allow him to remove the honey.*

The Poison Eaters

One riverine plant, *Dysoxylum angustifolium*, from the forests of the Far East, depends on fish, which love its fruit, to ensure its distribution. As an added reward, the seeds taint the flesh of the fish, rendering it poisonous and thus affording the fish some possible protection against predators. Of course, the fish depend on this and other fruits for their daily sustenance, closing again the cycle of interdependency.

We do know that certain plants contain obnoxious odors and tastes due to alkaloids and other substances. Certain fortunate insects, such as the bird-winged butterflies (*Troides* spp., *Ornithoptera*, and others), have overcome this repulsion and feed on these plants. They then taste and even smell like the plants, giving them protection from predators, while the plants benefit from the insect's pollination services.

In some cases, plants contain powerful poisons in the form of cyanide compounds. The foliage of the passion flower (*Passiflora* spp.) is such an example. Nevertheless, various caterpillars and butterflies are able to eat, metabolize, and retain these poisons, thus making themselves poisonous to predators. Most of these butterflies are very vividly colored and marked. Their protective coloration is, in turn, mimicked by certain other butterflies and moths that do not carry the protective poisons.

THE MIMOSA GIRDLER

The late essayist and medical educator Lewis Thomas (1913–93) was filled with awe at the teachings nature will undoubtedly reveal to us in time. He reminded us that the dimensions of human knowledge are dwarfed by the dimensions of human ignorance.

Thomas used mimosa girdler beetles (*Oncideres* spp.) as an example of preplanned "forethought" in a creature that lacks much of a central nervous system. An amazing scenario unfolds in the life history of this simple-looking beetle. First, the female likes only *Mimosa* trees and will not bother with any other. She will climb a tree, go out on a limb, and there make a longitudinal slit in the bark using her mandibles. She then lays her eggs in the cut, which almost immediately heals over to become invisible. Now, the eggs will not hatch in live wood so she intricately sets about girdling the limb—cutting through the bark right around the limb, so causing it to die. Baby girdlers then hatch out and sally forth across the land to girdle again.

Perhaps more than coincidental is the fact that many mimosa trees are short-lived, reaching only 20 to 25 years of age. They are, however, *very* responsive to pruning, and the activities of the mimosa girdler can extend the life of this tree by 100 percent. The relationship here is symbiotic: both tree and beetle accrue profound benefits from each other, without cost to either. If only we could emulate such clean thrift in our human relations with the environment!

Having broken the girdler-mimosa code, we should now ponder how evolution achieved these separate acts of behavior. The tree must produce an attractant scent to lure the girdler, having somehow "perceived" or at least responded to the fact that the beetle can help it. The girdler wants only a mimosa for her offspring, who cannot survive in live wood, and the neatest way to kill the wood (but not the whole tree) is by girdling the chosen branch.

Not all trees, however, appreciate girdling and other predation by insects, and many plants have defenses to avoid this. All of us are well aware of the commercial and recreational value of rubber, but few probably realize that latex, in this case tapped from the rubber tree (*Hevea brasiliensis*), is an adap-

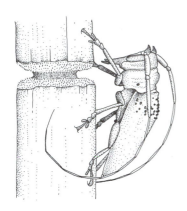

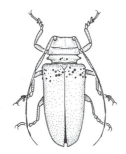

▲ *A superb example of specialization: a mimosa girdler* (Oncideres *sp.) rings the bark of a small side branch, simultaneously extending the life of the tree while creating a supply of dead wood for her larvae.*

tive defense. Most insects, after boring into the bark of the tree, find a snootfull of the sticky liquid (enriched with a natural insecticide) a repugnant, odious experience. There are no "free lunches." This goes for the rubber tree as well, which produces latex at considerable cost. When tapped commercially, the tree's growth slows markedly and it produces fewer seeds, suggesting that latex production has a high ticket price.

VITAL AND VARIED ROLES OF THE INSECTS

Insects evolved at least 350 million years ago, and survival over this period makes them infinitely successful. Outweighing the population of humankind by a factor of 12, their numbers are estimated at 10,000,000,000,000,000,000 (10 quintillion) and relatively stable due to crucially intricate natural controls.

Current research reveals that the management of the tropical forest is largely the responsibility of insects and lower life-forms, as they serve as food sources or provide pollination for fruit which in turn feeds animals further up the food chain. Perhaps if we come to better appreciate the insect, we can begin to gain a perspective on the full spectrum of creation in the biome.

Donald R. Davis, curator of entomology at the Smithsonian Institution, states, "Within the next 25 years we may witness the extinction of more than one-half of the world's insect species, about three million, even before they have been made known to science. The vast majority represent essential keys to future pest management programs, crop pollination, soil production, and in brief, healthy ecosystems . . ."

Consider that although we offhandedly effect mass extinctions of many species, paradoxically humans have never, despite their best endeavors, brought about the extinction of a single agricultural pest insect or other target insect species. The insect develops resistance to our most formidable pesticides in only a minimal number of generations, and because of this the gene pool of the tropical forests performs a critically valuable service to humankind. We can imagine that a prime reason for the insects' success has been their extreme resilience in adapting to ever-changing environmental conditions.

◀ Enter the real Tarzan. In what is probably the greatest weight-lifting feat ever recorded on film, this parasol ant (Atta cephalotes) carries his incredible burden with apparent ease through the forest of the Brazilian Amazon. Were a man to have the relative strength of an ant he would be able to carry 50 times his body weight—in his teeth. The ant's feat is possible because the hard plates of the exoskeleton store muscle energy like a taut bow, while the insect itself has more muscle per unit of body weight than any human.

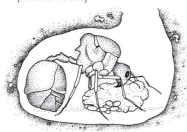

▲ ▶ In a dizzying column of moving leaf fragments a colony of leaf-cutter ants (Atta sp.) carries its bounty along forest routes kept meticulously clear of debris. In their underground nests they cultivate a specific fungus as their sole food source—and will ignore other fungi such as the Caripia montagnei visible in the photograph above right. [Costa Rica.]

▲ Having completed her nuptial flight, the new queen places a small piece of the food-source fungus in an underground chamber and manures it with fecal material. She then lays her eggs, the start of a new leaf-cutter colony.

LEAF CUTTERS AND CULTIVATORS

Leaf-cutter or parasol ants (*Atta* spp.) are fascinating creatures frequently seen in the neotropical forests. They climb certain trees and cut out dime-sized pieces of leaves and flowers with their sharp mandibles. They then carry these fragments, some 50 times their own body weight, incredible distances to their subterranean nests, often 15 to 20 feet (4.6–6.1 m) below the surface.

To avoid stripping entire trees in their gathering, these consummate conservationists travel hundreds of meters while foraging. Travelers to American tropical cities and towns often wonder why most of the tree trunks in streets, parks, and gardens are painted with white lime. The reason, quite simply, is to deter the leaf-cutter ant.

In the forest, neat and orderly highways are constructed on the ground, cleared of leaves, litter, twigs, and other debris. These highways are alive with moving leaf fragments and the visual effect is mesmerizing.

These ants were one of the first life-forms on Earth to engage in a form of agriculture. They do not eat the special leaves they have collected, but take them underground, add saliva to them by chewing, and dab the leaves with an anal secretion. This organic mulch is used to nurture the growth of certain mycelial fungi, which the ants cultivate and eat as their sole diet. They also weed their gardens of any other invasive fungi and use their body secretions to suppress bacterial growth. This is true cultivation in every sense: planting, fertilizing, weeding, pest control, and harvesting. In this mutualism, both the ant and the fungi are solely responsible for each other's survival. Oddly, the fungi appear to have lost (or perhaps never had) the ability to produce reproductive spores. They are found only under the ant's cultivation, and the *Atta* nest is their sole habitat on Earth. The growth of the fungus is never left to chance. When a new queen, who reigns for some twenty years, migrates to establish a new colony, she takes with her a small pellet of fungus with which to propagate a new garden.

The web of symbiosis is yet still more intricately woven. Networks of plant and tree roots pervade the leaf-cutters' labyrinth and lend structural support to their extensive catacombs. Recent research on the fungus grown by the ants shows that it exhibits biological activity against certain plant pathogens, thus protecting the supporting trees. This discovery, needless to say, could have enormous practical application in agriculture.

As if all this were not enough, the complex plot continues to thicken. It was recently found that the leaf-cutters' most serious threat comes from a small fly (*Apocephalus* spp.) related to the coffin fly. These flies hover above the laboring leaf cutters and try to lay their eggs on the backs of the ants' necks. If successful, when the larvae hatch, they eat away the ants' brains. The ants, not surprisingly, have evolved a response. A scientist working in the tropical forest of Trinidad has discovered that smaller worker ants called *minima* act as bodyguards. They hitch a ride on many of the larger "media" workers' leaf fragments. Riding upside down with their formidable pincers pointed skyward, they snipe at the treacherous flies, preventing them from parasitizing their fellow workers, who are otherwise defenseless while carrying their cumbersome burdens. (Certain aphids parasitized by wasps are now known to commit suicide by jumping to their death. Such "host suicide behavior" is attributed not to psychosis, but to the aphid's instinctive knowledge that such a sacrifice will kill the wasp's eggs as well, reducing the chance of further affliction to other aphids.)

CURIOUS PARTNERSHIPS OF ANTS AND PLANTS

Plants that share a symbiotic relationship with ants are called *myrmecophytes,* from the Greek word *myrmex* which means "ant." In the Indo-Malaysian rainforest, there exist certain curious epiphytes called *myrmecodia* (*Myrmecodia tuberosa*). They look very much like potatoes that have attached themselves to trees, but unlike most other epiphytes, they have no debris-catching facility by which to feed themselves. However, cutting one open reveals a catacomb of chambers housing ants (*Iridomyrmex myrmecodiae*). In the center of the interior are roots on which the ants "kindly" deposit the damp humus of their feces. Without this liquid and nutrient material, the myrmecodia would certainly perish. More amazing still, it is found that these very helpful ants gather ripe seeds from the host myrmecodia and plant them in detritus-filled areas around the roots of the epiphyte. If the mother myrmecodia dies or is dislodged, it may be replaced by offspring sowed by the ants—future security for both plant and ant.

The cecropia (*Cecropia* spp.) or trumpet tree of the New World tropical forests has fruits and leaves that are sought after by many and varying creatures. This quite successful species, however, has an army of protectors—the aggressive Aztec ants (*Azteca coeruleipennis, A. alfari,* and others). The cecropia's hollow-noded trunk and branches, similar in structure to bamboo, serve as a fortification for the Aztec ant colonies, who bore into these chambers to establish nests and living quarters.

This tree is a gracious host, providing not only shelter, but food as well. At the base of each leaf petiole are glandular nodules called Mullerian bodies which the Aztecs feed on. Made of 50 percent glycogen, these energy-rich capsules are a drain on the plants' energy resource. In fact, the Aztec ant is a predator species and requires food of animal origin. Wonder of wonders, glycogen is generally a product of animal metabolism; the cecropia is the only plant known to produce it! The ant repays this generosity by viciously attacking anything that touches the tree. Tapping on the trunk will cause legions of ants to boil out from the interior and cover the intruder in moments. Even a vine tip blown against the tree by the wind is chewed to shreds. Other encroaching vegetation is trimmed back also, thus ensuring the cecropia's competitive

Plant evolution has produced a remarkable array of structures apparently designed for the benefit of ants. The relationship is usually mutually beneficial: the plants offer the ants food and safe lodgings, and in return the ants provide protection and nutrient-rich detritus.

△ ▷ The cecropia tree
So beneficial are Azteca ants, here feeding on the cecropia tree's food-rich Mullerian bodies, that considerably higher than normal levels of calcium, nitrogen, and phosphorus are found in trees inhabited by these insects.

▷ Cordia nodosa
Azteca ants also make and defend their homes inside the swollen, soft, pithy stem tips of this common Amazonian forest bush.

▷ Anthurium gracile
Colonies of the ant Pachycondyla goeldii *often thrive in the hollow root balls of this South American epiphyte. The ants carry detritus into galleries among the roots, so providing the plant with nutrients.*

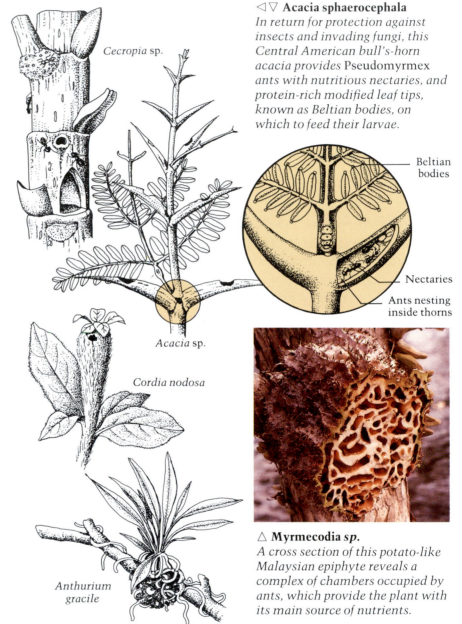

Cecropia sp.

◁▽ Acacia sphaerocephala
In return for protection against insects and invading fungi, this Central American bull's-horn acacia provides Pseudomyrmex *ants with nutritious nectaries, and protein-rich modified leaf tips, known as Beltian bodies, on which to feed their larvae.*

Beltian bodies

Nectaries

Ants nesting inside thorns

Acacia sp.

Cordia nodosa

Anthurium gracile

△ Myrmecodia sp.
A cross section of this potato-like Malaysian epiphyte reveals a complex of chambers occupied by ants, which provide the plant with its main source of nutrients.

advantage. The ants are so determined in their attacks that they will actually leap from trunk or leaf onto any unfortunate standing on the ground below. Their bites are treacherous. Only the sloth (Bradypodidae), protected by an extremely coarse hair coat, may safely climb the tree to dine on one of its favorite foods, the cecropia leaves.

It is astutely observed that where cecropias grow on Caribbean islands above 6,560 feet (2,000 m), altitudes where Aztec ants are not in attendance, the cecropias produce no Mullerian bodies. One cannot help but acquire a more profound respect for the mysterious adaptive aptitudes of the lesser life-forms of plant and insect.

These remarkable ants are also expert herders of livestock, and it is the habit of the Aztec to keep mealybugs (Pseudococcinae) inside the cecropian chambers. We are all familiar with the house and garden pest that sucks the life juices from our plants. The mealybugs produce a sugary nectar from this extract that is literally milked from them by the ants. In return, the otherwise vulnerable and defenseless mealybug is given shelter and undying allegiance.

The soldier Aztecs will give their lives in defending the mealybug from attack. Where aphids (Aphididae) are tended in the same manner, they are referred to as "ant cows." It is evident that humans were not the first to herd and tend livestock.

To Each a Place of Its Own

The very specific niches some creatures fill give some further insight into the intricacies of the web of life. Just recently identified by scientists of the American Museum of Natural History is a new species of mosquito, *Anopheles dirus*, from Thailand. Its sole known reproductive habitat is the rain-filled footprints of the Asian elephant (*Elephas maximus*) pressed into the soft forest floor.

Certain species become so successful in the forest that migration becomes unnecessary. It is common for the ranges of insects as well as other animals and plants to be extremely restricted. Often, a small valley or a single mountaintop holds the entire world population of a species. In 1973, the Po'o-uli (*Melamprosops phaeosoma*), a type of honeycreeper hitherto unknown to science, was discovered in the inaccessible forest clothing the northeastern flanks of Haleakala volcano on the Hawaiian island of Maui. The bird's entire range covers less than a square mile. More recently, 50 new species of plant were discovered on a mountaintop on the Panama-Colombia border. Forests of this size can be felled in an hour with the mega-equipment in use today, making the situation grave, with a far-reaching web of implications.

Though we often build preservation campaigns around, and become quite emotional over, the possible extinction of a higher, aesthetic vertebrate such as the gorilla, it is often the disappearance of insects and animals on the lower levels of the food chain that may be responsible for the demise of several dozen dependent plant, fish, bird, and mammal species. Unlike our northern and temperate forests, made up of one or only several, very rarely up to even several dozen tree species, a single hectare (2.47 acres) of tropical rainforest in the Cuyabeno Reserve in Ecuador contains 313 different tree species. Many of these and countless other plants are directly dependent on the quiet labors of insects (as well as higher animals) for their survival, and many more animals are dependent upon those plants.

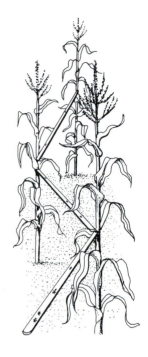

▲ *Capitalizing on the predatory habits of many native ant species, certain Asian tribes link their growing maize stems with split bamboo runways to encourage the ants to help rid their crops of destructive insect pests.*

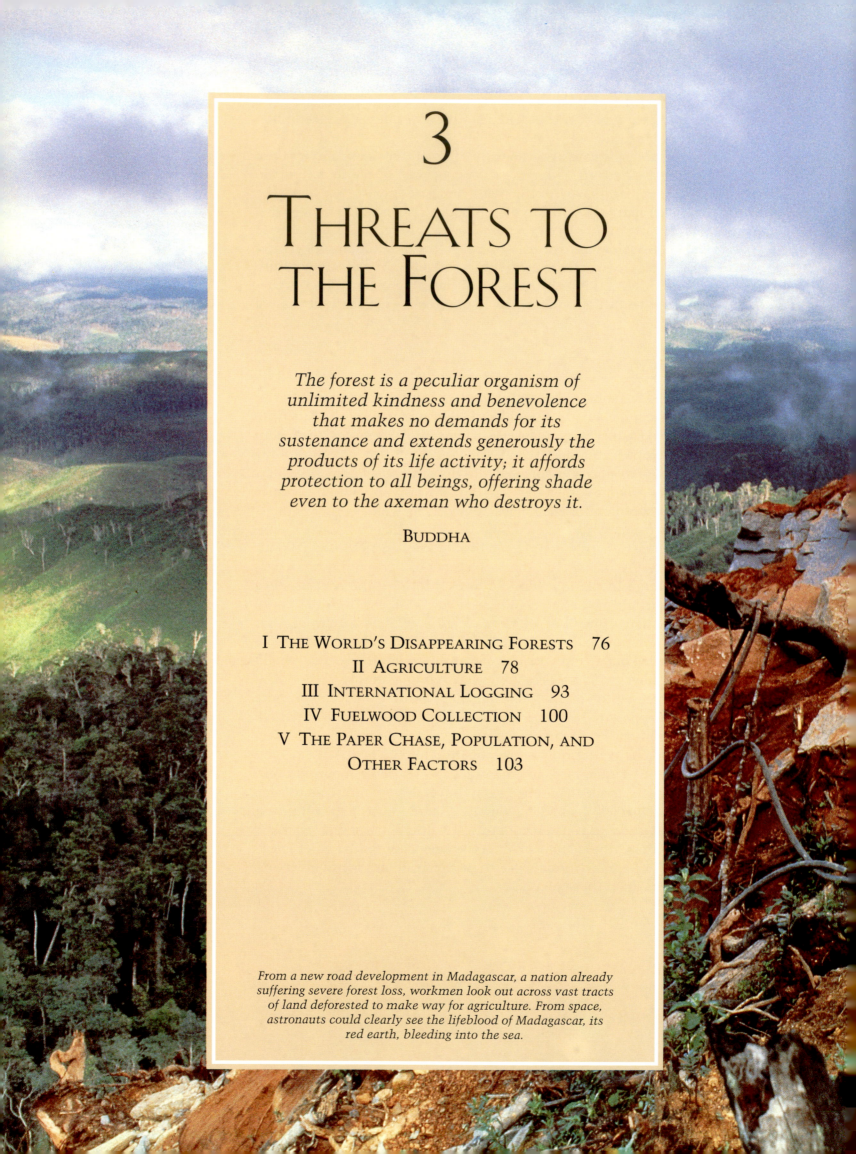

3
THREATS TO THE FOREST

The forest is a peculiar organism of unlimited kindness and benevolence that makes no demands for its sustenance and extends generously the products of its life activity; it affords protection to all beings, offering shade even to the axeman who destroys it.

BUDDHA

From a new road development in Madagascar, a nation already suffering severe forest loss, workmen look out across vast tracts of land deforested to make way for agriculture. From space, astronauts could clearly see the lifeblood of Madagascar, its red earth, bleeding into the sea.

I THE WORLD'S DISAPPEARING FORESTS

Each minute more than 69 acres (28 ha) of tropical forest are cut globally. Every year 56,462 square miles (146,225 sq km), an area larger than the Kingdom of Nepal, are removed or degraded. In 25 years, the tropical rainforest will be virtually extinct.

Today, forests cover more than 25 percent of the planet's land area, excluding Greenland and Australia. Slightly more than 50 percent of this total lies within the tropics. Tropical wet and moist forests, the subject of this book, comprise half of forests in the tropical region and cover 6 percent of Earth's land surface. The tragic reality is that 54 percent of the area that existed historically is now gone. While European and North American forests are stabilizing, deforestation (in the last 50 years) is occurring at an accelerating pace in the tropics. Virtually extinct already are the forests of El Salvador, Haiti, Côte d'Ivoire, Nigeria, Madagascar, and the Philippines. Are the great Amazon and Congo basins to follow?

The anomaly of the tropical rainforest has gained a life of its own. Perceived as belligerent in its levels of biological energy, and supporting an intimidating biomass, its soils, given the ample rain and heat of the clime, will—it is assumed—give forth a bounty to humans in any way they direct. Such a fantasy is easily supported by the astonishing regrowth of secondary species that materializes in the space of two weeks if the forest is opened up by a canopy-tree windfall. After a month one needs a machete just to turn around. So why not remove the hardwoods? Why not plant corn or cattle pasture?

One of the major disappointments of the tropics, and the unpalatable answer to those questions, is that the forest has an Achilles' heel. The closed cycle which perpetuates its productivity is quite easily broken, and this outflow of fertility cannot be harnessed sustainably by methods currently in use. (We will see later that, fortunately, technologies are available that will allow us to successfully manipulate or even mimic the primary forest without irrevocably breaking the closed cycle.)

But the myth lives on, especially in tropical governments encouraging wholesale colonization of their "great green realms." But we should not judge too harshly. I, and most readers of this page, would also cut standing forest and move on if this were the only means we had of feeding our families.

GLOBAL ENVIRONMENTAL MONITORING (GEM)

Before human influence (postglacial), tropical rainforests are thought to have covered 3,960,000,000 acres (1,603,000,000 ha) (Sommer 1976). Today only 72 percent of the original expanse remains. Tropical moist forests, both seasonal and evergreen (tropical closed broadleaved forests), once comprised

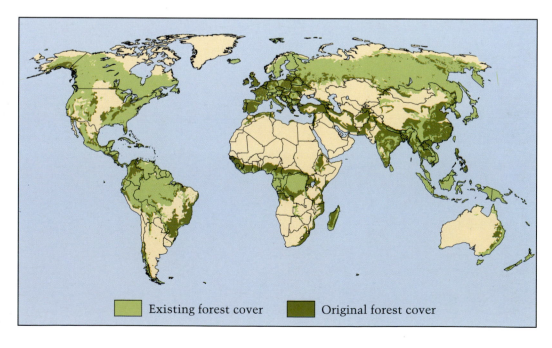

Existing forest cover   Original forest cover

some 6,177,000,000 acres (2,500,000,000 ha) (Terborgh 1993); today only 46 percent survive. Since essentially all forest clearance has taken place since 1950, this represents the fastest land-use change in the history of humanity.

In 1980, 3,061,421,000 acres (1,238,957,000 ha) (to convert hectares to square kilometers remove 2 zeroes) remained of *tropical closed broadleaved forests* globally (pantropical). In 1990, 2,845,891,000 acres (1,151,732,000 ha) remained at a decade loss of 215,530,000 acres (87,225,000 ha) or 21,553,000 acres per year (8,722,500 ha/yr) globally—an area larger than Austria. If we break the numbers down further on regional levels, the annual deforestation for Africa, including Madagascar, is 3,691,129 acres (1,493,800 ha) at 0.6 percent loss of the total remaining forest cover in that region in 1980; for Asia, including Oceania and Australia, the amount is 6,840,870 acres (2,768,500 ha) at 1.1 percent loss; and for Latin America, including the Caribbean, the amount is 11,021,002 acres (4,460,200 ha), at 0.6 percent loss.

To the above figures of total annual deforestation, we must add the 14.6 million acres (5.9 million ha) degraded by logging, as ascertained from unpublished Food and Agriculture Organization of the United Nations (FAO) data as a reassessment of *FAO Forest Resources Assessment 1990: Tropical Countries* (Dennis Dykstra, Deputy Director General for Research, Center for International Forestry Research, pers. comm. 1999) for a grand total of 36,132,000 acres (14,622,500 ha)—an area larger than the Kingdom of Nepal! Altogether, the rate of deforestation is estimated to have increased some 50 percent from 1980 to 1990 (FAO 1991). World Resources Institute predicts that 90 percent of total remaining forest left in 1990 will be lost by 2023.

ESTIMATES OF TROPICAL CLOSED BROADLEAVED FOREST COVER AREA AND RATE OF DEFORESTATION BY MAIN ECOLOGICAL ZONE AND GEOGRAPHICAL SUBREGION

| Ecological Zone | Forest Cover Area | | | | Annual Deforestation Rate | | |
| | 1980 millions | | 1990 millions | | 1981–90 millions | | |
	acres	hectares	acres	hectares	acres	hectares	%per annum
Africa and Madagascar							
Tropical Rainforest Domain	225	91	215	87	1.2	0.5	0.5
Tropical Moist Hill/Mountain Domain	86	35	81	33	0.7	0.3	0.8
Tropical Moist Forest (short dry season)	314	127	294	119	1.7	0.7	0.5
Total Africa and Madagascar	**625**	**253**	**591**	**239**	**3.7**	**1.5**	**0.6**
Latin America and Caribbean							
Tropical Rainforest Domain	1161	470	1114	451	4.7	1.9	0.4
Tropical Moist Hill/Mountain Domain	279	113	245	99	3.5	1.4	1.2
Tropical Moist Forest (short dry season)	348	141	319	129	3.0	1.2	0.8
Total Latin America and Caribbean	**1789**	**724**	**1678**	**679**	**11.1**	**4.5**	**0.6**
Asia, Oceania and Australia							
Tropical Rainforest Domain	509	206	455	184	5.4	2.2	1.1
Tropical Moist Hill/Mountain Domain	123	50	111	45	1.0	0.4	0.8
Tropical Moist Forest (short dry season)	12	5	10	4	0.15	0.06	1.2
Total Asia, Oceania and Australia	**645**	**261**	**576**	**233**	**6.7**	**2.7**	**1.1**
TOTAL GLOBAL (PANTROPICAL)	**3059**	**1238**	**2844**	**1151**	**21.5**	**8.7**	**0.6**

		Acres	Hectares (in millions)
Pantropical Annual Deforestation in Rainforest Domain		11.4	4.6
Pantropical Annual Deforestation in Moist Hill/Mountain Domain		5.2	2.1
Pantropical Annual Deforestation in Moist Forest (short dry season) Domain		5.0	2.0
Global Annual Clearance of Tropical Closed Broadleaved Forest	Subtotal =	21.6	8.7
Global Annual Logging of Tropical Closed Broadleaved Forest		14.6	5.9
Global Annual Tropical Closed Broadleaved Forest Deforested and Degraded	Total =	36.2	14.6

II AGRICULTURE

▲ Slash-and-burn across Africa

This satellite image shows the red band of fires caused by slash-and-burn farming that blaze across the continent of Africa. Farther north and with concentrations around the Persian Gulf, the burn-off from natural gas appears in yellow. Brightly lit areas on top are the heavily populated regions of Europe.

THE IMPACT OF "SLASH-AND-BURN"

Typically, the entire biomass of a future farm plot in the moist tropics is felled and burned to prepare for planting. Some nutrient matter in the ash remains on the surface, and in this enriched soil the farmer sows his seeds. Torrents of rain continue to fall, but the constant rain of leaves and other nutritious debris has suddenly stopped. Without the protective layers of tree cover, the tropical downpours pelt the bare soil, and existing nutrients are flushed away into rivers and out to sea in a reckless expenditure of soil fertility. In fact, the leading "export" of most tropical-forest nations is topsoil. A farmer may harvest only two or three crops on the same plot of land before he must move on to fell more forest and begin the destructive and wasteful process over again. That these same people must continue to sustain themselves year after year is too infrequently acknowledged, yet this is the essence of tropical deforestation issues. Where aboriginals practiced lengthy fallow periods, allowing fertility to build, today's land-hungry cultivators return too soon, recutting and degrading previously used areas, and all too often rendering the plots infertile. Increasingly, there is permanent degradation.

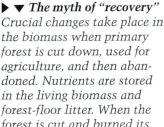

▶ ▼ The myth of "recovery"
Crucial changes take place in the biomass when primary forest is cut down, used for agriculture, and then abandoned. Nutrients are stored in the living biomass and forest-floor litter. When the forest is cut and burned its

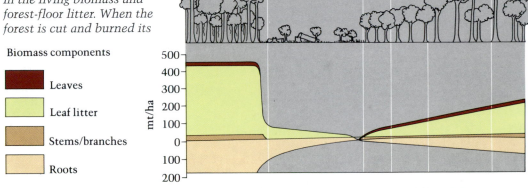

Biomass components

- Leaves
- Leaf litter
- Stems/branches
- Roots

mass is reduced to almost nothing and its nutrients exploited briefly before the plot is finally abandoned. Even 30 years later, the secondary forest that takes its place bears little resemblance to the original. It is poor in total biomass and also in species diversity. The paired photographs below compare the rich diversity of primary forest in the author's Cathedral Rain Forest Science Preserve in Costa Rica with an area of secondary forest—a vast expanse covered in just one species, Cecropia.

Soon, sheet and gully erosion of nightmarish magnitude rake the land. Studies show that in primary rainforest, even on undulating terrain, the erosion factor is almost negligible. Far less than a ton of soil is lost per hectare (2.47 acres) per year. Depending on slope, an identical plot under a dense tea plantation loses 20 to 160 tons; for man-made pastureland the loss is up to 200 tons; and on 70 percent slopes planted with annual field crops, losses have been measured at 268 tons per hectare per year and more.

It is significant that in the past, shifting cultivators lived in balance with the environment as long as the human carrying capacities of the land were not exceeded. The population density allowed fallow land sufficient time to recover—either to return to climax forest or at least to regain sufficient fertility to allow recultivation.

Remote-sensing imagery reveals that some *two-thirds* of global tropical deforestation is now due to those migrant dispossessed known as "shifted cultivators" (Myers 1995b; Billsborrow and Hogan 1996). As we shall see, these relative newcomers to the tropical forests are quite distinct from the forest tribes who have successfully practiced sustainable slash-and-burn agriculture.

The express reasons these marginal masses are shunted into marginal environments for food production are population pressures, overbearing poverty, lack of property rights and tenure regimes, preferential distribution of fertile farmlands, inequitable land-use systems, almost complete absence of funding

◀ *In the long-standing tradition of "slash-and-burn," this Cameroon woman burns the felled forest prior to planting. The infusion of nutrients will yield crops for only a few years; the soil will then be exhausted, and the family forced to move on and start again.*

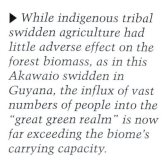 ▲ The shifting of fields instead of crops is labor intensive as well as wasteful of valuable resources. Felling, burning, planting, and harvesting can take 1,500 man-hours, and must be repeated every few years as the migrant farmer moves on. Here, an Amazonian farmer will grow manioc (Manihot *sp.*), a starch crop with low nutritional value.

▶ While indigenous tribal swidden agriculture had little adverse effect on the forest biomass, as in this Akawaio swidden in Guyana, the influx of vast numbers of people into the "great green realm" is now far exceeding the biome's carrying capacity.

and proliferation of sustainable agrotechnologies, and lack of employment outside of farming. The upper limits of sustainable carrying capacity of tropical forest farming ranges between 20 (Freeman 1955) and 48 (Conklin 1959) people per square kilometer; yet, the agricultural population density of tropical forest areas not yet altered by farming is 90 people per square mile (60 per sq km). Idaho, by comparison, has an agricultural population of 3 people per 0.4 square mile (1 sq km). It must be emphasized that population densities of tropical forest aboriginal cultures are far lower than shifting cultivators, varying from 1 (Denevan 1971) to 10 persons (De La Marca 1973) per square kilometer. These masters of the soil who would seem to have instinctive talents in coaxing sustenance from stringent resources are able, without fertilizers, to sustain a two-to-three-year cycle of agriculture by providing a 15-year fallow period for the regeneration of at least minimal nutrient stocks. This is their first priority, irrespective of any ecological concerns they, or we, may embrace. Yet such basic environmental limitations are rarely considered in the misguided resource development directions of our time. The United Nations Environmental Program (UNEP) estimates that by 2050 agricultural land area, much of which is currently forested, could nearly double in Africa and West Asia and increase by 25 percent in the Asia-Pacific region. On intriguing small aircraft trips into remote Amazônia, traversing a rolling carpet of forest canopy across the distant horizon, occasionally I have viewed an isolated patch of forest felled and planted adjacent to the infrequent Indian village, dugout canoes blissfully plying a river, a tranquil plume of blue smoke telling of women preparing an afternoon meal. A malignant black smoke now increasingly fills the air from the firestorms set by the hordes of unintentionally destructive migrant cultivators, and now large-scale commercial farming operations, not only in Amazon, but the global tropical moist regions—and these fires are now clearly visible from space.

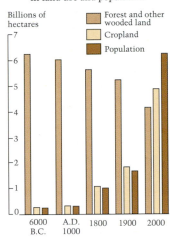

Historical and projected changes in land use and population

▲ Human activities have depleted half the world's original forest cover, with the greatest damage done since human numbers reached significant levels. Whether due to subsistence or commercial agriculture, cattle ranching, logging, fuelwood collection, or illicit drug production, the direct correlation between forest loss and population is poignantly apparent.

THE GRIM REALITIES OF GEOMETRIC PROGRESSION

These progressively roving masses total as much as 600 million in the tropical forest zone worldwide (Durning 1993; Pimentel, et al. 1996). They now represent more than 1 in 10 people on Earth and their growth rate is a phenomenal 4–6 percent.

Having been completely bypassed by the processes of development, the shifted cultivator is concurrently blamed for deforestation, as if he had exercised a conscious choice to desecrate the biome that begrudgingly gives up its resplendent opulence for fleeting sustenance. A hard line must be drawn in the eroded red clay of the abandoned farmlands that border the stately tropical forests globally—for until we address the grave problems of the "shifted cultivators" we will not have addressed, in any substantial way, tropical deforestation.

PROBLEMS OF HAPHAZARD COLONIZATION

The plight of the universal peasant is much the same throughout the moist tropics. His prime concern is to provide food and shelter for himself and his family, yet he faces the cruel reality of swidden agriculture—the bleak prospect that the vulnerable habitat that supports him could be reduced to a memory within his own lifetime. It is a great irony that in many parts of the tropics, millions of landless peasants are being directed into rapidly dwindling forest areas by government resettlement programs.

Indonesia's ambitious transmigration scheme from 1969 to 1994 resulted in the relocation of some 8.5 million peasants from the overcrowded island of Java to the virgin wilderness of Irian Jaya (the western half of the island of New Guinea) and other outer islands. Such an undertaking—in which some 1.2 million native Papuans face some 1 million migrants—will invariably lead to the destruction of much of the island's natural habitat and to the decimation of some of the most primal aboriginal tribes remaining on Earth, through dislocation from their tribal lands and from plagues of disease introduced by the immigrants.

In addition, colonizers typically fall victim to malaria and other lethal diseases for which they are ill prepared in terms of natural defenses, prophylaxis, or medication. Any benefits to the colonizers would be temporary at best, hardly balancing the loss of 7.4 million acres (3 million ha) to date, or 5 percent of the nation's forest. Much of this was funded by the World Bank until the institution, realizing the environmental and cultural degradation it had wrought, withdrew its support, admitting "irreversible impacts" on indigenous peoples. The annihilation of settlers in Sumatra, Kalimantan, and the Moluccas in 2001 is a direct result of transmigration to these islands. Several distinctive factors turn up here that are common to many resettlement programs.

1. Java, although extremely fertile, is severely overpopulated, with as many as 5,000 people living on 1 square mile (2.6 sq km).
2. Almost 45 percent of the people who reside in the countryside have no land at all; another 35 percent have insufficient land to produce enough food to support their families.
3. A glaring reason for this predicament is unfair land distribution. One-third of the land on Java is in the hands of 1 percent of the landowners.
4. Many of the new colonists have few farming skills. One study showed that up to 45 percent of the transmigrants had never grown rice, the staple crop of Indonesia.

The question is not one of whether to employ these people or have them sit idly by, but of *where* to direct them so that they may sustain their lives, and of *how* to prepare them for a measure of success, while at the same time adhering to principles that will prevent the environment from spiraling into irreversible degradation.

THE EXPLOITATION OF BRAZILIAN AMAZÔNIA

In December 1966, at the invitation of Brazil's President General Castello Branco, 300 of the most powerful Brazilian tycoons, real estate speculators, and beef barons, boarded the *Rosa de Fonseca,* a luxury cruise ship anchored off the Amazonian city of Manaus. Two years earlier, Branco had proclaimed, "Amazonian occupation will proceed as though we are waging a strategically conducted war." "Operation Amazônia" had been launched.

Through the filter of their own dreams, the entrepreneurs aboard the *Rosa de Fonseca* watched the forest slip by while the general laid out an offer few on board could refuse: tax holidays of 100 percent and for up to 17 years; loans providing subsidized credit at negative interest rates; and land grants of one million acres (404,700 ha), capped off with the promise of roads, airports and hydroelectric projects.

What finally evolved was a land rush, which became a handy hedge for investment portfolios against an insidious inflation rate. To establish ownership, land was cleared and cattle often unceremoniously dumped on it. Under the fever of the land grab, unprecedented in history, it no longer seemed to matter that others, be it *peones* or indigenous tribes, were there first. For the financiers, the ready remedy to prior occupancy and ownership was the hiring of gangs of *pistoleiros*. Hired for "cleaning or service" by the absentee industrialists, the gunmen insulted, provoked and generally harassed peasants, clergy, and organizers alike without discrimination. When these tactics failed to drive the stubborn off their land, the victims were tortured or murdered. Statistics compiled by the Catholic Church show that more than 1,000 innocents had been killed by the gunmen between 1985 and 1989 alone, and this accounts for only 3 percent of the total estimated incidents. That Chico Mendes, the now-legendary rubber tapper's union organizer and martyr to Amazonian deforestation, was only one of that multitude in some way brings home the enormity of the tragedy which continues today.

Yet the ranches created on board the *Rosa de Fonseca* are failures. One in three of the government-subsidized mega-ranches has since been abandoned, and almost 50 percent have never sold a steer. Despite this, however, given the huge government subsidies, they have all turned handsome profits for the magnates. The real winners in this vast development project are the powerful and influential construction companies and government bureaucracies, the recipients of international lending institution loans, largely due to appreciation of land values.

Today, the tribal groups, backwoods settlers, and rubber tappers have become high-profile allies in an effort to direct protective legislation through the difficult channels of political Brazil—a terribly steep task, given that those halls are the exclusive domain of entrepreneurial club members. In unprecedented cooperation, distant tribes of Kayapó, Yanomamö, and scores of others, have joined in a solidarity front against the theft of their lands.

It is clear that far more than a demand for fast-food hamburgers has been at work in Amazônia. The voices of the international anthropological community, environmental organizations, human rights movements, and many others, are now increasingly heard in outcry.

The Transamazon Highway

We have come to realize that a road cut through the forest has far more grave implications than the mere removal of a transect of trees. Not only does the artery infuse the region with misdirected agriculturists, breaching the region's integrity, but it is also found that many species will not cross open clearings, resulting in fragmentation and isolation of animal populations.

Back at its inception, the Transamazon Highway was envisioned as "the solution for 2001." It was not to be. Even if all of Brazil's legal Amazônia (defined in 1966, it encompasses nine states and covers 1.9 million square miles [4.9 million sq km] or 58 percent of Brazil's national territory) were designated as 100-ha (250-acre) parcels, as was the standard lot size along

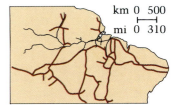

km 0 500
mi 0 310

——— Major highways

▲ *The tragic effects of the development of new roads through the virgin forests of Amazônia are dislocation of the indigenous people, and a reduction of the forest itself by more than 14 percent. In 1960, only 3,700 miles (6,000 km) of roads existed in the Brazilian Amazon, and only 180 miles (300 km) paved. In 1964, the Brasilia-Belem highway, 1,100 miles (1,900 km) long, was completed. By 1980, some 30,000 miles (45,000 km) of roads were installed. The "Brazil in Action" plan, intent on developing export corridors, has, since the beginning of 1997, put 42 road-building projects on its wish list, including inroads through Rondônia, Acre, and to Bolivia. The "link to the Pacific Port" project still looms on the horizon, with immense potential impact on Amazon forests.*

the highway, the entire region would be filled by only 5 million families, or 25 million people. This represents only eight years of Brazil's population growth from 1980 figures of 119 million at a rate of 2.4 percent per year. Although 25 million people are surely significant, this is not "the solution for 2001."

Given that only 4 percent of Amazon soils are fertile, and that only 7 percent of settlers prove successful, the highway is seen by many as a poison vein, bringing in the hopeful destitutes and carting out, for the large part, the same people with broken dreams and bodies. A 12-mile (20-km) wide area of forest all along the new highway has been designated for agricultural development, although the predicted numbers of settlers have not arrived due to the widespread crop failures and severe disease suffered by the original migrants into the area. Settlement names such as Tingo Maria, Jaci Parana, Belo Horizonte, Boa Vista, Vale do Xingu, then a new

▶ *Brazilian writer Euclides da Cunha's perception of Amazônia is of a last vestige of Eden, "The last unwritten page of Genesis." That page is now being set in type. The Transamazon Highway is now seen as a dagger plunged into the heart of the Amazon rainforest, infusing ill-equipped and unprepared farmers into a hostile hinterland of unproductive soil, and bringing out the broken results—humbled, often malarial families, leaving behind them the wreckage of failed farms.*

town named "Super Mama," belie the hardships of life awaiting the new settlers.

The chaotic infusion of settlers into the state of Rondônia by the road BR-364, where paving was funded by the World Bank, saw such lawlessness that in the town of Rolim de Moura in one month of 1984 there were more than 30 deaths by gunshot. Brazil's critical land tenure imbalance outside Amazônia, where soil fertility is high, has 5 percent of farmland owners possessing 70 percent of all farmland, while 70 percent are left to cultivate only 5 percent (Myers 1992). This is the true impetus for the Brazilian peasant to pick up his machete and matchbox and head for Amazônia. It should be understood that these "shifted cultivators"—shifted from fertile growing regions to the 90 percent infertile backwaters of the Amazon—account for 60 percent of deforestation, a figure on the rise.

We now have the benefit of hindsight in evaluating the transamazon colonization which began in 1970. Low-crop productivity due to low-soil fertility was specifically cited as the principal reason for a large degree of failure. Typically, a farmer will plant 20 acres (8 ha) of rice annually. Sales of the crop gross only U.S.$1,900, considered meager given the high cost of manufactured goods and the necessary wages paid for labor. The coffee and cacao cash crops were largely decimated by leaf rust and witch's broom. We shall see that alternatives to haphazard colonization do, in fact, exist, but for the present the world's peasantry, by following the path of least resistance, is relegated to the destructive process of slashing and burning themselves into their own future oblivion.

THE COCAINE CONNECTION

Oddly, the contribution of the illicit drugs trade toward tropical deforestation has in past years largely escaped analysis. In Peru alone, more than 2.5 million acres (1 million ha) of forest have been cleared over the past several decades for coca production. The National Agrarian University in Lima reports that 158 million gallons (600 million l) of caustic chemicals, equaling 2 metric tons per hectare, are dumped into the habitat and find their way into the water drainage, as does the herbicide used to clear the land for coca production. Tributaries of Peru's Huallaga River, which empties into the Amazon of Peru, Colombia, and Brazil, "are almost entirely devoid of many species of plant and animal life" (CIA 1992).

In Colombia, drug terrorists mounted an audacious armed attack on the judicial branch of government that left the world in disbelief. In a 1998 interview with the author, Brian Bachman, Colombian Program Officer of the U.S. Bureau of Narcotics Matters, stated that although all the major players of the cocaine cartels have finally been either jailed or killed, hundreds of minor players have now filled that void. He reports that the U.S. powder and crack cocaine epidemic is waning from its peak in the 1980s, especially as far as casual users such as high school and college students are concerned. The hard-core addict, however, is still there—as evidenced by an estimated U.S.$16 billion in cocaine exports from Colombia for 1998 compared with U.S.$11 billion for products like coal, petroleum, coffee, and bananas. Colombia currently supplies 80 percent of the worldwide cocaine supply (McGirk 1999) which continues to maintain a stranglehold on the nation. Colombia produced 66 metric tons of opium (6 mt heroin compared to 125 mt of cocaine

▲ *Largely unrecognized, deforestation is another of cocaine's devastating effects, one that accelerated as producers attempted to keep up with the demands of the "crack" epidemic. Here, farmers harvest the coca leaves (Erythroxylum coca), destined for clandestine laboratories deep in the forest ◄ where they are converted into the deadly white powder.*

The cocaine connection

■ Principal growing areas

➤ Main trafficking routes

▲ *The narcotrafficantes' deadly cargo crosses the globe on wings of money and murder. In a system called "plata o plomo"— "silver or lead"—more than* *200 judges and supreme court officers, and one presidential candidate, were ruthlessly assassinated for refusing the bribes of the all-powerful drug cartels.*

▲ *On the filter lies the partly processed coca extract. Below, and in drums behind, are the processing chemicals—noxious, highly caustic compounds which will be dumped after use in the nearest stream, often poisoning the water for many miles downstream.*

hydrochloride) in 1997, becoming the world's third largest illicit producer of heroin, next to Burma (Myanmar) and Afghanistan. In Burma, Laos, and Thailand, toxic chemicals used to produce heroin that end up in streams and rivers, amount to some 4 million pounds (1,800,000 kg) annually.

It should be noted that heroin and cocaine production in Colombia is one of the few instances where smallholder farmers in tropical moist forests practice intensive agriculture such as crop rotation and use of fertilizer. Cultivation of coca leaf on steep slopes, remote from observation, has also led to significant soil erosion, which in turn leads to silting of rivers and bays and the need to clear new slopes for production. Altogether, the major Andean players, Peru, Bolivia, and Colombia, listed in order of magnitude of cultivation, produced almost a half-million acres (194,000 ha) in 1997 for cocaine production which totaled 650 metric tons. In 2001, Colombian minister of environment Juan Mayr admitted that fully 30 percent of deforestation there is due to illegal crops. We can reasonably speculate that Peru and Bolivia exceed this figure—a daunting revelation.

THE CATTLE CONNECTION

An increasing demand in the United States and other developed nations for inexpensive beef for human convenience foods and pet food has had a direct effect on tropical forests by resulting in their conversion to short-life pastures. Thus far a more popular concept in Latin America than elsewhere in the humid tropics, the forest is clear-cut and seeded with aggressive grasses. This would seem innocuous enough, even a logical and productive use of land. After all, the North American West is legendary for its cattle production. The differences between tropical and temperate soils and climates are, however, dramatic. Moderate rainfall and reasonably stable soil fertility in the American West and many other regions allow for sustained pastures. The thin, fragile soil and torrential rainfall of tropical forest areas place them at the opposite end of the spectrum. Tropical pastures have a short life and new areas must be constantly encroached on. This continuing process results in a rate of deforestation third in direct impact after shifting cultivation and logging.

An increasingly large proportion of these commercial enterprises are owned by corporations outside the countries with tropical forests. One of the largest of such holdings included a 540-square-mile (1,400-sq-km) concession in eastern Amazônia, and when this tract of forest was put to the torch it produced the largest single fire ever deliberately created by humanity!

Cattle ranching was the cause of 72 percent of Brazil's deforestation up to 1980. Further, the World Bank, the U.S. Agency for International Development (USAID), and other development agencies have provided some U.S.$4 billion for beef-production expansion. The journal *Cultural Survival Quarterly* estimates that "at least two-thirds of Central America's arable land is now devoted to cattle production." This region alone delivered more than 800 million hamburgers to the United States in 1994.

Beef is produced almost exclusively for export in these countries, and surprisingly little is consumed domestically. Local consumption is commonly limited to less desirable parts such as the viscera. The average Brazilian, for example, consumes a mere 35 pounds (16 kg) of beef annually; less meat than a domestic cat is provided in the United States. Fed on coarse, nutrient-poor grasses, the cattle yield low-quality beef, and it is not surprising that fast-food chains in the United States are the largest importers. One of the most ludicrous aspects of this trade is that some 67 square feet (6.25 sq m) of forest are sacrificed for each standard quarter-pound hamburger. That area of forest would contain roughly 800,000 pounds (362,900 kg) of plant and animal material—comprising species as yet unknown to science.

There are convoluted reasons why conversion of tropical forest to cattle pasture is so ultimately destructive. By its very nature, cattle raising comes with built-in inequities that compute poorly into the lower-economic sector. Such industry promotes the concentration of large landholdings in relatively few hands, and this results in small farmers being displaced from their land, and thus to unemployment and social stratification.

Such dynamics drive the landless in large migrations to urban areas, where they contribute to escalating unemployment, or to new wilderness areas where they contribute to deforestation. And, as production of beef for export replaces production of staple food crops, protein deficiencies appear in the landless and food imports very soon become necessary.

To compound this extravagance, cattle production is the least productive use of the land and the worst environmental alternative in the wet tropics. Stocking rates are surprisingly low at only one animal per hectare. Fertility, and thus profit, often wears out after only five years. The soil is commonly trampled to compaction, overgrazed, oxidized, and sun-baked, and toxic weeds move into the pasture and compete more successfully than the grasses, especially as they are not grazed away by livestock. Fertilizer has not been a

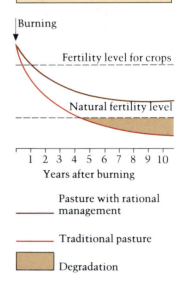

Burning

Fertility level for crops

Natural fertility level

1 2 3 4 5 6 7 8 9 10
Years after burning

Pasture with rational management

Traditional pasture

Degradation

▲ *Following forest clearance and burning, peak fertility levels plummet. Five years on, pastures are marginal, soon to be abandoned.*

THE BIGGEST FIRE LIT BY MAN

An environmental holocaust is currently sweeping the equatorial regions, brutally illustrated by the burning of Amazônia. Described by U.S. senators as "one of the great tragedies of history," images like the one below have finally awakened the world to the blight of deforestation.

◀ ▶ Rondônia
Over western Brazil the skies are darkened day and night. During the dry season, the forest is put to the torch to make way for unsustainable farming and cattle ranching. In the large map opposite, exploitation can be seen spreading out at either side of highway BR-364, laying waste to the forest and opening up areas that were formerly sacrosanct Indian tribal lands. On just 118 days in 1997, some 45,000 fires were counted—up 50 percent from 1996.

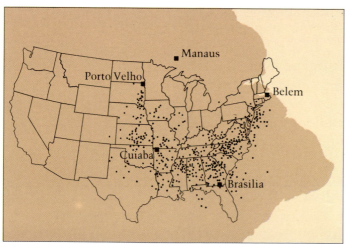

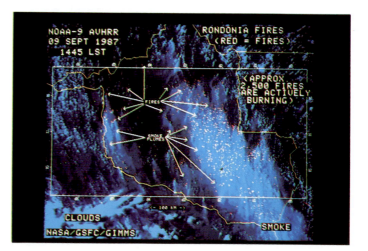

▲ The scale of the burning in Brazil
The horrifying extent of the assault on Brazil's forests can be seen when the affected area is superimposed on a map of the United States. The area suffering the brunt of the attack is roughly half that of the entire continental United States, and the destruction shows no sign of abating in the foreseeable future. In 1998 alone, an estimated 12,000 square miles (30,000 sq km), an area the size of Belgium, was burned.

▲ Satellite view of the state of Rondônia
The epicenter of Brazil's firestorm is the Amazon state of Rondônia. In this NASA satellite image some 2,500 separate fires are actively burning. Many times the smoke was so thick that the airport at the state capital was forced to close, often for days at a time. NASA scientists noted "indications that cloud formation may be suppressed in areas where smoke is present."

▶ Five-year legacy

The cumulative impact of the fires in Rondônia can be seen in these two NASA photographs. Areas outlined in red are largely deforested. Within those areas the white linear features are the ever-growing network of access roads spreading from highway BR-364. (Areas outside are natural savanna regions.)

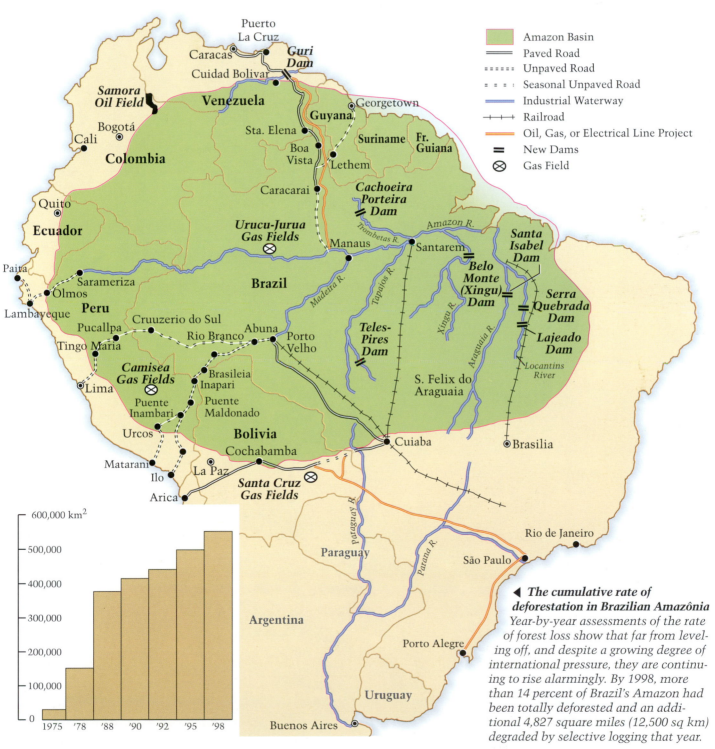

Legend:

- Amazon Basin
- Paved Road
- Unpaved Road
- Seasonal Unpaved Road
- Industrial Waterway
- Railroad
- Oil, Gas, or Electrical Line Project
- New Dams
- ⊗ Gas Field

◀ The cumulative rate of deforestation in Brazilian Amazônia

Year-by-year assessments of the rate of forest loss show that far from leveling off, and despite a growing degree of international pressure, they are continuing to rise alarmingly. By 1998, more than 14 percent of Brazil's Amazon had been totally deforested and an additional 4,827 square miles (12,500 sq km) degraded by selective logging that year.

cost-effective solution. Finally, it takes a full four years before steers are ready for slaughter weighing a scant 992 pounds (450 kg), and the severe epizootic problem is a constant harassment and constraint on productivity: this, after all, is the land of the parasite.

WHY INVEST WITH SUCH DISCOURAGING ODDS?

Since 1980, Rondônia's forest cover has dropped from 97 percent to 17 percent (INPE 1998), and it is still falling rapidly.

However, not all the news is bad. In 1987, highly successful broad-based grassroots environmental movements in the United States, coordinated by the Rainforest Action Network (RAN), have convinced Burger King (one of the major fast-food importers of Latin American beef) to cease the practice. Yet, RAN's Tamar Hurwitz informed me in 2001 that since imported rainforest beef loses that identity once distributed to fast-food chains and other outlets, it is currently unknown who retails that beef in the United States.

THE ECONOMICS OF HUNGER

The FAO estimates that 791 million souls suffer from persistent and chronic hunger and malnutrition. This shrouded killer takes the lives of 35,000 children under the age of five each day—one out of three in poorer countries! (UNICEF 1995)—not headline-breaking famine, but a day-by-day silent holocaust. In children alone that's more than 12 million per year—more than the total number of people who perished each year during World War II,

▲ *Land barons in Brazil clear immense tracts of land and then introduce cattle primarily to establish their presence there. Most ranches never sell a steer, but make their profit through inflated land prices. In Brazil, cattle ranching accounts for 30 percent of all deforestation, and nearly half of this was promoted by government subsidy. There are many who argue that such financial resources should be directed instead at the reclamation of degraded land and development of sustainable agriculture.*

◄ *Another high-profile ecological tragedy— the highlands of Madagascar are bare and scarred where once there was lush forest and a wealth of endemic wildlife.*

or equal to the number killed instantly by a Hiroshima bomb—every three days (Lappé 1998)!

In fact, there is enough food to feed the world—the problem is distribution. Yet in times of media attention to famine, the human and political will of developed nations is suddenly manifest to overcome even this formidable obstacle. It is surprising to learn that even the poorest of nations, Ethiopia, Somalia, and India, grow and export food—for animal feed. World Bank figures show that more than 40 percent of the world's grain (a volume of grain sufficient to feed everyone in the world) and 60 percent of its processed fish are fed, not to people, but livestock.

Brazil, whose Amazon is being consumed by dispossessed, hungry farming families, is the second largest exporter of food in the world. Where bananas, beans, corn, and fruit once grew in abundance, now more than 25 percent of the land is owned by large companies which grow soybeans for export (Flood 1995). In *Living Poor*, Moritz Thomsen recounts his experience during a drought in Ecuador. Parents "were selling their children before they died of hunger; autopsies on the ones who had died revealed stomachs full of roots and dirt." The stone wall of such untenable poverty often foments war.

Let us put ourselves in the tire tread–soled huaraches of an El Salvadoran campesino, as recounted by Charles Clements in *Witness to War.* "This year the money made from my crop of coffee, I will use to pay my mortgage. For one more year my farm cannot be taken from me. But if my child gets sick, I will have no money to pay for a bus to take me to the clinic for treatment and medicine. But without [my farm] my child will die anyway. With no farm, I have no money, no food. But today my youngest died, from fever and diarrhea. Take my farm. Take it; I don't care."

▼ *The bare, ravaged landscape of Haiti provides a stark contrast to the dense forest cover of the neighboring Dominican Republic. Only 0.8 percent of natural forest remain in Haiti, and with soil fertility washed away, the nation—now down to bedrock in many areas—is one of the world's poorest countries and is reliant on imports for much of its food.*

III INTERNATIONAL LOGGING

What is the place of human beings in the tropical forest biome? Are we inside or out? Are we intruders in the blissful rainforests or are we to consider ourselves part of this vast system? There are no ready black-and-white responses. Yet a moderate shade of gray is emerging out of the hard conglomerate of valiant ecological values on the one hand and fluid monetary incentives created by pressing raw-material demands on the other.

THE CONSEQUENCES OF LOGGING OPERATIONS

Tropical timber extraction by international companies obviously has a major impact on the viability of the remaining areas of rainforest. But unfortunately the impact does not stop there. FAO estimates that 70 percent of those forests cleared by landless settlers is made possible by logging roads. World Bank ecologist Robert Goodland states that "settlement along logging roads globally and [resulting] peasant agriculture may be the main causes of tropical moist deforestation." In many African nations more than 50 percent of logged forest areas were subsequently deforested, while virtually no deforestation took place on previously unlogged forest (Barbier, et al. 1994). Without the ingress of logging roads into new forest areas, migrant cultivation would be much reduced, possibly resulting in a more rational, intensified use of the original farm plot. For every 177 cubic feet (5 cu m) of logs removed by exploiters of timber, 2.47 acres (1 ha) are cut and torched by the follow-on cultivators; the implications are not evidenced by a subtly smoking gun, but by a 21-gun salute!

Although hard realities demand a clear differentiation between tropical and temperate exploitive strategies, extractive methods remain dictated by the price tag of each cubic meter of wood. Temperate trees produce seed yearly, but many tropical species flower and produce seeds infrequently, some only once in 35 years. To ignore reproduction cycles in the planning of cutting schedules is to ensure the demise of these and other tree species within a span of only a relatively few years.

As would be expected, logging puts discernible pressure on commercial as well as other species. The late Alwyn Gentry of the Missouri Botanical Garden found various trees in Ecuador to be close to extinction: *Persea theobromifolia*, formerly the most important timber tree species in its region, had already been reduced to fewer than four dozen mature individuals; of the lianoid, *Ducliptera dodsonii*, a single plant remained. In Perak, Malaysia, a number of tree species have been recorded only once, for instance *Burkilliodendron album*, and as their habitats have been converted to rubber plantations, they are presumed extinct. In 1992, Brazilian rosewood (*Dalbergia nigra*) was placed on Appendix I of the Convention on International Trade in Endangered Species of Wild Fauna and Flora (CITES), allowing no further trade (illegal trade continues). Furthermore, up to 10 percent of rainforest trees have extremely limited ranges, some occurring over as little as a few dozen square kilometers.

As conditions are so constant and hospitable inside the undisturbed forest, tropical tree species (as well as other biotics) have a marked intolerance

The forests of this planet are no longer to be regarded as the preserve of one industry for the production of a few commodities; rather, they are the habitat of millions upon millions of people whose intricate relationship to the forest must be of primary concern to those who would seek to manage forests more effectively.

THE FOOD AND AGRICULTURE ORGANIZATION OF THE UNITED NATIONS

▲ *Every year, 14.6 million acres (nearly 5.9 million ha) of closed tropical forests are logged. But because the canopy is interlaced with lianas, cutting 10 percent of the forest also destroys 50 percent of the noncommercial trees.*

Logging operations commonly target only the high-value commercial species, a gross underutilization that requires the logging of vast areas to fill company quotas. Globally, the forest resource is treated as nonrenewable, and many smallholders sell their logging rights for as little as U.S.$78 per hectare.

▲▲ Loggers near Korup in southwest Cameroon cut up a massive hardwood trunk.

◀ A tractor operator drags a felled tree in the Atlantic rainforest of Brazil. Mechanization of this kind has its own problems: the heavy machines leave a wake of destroyed vegetation and compacted soil, promoting erosion and reducing the forest's potential for recovery. Using oxen to haul logs would be a preferable alternative.

▲ The results of exploitive operations are evident. Sustained cyclic cutting of forests is still almost unknown in the tropics. [Osa Peninsula, Costa Rica.]

Developing nations in the tropics, often crippled by staggering debt, all too often export their principal asset, their forests. The implications of this shortsightedness are grave. We now increasingly see these former exporters of forest products becoming importers while losing the vast revenues sustainable harvesting could have allowed.

▲ A heavily laden truck makes its way through the rapidly diminishing Atlantic rainforest of Brazil, heading for the coast where ▶ the sawn timber will be loaded onto ships for export.

▼ In many parts of the tropics, broadrivers like the Solimões in Amazônia provide one of the main methods of transporting large numbers of logs from interior forest regions to coastal ports.

▲ *With latex bleeding from its wounds, another huge forest tree falls to the chain saw, having started its life as a seedling about the time Columbus discovered the New World, an event which eventually led to its undoing. Global demand for tropical hardwood is largely responsible for the felling of more than 16 million trees every day.*

toward disturbance. Seeds of temperate species survive hot summers and sub-zero winter temperatures, sometimes for periods of many years before germinating. Primary tropical forest species, on the other hand, often refuse to germinate after as little as 25 days. Further, certain dipterocarp species require a germination temperature of 73 to 79°F (23–26°C), yet after the forest is opened by loggers, ground temperature soars to 104°F (40°C).

Pollination is also precarious in the forest. In the still interior, very little pollen is carried on the wind. In Brunei only 1 in 760 tree species in 100 acres (40 ha) is wind pollinated, while globally each of 900 species of fig relies on a specific insect pollinator. Should disturbance remove a pollinator from the area, the dependent trees will not produce seed. This also removes from the area those animals that rely on the species for fruit, and this in turn may remove other pollinators, required for service to other tree species.

Because of such intricate relationships we can readily understand how fragile this habitat is and why it demands treatment far different from those in temperate zones. We can also see why 137 species a day are expunged from the global genetic reservoir (UNEP 1995).

There is as yet no indication of improvement. In 1961, the average timber harvested from closed broadleaved tropical forests was only 9,000 square miles (24,000 sq km), 245 percent less than that harvested in 1990 (Dykstra, CIFOR pers. comm. 1999). In the early 1980s the area of selectively logged tropical forest exceeded that of protected undisturbed forest by a ratio of 4 to 1 (Brown and Lugo 1984). By the early 1990s, this ratio had increased to 9 to 1 (World Bank 1991). Tropical closed broadleaved forest logged for timber amounts to 23,000 square miles (59,000 sq km) annually (Dykstra, CIFOR, pers. comm. 1999).

"Cut and Run" versus "Sustained Yield"

Clear felling is not generally practiced in the tropical forests, as only a small portion of the many species are commercially useful at present. Yet the damage levels to primary forests, even with selective logging, are of considerable magnitude, depending on harvest rates, which vary: Asia, 14–21 trees per hectare, Amazônia terra firma, 3–6 trees per hectare and Africa, 1–2 trees per hectare on average (Johns 1997; Nepstad 1999). Combining the effects of felling large trees, (which have both a knock-on and drag-on consequence to other trees in their path as well as to other neighboring trees due to the woody vines that bind them), destruction from skidding logs through the forest as well as clear felling for logging roads, the cumulative mortality to all tree size classes is on the order of 50 percent (Johns 1997). In Para state, Brazil, half the canopy cover was removed after selective logging, and the felling of single mahogany trees with mean log volumes of 5 cubic meters caused a mean loss of 31 other trees (Verissimo, et al. 1995). The need for tropical forest products is a reality, yet it is generally acknowledged that the logging industry could enjoy a longer and more profitable life if it synchronized its consumption to regeneration cycles instead of simply filling sales quotas.

The pitfalls of self-regulation become glaring in tropical logging. Regulations laid down by tropical countries on overcutting and the taking of undersize trees go largely unenforced. A common, circuitous, but somewhat justifiable complaint of the logging firms is, why should they be charitable by adhering to conservation regulations when other operators secure a competitive advantage by ignoring conscionable harvesting procedures?

FUTURE TREND OF
WORLDWIDE WOOD DEMAND

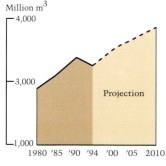

Million m³
4,000

3,000

Projection

1,000
1980 '85 '90 '94 '00 '05 2010

A recent United Nations hearing on multinational corporations reveals how the understandably appealing carrot of foreign skills and capital is often eagerly accepted by developing nations with large balance-of-trade deficits. The price tag on the carrot is often the handing over of enormous tracts of virgin forest, unencumbered by regulation, or a tacit waiver in practice of regulation enforcement. Yet the political and economic power wielded by the multinationals in the countries they exploit often exceeds and even undermines the governments of these nations. The question is raised: Why have we granted the multinational corporations such latitude?

Indonesia serves as a typical example of the logging industry's environmentally counterproductive flexing of its political muscle. With the use of proper cyclic methods, forest regeneration is *theoretically* possible in 30 years. The Indonesian government requires logging corporations to follow a 35-year cutting cycle, yet it grants them a 20-year lease. Most of Indonesia's accessible forests are already allocated to multinational timber corporations, and by 2011 Indonesia's accessible timber is expected to be completely overcut.

It is clear that both the importing and exporting nations have been irresponsibly inadequate in leaving the policy making, policing, and enforcing of regulations to the logging concerns. This could well be a major point of focus in the next decade. If much of this review appears critical of current timber industry practices it is to emphasize that the pivotal point is not whether extracting timber is an admirable endeavor, but rather how extensive tracts of tropical forest are currently being cut down without design, planning, or regulation. The goat, as they say in Russia, is in charge of the cabbage patch.

A recent Brazilian government forest policy meeting discussed that supply is the major timber company concern. Malaysia in the late 1990s had a demand for 9 million cubic meters of timber per year to meet Japan's import requests. Commonly, local shifting cultivators sell the commercial trees on their plots or in nearby forests to the loggers for a going rate (1997) of less than U.S.$2.50 (Brazilian R$5.00).

Clearly, economic programs that give tree poachers other viable options for a livelihood would be the front line of attack on the 80 percent of total timber extraction that is poached illegally in Brazilian Amazônia, where the Brazilian Institute for the Environment (IBAMA) has but a few hundred officials to cover an area the size of the continental United States.

While tropical timber nations will continue to rely on their forest sectors as a means of offsetting their balance-of-trade deficits, a glaring failure exists on every continent in actualizing the potential in processing raw logs, rents, stumpage fees, royalties, and revenues. Indonesia currently loses U.S.$1 billion annually, but could robustly reduce its overall cut if it captured these revenues.

The World's Major Forest Consumer

A sketch of one nation's harvest and use of tropical wood beggars belief. Although having only 2 percent of the total global population, Japan receives 36 percent of all tropical logs exported, more such wood than any other nation, and more than twice the amount of all Europe combined. Consumption per capita is also more, at 1,624 cubic feet (46 cu m) per 1,000 persons, with Europeans at 177 cubic feet (5 cu m) and the United States barely registering (ITTO 1998).

Surprisingly, for a nation known traditionally for its frugality, a conspicuous amount of waste is built into Japan's high-profile overuse. Up to 80

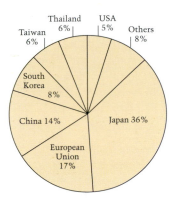

▲ If the world is now a "global village," there is a disproportionate consumption of resources by at least some of its villagers. With barely 2 percent of the village's population, Japan now consumes a staggering 36 percent of total tropical timber exports.

▲ The world is anxiously watching the "Brazil in Action" plan which recently funded U.S.$1 billion for road development and natural gas exploitation in its Amazon region. If the extension of highway BR-364 is paved through the pristine Amazonian state of Acre, it would link up with the Peruvian road to the Pacific coast port at Lima. Such a link would create a direct export "pipeline" from Amazônia to the Asian markets, with disastrous consequences for the Amazon Basin forests.

TOP TEN PLANTING COUNTRIES (TROPICAL)		
Countries	Total	Annual
		(000 ha)
1. India	18,900	1,700
2. Indonesia	8,750	100
3. Brazil	7,000	200
4. Vietnam	2,100	125
5. Thailand	756	40
6. Venezuela	362	30
7. Cuba	350	30
8. Bangladesh	335	10
9. Myanmar	335	40
10. Madagascar	310	5

percent of the wood is processed into plywood, most of which is used to make molds for concrete. These are then discarded and burned after only a few uses. Furthermore, coastal mangroves, the removal of which can be proved directly responsible for the serious depletion of Asian coastal fisheries, are used to make chipwood and to grill *yakitori,* a popular chicken dish. In Southeast Asia, natural forests are widely cleared and replanted with "more suitable" wood for the production of *waribashi,* or disposable chopsticks!

Part of Japan's official "foreign aid" is the construction of logging roads into Sarawak and other areas, and these are highly destructive to the Penan and other traditional tribes. Such roads are used solely as a conduit for wood to Japan, and the burden of cost must be repaid by the people of Sarawak. Japan, by use of high tariffs, discourages the importation of any finished products, taking only raw logs and thus ensuring the tropical forest nation's need to export large volumes of timber in order to accrue the necessary balance-of-trade revenues. During the 1990s, the Rainforest Action Network instituted a tenacious boycott on Japanese Mitsubishi Corporation products, as Mitsubishi is one of the major logging companies plying tropical forests.

Certain aspects of the 1996 "Brazil Action Plan" have shaken the global scientific, political, and environmental communities with the news of the nation's intent to implement a vast road infrastructure, which could include the connection of Brazil's infamous BR-364 highway with the Peruvian road that leads directly to the Pacific coast near Lima. In its short life, BR-364 has already had an enormous impact on the Mato Grosso and caused the destruction of 83 percent of the forests of Amazônia's Rondônia state. The proposed new 500-mile (805-km) paved road would go through the comparatively pristine Brazilian state of Acre at a cost of U.S.$300 million. It will connect the Amazonian borders of Brazil, Bolivia, and Peru—the major holders of the basin. One can envision logging spurs infiltrating the entire region, and reaching out into Colombia and other northern forest holders.

Brazil's Space Institute reports that more than 14 percent of its primary forests in Amazônia have been cleared in the past three decades (INPE 1998). Japan's major source of tropical wood imports is currently Indonesia, where the forests are rapidly approaching depletion. There is a visceral foreboding that should this highway connect the very heart of Amazônia with Pacific shipping access to Japan—the world's number one importer of tropical forests—it would quite literally extract every last commercial log, leaving Amazônia and the last of its traditional tribal cultures disenfranchised and effectively obliterated. It was to the halting of this road that the martyred Chico Mendes dedicated his life. Concerned individuals and organizations worldwide are closely monitoring this assuredly disastrous plan.

THE TREND TO REPLACE NATURAL FORESTS WITH PLANTATIONS

Plantations produce wood more uniform in size and quality, and in shorter production cycles (7 to 30 years), than those of natural forests (30 to 150 years). This facilitates harvest and transportation, and so there is a growing trend to replace natural forests, with their plethora of services and functions, with comparably sterile plantations. The key environmental strategy, however, is to establish plantations (at a cost of U.S.$400 per hectare in tropical nations) on deforested or otherwise degraded land, of which some 2 billion acres (800 million ha) exist. Yet primary forest is still typically the prime target for conversion.

So it is with mixed emotions that FAO reports that forest-rich countries such as Indonesia plan to increase the share of plantations for industrial wood production from 20 percent in 1990 to 80 percent by 2030. In the tropics, the estimated total area of plantations established by 1980 was 45 million acres (18 million ha). By 1990, that figure rose to 109 million acres (44 million ha), an increase of 150 percent at 2.61 million ha annually. The lack of forethought is even more glaring when one considers that there are presently 640,000 square miles (1,657,000 sq km) of watershed globally in the most dire need of repair. In 1997, however, Indonesia issued more forest-clearing concessions than ever before—mostly to large agribusiness families close to then-president Suharto, largely for oil palm and pulp wood plantations. Yet highly commendable community/social forestry, the growing of trees outside the forest for fuelwood and other local uses, is much on the rise, especially in India and other areas of Asia and the Pacific; this is the reason these regions are responsible for 75 percent of all established plantations in the tropics.

ENVIRONMENTAL PROBLEMS CAUSED BY TREE PLANTATIONS	
Problem	**Notes**
Loss of habitat	In many places, plantations have been established in the place of existing natural forest and natural or ancient heathland, etc. Some of the habitats replaced are themselves now scarce and require conservation.
Reduced biodiversity: trees	Plantations tend to use exotic tree species or selected strains of native trees (sometimes through use of tissue culture to develop identical trees), thus reducing genetic variability and hence adaptability of trees.
Reduced biodiversity: other wildlife	Replacing native or managed forests with plantations inevitably leads to a crucial reduction in biodiversity throughout the flora and fauna.
Introduction of exotic tree species	Exotics sometimes escape cultivation and compete with native species and have occasionally hybridized with native species, leading to loss of local provenances.
Soil erosion	Deep plowing during planting, especially in upland areas, can lead to excessive soil erosion, as can the impact of clear felling.
Acidification	Establishment of conifer plantations on base-poor soils has led to increased acidification of both soil and freshwaters, due mainly to the role of conifers in scavenging air pollutants, which are later washed down trunks, although conifers may have an additional acidifying role of their own.
Water table changes	Planting some species, e.g., eucalyptus, can lead to serious lowering of the water table in drought-prone areas.
Water quality changes	Drainage, plowing, and clear felling can all lead to an increase in water turbidity, which can damage the breeding success of fish, disturb other aquatic life, etc.
Changes to the fire ecology	Plantations can either increase fires through poor management, or artificially suppress fires (in fire climax habitats). Both can have serious ecological consequences.
Increased pest and disease attack	Monocultures are particularly prone to attack by pests and diseases. Introduction of exotic trees has sometimes resulted in parallel introduction of serious pests.
Agrochemical use	Pests and problems of decreasing fertility lead to greater use of pesticides and soluble fertilizers; both of these have a range of environmental problems including water pollution, damage to wildlife, etc.

IV Fuelwood Collection

Deadwood collected as fuelwood in tropical wet and very moist regions, usually by rural households, does not contribute significantly to deforestation beyond the removal of nutrients from the biome. However, some 3 billion people in developing countries worldwide depend on fuelwood, including charcoal, for all their household energy needs and consume half of all wood produced globally. As FAO projects, the 1993 level of demand which is responsible for 6 percent of global primary energy use (13.3 percent in Brazil, up to 30 percent in China and more than 90 percent in its domestic sector) (Nakicenovic, et al. 1996) will increase 25 percent by 2010 and more than double the current demand by 2050, an increase greater than total wood use. If 1.5 billion people cannot presently meet their fuelwood needs without overcutting tree stocks, 2.5 billion people will be ravaging their respective habitats due to self-need by 2010.

The World Wood Famine

The approaching fuelwood famine should be evaluated in a spirit of urgency, as in tropical regions, especially the dry formations, as much as 90 percent of total forest production is consumed as fuelwood (FAO 1993). But due to deforestation, by 2050, people of tropical nations will need 2 percent more wood as fuel than will be grown annually by that year (Solomon, et al. 1996). Signs of critical impending shortages are seen in current percentages of fuelwood cut in some countries as a percent of each country's total. They include: Bangladesh, 96 percent; Bhutan and India, 91 percent; Thailand, 89 percent; Nepal, 88 percent, Burma 84 percent; and the Philippines, 77 percent.

Yet demand in many nations, including some of the above, actually now exceeds fuelwood available. India requires 133 million tons of fuelwood but only 33 million is available, which means that some 100 million tons were illegally harvested from Indian forests. The shortages are now so critical that in some denuded rural areas, recently clothed in forest, a family member must now spend two days foraging for enough firewood to cook one hot meal for the family. Further, envision that the preponderance of human food consumption consists of grains and other starches which are indigestible unless cooked. Where, then, will that fuelwood come from? In many tropical countries, and essentially in the drier formations, because fuelwood costs are up 100 percent from 1980 levels (FAO 1998), it now costs more to heat the pot than to fill it. How will they afford both fuelwood and food?

The answer to the second question largely depends on the answer to the first. But lest we succumb to the inertia of negative velocity as demonstrated in the statistics above, we do have options we may exercise now (see chapter 5). It is also true that the longer we wait to implement them, the fewer the souls that will be able to slip through the closing door of

THE WORLD FUELWOOD CRISIS

The world fuelwood famine kindles grave concerns for the developing countries whose people rely on this dwindling resource for cooking and heating.

As forests of all types continue to diminish, in many of the world's poorest areas it now costs more in time and effort to heat the pot than it does to fill it.

CONSUMPTION OF FUELWOOD AND CHARCOAL (Million M³)				
	1970	1980	1990	1994
Africa	250.3	330.5	443.8	502.2
North/Central America	49.7	139.0	145.9	160.9
South America	155.6	195.5	234.4	258.0
Asia	569.2	675.1	816.0	878.2
Europe	67.9	52.1	52.3	51.8
Oceania	5.9	7.1	8.8	8.7
Former USSR	86.5	78.9	81.1	30.6
World	**1,185.0**	**1,478.1**	**1,782.3**	**1,890.4**

▲ ▶ The scale of the fuelwood crisis

FAO figures for 1980 and 2000 show the numbers of people, in millions, whose fuelwood supplies cannot be maintained. "Acute scarcity" means a lack of even the minimum requirement, while "deficit" means that needs can be met only by overcutting the resource and degrading the habitat. Here ▶ wood is collected in Guinea.

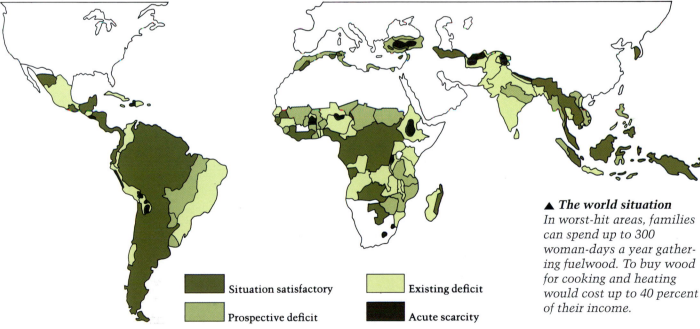

■ Situation satisfactory	■ Existing deficit
■ Prospective deficit	■ Acute scarcity

▲ The world situation

In worst-hit areas, families can spend up to 300 woman-days a year gathering fuelwood. To buy wood for cooking and heating would cost up to 40 percent of their income.

▶ Fuelwood's share of total energy use

While the developed world's consumption of fossil fuel gives cause for increasing environmental concern, most developing countries have few options but to use fuelwood as an energy source. Alternatives are too expensive, or simply not available.

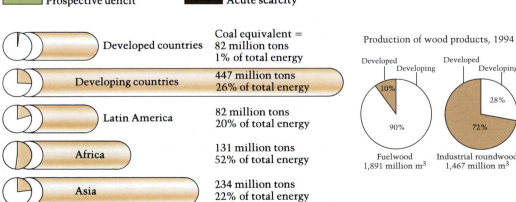

	Coal equivalent =
Developed countries	82 million tons / 1% of total energy
Developing countries	447 million tons / 26% of total energy
Latin America	82 million tons / 20% of total energy
Africa	131 million tons / 52% of total energy
Asia	234 million tons / 22% of total energy

Production of wood products, 1994

Fuelwood
1,891 million m³
Developed 10%
Developing 90%

Industrial roundwood
1,467 million m³
Developed 28%
Developing 72%

▶ *Dung patties drying on a wall in Calcutta. The growing reliance, currently by 250 million people, on cattle dung for fuel is robbing the developing countries' fields of desperately needed nutrients. Each ton of dung burned represents a loss of 110 pounds (50 kg) of grain production, and in Asia, the Near East, and Africa, 400 million tons are burned every year. To reduce this dependency, village tree-planting schemes should be introduced and established quickly on a wide scale.*

opportunity—and that opportunity can only be massive industry in plantation forestry on degraded lands in conjunction with population stabilization.

A Resource Goes Up in Smoke

While visiting Calcutta, India, as far back as 1962, I noticed patties of a strange material plastered to wall surfaces. In answer to my inquiry, I was informed that these were cow-dung cakes drying, to be used as fuel: a most common practice, I later found, as there is simply no wood available at all for the masses of this, one of the world's most crowded and certainly most impoverished cities.

A smoky pall of this interesting custom hangs over many Indian towns and cities as in many other developing countries, and the practice, unfortunately, is growing. The burning of dung and crop residues robs the fields of much-needed nutrients, and borrowing from Peter to pay Paul causes a continuous downward spiral in harvest yields at a time when, due to population pressures, increased production is demanded. Solid fossil fuels and oil appear to be out of the question as fuel sources due to their high cost. It is estimated that some 400 million tons of dung are burned as fuel in areas where firewood is scarce or nonexistent. The trade-off is highly illuminating. The task force convened to produce the Tropical Forestry Action Plan states that by loss of dung (fertilizer) in the fields, food-grain harvests are reduced by more than 14 million tons. This loss of food is nearly *double* the quantity of food provided annually in aid to developing countries!

V The Paper Chase, Population, and Other Factors

The consumption of paper (which includes newspaper and paperboard) is increasing faster than that of any other forest product; in fact, present consumption is five times the amount used in 1950. This volume is projected to double again by 2010. In 1997, some two-thirds of paper produced globally came from virgin logs, only 4 percent from nonwood sources such as straw or cotton, and the balance from wastepaper. Quite soon more than one-half of global industrial wood harvested will go toward paper production.

In standard practice, each citizen of the United States throws away in paper three whole conifer trees yearly. This represents only paper wasted, not the total amount consumed, and means that approximately 1 billion trees (6,725 square miles or nearly 17,416 sq km of forest, an area larger than the state of Hawaii) are being wasted each year by one country alone. In developing nations, the average person uses only 11 pounds (5 kg) each year, but most use less than 2.2 pounds (1 kg), the equivalent of one-third of the Sunday edition of the *New York Times*. (Conversely, one single run of the *New York Times* Sunday edition consumes 86,000 trees.) Incremental surges often elude perception. Yet the world is projected to use 11 times as much paper by 2050 than presently (FAO 1996). Paper production is driven solely by buoyant demand, and if it is currently unsustainable, the path to filling such future demand will be very hard to follow indeed.

Mineral Extraction

The extraction of mineral resources from forest lands is often accompanied by circumstances that produce far more damage than the mining process itself. The U.S.$5 billion, 347,000-square-mile (900,000-sq-km) Grande Carajás Project in Brazil's eastern Amazon pursues the exploitation of considerable deposits of iron ore, copper, manganese, bauxite, and nickel. The pig iron production scheme at full operation of 2.7×10^3 tons per year implies a charcoal demand equivalent to 386–580 square miles per year (1,000–1,500 sq km/yr) of deforestation (Anderson 1990). Despite the colossal nature of the Carajás project, it has done very little to alleviate the pernicious poverty in the Amazon. Beginning with the late 1980s influx of 40,000 Brazilian gold miners into Ῠanomamö territory, malaria became responsible for 25 percent of the tribe's deaths over the next few years. It is estimated that 1,000–2,000 tons of poisonous mercury has been released into the Amazon through mining, mostly for gold. Mercury contamination continues today and is found in the commercial-fish food chain in all major Brazilian rivers with the exception of the Madeira (UNIDO 1999). It is sad to note that multinational corporations make use of the World Bank and International Monetary Fund for mining-project funding. By 1996, 60 percent of the total Carajás area was deforested or seriously degraded.

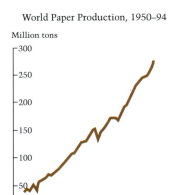

World Paper Production, 1950–94

Million tons

▲ *Soaring world paper production and consumption is glaring proof of the destruction of close to half the world's original forest cover over the past century.*

Hydroelectrical Debacles

It is understandable that tropical nations with major rivers will wish to consider their hydroelectric alternatives. A disturbing pattern emerges, however, of vast projects launched without a thorough evaluation at the outset of factors such as the projected longevity of the dam, the actual need for electricity production, environmental destruction, and the displacement of indigenous cultures with few satisfactory options for their future.

In any conversion from one form of land use to another, there will, of necessity, be trade-offs which must be carefully evaluated. All too often the more obvious merits of hydroelectrical projects are, for lack of more tactful description, wanton infusion of capital, commonly out of political expedience. USAID, World Bank, and other international lending institutions were duly challenged on such policies toward the end of the 1980s. However, the promise of future environmental impacts through major dam projects unfortunately still exists.

Brazil's "Plan 2010" dictates the construction of 136 high dams, 22 of them in Amazônia, that will flood a rainforest the size of the United Kingdom. This includes the highly controversial 11,000 megawatt Belo Monte dam on the Xingu River. If built, this project would destroy part of the Kayapó reserve, flooding the lower sections of the city Altamira (inhabited by some 50,000 people) and will flood 390 square miles (1,000 sq km) of forest. The environmental atrocities aside, the dam is criticized economically, as electricity generated would be less than 50 percent of the installed capacity due to the paucity of water in the dry season. Price tag: U.S.$11.5 billion. In Bolivia, more plant and animal species grace the new Madidi National Park than any other preserve in South America. Yet the government plans to build a new hydroelectric dam here, endangering this pristine ecosystem.

Various factors conspire to differentiate the feasibility of dam construction in temperate areas and tropical forest regions. Erosion, and subsequent siltation, has been consistently problematical. The ludicrously accelerated obsolescence due to this factor can be easily demonstrated by the example of

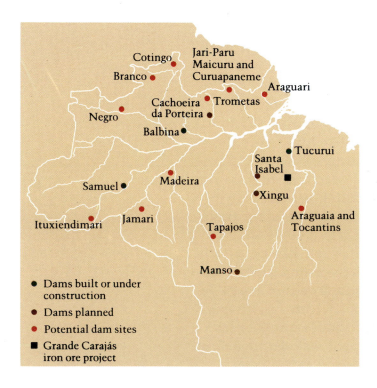

- ● Dams built or under construction
- ● Dams planned
- ● Potential dam sites
- ■ Grande Carajás iron ore project

◀ ▲ **Hydroelectric schemes** *Vast areas of Brazil's forests are being flooded by hydroelectric schemes. The victims are many of the country's indigenous tribes. Criticisms focus on the* *politically motivated international bank loans that are used to finance the schemes, and the low output of energy and inappropriate location of many of the projects.*

Colombia's Anchicaya Dam, which lost a full quarter of its storage capacity within only two years of its completion. Seventeen of India's major reservoirs are silting at up to three times the rate expected. Another concern is the overgrowth of water-surface vegetation. This matting chokes off primary production, oxygen production, and animal life, in that order.

Of major consequence, and a factor regularly overlooked, is that due to unvarying temperatures, the layers within impounded tropical water bodies do not mix. Due to anoxic (oxygen-deficient) conditions, submerged vegetation produces hydrogen sulfide, and this in turn often produces water of such extreme acidity that turbine blades in hydroelectric generating stations corrode, critically shortening the life of such installations.

It should be especially noted that such projects commonly *reduce* employment opportunities in rural agriculture, small-scale village industries, and other traditional livelihoods. For example, bank-funded rural electrification projects in Bangladesh and Indonesia have taken employment from millions of women who formerly earned their living husking rice by hand. In the bank's "one step forward, two steps back" approach, it is just such displaced rural masses who are then forced to try to cultivate steep hillslopes and other inappropriate areas in an attempt at survival.

POPULATION GROWTH AND TROPICAL FORESTS

October 12, 1999, was the "Day of Six Billion," (U.S. Census Bureau 1999)—the day the 6 billionth individual joined the human family! To accumulate its first billion it took world population from the dawn of humanity until 1820, the second billion, 110 years, from 1820 to 1930. Each succeeding increment of 1 billion has taken 30 years, 15 years, and 12 years respectively. The world's population has doubled in the last 40 years. In less than three decades, the global total will reach 8 billion with a full 80 percent living in tropical forest countries—or more than the global total today! This now brings the population density of the earth to 105 people per square mile. A large percentage of those unfortunates will be relying for their sustenance on slash-and-burn agriculture in quickly receding tropical forests. On that observation, and recognizing that such warnings are written on the wall in blood, Peter Raven, director of the Missouri Botanical Garden and a prominent voice among concerned scientists, in testimony before a congressional subcommittee, stated, "Since [virtually all] the tropical forests will be destroyed during the next 25 years, it is difficult to avoid the conclusion that up to one billion people will be starving to death in the first two decades of the [21st] century."

The direct relationship between human population growth and species extinction is clear. Is the human species on the same slippery slope as the balance of species we share this planet with? What does that portend for us? If we, as a species, are unable to craft a viable response to such visceral, long-term threats to humanity's long-term survival (as population growth, soil erosion, and global warming with 6 billion souls), how will we contend with these lethal debacles in 2050, with a median projected population of 8.9 billion (United Nations 1999) fueling the decay of our environment? As 1.86 billion (31 percent) people are under 15 years of age, tomorrow's mothers are already present—and 95 percent of these reside in developing countries.

It should also be abundantly clear that nothing is more firmly at the heart of the issue than population pressure, and that family planning can in no way

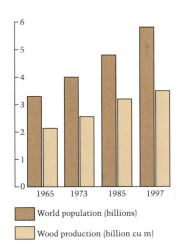

▲ *The connection between population increase and deforestation is clearly shown in this graph, leaving little doubt that those who would seek answers to the problem of tropical deforestation must also address the problem of population pressure—one of the root causes.*

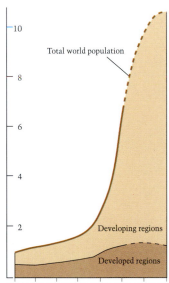

▲ *If runaway population is the disease, then tropical deforestation is one of the main symptoms. An increase of some 78 million souls per year is a reflection of the need of peasant parents in many parts of the world for help on the farm and security in old age.*

FOREST AREA, POPULATION, AND AVAILABILITY OF FOREST AREA PER PERSON IN THE TROPICAL FOREST ZONE

LATIN AMERICA COUNTRY	Brazil	Colombia	Costa Rica	Ecuador	Guatemala	Guyana	Honduras	Mexico	Nicaragua	Panama	Peru	Suriname	Venezuela
1980 FOREST AREA (thousands of hectares)	600,762	57,771	1,925	14,372	5,049	18,597	5,720	55,423	7,255	3,764	70,714	14,901	51,768
Population (thousands)	121,672	28,447	2,284	7,961	6,820	759	3,569	67,570	2,921	1,950	17,324	355	15,091
Per Capita Forest Area (hectares)	4.94	2.03	0.84	1.81	0.74	24.50	1.60	0.82	2.48	1.93	4.08	41.95	3.43
1995 FOREST AREA (thousands of hectares)	551,139	52,988	1,248	11,137	3,841	18,577	4,115	55,387	5,560	2,800	67,562	14,721	43,995
Population (thousands)	159,346	38,542	3,554	11,460	9,976	830	5,654	91,145	4,426	2,631	23,532	409	21,844
Per Capita Forest Area (hectares)	3.46	1.37	0.35	0.97	0.39	22.39	0.73	0.61	1.26	1.06	2.87	35.99	2.01
2025 FOREST AREA (thousands of hectares)	480,358	45,761	497	6,832	2,084	18,321	2,039	42,322	2,592	1,468	61,408	14,360	31,509
Population (thousands)	217,930	59,758	5,929	17,796	19,816	1,045	10,656	130,196	8,696	3,779	35,518	525	34,775
Per Capita Forest Area (hectares)	2.20	0.77	0.08	0.38	0.11	17.54	0.19	0.33	0.30	0.39	1.73	27.37	0.91

▲ *Population in the tropical forest zone*
The projections in this chart show the vulnerability of the tropical developing countries. One-half of the region's people are 15 years old or less, and population growth rates continue to rise, putting ever more pressure on the region's natural resources.

be subjugated to more direct causes, such as commercial timber extraction, migrant cultivation, fuelwood collection, or the hamburger connection. It is no mere coincidence that Ethiopia was some 45 percent covered with forest in 1920 with a population of 5 million. That was 123 acres (50 ha) of natural forest per capita. In 1994, with only 0.8 percent of forest left, each person of a population of 55 million is left with a minuscule 0.62 acres (0.25 ha) of natural forest for his or her needs and ecosystem maintenance.

Madagascar, with a population of 13.4 million and a phenomenal growth rate of 2.9 percent from 1960–92, could nearly triple its numbers by 2020. Its forests are presently under siege and 74 percent deforested. Already one of the most heavily eroded places on Earth, Madagascar's topsoil is vanishing eight times faster than Ethiopia's. Given such bleak austerity, it is regrettable, but not surprising, that infant mortality has soared to 93 per thousand. Of all the major environmental debacles plaguing the Earth, overpopulation is the greatest. In many respects it is the fundamental disease; most other problems are in reality only the symptoms. It is estimated that 600 million people in rural zones are landless, and that they farm one-fifth of the entire tropical forest biome, including secondary forests. The death toll for these landless people in times of food shortages is fully three times higher than that for people who own a plot, even one as small as 3.7 acres (1.5 ha).

"WHOSE HAND IS ON THE CHAINSAW?"

Those in the environmental sciences are increasingly concerned that sufficient world resources are not being allocated to the population problem. As more people populate tropical moist nations, the more food must be sustainably cultivated to feed them, as food imports for that purpose in developing tropical nations are a minor factor. Many assume the "green revolution" will fill the coming void, but the marvelous gains of those technologies are already

	Bangladesh	Myanmar (Burma)	India	Indonesia	Malaysia	Papua New Guinea	Philippines	Thailand	Vietnam		Cameroon	Côte d'Ivoire	Democratic Rep. of the Congo	Gabon	Madagascar	Republic of Congo
ASIA										**AFRICA**						
	1,258	32,901	58,259	124,476	21,564	37,145	11,194	18,123	10,663		21,573	12,128	120,613	19,411	17,314	20,200
	88,221	33,821	688,856	150,958	13,763	3,086	48,317	46,718	53,711		8,655	8,194	27,009	692	8,873	1,669
	0.01	0.97	0.08	0.82	1.57	12.04	0.23	0.39	0.20		2.49	1.48	4.47	28.05	1.95	12.10
	1,010	27,151	65,005	109,791	15,471	36,939	6,766	11,630	9,117		19,598	5,469	109,245	17,859	15,106	19,537
	118,616	42,877	933,665	197,464	20,108	4,301	68,354	58,610	73,866		13,182	13,528	45,421	1,077	13,744	2,561
	0.01	0.63	0.07	0.56	0.77	8.59	0.10	0.20	0.12		1.49	0.40	2.41	16.58	1.10	7.63
	782	17,956	65,221		82,216	7,457	33,184	2,336	5,254		16,133	4,630	89,451	15,357	11,732	18,334
	178,751	58,120	1,330,449		273,442	30,968	7,460	108,251	72,717		26,484	23,345	104,788	1,981	28,964	5,689
	0.00	0.31	0.05		0.30	0.24	4.45	0.02	0.07		0.61	0.20	0.85	7.75	0.41	3.22

realized, and, in many cases, are receding due to soil loss caused by machinery and systems too reliant on costly chemical fertilizers.

Population density—the numbers of people per thousand hectares—is the barometer. For example, a value of 25 (per 1,000 ha) for Suriname is one of the world's lowest; the nation enjoys the highest area of primary tropical forest per capita globally. Cuba, Indonesia, and Uganda, each with a value of 800 to 1,000 suffer staggering rates of deforestation. El Salvador and the Philippines, at values of 2,000 to 3,000, are virtually deforested. Compare some temperate nations' rates, such as Canada at 29 and the United States at 269. On balance, it should be realized that we have little latitude of choice in this issue, for if we fail to control population, it will, by the most natural and odious of processes, provide its own control.

It is quite clear that given the very high rates of infant and child mortality, parents in developing countries exhibit a very deliberate will to produce more rather than fewer children. A large number of children provides more than just workers in the fields (workers whom the parents could certainly not afford to hire as paid labor); it also provides a degree of insurance against old age.

Given these cultural realities it is essential to parallel our efforts to promote birth control with equally determined efforts to increase soil fertility, crop yields, and farm plot productive life. A real decrease in birth rate cannot be achieved until there is real progress in the improvement of food supply, child health, longevity, and overall well-being in the populations of developing countries. If we gain ground here, we will, at the same time, be attacking the root causes of tropical deforestation.

In the following chapters, we will investigate what is at stake if tropical deforestation goes unchecked. We will also see that the fate of these forests is not inexorably sealed. Humanity does have viable options. Will we employ them?

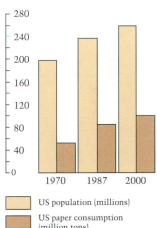

US population (millions)

US paper consumption (million tons)

▲ The United States population produces more waste per capita than any other nation. While less than one-third of all newspapers are recycled, recovering just one run of the Sunday New York Times would save 86,000 trees. It is a sobering thought that recycling one ton of paper can save 17 trees, 25 barrels of oil, 7,000 gallons of water, and 3 cubic yards of landfill space.

4
WHAT DO WE LOSE?

The action for which our descendants are least likely to forgive us is the loss of genetic and species diversity by the destruction of natural habitats. Unless we curtail our activities in these areas, the effects of the loss of such a large portion of species will have the most serious long-term consequences, of even longer duration than the unthinkable outcome of nuclear war, famine, and political turmoil.

EDWARD O. WILSON
National Medal of Science Recipient, Harvard University.

Humanity is so closely related to the mountain gorilla that we can instinctively interpret its every gesture with crystal clarity. Here, glaring fiercely at me just before launching a harrowing charge, this silverback troop leader demands that I lower my camera and behave submissively. Discovered just 100 years ago, only some 600 survive today—on the precipice of extinction.

I BIOLOGICAL DIVERSITY

The whales, the rhinos, the tigers, the elephants, these are the visible tip of the iceberg. But what we're really talking about is the biological impoverishment of this planet.

RUSSELL E. TRAIN
PAST PRESIDENT, WORLD WIDE FUND FOR NATURE—USA

H. G. Wells once said, "Human history more and more becomes a race between education and catastrophe."

What then does it mean to us when we hear that some 69 acres (28 ha) of tropical forest disappear every minute? Are the figures and the problems of tropical deforestation so enormous that they elude comprehension?

THE COPIOUS PRODUCTIVITY OF THE FOREST

The tropical forests are responsible for a conspicuous percentage (up to 69 percent) of Earth's biological productivity. Nothing could demonstrate the significance of our dependence on this biome more than to recall the transpiration dynamics of a single large emergent forest tree—pumping some 200 gallons (760 l) of water per day into the atmosphere. Through this process, 1 acre (0.4 ha) of tropical rainforest releases 20,000 gallons (76,000 l) of water into the atmosphere daily for cloud formation—20 times the amount the sea contributes through evaporation from the same surface area.

Were we to search for a single mechanism to preserve soil fertility; percolate water evenly through the seasons, and so prevent flood, erosion, and drought; release atmospheric water; store atmospheric carbon; cleanse the air; moderate global temperature and climatic balance; beautify the terrain, and support a varied fauna and flora, none could be found to serve better than a

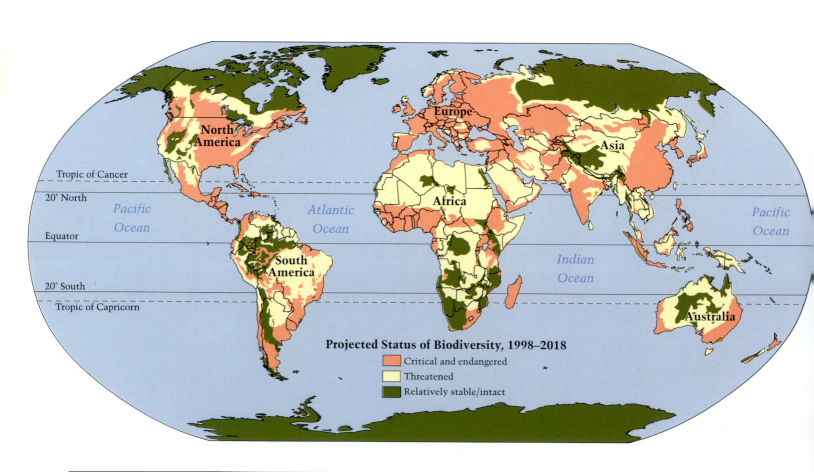

Projected Status of Biodiversity, 1998–2018
- Critical and endangered
- Threatened
- Relatively stable/intact

PRODUCTS OF THE RAINFOREST

At the current rate of tropical deforestation we face a cumulative loss of 10 million species by 2020. We already derive a wealth of benefit from the forest resource and can only speculate on the countless medicinals, food, and other useful plants we stand to lose before even knowing they exist.

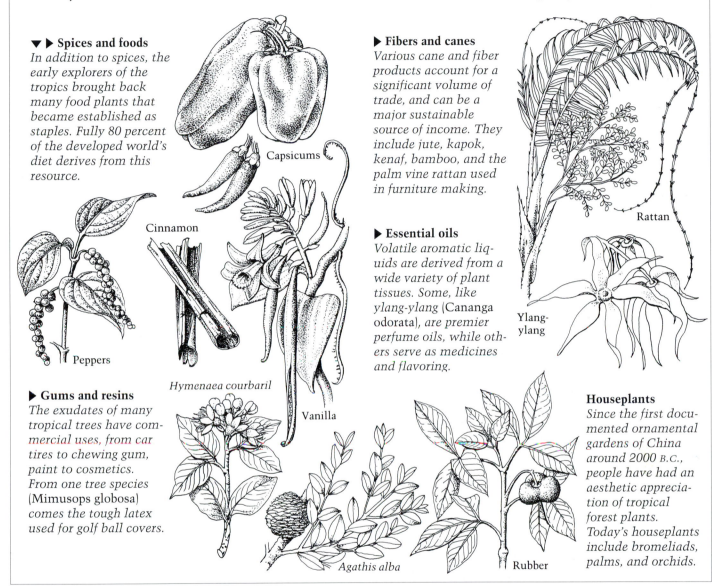

▼ ▶ Spices and foods
In addition to spices, the early explorers of the tropics brought back many food plants that became established as staples. Fully 80 percent of the developed world's diet derives from this resource.

Capsicums

Cinnamon

Peppers

Hymenaea courbaril

Vanilla

▶ Gums and resins
The exudates of many tropical trees have commercial uses, from car tires to chewing gum, paint to cosmetics. From one tree species (Mimusops globosa) comes the tough latex used for golf ball covers.

Agathis alba

▶ Fibers and canes
Various cane and fiber products account for a significant volume of trade, and can be a major sustainable source of income. They include jute, kapok, kenaf, bamboo, and the palm vine rattan used in furniture making.

▶ Essential oils
Volatile aromatic liquids are derived from a wide variety of plant tissues. Some, like ylang-ylang (Cananga odorata), are premier perfume oils, while others serve as medicines and flavoring.

Rattan

Ylang-ylang

Houseplants
Since the first documented ornamental gardens of China around 2000 B.C., people have had an aesthetic appreciation of tropical forest plants. Today's houseplants include bromeliads, palms, and orchids.

Rubber

tree. The forest is a community of such benefactors and its list of credentials is imposing.

As a self-sustaining cornucopia, undisturbed and without our management, Earth's most productive biome converts ground litter, carrion, and offal to sustain an infinite supply of forest plant and animal produce, including medicinals, fruit, seeds, berries, nuts, leaves, roots, teas, perhaps 30,000 edible plants, fuel, latex, oils, spices, gums, resins, turpentines, varnishes, lubricants, inks, flavoring and scenting agents, drugs, bamboo, barks, polishes, insecticides, cosmetics, clothing, thatch, insulation, packing materials, rattan, flowers, soaps, dyes, tanning agents, fish, animals, animal skins, meat, honey, decorative plants, plant genetic resources, fodder, wood, pulp, paper, jute, and

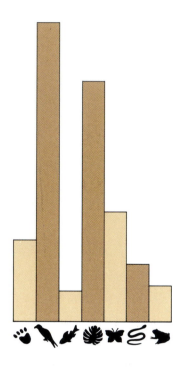

▲ *The astonishing species diversity of the tropical rainforest biome is well illustrated by the species count taken in La Selva, a Costa Rican biological reserve of only 1,800 acres (730 ha). The tally of 1,125 species is roughly half as many again as in the whole of California's 158,313 square miles (410,000 sq km).*

countless other diverse products with a potential market value of many billions of dollars annually. In addition, this priceless resource serves as the bounteous provider of scientific, cultural, educational, recreational and aesthetic riches and human habitat, pollination and pest control. More incredibly, it performs all these varied and essential services at once, in perpetuity, *and* renders them cost free. Dependent on which course humanity takes in the next decade, or perhaps two, it is probable that at no other time in our history will we risk losing—yet conversely have a better opportunity to preserve—so many vital assets.

POCKETS OF ENDEMISM

Of up to an estimated 100 million species that share the planet with us (Erwin and Wilson in Swerdlow 1999), at least 50 percent to perhaps as high as 90 percent (Erwin 1988; Wilson 1992), is found in the tropical forests. Harvard's Edward O. Wilson eloquently alerts us that "life is more diverse and plentiful than anyone had previously known" as only 1.75 million species have yet been described, which in the major groups includes, approximately 750,000 insects, 47,000 vertebrates, and some 270,000 plants.

Peter Raven sadly observes that at least eight animal species that serve as official symbols of their national lands are today on the brink of extinction. The American bald eagle was included in that austere membership and through concerted efforts on its behalf was reclassified as threatened in 1999.

A pocket of endemism is a relatively small area to which the entire distribution of a species is relegated. Examples include the snail darter, Miss Furbish's lousewort, and the mountain gorilla. Such limited range is a common feature of the tropical rainforest.

Under the constant environmental conditions of the tropical rainforests, a large number of species have become so specialized over the millennia that their ranges are restricted to certain niches and often to surprisingly small areas. A single square mile (2.6 sq km) or less is not uncommon for the entire range of a species, and this makes them extremely vulnerable. The spectacular golden toad (*Bufo periglenes*), for instance, discovered in 1964, inhabited a single mountaintop (Monteverde) in Costa Rica. It would take just half an hour with modern logging techniques to completely obliterate this particular gem of creation which took millions of years to evolve. It is with great sorrow that I report in this revised edition that the golden toad has not been seen since 1989 and is now declared extinct, demonstrating far more succinctly than even I would have wished to, the excruciating fragility of so many of these species. (For further discussion see page 160.)

Such creatures do not serve solely as zoological curiosities or to stimulate natural history tourism. For instance, tetrodotoxin, derived from certain Central American and Caribbean rainforest frogs, is employed as a painkiller and muscle relaxant for victims of neurogenic leprosy and terminal cancer. As an anesthetic it is 160,000 times more potent than cocaine, a fact not lost on Haitian voodoo practitioners who, it was recently discovered, use tetrodotoxin as the primary ingredient in potions designed to create "zombies"! Another unlikely drug is capoten. Derived from a South American viper, it is responsible for millions of dollars' worth of sales globally as a highly effective blood pressure inhibitor.

Species Rich and Interdependent

While a relatively rich temperate forest may have 20 different species of tree to the hectare (2.47 acres), but more often only two or three, the same-size area of tropical rainforest may have as many as 313 different species of tree (Richards 1996) and many thousands of other plant and animal species. A case in point is a single volcano in the Philippines which contains more species of woody plant than the entire United States. Another is a minute 5.4 square-foot (0.5 sq-m) quadrant of ground in the Peruvian lowland tropical forest in which are found the leaves of 50 different species of tree.

This luxuriant diversity has proved to be a severe liability when these forests are exploited. Cutting can leave too few individuals scattered over too wide an area to successfully propagate the species, and extinction may become imminent. This is but one reason why the tropical rainforest, exploited by classical methods, has been referred to as a "nonrenewable resource." Raven alerts us that a single plant species can take 10 to 30 dependent insect, higher animal, and other plant species with it to extinction.

There will, without a single exception that I am able to cite, be ramifications up and down the food or dependency chain with the demise of any one of Earth's species. Paul and Anne Ehrlich, authors of *Extinction*, have likened this to rivets popping out of an airplane you are piloting. The aircraft remains aloft until the critical point is reached when too many rivets have been lost. At that point, disaster is inevitable.

The Black Hole of Extinction

It took 100 million years for the flowering plants to evolve and clothe the Earth, yet the past 20 years alone have put a sizeable portion of them in mortal jeopardy. The Threatened Plants Committee of the International Union for Conservation of Nature and Natural Resources (IUCN) has decreed 10 percent (20,000–30,000) of the world's known flowering plants to be "dangerously rare or under threat." The great majority of these life-forms will never have been identified. "This crisis is not about saving a handful of species; it is not an endangered species program," says William Rodriguez, who heads the botany department at the Institute for Amazonian Research in Manaus, Brazil. "We are talking about the source of species diversity itself, the machine that cranks them out and ultimately protects us from calamity." "Death is one thing; an end to birth is something else" (Soule and Wilcox 1980). Furthermore, it has been extrapolated that as a result of the disturbance of the tropical forest biomass to date, it is unlikely that another *conspicuous* animal will ever again evolve on Earth.

It is now all too clear that deforestation in the tropics has far-reaching, even global, effects. Between 1940 and the 1990s, the population densities of migratory songbirds in the mid-Atlantic United States dropped more than 50 percent with many species becoming locally extinct, a grim phenomenon accelerating more recently, as are the strong declines in Great Britain and Central Europe, with waterfowl sharing similar patterns. A major cause is the compounding deforestation in Latin America and the West Indies (and Africa for European birds), the principal wintering grounds of many of the migrants. Almost one-third of the 53 species that winter in Central America from North America are decreasing in number. Many of these spend their

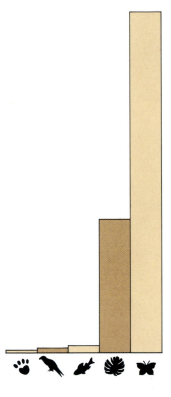

▲ *Birds and mammals are highly visible, and we have a considerable fund of knowledge about them. The tragedy of extinction now is that hundreds of species are lost without ever being studied or named. For every bird that disappears, we lose 2 or 3 fish, 35 plants, and about 90 insects: and for every 2 birds lost, a mammal species disappears forever.*

nonbreeding season in the quickly receding Pacific coastal forests of Central America. These birds serve us in more ways than to brighten the landscape or delight us with their song. U.S. farmers have always relied on them for free services such as pest control.

GLOBAL EXTINCTION SPASMS

By examining the fossil record of marine invertebrates, it is established, with reasonable accuracy, that the "background" rate of extinctions over millions of evolutionary years has been between one and three species per year. In stark contrast, The United Nations Environmental Program's (UNEP) Global Biodiversity Assessment (1995) places current species loss, mostly in tropical forests, at 6 per hour, 137 per day, and some 50,000 per year, or approximately 25,000 times the historical and acceptable background rate. Currently, the world *adds* 78 million people per year to its numbers. E. O. Wilson states that "clearly, we are in the midst of one of the greatest extinction spasms in geological history." Unlike the dinosaurs, which were victims of such a spasm, we are the cause of it! UNEP warns that "the breakdown of rainforest ecosystems will likely lead to the disappearance of up to 10 percent of the world's species (by 2020)," unless we take viable corrective action. That could well mean between 5 and 10 million species. "We are surely witnessing the imminent demise of . . . as much as two-thirds of all species" (Wilson 1992; Myers 1994b). If it will take natural selection at least 5 million undisturbed years to replace those lost species, it means the number of people affected by our actions—or inactions—to conserve these forests total some 500 trillion, or 10,000 times more people than ever existed on Earth until now!

Due to the recently discovered extreme diversity of arthropods (insects, spiders, crustaceans, etc.) in the rainforest canopy, which number between 30 and 80 million, the total number of species on Earth may well number 100 million (Erwin, in Swerdlow 1999). Thus far only 750,000 insects have been described, 47,000 vertebrates, and some 270,000 plants, for a round total of 1.75 million. While the IUCN's red list of threatened animals reports 11 percent of birds and 33 percent of fish are endangered with extinction, their 1996 assessment of mammals grimly observes that of 4,400 mammals, 11 percent are presently critically "endangered" while another 14 percent are vulnerable to extinction. Due to deforestation of tropical rainforests, the principal habitat of primates, our closest relatives, fully half their species are threatened with extinction.

Of the herpetofauna, reptiles, currently numbering 6,300 species and 4,000 for amphibians, there are indications that 25 percent of their numbers are also endangered or vulnerable. Amphibians, in particular, are known as environmental "litmus species" (as are lichens on trees or rocks)—ubiquitous indicators of global environmental health. Beginning in the early 1990s, herpetologists in such diverse locations as the Sierra Nevada in California, rainforest areas of Australia, Costa Rica, Puerto Rico, and elsewhere, have reported their alarm at the mysterious decline in amphibian species, especially frogs. Habitat destruction, global warming, ozone depletion, pesticides, and chytrid fungus are implicated. Many scientists liken the debacle to the miner's canary whose death is a first warning of dangerous levels of poisonous gases in the mine shaft. If frogs are finding

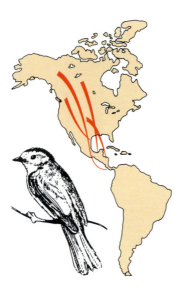

▲ *Migrating songbirds like this Wilson's warbler* (Wilsonia pusilla) *are increasingly affected by habitat changes in their tropical winter quarters.*

◀ *Every individual must now take responsibility for the consequences of the choices he or she makes. If we buy curios like these on sale outside Acapulco, Mexico, we create a market for them. The fate of these animals is firmly in our own hands. Without a market, the traders and the hunters who supply them would have no viable business.*

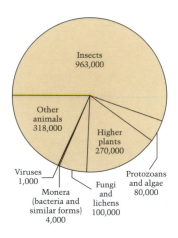

▲ Creation's rich legacy
Estimates of existing species are as high as 100 million, yet only 1.75 million have been officially classified. As we can see, the tapestry of life is woven together by the diminutive, yet no less miraculous creatures. The majority of these species inhabit the largely unexplored elevated frontier of the rainforest canopy.

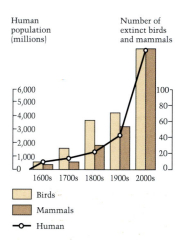

▲ Extinctions increase as the human population grows
At the apex of our orbit of development, we must ask ourselves whether our species, one of perhaps 100 million, will be but a locust on our planet—or will we bring our formidable intellect, propensity for morality, and aesthetic appreciation to bear in time to coexist with the balance of life that makes Earth so uniquely wondrous in the known universe.

the planet an increasingly hostile home, what does that portend for other occupants, including humans?

INCONSPICUOUS SPECIES

How fragile the tropical forest ecosystem is, and how dependent the whole is on its parts, may be demonstrated by a typical interrelationship. Many tree species depend directly on the sole pollination services of individuals of distinct species of hummingbirds, wasps, bees, and butterflies. If deforestation removes from a pollinator's range the last tree that flowers during certain months, then the creature is forced to abandon its territory. The remaining trees in that area will consequently fail to produce fruit, and a variety of herbivorous species dependent on that food source may also succumb, leading to the potential demise of predators who preyed on those species, and so outward through the food web to other plant and animal species.

In *Extinction*, the Ehrlichs emphasize this by stating, "It seems certain that over 95 percent of the organisms capable of competing seriously with humanity for food or of doing us harm by transmitting disease are now controlled *gratis* by other species in natural ecosystems." While many would quickly dismiss the potential effects of the disappearance of many insect species, future use of these minute life-forms could have highly significant impacts. For example, Malaysian oil palm (*Elaeis guineensis*) plantations used to require inefficient and labor-intensive hand pollination. Research indicated that a weevil from West Africa, where the palm is indigenous, was responsible for pollination—and so imported insects were released into the Malaysian plantations. They now generate U.S.$110 million in savings annually.

The lowly pokeweed was found to contain a snail-killing chemical, and this is now used to battle schistosomiasis, the lethal, snail-borne parasitic disease that infects more than 200 million people in the tropics. We can be quite sure that in times past no one had much use for the unsightly mold we now know as *Penicillium notatum*, from which the drug penicillin is made, yet today most of us are indebted to the discovery of its amazing properties.

THE "NOAH PRINCIPLE"

Certainly, though, there are many species that have thus far demonstrated no proven value to man. In these cases David W. Ehrenfeld, Rutgers University biologist, argues for a noneconomic approach to the issue. "Longstanding existence in nature is deemed to carry with it the unimpeachable right to continued existence. Existence is the only criterion of value." Ehrenfeld's ethical justification for species preservation is known as the "Noah principle." Noah admitted into his ark "everything that creepeth upon the earth." No creature was turned away for lack of apparent economic value.

Félix Houphouët-Boigny, former president of Côte d'Ivoire, amplified the "Noah principle" when he stated, "Man has gone to the moon but he does not yet know how to make a flame tree or a bird song. Let us keep our dear countries free from irreversible mistakes which would lead us in the future to long for those same birds and trees."

II A Wealth of Natural Resources

Medicinal Value of Tropical Plants

At various stages in the disintegration of the forest life chain, human beings most definitely suffer. For example, fully 50 percent of the medicines we use are derived from plants, and 25 percent of all prescription drugs have their origins in tropical forests. Should trends of habitat loss continue, by the middle of the 21st century we can expect to lose 25 percent of all higher plants—approximately 60,000 species.

Although only about 7 percent of tropical plants have been screened for possible usefulness to humans and only 1 percent intensively investigated, an even lesser share of sparsely studied groups such as microorganisms (the source of more than 3,000 antibiotics), have been evaluated. Yet many of our "wonder drug" botanicals have been used for centuries by primitive tribes. This has "sparked a revolution," noted the late Richard Evans Shultes (1915–2001), former director of the Harvard Botany Museum, who reported with enthusiasm that "it crystallized the realization that the plant kingdom represents a virtually untapped reservoir of new chemical compounds, many extraordinarily biodynamic, some providing novel bases on which the synthetic chemist may build even more interesting structures." The simplest bacterium can synthesize more organic compounds in its brief life than can all the world's chemists combined.

Let's take a self-serving look at just one plant-derived class of compounds, our proven friends the alkaloids, used extensively by the medical profession. These versatile and biologically active chemicals are employed as cardiac and respiratory stimulants, blood pressure boosters, narcotics, hallucinogenics, antimalarials, local and general anesthetics, painkillers, muscle relaxants, pupil dilators, tumor inhibitors, and antileukemic drugs, to name only the most prominent applications.

Of the 10,000 or so alkaloids known in 2001, the vast majority have not yet been subjected to critical pharmacological screening. Yet it is known that plants in the tropics are twice as likely to contain these versatile chemicals as those in temperate zones.

The Life-Saving Cinchona Tree

Had the cinchona tree (*Cinchona* spp.) of the eastern Andean tropical forest not yielded quinine, this world's tropical, subtropical, and even some temperate climate residents would be laboring under the scourge of unmitigated endemic malaria. Even now responsible for more deaths than any other transmissible disease, malaria afflicts 500 million people worldwide.

During fieldwork in Zaire, both myself and a colleague, Roxanne Kremer, came down with falciparum malaria (*Plasmodium falciparum*), the most dangerous of several malaria strains which may be lethal on the first attack. We were in an extremely remote sector of the Ituri Forest and the attacks raged day after day, with chills, pain, paralyzing hallucinations, and fever hovering

ACTIVE COMPOUND	MILLION PRESCRIPTIONS	PERCENTAGE OF TOTAL
Steroids (95% from Diosgenin)	225·050	14.69
Atropine	22·980	1.50
Reserpine	22·214	1.45
Pilocarpine	3·983	0.26
Quinidine	2·758	0.18
Total	**276.985**	**18.08**

▲ *These 1973 figures show the extent of our debt to the rainforest biome: more than 276 million medical prescriptions issued in the United States alone were solely based on five pure compounds derived from rainforest plants. Drugs with active ingredients derived from forests totaled more than U.S. $100 billion annually in the 1990s. Fully 70 percent of all plants identified by the National Cancer Institute as having anticancer properties occur only in tropical forests. Researchers feel Ancristocladus korupensis may hold a key to a new AIDS treatment. [Global Biodiversity Strategy 1992.]*

▲ *On Costa Rica's Caño Island, the author picks a* Costus *species, widely used by past cultures as treatment for kidney ailments. He also found it remarkably effective as a dentifrice.*

▼ *Machiguenga Indians in a remote Peruvian forest presented the author's expedition with myriad traditionally used forest plants after expedition members had saved the lives of two tribesmen with modern medicines. The cultural exchange was completed when the* brujo, *or tribal medicine man, using local herbs, cured the author and others of a crippling reaction to blackfly bites when the expedition's medications proved quite ineffective. WHO estimates that 80 percent of people in the developing world rely on plant-based traditional medicines.*

near 107°F (41.6°C). Fortunately, my son Gandhi, the third member of our party, who had a lower blood count of the parasite, nursed us both until we could make radio contact with Nyankunde Mission Hospital in the Ituri region, to which safe haven we were subsequently airlifted for treatment just in time to save our lives.

You may be able to appreciate my profound respect for quinine. Synthetic drugs such as chloroquine, quinacrine, and primaquine were produced only after quinine, and this accomplishment was made possible only by using the original compound as a model. Yet even now an ever-growing number of tropical areas have developed strains of malaria resistant to synthetic chloroquine drugs (the strain we incurred was of this type), and our prophylactic antimalarials are becoming largely ineffective. Physicians and biochemists therefore again return to quinine. The multifaceted quinine is also used in the treatment of headache and neuralgia, for cardiac arrhythmia, as a sclerosing agent in the treatment of varicose veins, as a substitute anesthetic for cocaine, in the treatment of bacteriological infections, including pneumonia, and as a stomachic and labor inducer as well.

Another plant, the Mexican yam (*Dioscorea* spp.), found only in tropical forests, yields diosgenin used in the manufacture of cortisone and hydrocortisone for the treatment of a wide spectrum of ills including rheumatoid arthritis, rheumatic fever, ulcerative colitis, various allergies, sciatica, Addison's disease, and certain skin diseases. This versatile species is also used in the preparation of various sex hormones, including "the pill." Potential over-the-counter sales of this one product alone exceed U.S.$700 million.

As an example of the potential impact on humanity of a single plant, (nontropical) purple foxglove (*Digitalis* sp.) gave us digitalis—without which more than 3 million people in America alone would expire of congestive heart failure in as little as 72 hours. From the skin of the African clawed frog exudes a family of antibiotics called *magainins*, from the Hebrew world for shield, that kills virtually all known bacteria (Swerdlow 1999). In addition, the rainforests of the world have witnessed an explosive international surge in the use of its herbal remedies, which if not judiciously collected sustainably for market purposes, will soon put many of these species in jeopardy of extinction. The traditional harvesting and sale of unprocessed marketable medicinal plants from a 50-year-old secondary (not primary) hardwood forest site in Belize generated U.S.$1,347 per acre (U.S.$3,327 per ha) on an arbitrary 50-year rotation, report Balick and Mendelsohn (1992) who estimate (1995) that future drugs awaiting discovery in tropical forests have a theoretical value to society of U.S.$147 billion.

THE CANCER CONNECTION

Another plant, the rosy periwinkle (*Catharanthus roseus*) from the tropical Madagascan forests, where it was rescued only a year or so before its extinction, produces 75 different alkaloids. Two, vincristine and vinblastine, have produced a major breakthrough in the treatment of cancer. Chemotherapy involving these drugs achieves 99 percent remission for acute lymphocytic leukemia and 80 percent remission for Hodgkin's disease (and in an impressive number of cases, complete cures) where previously there existed only a 19 percent chance for remission of this dreaded disease. In addition, the two drugs are responsible for 50 to 80 percent remission for several other forms of cancer. The National Cancer Institute is presently testing four plant compounds that have demonstrated 100 percent protection against the replication of the HIV-1 virus. One compound, calanolide A, is derived from leaves and twigs of a Bornean rainforest tree (*Calophyllum lanigerum*). Tragically, the original tree was felled and as it is a commercially logged species now too rare to accommodate botanical collection. Fortunately, the active compound was synthesized and is now undergoing promising medical trials, another example of a potentially lifesaving species giving forth its benefits to humanity at its eleventh hour.

A CORNUCOPIA OF NEW FOODS

Almost all our food originates from hybridized wild plants. Indeed, most all of us are partaking daily in the bounty of the tropical forests without ever

▲ *A miracle plant from Eden, this* Dioscorea, *half-hidden in the ground litter of the author's Cathedral Rain Forest Science Preserve in Costa Rica, is the source of diosgenin, a compound with a wide range of uses including the birth control pill.*

▲ *The rosy periwinkle of Madagascar (*Catharanthus roseus*) now gives 99 percent remission from some forms of childhood leukemia, and is also effective against Hodgkin's disease.*

▲ *Photographed wild in its native Javan jungle, this banteng bull (*Bos banteng*) is the ancestor of our familiar domestic cattle. Without our help the species would soon be extinct; without the wild bovine we have no gene stock for future hybridization.*

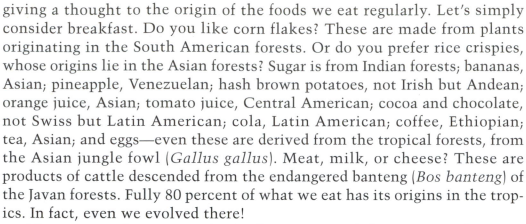

giving a thought to the origin of the foods we eat regularly. Let's simply consider breakfast. Do you like corn flakes? These are made from plants originating in the South American forests. Or do you prefer rice crispies, whose origins lie in the Asian forests? Sugar is from Indian forests; bananas, Asian; pineapple, Venezuelan; hash brown potatoes, not Irish but Andean; orange juice, Asian; tomato juice, Central American; cocoa and chocolate, not Swiss but Latin American; cola, Latin American; coffee, Ethiopian; tea, Asian; and eggs—even these are derived from the tropical forests, from the Asian jungle fowl (*Gallus gallus*). Meat, milk, or cheese? These are products of cattle descended from the endangered banteng (*Bos banteng*) of the Javan forests. Fully 80 percent of what we eat has its origins in the tropics. In fact, even we evolved there!

Now we see why conservationists have compared the present exploitation and extinction of species for transient benefits to the burning of a Rembrandt masterpiece for an hour's warmth.

UNTAPPED FOOD RESOURCES

Humankind's dependence on the tropical forest genetic pool is marked by the little-known fact that 90 percent of the world's food is produced from only 20 plant species and a dangerously few seed varieties, yet many thousands of species are believed to be edible. Through hybridization, a few wild species of one genus have produced a whole range of familiar vegetables—cabbage, broccoli, kale, cauliflower, and brussels sprouts.

Botanical breeding programs turn increasingly to wild plants to find genetic traits that can be integrated into the 20 crop species upon which most of the world's people depend. Yet 30,000 plants are known to contain edible parts and some 7,000 species to have been collected or grown as food. Some plant hybridizers already warn that the potential for improvement in only 20 crop species may be reaching its limit. It is time, they say, to go back into the wild and find new plant species that can be domesticated for food. (So narrow is the tolerance of modern hybrid-crop varieties that a 1.8°F [1.0°C] drop in global temperature could cause rice production to fall by a catastrophic 45 percent.) In the forests of southern China grows a vine known as the gooseberry (*Actinidia chinensis*). The juice from its fruit, now known popularly as the kiwi, is up to 18 times richer in vitamin C than orange juice. The West African serendipity berry (*Dioscreophyllum cumminsii*) is 3,000 times sweeter than sucrose, but its active ingredient is a protein instead of a high calorie sugar.

From Amazônia, *tucumã* palm fruit (*Astrocaryum vulgare*), has a vitamin A content three times that of a carrot, previously thought one of the best sources of vitamin A. From the same forest, the peach palm fruit (*Bactris gasipaes*) has twice the protein of banana and will produce more carbohydrate and protein per acre than maize. Yet another Amazonian palm fruit, *patauá* (*Jessenia bataua*) has revealed its protein to be comparable to good animal protein, and appreciably better than most grain and even legume sources. In fact, the biological value of its protein is 40 percent higher than that of soybeans.

From the forests of Southeast Asia a previously uncultivated fruit called the mangosteen (*Garcinia mangostana*) is purported to be "perhaps the world's best tasting fruit." But on that point perhaps I would take issue. I

▲ *A wild dwarf pineapple plant (*Ananas sp.*) stands unobtrusively in the upland forests of Venezuela. This small and seemingly insignificant plant should remind us of the enormous debt we owe the forest. Commercial pineapple cultivation today is a multibillion-dollar world-wide industry.*

<table>
<tr><td>

Fruits and vegetables

lemon, papaya, rambutan, breadfruit, grapefruit, lime, passion fruit, avocado, cucumber, jack fruit, orange, plantain, banana, durian, tangerine, coconut, guava, mango, pineapple, yam, sorghum, potatoes, sugar beet, rapeseed, olives, grapes, tomato, cabbage, oats, brussels sprouts, wheat, soybeans, maize, barley, apples, rice, orange juice, tomato juice, cassava, corn

Spices

cinnamon, nutmeg, cardamom, cloves, paprika, allspice, chili pepper, mace, vanilla, black pepper, cayenne, ginger, turmeric

Other foods

coffee, cocoa, eggs, millet, okra, tapioca, cashew nuts, cola, Brazil nuts, chocolate, manioc, sesame seed, cane sugar, peanuts, tea, chayote, hearts of palm

</td><td>

Fibers

bamboo, jute, kapok, raffia, ramie, rattan, cotton

Plants

palms, African violets, begonia, croton, fiddle-leaf fig, philodendron, snake plant, umbrella tree, aluminum plant, bromeliads, dieffenbachia, orchids, prayer plant, spathe lily, anthurium, gooseberry, Christmas cactus, dracaena, parlor ivy, rubber tree plant, Swiss cheese plant, zebra plant

Other products

Chicle (chewing gum), copaiba (perfume, fuel), copal (varnish, paint, printing ink), dammar (varnish, lacquer, printing ink), gutta-percha (golf ball covers), tobacco, rubber

Oils

bay (perfume), camphor, cascarilla (confectionery, beverages), coconut, eucalyptus, guaiac (perfume), palm,

</td><td>

patchouli, rosewood, sandalwood, star anise, ylang-ylang (perfume), cottonseed oil, linseed, sesame, flax

Medicines

All the herbs and medicines are too many to list; the following is only a sampling: curare (muscle relaxant for surgery) diosgenin (steroids, asthma, and arthritis treatment), quassia (insecticides), quinine, reserpine, strophanthus, strychnine, vincristine & vinblastine (cancer drugs), calanolide A, B, and C (AIDS drugs)

Woods in plantation forestry

balsa, sandalwood, mahogany, teak, rosewood

RAINFOREST LESSONS TOWARDS A GLOBAL UNDERSTANDING (1995) BY ILENE MILLER AND LAURIE AGOPIAN.

</td></tr>
</table>

recall sampling the most delectable fruit I have ever tasted from a small tree on my Cathedral Rain Forest Science Preserve in Costa Rica. Consuming a small portion and feeling no ill effects, I was anxious to return to the tree early in the morning for much more of the same. The tree, to my enormous disappointment, had been completely stripped by a troop of monkeys during the evening. In my despair, I found myself nibbling the monkeys' leftovers, lying half-eaten on the ground.

Although I marked the tree for future identification when in flower, it was subsequently lost when a squatter deforested the very acre on which the tree had stood. In the 25-year period since then I have been unable to locate another specimen of the species, and not once have I seen the fruit in a native market. The potential for loss in such a scenario is easily extended to the whole biome.

In the forests of New Guinea grow 251 tree species that are known to bear edible fruit, yet only 43 have so far been ushered into cultivation. One East Indian tribe regularly uses no fewer than 17 forest plants as a source of fruit drinks—significantly more varieties than can be found on any modern supermarket shelf!

The forests of Southeast Asia and New Guinea have also given us the winged bean (*Psophocarpus tetragonolobus*). With up to 42 percent protein, more amino acids than any other staple vegetable food, and leaves containing up to 20,000 units of vitamin A, it is no wonder the U.S. National Academy of Sciences stated, "Of all the plants examined, the winged bean emerged as most capable of relieving protein hunger [in the developing world]."

DESSERT FOR SOME, STAPLE FOR MANY

Manioc (*Manihot utilissima*) is a multipurpose, rampantly growing tuberous root that serves as a cheap, abundant staple food in tropical developing

▲ *The giving forest*
Almost 80 percent of our food crops are derived from tropical stock, and it is to that biome we must return for the genetic resources we will need if we are to produce new food crops, resistant to disease, insect pests, and climatic constraints, in the fight against world food shortages.

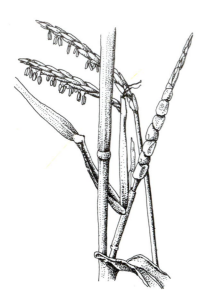

▲ *The potato blight of 1846 wiped out virtually the entire Irish crop in one season and resulted in the starvation of 1.5 million people. The recent discovery of an ancient perennial corn in the mountains of Mexico holds promise of new food-crop strains that will be less susceptible to failures of such tragic scale.*

▲ *Rafael Guzman, a young Mexican botany student, and his discovery* Zea diploperennis—*not only perennial but also resistant to five of the world's seven major corn viruses. For example, a leaf fungus blighted cornfields throughout the eastern United States causing a 15 percent and U.S.$2 billion loss in 1970 alone. The introduction of blight-resistant plant stock from its native habitat in Mexico now eliminates that threat.*

nations. We know it as the dessert tapioca. Yet it is a "cheat" starch, containing but 1 percent protein and few vitamins; its consumption results in malnutrition for those who depend on it. Botanists are now attempting to develop high-protein strains in wild populations still existing in virgin habitat. In this endeavor there is a race to discover the ancestors of manioc and other common agricultural crops being lost through habitat destruction as we slash and burn our genetic bridges behind us.

We have seen the tragic vulnerability of disease-susceptible cultivars in the Irish potato famine of the 1840s when an estimated 1.5 million people perished, and in the United States corn blight of 1970. These issues transcend academics and strike at the very heart of human survival. A new genetic constitution must be bred into food-crop varieties about every five to 15 years as diseases infiltrate the plants' defenses. We are now, it is feared, on the brink of losing this flexibility.

PERENNIAL CORN—THE FARMER'S DREAM

Not long ago, a young Mexican botanist exploring a mountainous area in Mexico came upon a small, high valley, where he encountered clumps of a shaggy, corn-like grass. Previously unrecorded in science, this wild grain may soon completely revolutionize the cultivation of corn worldwide.

This priceless discovery was a new perennial species of teosinte (*Zea diploperennis*), a member of the grass family (Gramineae) and a distant relative of annual teosinte, the ancestor of modern corn (*Zea mays*). Such distant relatives of corn may have special value, in this case an almost complete resistance to most of corn's major diseases. While it has been suggested that the new find may lead to the development of a hybrid corn that will send up new shoots each year without replanting, thus saving labor, time, money, and fertility by avoiding the necessity of plowing fields and replanting new seed, this development would produce very low-yielding crops. On the other hand, the above-mentioned disease resistance may in time save enormous proportions of future corn crops.

This new discovery by University of Guadalajara botanist Rafael Guzman, and Hugh Iltis and colleagues at the University of Wisconsin, is but one of scores of new and valuable biological breakthroughs based on utilizing newly discovered genetic material from the Earth's remaining natural areas. It is gratifying to know that in 1987 the Mexican government declared the whole mountain range the UNESCO Reserva Biosfera de la Sierra de Manantlan, comprising 350,000 acres (141,650 ha) and ranging from 1,300 feet to nearly 10,000 feet (400 m to nearly 3,000 m). Here a marvelous diversity of plants and animals will be protected as will the ancestral corn.

Vast areas of the world have soils too salty for grain production. By hybridizing with standard rice a variety of wild rice that grows in salt water, scientists are now producing a commercial rice that is perfectly adapted to these regions of saline soils that exist, "unused," globally. (It should be recognized in balance that these areas are not, however, wastelands but valid and precious habitats themselves, supporting rich and varied floras and faunas.)

Geneticists also hope to avert much of the 40 percent loss of food crops currently incurred in the field and in storage through the ravages of pests.

They look to the tropical rainforest for cross-breeding stock to induce pest resistance in plants (almost a prerequisite for survival in tropical plants and usually effected by means of "fur," spines, or chemical repulses) to develop more permanent *natural* biological controls on pests in lieu of dependence on toxic chemicals. Monetary returns with these methods have yielded U.S.$30 for each U.S.$1 outlay, and have increased crop yields exponentially.

Improving Animal Husbandry

Geneticists also look to the tropical forests for improved animal stock. Near the Thailand/Kampuchea border lives a very rare and elusive bovine, the kouprey (*Bos sauveli*). It is presumed to be one of the wild ancestors of the humped zebu cattle used for beef production in many areas of the world. This and other wild cattle such as the gaur (*Bos gaurus*), anoa (*Babalus depressicornis*), and tamarau (*Bos mindorensis*) could markedly increase world beef production by revitalizing domestic breeds in cross breeding. Their habitats, however, have been war-ravaged, defoliated with lethal herbicides, and otherwise disturbed by human activities for a protracted period of time, so that ultimate survival of these creatures will require immediate concerted action.

The Forest's Industrial Potential

From what we now know of ecotourism, medicinals, foods, and other non-timber forest products derived from the tropical forest, it is apparent that vast potential economic resources remain unutilized. Taking this all-important point into consideration, Charles Peters of the New York Botanical Garden, the late Alwyn Gentry of the Missouri Botanical Garden, and Louis and Robert Mendelsohn of Yale use a "net present value" to reflect the human tendency to see advantage in taking an "all-at-once" harvest, placing a current value on an infinite harvest, and discounting present monetary value to expected inflation. Their results are illuminating. Not only are tropical forests worth considerably more than was previously supposed, but the actual market benefits of timber are quite small in relation to other nonwood forest resources. For instance, 2.47 acres (1 ha) of forest will produce, annually, U.S.$400 in fruit and U.S.$22 in rubber. But as these trees produce every year, the true value far exceeds those figures. For those products alone the net present value is U.S.$6,330. In contrast, the one-time nonrenewable exploitation of the plot's timber would net a revenue of U.S.$1,000, periodic cutting of selected trees would yield a net present value of U.S.$490, while a tree plantation on the same plot would have a net present value of U.S.$3,184. Converted to pasture it would yield less than U.S.$2,960, or less than half the value of the fruit and rubber that could be judiciously cropped from the climax forest (Mendelsohn, pers. comm. 1989). Climax forest used in this way would go on to serve humankind and the environment indefinitely. Rattans alone, collected in Old World tropical forests, generate a global trade totaling U.S.$2.7 billion and employs a half-million people in Asia alone (Brown 1999).

In his Earthscan briefing document *What Use is Wildlife?*, Norman Meyers suggests that the United States may even be more crucially dependent on

I wonder what's around the bend!
    said the explorer.
I wonder what that plant is!
    said the collector.
I wonder what's in it!
    said the chemist.
I wonder what activity it has!
    said the pharmacologist.
I wonder if it will work in this case!
    said the physician.
I hope she lives!
    said the father.
Please God!
    said the mother.
I think she'll be all right in the morning,
    said the nurse.

Green Medicine: Search for Plants that Heal (1964) by Margaret Kreig.

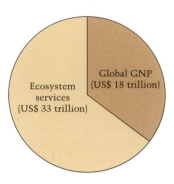

Ecosystem services (US$ 33 trillion)

Global GNP (US$ 18 trillion)

Estimates of various ecosystem services	
Ecosystem services	**Value** (trillion US$)
Soil formation	17.1
Recreation	3.0
Nutrient cycling	2.3
Water regulation and supply	2.3
Climate regulation (temperature and precipitation)	1.8
Habitat	1.4
Flood and storm protection	1.1
Food and raw materials production	0.8
Genetic resources	0.8
Atmospheric gas balance	0.7
Pollination	0.4
All other services	1.6
Total value of ecosystem services	**33.3**

▲ *An international research team from the United States, Argentina, and the Netherlands quantified an approximation of fundamental ecosystem services—heretofore largely taken for granted, as they are free—showing their value to humanity as almost twice the global gross national product of U.S.$18 trillion.*

foreign plants and animals for food, medicine, and industry than on foreign oil. Their importance cannot be underscored strongly enough.

CORNUCOPIANA

Rainforest-derived products are used in surprising places. We are all quite familiar with the myriad uses of rubber from the Brazilian tree *Hevea brasiliensis* (the fourth largest agricultural export of the developing world), yet few recognize that the latex of other rainforest trees produces chicle (*Manilkara zapota*) from Central America, the main component in chewing gum; balata (*Achris balata*) from northern South America, the uniquely durable, tough, and elastic covering on golf balls unmatched by synthetic alternatives; gutta-percha from the Asian tree *Talaquium gutta*, used as superhard dental filling as well as covering for the trans-Atlantic cable.

Photosynthesizing plants offer an elegantly simple process for humankind to tap into solar energy to produce "phytoleum." In fact, each year the process stores energy in the global floral biomass equivalent to 80 billion tons of coal, some 10 times the world's consumption of fossil fuels. Melvin Calvin, the late Nobel laureate chemist, discovered that the Brazilian copaiba tree (*Copaifera langsdorffii*) when tapped produced 6.6 gallons (25 l) of hydrocarbon fluid from a single bunghole in two hours at six-month intervals. The sap is so similar to diesel fuel that it can be put directly into the fuel tank of diesel trucks (Taylor and Otvos 1998). Brazilian experimental "petroleum plantations" are projected to produce 60 barrels of fuel per hectare per year. During World War II, the Japanese used the "petroleum nut tree" (*Sapium sebiferum*) of the Philippines for tank fuel. For household use alone, a half-dozen trees planted in a rural backyard produces 80 gallons (300 l) of fuel annually for cooking, lighting, etc.

TROPICAL DEVELOPING WORLD FUTURES

As a result of the expansion of the world economies, since the mid-20th century, demand for forest products has increased several times, lumber use has tripled, paper use has grown sixfold, and fuelwood use has soared. The West African economy of Côte d'Ivoire flourished in the 1960s and 1970s, due significantly to timber exports. But as timber was not sustainably harvested, export earnings from forest products have plunged to virtually zero today. Nigeria, the Philippines, and Thailand, whose forests are now critically depleted and who were once considerable exporters of tropical hardwood, are now net importers of forest products. The Malaysian Peninsula's timber companies are arguably the most perniciously aggressive in the industry. They decimated once lushly forested Asian nations and are now looking to Latin America. Indeed, beginning in the mid-1980s, imports into tropical countries began to exceed the value of their exports by 30–50 percent. Soon into the 21st century, only some 10 tropical countries will be net exporters (Brown 1998). To many of those nations, the added economic imposition of being transformed from net exporters of timber to net importers will be prodigious.

III ATMOSPHERIC STABILITY: THE HEAT IS ON

THE GREENHOUSE EFFECT—A BRIEF PRIMER

Imagine Earth's atmosphere as a greenhouse that allows the Sun's short-wave radiation to pass through. Earth's surface then radiates some of this energy back through the atmosphere into space in the form of long-wave infrared radiation. While almost all of Earth's atmosphere is composed of nitrogen and oxygen, which allow this transference, greenhouse gases (GHGs) markedly retard this process. As a result of the build-up of these gases, an increasing amount of radiation is reflected back down to Earth's surface and lower atmosphere—increasingly warming both. In addition, warmer air will contain more water vapor, actually the most potent GHG (UNEP, WMO 1996). This indirect effect is called a *positive feedback* and causes an automated forcing on the process, imbuing it with a life of its own. GHGs have been an atmospheric reality since our planet formed and stabilized eons ago. They have, however, been consistently regulated by Earth's steady-state systems—without the presence of these gases, the planet would be approximately 61°F (34°C) colder.

The 2,000 scientists of 100 nations which make up the Intergovernmental Panel on Climate Change (IPCC) have confirmed that global warming is presently destabilizing the climate that has supported humanity, civilization, and the conglomerate of species up to this time: deep and cold oceans are warming, fracturing ice repositories and shelves on both poles, disrupting rainfall patterns; glaciers are melting worldwide; ocean levels are rising and tropical disease is spreading—all with compelling scientific verification. The IPCC report of 2001 states that "human influence . . . has contributed substantially to the observed warming over the past 50 years." Michael Oppenheimer, an atmospheric physicist and coauthor of the report, stated that the new warming estimates pose "a risk of devastating consequences within this century."

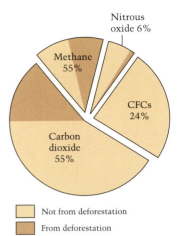

▲ *Radiative forcing (radiation energy absorbed and given off by Earth) for the 1980s shows that contributions of the major human-released greenhouse gases from tropical deforestation and subsequent changes in land use account for some 25 percent of heat-trapping emissions globally.*

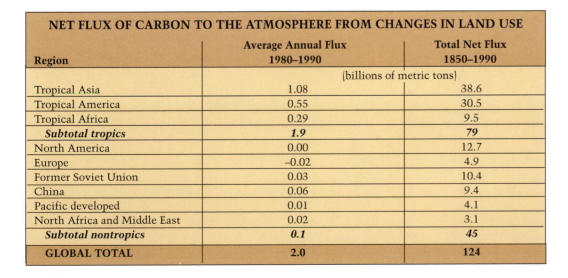

NET FLUX OF CARBON TO THE ATMOSPHERE FROM CHANGES IN LAND USE		
Region	Average Annual Flux 1980–1990	Total Net Flux 1850–1990
	(billions of metric tons)	
Tropical Asia	1.08	38.6
Tropical America	0.55	30.5
Tropical Africa	0.29	9.5
Subtotal tropics	*1.9*	*79*
North America	0.00	12.7
Europe	−0.02	4.9
Former Soviet Union	0.03	10.4
China	0.06	9.4
Pacific developed	0.01	4.1
North Africa and Middle East	0.02	3.1
Subtotal nontropics	*0.1*	*45*
GLOBAL TOTAL	**2.0**	**124**

◄ *Of the total net flux of carbon to the atmosphere from land use changes, agricultural expansion looms as largest with croplands accounting for 68 percent, pastures (from forest) 13 percent, and shifting cultivation 4 percent. Harvest of wood is responsible for 16 percent of the long-term flux, and the establishment of plantations removed carbon from the atmosphere equivalent to 1 percent of the net flux.*

▲ The aftermath of forest burning in Amazônia. Within this dismal landscape is the long-awaited dawning of humanity's acceptance of responsibility for the CO_2-climate connection and, we anticipate, a global resolve to come to grips with the phenomenon. As one-half a tree's mass is carbon, tropical deforestation looms large as a force in global warming. Forests worldwide hold twice the volume of carbon contained in the atmosphere.

TROPICAL FORESTS—LUNGS OF THE PLANET

It is estimated that the tropical forests are responsible for a major portion of Earth's biological productivity, which may seem surprising, as they encompass but 6 percent of the planet's land surface. Each 2.47 acres (1 ha) produces 28 tons of oxygen per year (an amount roughly consumed during vegetative respiration and decomposition) representing a monumental exchange of gas. These forests are responsible for the highest net primary production of carbon per unit area found on Earth. This, of course, represents a vast yearly intake (through photosynthesis) of carbon dioxide, which is stored in the form of carbon in the trees' tissues. Carbon makes up 50 percent of a tree's biomass.

The significance of deforestation in GHG buildup can be underscored as follows: global forests in all categories presently hold some 1,200 billion tons (1 billion metric tons is a gigaton or Gt) of carbon in their plants and soils (all

CARBON STOCKS IN VEGETATION AND SOILS OF DIFFERENT TYPES OF ECOSYSTEMS WITHIN THE TROPICS (TONS OF CARBON PER HECTARE)			
	Closed Forests		Open Forests or Woodlands
	Moist Forests	Seasonal Forests	
VEGETATION*			
America	129	122	27
Africa	167	126	53
Asia	193	120	50
SOILS			
All tropics	100	90	50
*Values are averaged from estimates of both destructive sampling of biomass and estimates of wood volumes.			

terrestrial plants and soils combined contain 2,000 Gt). Dramatically, the total amount of carbon held in forests worldwide is almost twice the volume contained in the atmosphere (750 Gt) (Houghton, et al. 1990; Woodwell 1993). When trees burn or decay, carbon is released into the atmosphere, where it combines to form carbon dioxide (CO_2), which comprises 50 percent of total GHGs. While tropical forests account for slightly less than half the world's forests, due to the much higher biomass volume, they hold 65 percent more carbon than temperate and boreal forests combined. Therefore, deforestation in the tropics releases considerably more carbon into the atmosphere than do other forest categories of equal area (Houghton 1993). The IPCC calculates that most of the carbon (5.5 GtC) released into the atmosphere per year is produced by combustion of fossil fuels, but a significant 27 percent or 2.1 GtC per year (plus or minus 0.8) is released as a direct result of the torching of forests, virtually all in tropical developing nations (Houghton 1999).

Total current emissions of 7.7 GtC per year have increased fourfold since 1950, which is 29 percent above the preindustrial (circa 1750) level—the highest level within the past 160,000 years. From measuring the composition of air bubbles trapped in ice cores from Antarctica and Greenland, we know that preindustrial levels of CO_2 ranged between 190 and 280 parts per million (ppm) and have now reached 367 ppm—and climbing (IPCC 2001). Humanity's activities have generated these increases with alarming speed, about one-quarter this amount in the past decade alone. A particularly sobering consideration is the fact that even if CO_2 levels were kept down to 1994 levels, by the end of the 21st century we would still reach 500 ppm, virtually double preindustrial levels (IPCC 1995). This projection prompted Jerry Mahlman of the National Oceanic and Atmospheric Administration (NOAA) to observe, "The best Kyoto [Protocol on Climate Change] can do is produce a small decrease (only 0.1°F or 0.05°C [Monastersky 1999]) in the rate of increase." Other GHGs include methane (CH_4), up 145 percent, and nitrous oxide (N_2O), up 15 percent. In 1995, the IPCC confirmed "a discernible human influence on global climate" and "the longtime scales governing both the accumulation of the GHGs in the atmosphere and the response of the climate system to those accumulations, means that many important aspects of climate change are *effectively irreversible*" [author's emphasis].

TEMPERATURE AND SEA LEVEL

The 16 warmest years since record keeping began in 1860 have occurred since 1979, which may be unprecedented in the last 1,200 years, according to Jonathan T. Overpeck of NOAA. Of those 16, the nine warmest years have occurred since

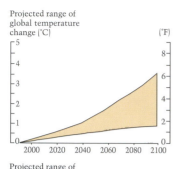

Projected range of global temperature change (°C) (°F)

Projected range of global sea level rise (cm) (inches)

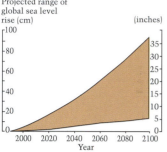

Year

▲ *The compelling link between the Intergovernmental Panel on Climate Change's projections of temperature increases and sea level rise from polar/glacial ice melt and thermal sea expansion is evident.*

PERCENTAGE OF INITIAL CARBON STOCKS LOST WHEN TROPICAL FORESTS ARE CONVERTED		
Land Use	Vegetation	Soil
Cultivated land	90–100	25
Pasture	90–100	12
Degraded croplands and pastures	60–90	12–25
Shifting cultivation	60	10
Plantations	30–50	·
Degraded forests	25–50	·
Logging	10–50	·
Extractive reserves	0	0
·Unknown.		

▲ *In 2001, GHG buildup was verified by comparing satellite data from 1970 and 1997, which clearly showed less infrared light from Earth's surface escaping into space in 1997 (Harries 2001).*

1990. As of 2000, 1998 has been declared the hottest year on record, with 1997 coming in second, prompting James Baker, NOAA administrator, to state, "There is no time in recorded history that we have seen this sequence of record-setting." He also called the findings "remarkable and sobering."

The World Meteorological Organization (WMO) reports that global temperatures are now up almost 1.08°F (0.6°C) since the late 19th century and that over the same period the sea level has risen by about 4 to 10 inches (10–25 cm), based on analysis of tide gauge records. This rise is a combination of causes that include thermal expansion of seas due to warming and to observable retreat of glaciers and ice caps. The IPCC projects a temperature increase, relative to 1990, of about 2.5 to 10.4°F (1.4–5.8°C) by 2100, a record for the past 10,000 years, with continued temperature increases and sea level rise thereafter—and notes that the sea level rise will continue even after emissions are stabilized. The prospect of virtually complete melting of the ice caps is not an unlikely scenario. While this incremental temperature rise may not appear severe, a perspective is gained knowing that during the height of the Ice Age, the average temperature was only 9°F (5°C) cooler.

Sea level is estimated to rise by a further 4 to 35 inches (9–88 cm) by 2100. With 50 percent of the world's population and 30 of the world's 50 largest cities near coasts, this would leave billions of people vulnerable to the increased flooding that climate change will produce. Further, sea level rise could flood 50 percent of the world's wetlands within the next century, an already documented trend along the Gulf of Mexico and the Atlantic seaboard of the United States.

CARBON MONOXIDE

Carbon monoxide (CO), while not a greenhouse gas per se, effects the oxidizing capacity of the atmosphere through its crucial interaction with hydroxyl radicals (OH) which cleanse the lower atmosphere by reaction with nearly all pollutants. An excess of CO, however, will deplete OH and allow pollutants as well as GHGs to build. While there is nothing in future scenarios to suggest that people will ever be suffering for want of oxygen, or succumbing to lethal concentrations of carbon monoxide, potential effects could include suffocating or runaway killer smogs, long-lived phenomena more severe than the historical lethal London smogs caused by the burning of coal.

Tropical deforestation and subsequent burning released an estimated 40 to 170 trillion grams, or teragrams (Tg or 1 million metric tons), carbon as CO in 1990 (Houghton 1993). Additionally, the repeated burning of pastures and savannas in the tropics is approximated to release 200 Tg of carbon as CO annually (Hao, et al. 1990). Significantly, these emissions combined from tropical forest burning equal industrial emissions. Paul Crutzen of the National Center for Atmospheric Research in Boulder, Colorado, explains that CO produced by burning vegetation is three times the amount caused by burning fossil fuels. Adding the emissions from tropical deforestation and subsequent land uses, and taking into account radiation energy absorbed and given off by the Earth and affected by these gases (radiative forcing) as well as their residence times in the atmosphere (Ramanathan 1987), it is apparent (see page 130) that tropical deforestation is responsible for some 27 percent of the heat-trapping emissions worldwide (Houghton 1993).

Richard A. Houghton, senior scientist at Woods Hole Research Center, projects that of 4.6 billion acres (1.9 billion ha) of tropical forests, both open and closed canopy, that existed in 1985, 80–98 percent will have disappeared by 2100. The projections of carbon release for this volume of deforestation are within the ranges of 120 to 335 Gt. These amounts are equal to—and up to—triple the volume of carbon estimated to have been released by worldwide deforestation in the 135 years previous to 1985 (Houghton & Skole 1990). The highest estimate is far higher than the amount of carbon emitted into the atmosphere to date by humanity's worldwide use of fossil fuels (some 200 Gt carbon).

POLAR MELTDOWN—ARCTIC

True to IPCC projections, Arctic temperatures have increased more than 2.7°F (1.5°C), more than twice the global atmospheric rate. In fact, the "polar melt-down" is already in process as measurements of the Arctic ice caps (containing enough water to raise sea level 25 feet [7.5 m]) reveal that more than 15 percent of sea ice volume, over 116,000 square miles (300,000 sq km) has been lost, threatening unique, ice-dependent animals such as polar bears, Arctic foxes, seals, and walrus, according to Arctic researcher Vera Alexander. Increased snow due to added moisture levels in a warming atmosphere threaten caribou and reindeer populations, essential to northern indigenous people's survival and to the region's food chain.

Arctic temperatures are expected to increase 7°F (3.9°C) in summer and 12°F (6.6°C) in winter. Arctic sea ice could be a catalyst of significant magnitude. If this ice reservoir and that of Greenland were to melt, warns Hermann Flohn at the University of Bonn, an ice-free Arctic Ocean would most probably lead to the displacement of Earth's climatic zones by 250 to 500 miles (400 to 800 km), drastically changing freshwater supplies and agricultural productivity. Ocean fish production would likely diminish at a time when the resource would be heavily relied upon.

During the last major U.S. Arctic Initiative in the 1970s, pack ice measured 9.8 feet (3 m) thick. In the 1997–98 Surface Heat Budget of the Arctic (SHEBA) expedition involving 170 scientists, ice was found only 4.9 to 6.6 feet (1.5–2 m) thick, reported Donald K. Perovich, the concerned chief SHEBA scientist of the U.S. Army Cold Regions and Engineering Laboratory in Hanover, New Hampshire.

Due to its brightness, the ice reflects more than half the sunlight that hits it during the summer. By contrast, says Perovich, the dark water absorbs 90 percent of the incident sunlight, which would rapidly warm the ocean, melting more ice—potentially a runaway, self-perpetuating process which could strip the ocean of its protective cap, causing the Arctic to warm much more than the balance of the globe, according to climate models. This "Arctic shift" would produce a domino effect, irreversibly rerouting ocean currents as well as weather patterns further south over untold millennia (Monastersky 1999). In yet another indelible benchmark to this ongoing meltdown process, European and South American glaciers are simultaneously retreating to levels unseen in the past 5,000 years.

ANTARCTIC

Antarctica may present the most chilling threat, as it contains 90 percent of the world's glacial ice. By the end of the Antarctic summer, March 1999,

THE GREENHOUSE EFFECT

Is humanity viewing the tunnel at the end of the light? There are many in the scientific world who now believe it is. While ignorance may have excused us in the past, we are now fully aware of the consequences of human activity, and the future of the global environment is now dependent on human wisdom. How will we measure up?

▲ Point of attack

The major sources of greenhouse gases (GHGs) are the industrialized regions of the world, but reducing current output will be difficult and slow. A more promising attack could, however, be made on tropical forest burning, already contributing 27 percent of carbon released.

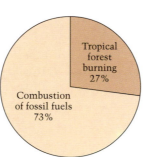

Tropical forest burning 27%

Combustion of fossil fuels 73%

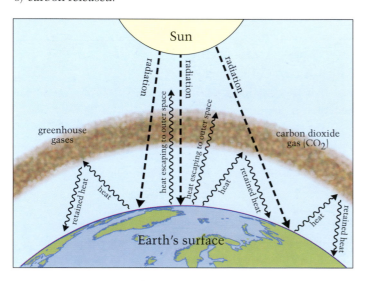

Sun

radiation

radiation

radiation

greenhouse gases

heat escaping to outer space

heat escaping to outer space

carbon dioxide gas (CO_2)

retained heat

heat

retained heat

heat

retained heat

heat

retained heat

Earth's surface

◄ The greenhouse effect

Human impact on the environment has greatly impaired our planet's equilibrium and its ability to compensate effectively. The Sun's radiation warms the Earth which then itself releases energy as infrared radiation. The increasing buildup of GHGs, however, is deflecting ever-greater amounts of that energy back to Earth, creating a heat trap. It is now known that chlorofluorocarbons (CFCs), a group of gases recognized in 1974 to destroy atmospheric ozone, also trap thermal radiation 10,000 times as effectively as CO_2, thereby compounding the problem. With currently projected increases in world population, even if we double our energy efficiency and reduce our use of CFCs, total output of greenhouse gases will still be increasing at a dangerous pace.

▶ Turning up the planet's thermostat

Temperature increases will not be uniform over Earth's surface. The polar regions will probably warm three times as much as the global average, resulting in changes to wind patterns which will have profound effects on agriculture. For example, with a rise of 7°F (4°C) by 2030 (a temperature increase never before experienced by the human species) many of the mid-latitude grain-producing regions—the bread-baskets of the world—could become arid.

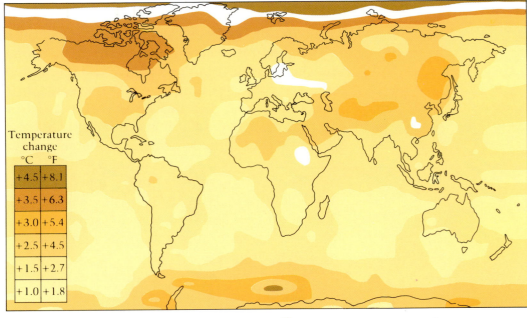

Temperature change

°C	°F
+4.5	+8.1
+3.5	+6.3
+3.0	+5.4
+2.5	+4.5
+1.5	+2.7
+1.0	+1.8

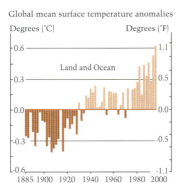

Global mean surface temperature anomalies

Land and Ocean

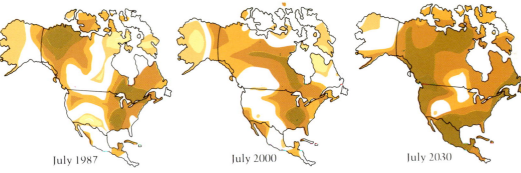

July 1987   July 2000   July 2030

▲ Record warmth

Including 2000, NOAA reports 22 consecutive years with above-normal average surface temperatures. Scientists agree that the trend started with the Industrial Revolution, but the past 30 years have shown a marked acceleration.

▲ An endless summer?

The Intergovernmental Panel on Climate Change (IPCC) predicts the greenhouse effect will produce a rise of 2.4 to 10.4°F (1.4 to 5.8°C) over the next 100 years. While this may appear to be a small increase, the 2,000 scientists of the IPCC warn that the average rate of warming will probably be greater than any experienced in the last 10,000 years. One consequence of the scenario could be a 50 percent reduction in rainfall in America's grain belt—shifting prime production north into Canada.

Temperature increase

°C	°F	°C	°F
−3.0	−5.4	1.0	1.8
−2.0	−3.6	2.0	3.6
−1.0	−1.8	3.0	5.4
0.0	0.0	5.0	9.0

▶ Flood scenarios

The maps on the right show the kind of impact that major sea-level changes could have on some of the world's most densely populated low-lying coastal regions. In the case of Bangladesh, a 10-foot (3-m) rise would affect most of that country's population.

Ocean today

Predicted flooding

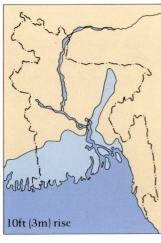

10ft (3m) rise

Bangladesh

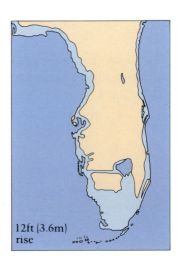

12ft (3.6m) rise

Florida, USA

10ft (3m) rise

Netherlands

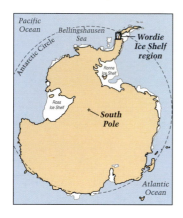

▲ *Glaciers are retreating everywhere in the world including Antarctica, Earth's coldest continent.*

656 square miles (1,700 sq km) was lost from the Larsen B Ice Shelf, and earlier in 1998, the Wilkins Ice Shelf lost 425 square miles (1,100 sq km), a combined area half the size of Delaware, reported Ted Scambos of the University of Colorado's National Snow and Ice Data Center (pers. comm. 1999). In April of 1999, David Vaughn, speaking for the research team of the British Antarctic Survey, stated that a warming Antarctica is responsible and that average temperature for the region has risen about 4.5°F (2.5°C) since the 1940s, 10 times the global average, bringing the average summertime temperature, critically, to just above freezing. From 1927 through 1997, some 3,000 square miles (8,000 sq km) has disappeared from the Antarctic peninsula, which is considerable. But a total loss of almost 1,200 square miles (3,000 sq km) in the 1998–99 season is considered alarming; thousands of square miles more appear ready to go (Petit 2000). Then in March 2000, a massive iceberg known as C-15 broke off the Ross Ice Shelf. The largest ever observed, it measured 170 miles (273 km) long by 25 miles (40 km) wide, a total of 4,250 square miles (11,000 sq km) of ice—almost the size of Connecticut.

Satellite radar images of Antarctica's Pine Island Glacier between 1992 and 1996 showed the glacier is shrinking. Eric Rignot of the Jet Propulsion Laboratory in Pasadena, California, study leader of a report published, stated in a *Los Angeles Times* article, "It's important because it could lead to a collapse of the west Antarctic ice sheet" which would raise sea levels as much as 20 feet (6 m). Rignot declared that "we are seeing a glacier melt in the heart of Antarctica." The IPCC has urged that for purposes of stemming the ever increasing greenhouse effect, there should be a vastly increased effort to halt the torching of tropical forests!

IMPACT ON FOOD PRODUCTION

Anticipated temperature increases have worrisome implications for the one-third of the world's population that relies on rice as a staple. University of Florida researchers reported in 2000 that above-average temperatures interfere with the life cycle and pollination process in rice plants. Modest temperature increases predicted by some climate change scenarios would reduce rice yields by 20–40 percent by 2100, while the most severe predicted temperature increases could force yields to zero. Ominously, it is projected that precipitation over the U.S. grain belt will be reduced by 50 percent. A similar fall-off of ocean food-fish production has been predicted (Wunsch, pers. comm. 1999).

The greenhouse effect is also suspected of contributing significantly to desertification, thereby consuming former agricultural areas. Environmental refugees now number 25 million—more than all other types of refugees combined, a figure projected to double in the next decade (Earth International 1999). The U.S. Central Intelligence Agency is presently assessing potentials for political destabilization which would result from climate related disruptions.

MORBIDITY PROJECTIONS

Both UNEP and WMO state, "the projected increase in the duration and frequency of heat waves is expected to increase mortality rates." They also report on expected increase in the transmission of many infectious

NEWS FLASH: DATELINE 2040

The formerly disparate nations of the Middle East, North Africa, and the United States meet in emergency session in Cairo to discuss a common cause—runaway heat! Most delegates report more than four weeks of temperatures over 130°F (54°C), yet no resolve is established on a plan to envelop major metropolitan areas in air-conditioned domes. The hole in the ozone layer, first detected in the 1980s and now referred to as the ozone blowout, has been proven responsible for 17 percent skin cancer mortality worldwide.

The major part of most national defense budgets is now allocated to the protection from plunder by masses of refugees of the remaining tropical forests, which now comprises only 1.5 percent of the earth's surface. Major shifts in world power have resulted from similar shifts in major grain-growing areas—this aggravated by several major nations having to finance, at staggering cost, seawalls around the perimeter of their national coastal boundaries.

Not all these projects have been successful. Holland is completely underwater, as are Bangladesh and many Caribbean, Oceanian, and Indonesian islands. The Mississippi River has a distinct reverse flow at high tide—its overflow has turned the entire delta, along with most of the U.S. southeastern gulf area, into an enormous, infertile, brackish marsh.

The state of Florida is likened to a mausoleum presenting a particularly macabre specter. Deserted hotels on Miami Beach, as well as state-of-the-art techno-exhibits of the Epcot Center and Disney World, are saltwater tombs.

While almost 1 billion have perished from starvation, as former agricultural areas wither in unprecedented heat, many more environmental refugees have, for the past decade and a half, been on a relentless trek northward—a tragic spectacle, infinitely dwarfing the sub-Saharan droughts and famines which, more than 50 years ago, gave a warning of far greater catastrophes to come.

---

diseases, including malaria, dengue, and yellow fever, due to extension of the range of the mosquitoes that transmit these diseases into the temperate zones of the United States, Europe, and Asia. This is projected to increase the range of these diseases from 45 percent of world population to 60 percent, resulting in an additional 50 to 80 million cases of malaria per year by 2100.

Some of these increases are already documented in small outbreaks of malaria in New Jersey, New York, and Texas, with dengue now directly on the southern border of the United States. In the tropics, a 7.2°F (4°C) rise in temperature, and no change in rainfall, is expected to reduce crop yield, with a decline of 30 percent in already hard-pressed sub-Saharan regions, putting an additional 40 to 300 million people at risk of hunger by 2060 (McMichael, et al., WHO 1996). Between 1973 and 1991 the incidence of malignant melanoma among Caucasians doubled; in 1996 there was a 12 percent increase over 1995—during an era when sunbathing's popularity is waning!

▲ *Flight of fancy—or closer to the truth than comfort would admit! At this stage no one can say with any certainty, but this is the kind of future that some are predicting the world could face if the international community fails to address the problems of global imbalance that now face us.*

SEASICKNESS

By 1999, ongoing research of the past two decades points to a sickening sea with coral colonies, vegetation and sea turtles suffering en masse, globally, from maladies including infections, tumors, obscure lesions, and fungal plaques. This phenomenon has markedly worsened in the late 1990s; searches of photography going back to the 1930s show no signs of several dozen new diseases (Raloff 1999).

Coral reefs are the richest ecosystem in the ocean and second richest on Earth, following tropical forests in species diversity. At least 65 percent of all marine fish species are dependent on coral reefs during some stage in their life

MAJOR TROPICAL VECTOR-BORNE DISEASES AND THE LIKELIHOOD OF CHANGE IN THEIR DISTRIBUTION AS A RESULT OF CLIMATE CHANGE

Disease	Vector	Number at Risk (millions)	Number Infected or New Cases per Year	Present Distribution	Likelihood of Altered Distribution with Climate Change
Malaria	Mosquito	2,400	300 million to 500 million	Tropics/subtropics	Highly likely
Schistosomiasis	Water snail	600	200 million	Tropics/subtropics	Very likely
Lymphatic filariasis	Mosquito	1,094	117 million	Tropics/subtropics	Likely
African trypanosomiasis	Tsetse fly	55	250,000 to 300,000 cases/year	Tropical Africa	Likely
Dracunculiasis	Crustacean (copepod)	100	100,000/year	South Asia/Middle East/ Central and West Africa	Unknown
Leishmaniasis	Phlebotomine sandfly	350	12 million infected, 500,000 new cases/year	Asia/South Europe/ Africa/Americas	Likely
Onchocerciasis	Blackfly	123	17.5 million	Africa/Latin America	Very likely
American trypanosomiasis	Triatomine bug	100	18 million to 20 million	Central and South America	Likely
Dengue fever	Mosquito	2,500	50 million/year	Tropics/subtropics	Very likely
Yellow fever	Mosquito	450	<5,000 cases/year	Tropical South America and Africa	Very likely

▲ *Altered temperature and rainfall patterns will change infectious disease patterns.*

cycles. Noted tropical marine invertebrate authority Gandhi James Newman (pers. comm. 1999), explains that the increase in ocean temperatures during El Niño events since the early 1980s caused an extensive bleaching and, in many cases, a severe dieback of the corals due to an expulsion of the symbiotic algae for which they depend on photosynthesis. These massive events resulted from only temporary heat spasms. Newman cautions us that the effects on coral and other marine organisms from the expected, more prolonged ocean temperature increases are easily demonstrated in controlled aquariums. The cumulative result, he warns, is of organisms perishing from hypermetabolic rates—a bleak specter—transforming the gloriously fanciful diversity of coral reefs into the wasteland of a barren seascape. In addition, massive coral reefs dieoffs produce increased nutrient levels, causing algae and red tide blooms, and potential cyanobacteria outbreaks which would form smothering mats, sealing the possibility of regeneration of coral reef regrowth in many areas.

The IPCC confirms Newman's scenario of the implications for coral and continuing warming of tropical seas projected at more than 3.6°F (1–2°C) by 2100: "The magnitude of such an increase, in addition to the rate of change, leaves virtually no margin for corrective action." Recent evidence implicates global warming over the past quarter-century for increasing amounts of dust transported by the great seasonal winds of the African harmathan. Hitching a ride on that dust from the Sahel are vast quantities of soil fungus spore, estimated at several hundred million tons per year, which have attacked and decimated sea fan coral across the Caribbean Basin all the way to Florida (Pratt 2001).

John Holdren of Harvard, a member of the President's Committee of Advisors on Science and Technology, clearly stated that in regards to global warming "the world's energy-economic system is a lot like a super tanker, very hard to steer and with very bad brakes, and we know from the science that has been reviewed that the super tanker is heading for a reef which will rip out its bottom. It's a very bad idea in these circumstances to keep on a course of full speed ahead."

IV A Dwindling Land Resource

Tropical forests form new soils even as they prevent erosion, another factor of prominent concern which should be considered, but most often is not, when decisions are taken on converting forest to other land uses. By a sponge effect they release a sustained flow of water during dry seasons and prevent flooding in wet seasons, thus protecting watersheds over immense areas. A closer look at the Amazon, the mightiest river in the world, will illustrate this.

Remarkably, the Amazon River contributes nearly one-fifth of all the fresh water that flows on Earth. From its mouth, an average daily flow of over 4 trillion gallons (15.4 trillion l) of nutrient-rich water rush into the Atlantic. Mightier than any other river, its output would fill Lake Ontario in three hours. The volume is such that it colors the ocean 20 miles (32 km) out to sea, and vastly reduces the ocean's salinity for more than 200 miles (320 km). Its nutrients, which are fed upon by plankton and form the base of a food chain up through the big fish, are carried by currents into the Caribbean, from where the Gulf Stream delivers them along the Atlantic coast all the way to the Grand Banks of Newfoundland. Thus, some of the most fertile fishing grounds in the world are fed directly by the Amazon.

▼ *Behind the dramatic image of the demarcation between the silt-laden Amazon and the clear dark waters of the Rio Negro near Manaus, Brazil, lies a somber warning. Some 40 percent of developing-world farmers depend on the regular flows and erosion control of healthy watersheds for crop production. In India, the value of forests in insuring that service has been calculated at U.S.$1,125 per 2.5 acres (1 ha) or U.S.$72 billion annually for the nation (Panayotou and Ashton 1992). What will be the price for those services in 2025 when 3 billion people in developing countries will be suffering water shortages (Postel 1992)?*

The truly massive erosion caused for the most part by tropical deforestation can be illustrated by the following. To match the transportation of topsoil caused by erosion, every person on Earth would have to load 4.9 tons of soil, and then cart it to and deposit it in the nearest body of water—every year! Instead of the regulated, constant year-round flow that results from the "sponge effect" of forest cover, deforested streams and rivers now alternately swell to disastrous flood or shrink to no flow at all. This is compounded by the die-off of biological activity in silted rivers and the land-building coral reefs smothered by the silt.

The deforestation of the Himalayas has resulted in devastating erosion downslope and into the lowland plains, even into India. During rains, unchecked flooding has wiped out agriculture and swept entire villages away, causing tragic death tolls. Presently, it is reported that no one sleeps at night in these regions when it rains—and no wonder. In Bangladesh, such floods have resulted in yet-uncounted numbers of dead and 25 million homeless, leading researchers there to declare, "We are no longer dealing with disaster events, but with disaster processes."

In India, one in 20 people are at risk, while during the dry season the other edge of the double-bladed axe of deforestation, drought, takes its toll. In the single Indian state of Maharastra, denuding of watersheds has resulted in the drying up of water supplies in 27,000 villages.

In 1998, the cutting of the Chuanxi Forest, near the source of the Yangtze River in China, caused the fiercest floods the nation has seen in 44 years,

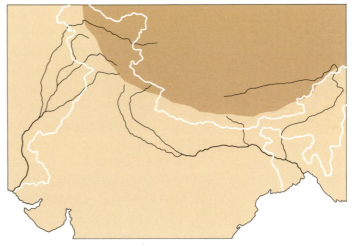

leaving 15 million homeless and almost 4,000 dead, at a cost of U.S.$24 billion. As a result, 100,000 timber industry workers will retire or take up new occupations. Throughout China the slogan is, "Tree cutters should now become tree planters."

An analysis by Oxfam America of 1998's Hurricane Mitch revealed that as destructive as a storm of this magnitude would normally be, when its fury and voluminous rainfall (6 feet [1.8 m]) passed over highly deforested regions of Central America, unmitigated runoff coalesced into raging floods resulting in a piteous and unprecedented 15,000 dead, more than 1 million homeless or displaced, and U.S.$8 billion in damage.

While humankind could manipulate its current dependencies on such things as fossil fuels, tropical wood, hydroelectric power, and the like, it is inconceivable that our species could flourish without the largesse of Earth's topsoil—the basis of our culture. Toward the close of the 1990s, Earth is losing each year, through erosion, 25.4 billion tons more topsoil than it produces! Over the last half of the 20th century, that is a 20 percent loss of global agricultural land and 25 percent of our topsoil (Raven, in Beardsley 1999). This same soil is the very namesake of our planet.

ONE THOUSAND YEARS FOR THE FOREST'S RETURN

Only if conditions permit, and a large enough seed reservoir of original forest is left standing nearby, will the successive generations of secondary species slowly die off and permit the original flora to return to a reasonable semblance of climax growth. This process probably requires 200 years at a minimum, but perhaps 1,000 years or more pass before the forest is restored. Forests 100 to 150 years old have only one-half the birds, mammals, and trees of mature forest and diversity is poor (Terborgh 1992). Beyond this, however, is the concern for the regeneration of large tracts where the nearest source of climax species seed is some kilometers away. For such cases, *The Ecology of Sumatra* speculates a time scale of "hundreds if not thousands of years" for regeneration.

GREEN MANSIONS TO RED DESERT

Once primary forest is removed, the prognosis for the future depends on several factors. When secondary growth is deflected by human disturbance, succession is, of course, retarded. We now increasingly see in areas where the

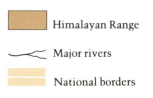

Himalayan Range

Major rivers

National borders

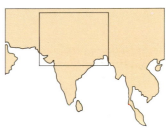

▲ *The water catchment area of the Himalayan Range has lost more than 40 percent of its forest cover and is now the greatest single ecological hazard on Earth in terms of numbers of people involved. The Ganges plain alone is home to more than 500 million people, and inundation is an inevitable feature of life. Year by year the floods become more severe. In one year some 65,700 villages were flooded, 2,000 people drowned, 40,000 cattle were lost, and property damage ran to more than U.S.$2 billion.*

clay subsoil is abused by cattle or machinery—compacted, leached by rain, and so parched and baked by the tropical sun—that not even aggressive grasses will grow again. In fact, where cement is unavailable or unaffordable, the laterite soil itself serves very effectively for the construction of airstrips and roads. We have managed to create useless, barren, red deserts where bountiful luxuriance once flourished.

An apt illustration of the permanence of the void that may result is that the bricks used to build the Angkor Wat temples in Cambodia were made from the red laterite forest clay. The temples still stand after more than 1,000 years, through war and weather. Incredibly, the forest in the Angkor vicinity was widely cleared and then abandoned in 1431. Today, some 560 years later, the forest still has not returned to a climax state.

Mounting pressure from an ominously expanding world population is putting severe stress on the tropical forest biome. This current situation holds a clear parallel to an ancient tragedy, and, as it is said that "he that does not pay heed to history is condemned to repeat it," we might profit from a brief review of an historical puzzle.

THE HYDROLOGICAL CYCLE AND THE MYSTERY OF THE MAYAN COLLAPSE

The Mayan civilization in northern Guatemala was at its peak just over 1,000 years ago, and supported some 5 million people. Then, within a relatively short span of three or four generations, there occurred a total collapse that is to this day one of the great mysteries of historic times.

Archaeological evidence indicates that environmental degradation caused by overpopulation and mounting pressure on the fragile tropical ecosystem may have been its undoing. According to field studies conducted by the University of Florida and the University of Chicago, the Mayan population in the Guatemalan rainforest grew slowly over 17 centuries and took 400 years to double until its collapse around A.D. 800. (By contrast, it now takes 20 years for the population to double in some developing countries.)

Direct evidence of forest abuse comes from a study of soils in lake beds in the major Mayan population centers of northern Guatemala. Extremely high levels of phosphorus in the lake sediments can be explained only by overwhelming soil erosion that would have placed an "undoubtedly severe" strain on the Mayan agricultural resource, thus causing the inevitable catastrophic decline.

We know that pasture converted from forest absorbs less than one-tenth the water resulting in runoff. Thus, 90 percent of the water exits the cycle and becomes unavailable for direct return to the atmosphere. Climatologists now have ample evidence that approximately one-half of the total precipitation in the Amazon Basin is transported by winds from the Atlantic Ocean. The remaining 50 percent is provided by evapotranspiration from the forest itself. In the rainforest proper (compared with other forest forms and savanna) the figure for evapotranspiration may be as high as 75 percent of total rainfall (see page 41). There is considerable concern that the continued reduction of forest cover by human activities will reduce rainfall on remaining forest in a continuing downward spiral that could soon fall below the minimum required to support the forest formation, and so effectively seal its fate (Salati and Vose 1984). Deforestation associated changes

Deforestation

Reduction in rate of evapotranspiration.

Increased exposure to wind and direct sun.

Loss of protection from impact of rain.

Drying and baking of surface soil.

Increased leaching and soil erosion.

Rate of nutrient recycling much reduced.

Destruction of leaf litter and associated micro-organisms.

Animal populations drastically reduced.

Number of insect predators reduced.

More extreme microclimate created.

Water retention of soil reduced.

Soil fertility reduced.

Number of animal pests increases.

Harsh conditions favor spread of weeds.

Crop failure

▲ *Downward progression from deforestation to total crop failure or land exhaustion is an inescapable consequence of short cycle shifting cultivation and cattle raising on tropical forest soils.*

The slow process of healing begins on a clear-cut patch of hillside in Panama. First to show are light-loving species such as Heliconia and Cecropia (Musanga cecropioides in Africa and species of Macaranga in Asia are analogous) which will mature into secondary forest and provide essential cover for the primary forest species that will follow. Recovery to mature primary forest will take hundreds, more probably thousands, of years.

▲ This Mayan temple ruin in the Petén Forest of Guatemala is a monument to an advanced civilization capable of sustaining a population of 5 million on agriculture and the utilization of the natural forest. The abrupt end of this ancient culture may have been caused by population growth, leading to stress on the land, a critical fertility loss, and the forced dispersal of the Mayan people.

in regional rainfall have been much documented (Salati and Nobre 1992). Notable among these are the regions of southwest India, much of the Philippines, montane Tanzania, southwest Côte d'Ivoire, northwest Costa Rica, and the Panama Canal Zone (Meher-Homji 1992). The overexploitation of scarce nutrients and excessive deforestation, resulting in precipitation fall-off, ominously mirrors the ancient Mayan agricultural collapse which could have been precipitated by the same agricultural/environmental processes.

Naturalist explorer Alfred Wallace once remarked to his colleague Charles Darwin that the English working class lived in squalor unknown to the "primitives" he studied in the Amazon.

A century later, we are now transforming that Amazonian Eden into squalor just as expeditiously as our numbers and technology allow.

The microbe is nothing; the terrain is everything.

LOUIS PASTEUR

TROPICAL DEFORESTATION AND THE RAMPANT EXACERBATION OF PANDEMIC DISEASE

"Disease is the retribution of outraged Nature"—Hosea Ballou. Never before has this dictum had more meaning than in the theater of deforestation in the moist tropics. The visceral, often appalling impact, both to incoming settlers and to the existing forest tribes, illuminates a terribly dark aspect of colonization that is as unfortunate as it is horrific.

Just as the intriguing fieldwork of medical detectives of the past found conditions that caused plague (rat infestation) and malaria (mosquito borne, not the bad air, or "mal' aria" swamps), so does that sleuthing continue today, with a focus on tropical deforestation and its effects. The lurid results are just now coming to light.

MALARIA

The ancient Hindus called malaria "King of Diseases." The Chinese called it "Mother of Fevers."

Gro Harlem Brundtland, the director-general of the United Nations World Health Organization (WHO), states that malaria infects up to 500 million people of tropical regions and kills up to 2.7 million annually, including 3,000 African children per day, the largest cause of death of any transmissible disease. Five species of Plasmodium parasites transmitted by a number of species of *Anopheles* mosquitoes consume large volumes of red blood cells, causing fevers in excess of 108°F (42°C), chills, muscle pain, and an all-consuming lethargy (Young 1961).

Malaria is a growing global concern rather than a receding one. Increasingly, since the early 1960s when malaria eradication campaigns were on the offensive, the Anopheline vectors have developed resistance to insecticides, and the plasmodium have continually evolved resistance to the drugs used in prevention and therapy, especially the dangerous *Plasmodium falciparum* strain, which is so virile it can kill a victim in the first attack (McGreevy, et al. 1989). In what was then Zaire, where I contracted Falciparum malaria, native villagers were begging for chloroquin tablets (instead of food or money) to save family members afflicted with the disease.

J. W. Mak's pioneering work at the Institute for Medical Research in Kuala Lumpur, Malaysia, made the direct malaria/deforestation connection as follows: Many species of the Anophelene vectors prefer the sunlight of the canopy and raise larvae in the water trapped in crotches and hollows of large canopy trees and primarily prey on arboreal animals for blood meals. These natural sites generally kept many species of mosquitoes high in the canopy and safely out of human contact. When those trees are felled, the *Anopheles* finds new niches in lower forest strata, close to humans at work or rest, often finding human dwellings an improvement to natural habitat. In addition, logging is associated with silting of rivers, which can cause them to burst their banks, contributing to the creation of more *Anopheles* sites (Marques 1987).

Add to this mix the depressions and scarred earth from logging machinery and hauling, road ruts, drainage ditches, even the ever-present auto tires and discarded tin cans in settlement areas, all of which provide inviting pools of stagnant water for mosquito breeding (previously rare in virgin forests except in bromeliads, a minor number of other plants, and the odd crotches in trees) and habitat formerly in equilibrium is transformed into a veritable malarial petri dish. Increasingly, in remote regions diseased settlers now share an environmental interface with tribal peoples of the interior who have an extremely low tolerance, and who die rapidly in large numbers from the disease. The bone-chilling wailing of these people as a loved one dies in the midst of an epidemic still reverberates within my soul.

Each year along the Transamazon Highway, 5–25 percent of the population contracts malaria. Two hospitals associated with the highway, which could well be rechristened the *Transmalaria Highway*, reported that malaria represented 41 and 53 percent respectively of the total patient cases (excluding maternity) and, as these are predominately agriculturists, an obvious factor in reducing crop yields. All evidence suggests that as deforestation increases in Amazônia, so will its lethal and silent partner, malaria (Walsh, Molyneux, and Birley 1993). So many Indonesian transmigrants died of malaria in areas such as Irian Jaya, that others retreated home to Java carrying the disease with them to previously malaria-free areas (Abisudjak and Kalenegara 1989).

Medical investigation now unveils the direct link between tropical deforestation and tragically disfiguring and life-threatening diseases such as these.

▲ *This once-proud Samoan chieftain now takes refuge within the protective shadows of his hut, coming out only under the cloak of darkness, so sensitive is he to the deformities of elephantiasis. He has allowed himself to be photographed only to teach villagers about the danger of this horrible affliction.*

▼ *This Peruvian villager, living on the edge of deforested territory, is suffering the dangerous mucocutaneous form of leishmaniasis which, if left untreated, will completely consume his face and his nasal and throat passages, with terminal results.*

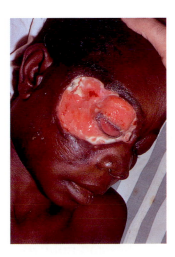

▲ *Buruli ulcer is a fiendish affliction infecting growing numbers globally. As yet there is no highly effective treatment.*

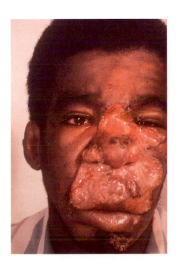

Wars and accidents aside, malaria has killed 50 percent of all humanity since the Stone Age. In 1999, trials began on a vaccine against the disease.

ELEPHANTIASIS

This frightfully deforming advanced stage of lymphatic filariasis affects limbs, genitals, vulva, breasts, and internal organs and is caused by the parasites *Wuchereria bancrofti,* and *Brugia malayi,* which live almost exclusively in humans. The vectors are species of *Anopheles* and *Aëdes,* which prefer seepage water on hill slopes open to light and so "are rare in uncleared primary forest, but they proliferate when deforestation occurs" (Cheong 1983), greatly increasing the likelihood of the spread of this disease in neighboring human populations. In addition, many of the aspects of deforestation detailed above that favor malaria transmission also apply to elephantiasis. The grossly dehumanizing aspects of this disease often include, in the case of the male victim, a horrendously distended scrotum which often must be carried before him in a wheelbarrow. It puts at risk more than 1 billion people in 73 countries and infects more than 120 million presently (WHO 1998). In endemic communities up to 50 percent of men and 10 percent of women can be infected. Chronic and acute manifestations of the disease tend to develop more often and sooner in newcomers rather than local populations (WHO 1998), "shifted cultivators" being prominent in that high-risk group. Needless to say, the psychological and social stigmata that accompanies this disease are immense and paint a sad tableau of destroyed lives.

KYASANUR FOREST DISEASE (KFD)

This rare forest arborvirus, or arthropod-borne (mosquito, tick, etc.) disease attacks both primates and humans, resulting in a prolonged, prostrating febrile illness with a 5 percent death rate. It is transmitted by ticks (*Haemaphysalis* spp. which inhabit *Latana* thickets of secondary growth only, resulting from deforestation (Walsh, et al. 1993). In addition, the clearing of forest for cattle grazing in southern India's Shimoga district led to a tick population explosion resulting in a serious KFD outbreak in the 1980s.

LEPROSY

In 1998, WHO reported that 5.33 persons per 10,000 in Brazil are afflicted with leprosy (Hansen's disease), more than most other nations, including India. Caused by a bacillus, *Mycobacterium leprae,* if untreated leprosy can lead to progressive damage to the skin, limbs, eyes (blindness), and nerves. The last results in loss of sensation in fingers and toes, leading to repeated injury, trauma, and atrophy. Of those infected, only 61 percent receive treatment—despite the fact that drug therapy is available to terminate infection and effect cures. This disfiguring disease, which infects 1.3 million people worldwide, spreads as population density increases with resettlement schemes and resulting deforestation. Research has shown that Pygmy tribes which inhabit primary rainforest contract leprosy only rarely and then apparently only by contact with Bantu natives who practice slash-and-burn agriculture, reside outside the forest, and who commonly suffer the disease (Wayne M. Myers, pers. comm. 1999).

YELLOW FEVER

Similarly, it has been documented with a particular note of caution to the timber industry that forest clearance exacerbates this *Aëdes*-transmitted arborvirus (Fiennes 1978). Initially this disease was considered a "jungle zoonosis" involving forest canopy primate communities and was passed under natural conditions to humans with far less frequency.

AFRICAN SLEEPING SICKNESS

Trypanosomiasis infects up to 500 million people annually and has been well documented to have had its range greatly increased by deforestation and fuel-wood collection, which are responsible for the open habitat favored by its vector, the tsetse (*Glossina*) and other biting flies (Malyneux 1982).

CHAGAS' DISEASE

A particularly insidious even if fascinating disease due to its life history, Chagas' disease puts 100 million people at risk and leaves 18 million infected. It is spread by assassin bugs, principally *Triatoma infestans.* In the past, it transmitted the parasite *Trypanosoma cruzi* to Central and South American forest burrowing mammals, it developed a penchant for open vegetation, in particular the thatch roofs of human dwellings. Those who sleep on the floor are the assassins' target. At night, the bloodsucking kissing bug approaches the sleeping human, makes a small bite and defecates near the minute opening. The bug's saliva causes an allergic itch; the disease is actually spread by the victim's unconscious scratching of the wound, moving the nearby feces, with the pathogen which causes Chagas', into the bloodstream. The clearing of forest regions and closely related outbreaks of Chagas' have been dramatically documented over the past 100 years (Barratt, et al. 1979; Schofield 1988).

LEISHMANIASIS

Another grotesquely disfiguring tropical disease, leishmaniasis (or "mountain leprosy") is spread by several species of the phlebotomine sand fly, of the genus *Lutzomyia.* Visceral leishmaniasis, normally more frequent in the drier areas of Venezuela and northeast Brazil, is now well documented to be spreading to parts of the Amazon where it was formerly rare and sporadic, thus extending its range in pace with deforestation there (Lainson 1989). The sand fly vector has quite enthusiastically adapted to the tractor impressions and hauling scars of logging, road ruts, and drainage ditches that are elemental to the invading colonizers' environment. One sand fly species causing Leishmaniasis braziliensis was found in catches distributed 99 percent inside houses and only 1 percent in the nearby Atlantic forest of southeast Brazil.

Research on the Peruvian Amazon concluded that the most significant risk to contracting the disease was exposure to forest clearing. "Extensive slash-and-burn agriculture on poor soils, absence of irrigation, production of annual crops, almost no manuring and greater plot size all correlated with more leishmaniasis," (Bartolini, et al. 1988).

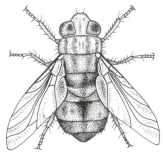

▲ *The human botfly (Dermatobia hominis) is a largely unrecognized but rapidly growing public health threat in moist tropical areas due to the influx of cattle. Eggs laid in the skin develop into larvae that burrow deep and are difficult, and risky, to remove as they contain toxins. Public information campaigns like the one illustrated above, from Mexico, are still all too rare.*

▲ *River blindness (onchocerciasis) is a tragic disease now spreading due to logging operations and the building of dams in many tropical areas.*

HUMAN BOTFLY

A fascinating if repulsive parasite, the adult botfly (*Dermatobia hominis*) is a New World tropical forest resident. Its larvae grow into large and painful maggots under human skin. Needing warm-blooded animals as intermediate hosts, the botfly now finds an abundance in cattle herds newly introduced into tropical deforested regions. The result is that where human parasitation by the botfly was formerly rather a rarity, it is now a growing public health reality in cattle country.

RIVER BLINDNESS

Also known as *onchocerciasis*, river blindness is one of the leading causes of blindness in the developing world. It occurs widely in tropical Africa and is now invading Latin America.

Caused by the filarial worm *Onchocerca volvulus*, the disease afflicts an estimated 18 million people at present and threatens another 120 million people globally, according to WHO. The two-foot-long (60 cm) parasitic worm causes eye lesions, and up to 20 percent of the population of heavily infested areas are permanently blind as a result. In some villages of west and central African nations, 60 percent of people over 55 years of age are either completely or partially blind. All too common is the sordid spectacle of long chains of people of all ages linked together, holding onto sticks or a rope, led by a sighted child. Hydroelectric projects are primary causes of the spread of river blindness, as the blackfly (*Simuliidae*) vector finds the fast-moving waters of the raceways of dams to be ideal breeding spots. Similar raceways are created by logjams that often build up downstream from logging operations and favor blackfly breeding, as does erratic stream flow, the result of widespread deforestation (Burnham 1991).

OROPOUCHE

In Amazonian Brazil, the 1980s brought record-breaking epidemics of this recurring viral disease which can cause inflammation of the tissues around the brain. This event coincides with Brazil's influx of colonizers into the region. Health officials have linked the epidemics to huge piles of cacao husks, a result of cultivation, which hold pools of water ideally suited to the breeding habits of the flies that spread the disease.

BURULI ULCER

Yet another grossly disfiguring disease, buruli ulcer is caused by the bacterium *Mycobacterium ulcerans*. It causes massive open ulcers, often necessitating amputation. Now widespread in the tropics, it has made its appearance in Melbourne, Australia, which cautions us that its range is potentially quite wide. A leading researcher of buruli, Wayne M. Meyers, Chief Mycobacteriologist at the Armed Forces Institute of Pathology in Washington, D.C., informs me that the organism is associated with water bugs found in the deep mud of swamps, often the result of flooding related to deforestation. There is also an apparent relationship between the disease and increases in basic agricultural activities (Meyers and Porlaeis 1999). S. G. Browne, who practiced medicine in deeply forested areas of Zaire, did not see a single case of buruli, which is common in deforested regions impacted by flooding and water impoundment as a result (Browne 1965). Meyers's work in central and west Africa found no incidence of buruli in deep forest Pygmy tribes, but was so widespread among shifting cultivator tribes that in a rural hospital in Ghana, for example, 58 of its 100 beds held people suffering the disease.

SCHISTOSOMIASIS

Also known as *bilharziasis*, schistosomiasis ranks second behind malaria in terms of socioeconomic and public health importance in tropical and subtropical regions and is the second most prevalent tropical disease, after malaria, afflicting some 200 million people. The disease has long been acknowledged to have increased its range. It is now endemic in 74 developing nations, in direct response to hydroelectric dam and irrigation projects in the tropics, which increasingly present a problem in rainforested areas (WHO 1990).

Schistosomes, the causative organisms, are associated with snails that generally avoid both strong sunlight as well as deep shade. The latter observation suggests the necessity of reforestation of streams and, of course, leaving forested streams unviolated to reduce incidence of the disease (Loreau and Baluku 1991). In many rivers and streams, let alone impounded water, one cannot even let a hand or foot trail in the water without risking infection. In undisturbed forest areas of equatorial Africa, schistosome vectors are rare or absent (Brown 1980).

It should be said here, in spite of all the horror defined above, that it is the rare traveler to the tropics who returns home with anything more serious than a bit of traveler's diarrhea, especially if normal and prudent health precautions are taken. This is essentially the case when visiting undisturbed tropical rainforests, which are safer than most urban areas. Having said that, I will make a feeble excuse for not having followed my own good advice to avoid spending time in agricultural villages. As a result, I have contracted (in over four decades of exposure) two strains of malaria, leishmaniasis, dengue hemorrhagic fever, and botfly maggot infestation, all clearly linked to deforestation, migrant cultivation, or cattle. With knowledge of these maladies and their vast impact on such a broad spectrum of humanity, a clearer image comes into focus of the human-made arenas of pestilence that tropical deforestation transforms from habitats in equilibrium.

I am pleased to report that in a highly lauded act of philanthropy, pharmaceutical firms SmithKline Beecham and Merck & Co. have both introduced drugs, albenadazole (for elephantiasis) and invermectin (for river blindness) respectively, and donated these in unlimited supply to WHO to effectively combat these diseases.

▲ *Puddles and road ruts in the squalid conditions of many tropical settlements provide an ideal breeding habitat for disease-carrying insects.*

THE LAST OF THE FOREST NOMADS

ARCHAIC HUMANITY—THE MIRROR OF OUR PAST—AN ENDANGERED SPECIES

Whether viewing documentary films, photographs within this book, or enjoying the rare experience of personal contact with these cultures, there is a quite common and almost instinctive tendency to assign them an almost

It is curious to note that tribes who became acculturated fastest also disappeared quickest.

—AMAZON EXPLORER HENRI COUDREAU, 1886

mystical splendor; the "noble savage," as it were. There is nothing new in this perception. In April 1500, the Portuguese explorer Pedro Alvares Cabral, destined for India, was blown too far to the west and arrived in Brazil where he was stunned by people as beautiful as birds, living in harmony with nature. "Their innocence is as great as Adam's," Cabral exclaimed.

The author admits he has been as deeply impressed by our forest relations as anyone, and, even as it is fashionable to do so, cannot here dispel the "myth" of the "noble savage" as he has, by and large, found in them a palpable nobility. That these cultures have existed and grown in a relative vacuum offers remarkable insights into our own humanity.

It should be known that we are rapidly losing this profound cultural resource in a process social scientists have termed *marginalization*. In 1967, the Indonesian government declared that it had sole legal jurisdiction over the nation's forests, 74 percent of its land area. Subsequently, the generations of complex and successful customary rights of its forest residents were rejected and the theory of "the tragedy of the commons" became a reality. With the government's absolute inability to police its extensive forest holdings and the forest peoples' lack of authority to halt both licensed and illegal exploitation by invading commercial loggers, one lucid interpretation concluded that "the traditional rights of millions of people have been handed over to a relatively small number of commercial firms and state enterprises." As a result, the tribal peoples' standard of living has been remarkably reduced in deforested areas. This, unfortunately, can be directly applied to the remaining tropical forest–dwelling humanity globally. In the Philippines, the liquidation of 90 percent of its primary forest by the Marcos regime enriched some 400 favored families by U.S.$42 billion, yet impoverished more than 18 million forest tribals.

The Brazilian government Indian agency, FUNAI, holds legal control over indigenous policy. While Brazilian decree #1775 lists 364 tribal lands, only 175 have been legalized by demarcation of their traditional tribal territory. (As of 2000 Brazil's indigenous policy had markedly improved.) In 1987, an invasion of gold miners known as *garimpeiros* descended on Yąnomamö Indian territory in both Brazil and Venezuela. A decade later, a quarter of the 25,000-strong tribe in all villages were dead of malaria and measles, also introduced by extensive and intensive anthropological studies (Tierney 2000). In 1993, *garimpeiros*, now numbering more than 40,000, invaded the 25-million-acre (10-million-ha) Yąnomamö reserve and slaughtered at least 12 Indians, including children in the northern Brazilian state of Roraima, who were beheaded. Yąnomamö girls as young as nine years old have been documented with hepatitis after being forced into prostitution by the miners.

Of international concern is the Venezuelan government's tentative decision to open almost 4 million acres (1.6 million ha) of forest lands in the vicinity of Yąnomamö land, including the tepuí mesa formations which tower over the forest in the magnificently scenic Angel Falls region to private mining concerns (Tierney 2000).

Such is the sordid state of this tribe that John Walden, who heads Marshall University's international health department and works with the tribe, states, "if we continue to just study the Yąnomamö, they're going to die." He goes on: "In my opinion the Yąnomamö are the number one priority for South American emergency relief right now."

Numbering in the many thousands until recently, the Urueu-Wau-Wau of Rondônia, and the Waimiri-Atroari of the Central Brazilian Amazon are on

▲ *Perhaps the gentlest of the world's people, the Pygmies of Africa live a nomadic yet highly ordered life, even while the forest around them is shrinking. Their mutualistic relationship with the Bantu people outside the forest hints at the possibility of coexistence on a wider front between such pristine cultures and our own.*

the brink of extinction; only several hundred have survived the invasion of their homelands (Miller and Agopian-Laing 1995). Perhaps 1,000 South American tribal languages have vanished (National Geographic Society 1999).

THE IMPACT OF ASSIMILATION

An unacceptably high percentage of the traditional tribal people who do survive the immediate effects of invasion of their lands, and forced transportation to relocation settlements or reservations, die in plagues of new diseases such as tuberculosis, influenza, parainfluenza, measles, mumps, rubella, poliomyelitis, and the common cold, to which they have no natural resistance. A series of epidemics often result in 85–90 percent mortality (Posey 1994). Moreover, it is readily apparent that the survivors of this morbid gauntlet of assimilation into the modern world all too often become the dregs of civilization, riddled particularly with alcoholism and venereal disease, often unable, even in the long run, to adjust to and become useful members of the new society.

From epidemiological data gathered by UNESCO, certain relationships clearly exist between observed declines in public health, and forest removal. UNESCO's Tropical Forest Ecosystems Report sums up its findings with the following conclusions: "Semi-nomadic hunter-gatherers are relatively little affected by malaria and other vector-borne disease. Their nutritional status is also generally satisfactory. Settlement appears to bring a deterioration of health. Man-made changes in the forest create situations favoring transmission of malaria, intestinal parasites, schistosomiasis and other water and vector-borne infections." (See previous section, "Tropical Deforestation and the Rampant Exacerbation of Pandemic Disease.")

Immediately apparent to any visiting lay person or medical anthropologist is the relatively uniform excellent physical and mental health, and general well-being, that the traditional people so commonly display. There are, of course, various virulent parasitic infections that do take their toll and effect a population control. Many studies have shown, however, that these tribes do not seem to suffer many of the fatal degenerative diseases with which we in the developed world are afflicted in epidemic proportions. Arteriosclerosis and its related heart attack, high blood pressure, stroke, and diabetes, are the number-one killers in our society. Most of us will eventually die of one (or a combination) of these diseases, while these conditions are largely absent in archaic cultures. That Nathan Pritikin based his longevity diet on that of the traditional Tarahumara tribe of northern Mexico's rugged hill country is a splendid example of applied anthropology.

A REPOSITORY OF KNOWLEDGE

The erosion of these cultures, principally through deforestation, entails the very real and major loss for global society of literally thousands of years of diverse traditions, languages, and philosophies, as well as vast unwritten catalogs of botanical, animal, and mineral pharmaceuticals and foods. Invading agriculturists are, to be conservative, having a very difficult time finding any meaningful measure of success in developing sustainable colonization in the moist tropics. As the interior-forest people of these zones have evolved, out of sheer necessity, an infinite understanding of the ecological interdependencies and resources available there, and moreover, how

▲ *In a wary first contact a remote band of Peruvian Machiguenga Indians (translated, "the people") are aware for the first time of a world beyond that of their forest home. Their garments,* manchakintsi, *are woven from wild cotton and are the result of six weeks of proud work by the women. In the lower photograph a young man returns home after crossing a swollen river.*

to ply them without degrading the environment, there is ample justification to view them as tenured professors.

A single village in the north of Thailand, for instance, makes use of 295 varieties of plant for food, and 119 separate plants for medicine. (It is noted that many indigenous remedies, such as the oils used to remove stomach parasites, are impressively effective and carry none of the severe side effects of Western prescription pharmaceuticals processed from those primary source materials.)

The World Health Organization is presently searching for new and improved contraceptives and finds that more than 3,000 plant species are used by forest tribes for purposes of antifertility.

The revolutionary protein-rich winged bean (*Psophocarpus tetragonolobus*) and the giant wax gourd (*Benincasa hispida*), which are now dramatically upgrading diets in more than 50 countries and are predicted to put a significant dent in world hunger in the future, were found being used by forest tribes in Southeast Asia.

How did we come to discover quinine, used by millions of people globally to treat malaria? The answer is that South American Indians were found using the bark of the cinchona tree (*Cinchona* spp.) medicinally.

A survey, though grossly incomplete, shows evidence of at least 4,000 plant species in Indonesia alone that have served the area's native people. Yet less than one in 10 of these are used widely today by modern cultures. Leaves of more than 1,650 tropical forest plants have been found to be "highly nutritious," yet very few are presently in use outside the forest biome. How many plants are thought to be edible? Far more than 30,000!

When Columbus reached the Americas, between 6 and 9 million Indians occupied Amazônia. Of 270 Brazilian tribes which existed in 1900, 55 have vanished. Two-thirds of those remaining contain a population of less than 1,000, leaving a total population of 360,000 (FUNAI 2000).

Brazil's Villa Boas brothers, Orlando and Claudio, who were famous for their initial pacification work, and often mentioned for the Nobel Peace Prize, now refuse on moral grounds to pursue the practice because of the pattern of violence that almost invariably followed. Orlando has recently said that "an integrated Indian is no longer an Indian, but just a lesser citizen of the Brazilian nation." In despair over the quintupling of the Brazilian population in his lifetime, and the vast numbers of those shunted into Indian lands, he cryptically states that "all we can do is pick up the hat of a drowning man and marvel that we lived to witness the last days of Eden." In Brazil, only 53 Asurinis Indians are left, the balance of the tribe destroyed by intruders to their homeland. The late anthropologist Berta Ribeiro states, "They want no more children; they know they are finished." The tribal-rights advocacy organization Cultural Survival informed me that in 1988 alone more than 200,000 developing world indigenous people were killed, and that more than 2 million were forced to flee for their lives, leaving behind shelter and gardens.

The 1987 Malaysian government's expropriation of the native lands of Sarawak forest tribes, and their subsequent handing over as timber concessions to logging companies, sparked the resistance of Penan tribal members, who blockaded the loggers' access roads. Subsequent arrests, and the illegal detention of the forest people, precipitated demonstrations at Malaysian consulates around the world and investigative missions by human rights and environmental groups, which continue to this day. In May of 2000, Bruno Manser, Swiss advocate for the Penan for almost two decades, was missing in the Malaysian forest, and foul play is suspected.

▲ *Blending the magic of the forest into religious and cultural practices, a Yąnomamö medicine man, assisted by another tribal member, has* epená, *a powerful hallucinogen prepared from the virola tree (*Virola elongata*), blown into his nasal passages. After suffering violent nausea the man then symbolically drew an evil spirit from the chest of a seriously ill child—an act of such passion and conviction that it will remain forever in my memory. In many cases the patient believes so deeply in the shaman's powers that a cure is effected.*

◀ *Is this the last glimpse of Eden? This Yąnomamö girl is so completely a part of her forest home near the headwaters of the Orinoco River in Venezuela that it is difficult for the few who know this fiercely independent people to visualize one separated from the other.*

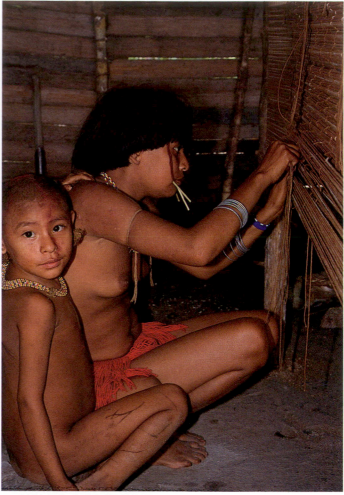

A window to our past. The insulation and isolation of the tropical rainforests have provided vital refuges for the few remaining pristine human societies. Will we choose to protect this unique resource or squander the opportunity in a headlong rush to rape the forests for a quick flush of nonsustainable profit? We can learn much from forest people about utilizing the forest without degrading it.

▲ ◀ After taking the drug epená, a Yanomamö man recovers in his house, built from, and filled with, produce of the forest. Nearby ▲ a young woman continues weaving. The hunter ▶ stands proudly with an ocelot he has killed with his longbow. The Machiguenga boy ◀ from the Peruvian jungle is making a hunting arrow.

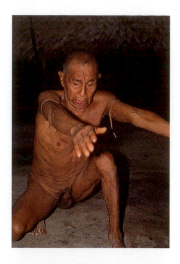

▲ *In 1988, more than 40,000 gold miners invaded Yąnomamö territory spreading malaria and other diseases. Here Chief Ciacho Awar A-Teri addresses the tribe in a "big talk" warning them of the coming malaria. Within three months the revered chief died, a victim of the epidemic.*

Typical of the frustration of tribal peoples against the great magnitude of forces that logging companies and the government represent, is the statement by Indonesian Forest Minister Hasrul Harahap, that "in Indonesia the forests belong to the State not the people." That these were ancestral lands does not give the people ownership, he said. When logging destroys the forest on which they depend "they have no right to compensation." In Sarawak that has recently included logging roads plowing through burial sites as well as natives' agricultural fields, for which they depend on harvest to survive. The Penan tribe has no word for "thank you" because sharing is a cultural obligation. Nor have they a word for "forest." Their universe is delineated sharply between *tana' lihep, lalun, tana' lalun*—land of shade, land of abundance—and *tana' tasa'*, the land that has been destroyed.

Stating Indonesian policy at a 1990 meeting of European and Asian leaders, Prime Minister Mahathir Mohamad remarked, "it is our policy to eventually bring all jungle dwellers into the mainstream. . . . There is nothing romantic about the hapless, half-starved and disease-ridden people." "We don't want them running around like animals," stated James Wong, Sarawak's Minister for Housing and Public Health. "No one has the ethical right to deprive the Penan of the right to assimilation into Malaysian society."

As a matter of record, the vast majority of Penan who have been placed in resettlement camps languish in squalor and food scarcity while commonly awaiting 30-year-old government promises for the building of schools (Davis 1999). Malaysian policies have drawn global criticism from anthropologists, environmentalists, and human rights advocates including David Maybury-Lewis, Harvard professor of anthropology and president of Cultural Survival, an indigenous peoples' rights organization. He sees the Penan as symptomatic of the global dilemma: "Genocide, the physical extermination of a people, is universally condemned," he explains. "But ethnocide, the destruction of a people's way of life, is not only *not* condemned when it comes to indigenous peoples, it is advocated as appropriate policy."

Benjamin Franklin noted that in colonial America, whites kidnapped by Indians almost never readjusted to civilized life, whereas Indians taken from the tribes took the first opportunity to rejoin their tribe even after years of education. "There must be something very superior in the nature of their social bond," Franklin concluded. This trend is commonly seen today.

If there are, understandably, economic sacrifices to be made by home governments in honoring tribal sanctity, these may be balanced by a format of supportive aid. Such a policy would be consistent with viewing these cultures as a common universal treasure, at the very least as precious as any other endangered species and deserving of the protection that only an enlightened international agreement can afford them.

By their very nature these tribes are typified by a lack of political power, with little chance to participate in a meaningful way in the decisions that decide their fates. This facilitates the processes of ancestral land expropriation, economic exploitation, and ensuing violence. Should not an avenue be opened for governmental agencies, assisted by developed nations' funding, to allow the tribes the self-determination to adapt at their own pace and to do so with a dignity they are accustomed to, but which is all too often denied them? In that incandescent spirit of statesmanship, the Colombian government in 1989 installed one-half of its Amazon forests, more than 45 million acres (18 million ha), to 50 tribal groups totaling some 70,000 souls, in light of their ability to sustainably make their living from the forest without annihilating it. The United Nations General Assembly declared 1995–2004 the International Decade of the World's Indigenous People, perhaps initiating the process of integrating them into the human rights forums.

In 1854, Chief Sealth said, "What is man without the beast? If all the beasts were gone, man would die from a great loneliness of spirit. For whatever happens to the beasts happens to man."

The chief's words are as true today. The human being, as the last of the archaic cultures, is as rightfully part of the global environment as other species. Such considerations go far beyond moral or ethical assertions. Many of those now living on the brink will perish. Others will move in to take their place on the margins. And if we take no action, it will simply be a matter of time before we too face the abyss.

▼ *In an echo of human prehistory, a New Guinea highland medicine man infuses village life with his mystical rituals. Though still using stone axes, the tribe is in many ways rich beyond our comprehension. The young girl, adorned in paints of earth tones, reflects the health and harmony of a people to whom heart disease and most degenerative diseases are virtually unknown.*

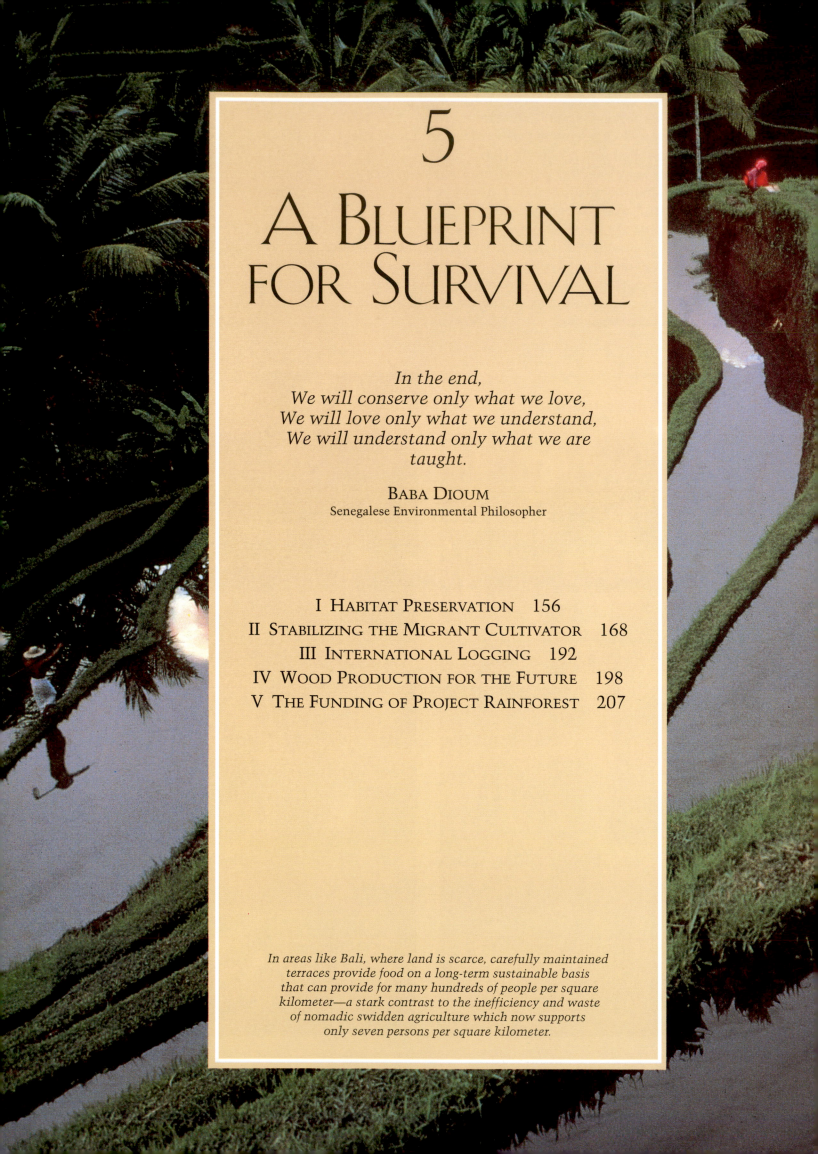

5

A BLUEPRINT FOR SURVIVAL

In the end,
We will conserve only what we love,
We will love only what we understand,
We will understand only what we are
taught.

BABA DIOUM
Senegalese Environmental Philosopher

In areas like Bali, where land is scarce, carefully maintained
terraces provide food on a long-term sustainable basis
that can provide for many hundreds of people per square
kilometer—a stark contrast to the inefficiency and waste
of nomadic swidden agriculture which now supports
only seven persons per square kilometer.

1 HABITAT PRESERVATION

There is a consensus among conservationists and scientists that nowhere can the conservation dollar be stretched further than in the tropical forests through habitat preservation. By the end of the 20th century, however, barely 8 percent of the tropical forest biome had been set aside as conservation areas. The goal still remains very much ahead of us.

A lily pond, so a French riddle goes, contains a single leaf. Each day the number of leaves doubles—two leaves the second day, four the third, eight the fourth, and so on. Question: If the pond is completely full on the 30th day, when was it half full? Answer: On the 29th.

The global lily pond in which more than 6 billion of us live may already be well over half full. Clearly, population stabilization must be the highest and most immediate international priority. Tropical deforestation and its consequences are but one of the corrosive results of overpopulation, and it is unlikely that environmentally oriented advancements will remain permanent without finally stabilizing global numbers.

The World Commission on the Environment and Development, in its report *Our Common Future* (the Brundtland Report), states, "Humanity has the ability to make development sustainable—to select paths or progress to ensure that it meets the needs of the present without compromising the ability of future generations to meet their own needs."

The author is one of many who feel humanity is empowered to preserve the many crucial values held in the tropical forest biome. We hope to illustrate in this chapter that the aims of controlling population growth, addressing global hunger, and achieving sustainable levels of wood production, while simultaneously striving to conserve vast portions of our biosphere are not contradictory, but are by necessity complementary.

APPLIED TECHNOLOGY

We know that with applied use of our advances in technology we can increase and then maintain the productivity of land in use, and that the sun must set on the tropical norm of rotation of fields. Agriculture, animal husbandry, and the logging industries in the tropics must leave behind the inefficiencies and wastefulness of the past.

Many parts of the humid tropics are quite unsuitable for sustained agriculture and, as we have seen, attempts to utilize these areas can quickly lead to permanent degradation of the site. In other areas, however, as demonstrated in parts of Indonesia, Thailand, Brazil, and Rwanda, productive forms of agriculture have been developed which have retained the fertility of the original forest soil and leave more options open to development. It cannot be the objective of enlightened conservation to preclude development from future planning, but a thorough review of alternatives can assure that the best possible course is charted so as to maximize the forest's ability to provide a continual flow of goods and services side by side with sustained agriculture that will not only provide sustenance, but a degree of prosperity to peasant farmers for the first time.

STEMMING THE TIDE OF EXTINCTION

While preserving habitats and their resident species in situ will come at some sacrifice, it is sobering to first consider the alternatives of attempting to preserve species as separate entities, in many cases outside their natural habitats (ex situ). These measures might include an *Endangered Species Task Force* assigned to the collection and germination of seed, and the transportation of animal and plant species from areas under exploitive pressure to appropriate "safe port" habitats, while ensuring that exotic transplants (if that is the case) will not be detrimental to their new environments. Although such a program would naturally be expensive, some of the cost might be saved by incorporating a curriculum for academic credit utilizing students or lay volunteers, as has been applied to other scientific fields. No finer example could be found of this hands-on approach than the field courses run by the

◄ *"Operation Rescue, 1971." Aware of the high degree of endemism among tropical species, and the threat of extinction facing so many of them, the University of Papua New Guinea launched a major salvage operation when the Segeri Plain was flooded as part of a hydroelectric plan. I was pleased to have participated in this rescue, in which thousands of plants were collected for study. Where development is imminent, such rescue missions can translocate flora and fauna to safe zones.*

indefatigable, now sadly late, Mildred Mathias, Professor Emeritus at the University of California, Los Angeles. Often working under the auspices of the Organization for Tropical Studies, this pioneer biologist led students and interested laymen on crash field courses to the forests of Central and South America. Among her former students are scientists, administrators, and decision makers far more aware than those of even a decade previous of the huge potential of tropical forest conservation.

It should be acknowledged that in many cases, species possessing commercial value increase in market demand sharply as those species move closer to extinction. Such species require heroic efforts in the black-market place of origin and at the export destination, as well as in the habitat, in order to effect their survival. All the rhinoceros species and African elephant, both now under the most serious threat from poachers, are classical and highly topical examples.

There are many situations, however, in which the remaining natural population is already too small to ensure continued survival of the species. In such cases a captive breeding pool may be the only alternative, with the goal of rereleasing animals into suitable habitats when and if increases are realized, while holding back sufficient numbers as a hedge against failure.

William Conway of the New York Zoological Garden considers that a population as small as 50 to 100 specimens of a given mammal species may be adequate as a breeding stock. Presently, a breeding stock of some 540,000 individuals of 3,000 species of mammals, birds, reptiles, and amphibians are maintained in global zoological gardens, representing some 13 percent of the known land-dwelling species of vertebrate animals. Naturally, the ideal situation is to make national parks profitable, since it has already been shown in Kenya that a maned lion is almost 450 times more valuable as a living tourist attraction than it is as a hunting trophy.

In some cases, however, such as the European bison (*Bison bonasus*) and Pere David's deer (*Elaphurus davidianus*), the only surviving individuals reside in zoos. These species walk a tightrope. Ironically it was war and flood that annihilated the last of Pere David's deer from its wild habitat in China at the turn of the 20th century. Bred in England since that time, a breeding stock was sent back to China not long ago.

Clearly, however, gene banks should be maintained for as many endangered species as possible in case the more natural and practical measures ultimately fail. The seeds of many plant species can be kept viable at 5 percent humidity and –4°F (–20°C) for long periods. You may call such facilities "frozen zoos" and "iceberg botanical gardens," but their time, unfortunately, has come. Yet given acts of God or man, such facilities as the Fort Collins Seed Laboratory (Colorado), the Northwest Germ Plasm Repository (Oregon), and the Potato Station (Wisconsin) offer a priceless if precarious insurance.

At best, however, such arrangements conserve the species but not the interactions between them that are so essential to healthy ecosystems. There can be no doubt that the greatest economy both in species preservation and the environmental dollar will be in the maintenance of holistic, biotic communities in the wild.

I doubt if anyone better appreciates the merits of preserving intact habitat, against the finances and energies required in bringing back a forest already gone, than Daniel Janzen, the "dean of tropical biology" who, with the able assistance of his colleague and wife, Winnie, have created the Guanacaste

▲ *In an FAO-sponsored study program, an Indian forester records the breast-height diameter of a tree. Research and monitoring activities like these are essential to management of global forest resources. The Royal Botanical Gardens, Kew, in Richmond, England, have set their sights on collecting the seed of 24,000 plants, some 10 percent of the world's flora by 2010 through the Millennium Seed Bank Project (Morell 1999).*

Conservation Area, a 323,600 acre (130,960 ha) preserve of rare dry-forest habitat (of which only 2 percent remains globally) in Costa Rica, actually regenerating the forest, largely by hand, in large areas of degraded pasture that surround the remnant undisturbed habitat. Janzen calls it "absorbing the human footprint."

ENVIRONMENTAL TRIAGE

While the agonies of triage can be jolting, such imminently threatened, highly visible charismatic species as the orangutan, African forest elephant, various rhinoceros and tiger species, and rafflesia flowers, to name only a sampling, serve well as central targets for swift action. Not only are they highly worth the effort of preservation, they garner easily won support from the public and political sector as well—a cogent scenario of the species preserving its own habitat. Pleistocene "refugia"—areas of great evolutionary diversity—are also prioritized. Norman Myers has defined the following 14 areas as "hot spots": western Ecuador, western Amazônia, the Chocó strip of Pacific-coast forest in Colombia, the Atlantic-coast forest of Brazil, southwestern Côte d'Ivoire, montane forests of Tanzania, Madagascar, the Western Ghats of India, southwestern Sri Lanka, eastern Himalayas, peninsular Malaysia, northeastern Borneo, the Philippines, and New Caledonia.

These areas comprise 120,000 square miles (311,000 sq km), an area of forest the size of New Mexico, or less than 4 percent of remaining tropical forests, and are under severe threat. They house far more than 37,000 endemic plants, 15 percent of all plant species on Earth within a scant 0.2 percent of Earth's land surface, as well as an estimated 750,000 (but probably several times more) endemic animal species and represent a "silver bullet" conservation strategy. Under the blazing gun of increasing habitat destruction and species extinction, Conservation International during the 1990s has conducted the Rapid Assessment Program (RAP)—flying in specialists to evaluate a remote, but potentially biologically superrich, often isolated habitat—with great success, in one instance culminating in the establishment of the 4.5-million-acre (1.8-million-ha) Madidi National Park in Bolivia in 1995. In 1993, a RAP also tragically resulted in a plane crash in the Ecuadoran forest that took the lives of Alwyn Gentry and Theodore Parker, two luminary biologists whose loss will be felt in tropical conservation for eternity.

An ideal solution to the problem of the limited financial resources available to establish and maintain tropical forest parks exists in having the tribal peoples themselves patrol and maintain their own homelands as national parks, reporting to senior officers employed by national parks departments. This, of course, keeps inviolate both tropical forest habitat *and* the tribal lands. The Kuna Indian Forest Park in Panama is an outstanding example of this arrangement. Funds generated from visiting scientists and tourists are used to support the park, which is the first in the world to be created by an indigenous group.

COSTA RICA—THE PILOT PROJECT

Here we might take heart in the Costa Rican example. This remarkable country covers only 19,575 square miles (50,695 sq km), or roughly the area of Denmark, but it has one of the richest biological heritages of any nation in the

We hope Edward O. Wilson's notions ring true into the dawning century, among which is biophilia, *a phrase he coined (just as he popularized the word* biodiversity), *alluding to an innate passion for nature that draws people to love and preserve nature. He states, "There's one good thing about our species: We like a challenge."*

▲ *In establishing the Cathedral Rain Forest Science Preserve on the Osa Peninsula in Costa Rica in 1972, I inadvertently cut off the only access of an American logging firm to a vast area of their Pacific coast forest holdings. The ensuing bitter battle resulted, eventually, in the expropriation by the state of the firm's entire holding—much of which is thankfully now protected by the Corcovado National Park. The Costa Rican government enjoys wide recognition as a prominent world leader in tropical forest conservation.*

▲ *"The golden toad* (Bufo periglenes) *perfectly exemplifies the fragility of endemism. The toad's sole habitat on Earth is the wooded peak of Monte Verde in Costa Rica, which could be deforested in a matter of hours with modern logging equipment."* (That was the caption for this book's first edition! This flamboyant toad was a leading ecotourism attraction but it has not been sighted since 1989. To universal sorrow, it is now declared extinct. Research indicates global warming, as dry weather pushed moisture laden clouds beyond its cloud-forest range. The loss tragically demonstrates the fragility of endemism prophesied above.)

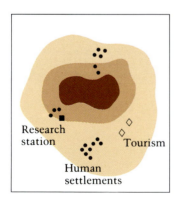

■ Core area

■ Buffer zone 1

□ Buffer zone 2

▲ *A popular and effective form of reserve consists of a totally protected core area surrounded by buffer zones in which scientific research and limited human activity is permitted.*

world. It contains 850 bird species, of which fewer than 140 migrate. This avifauna contains more bird species than exist in the whole of North America north of the Tropic of Cancer. Plant species total in excess of 12,000, with orchids numbering more than 1,200.

As a result of decade-long conservation efforts on many fronts, Costa Rican leaders, many subsequently the recipients of international conservation awards, have protected in some form or other approximately 26 percent of the country's national territory, with 22 parks and preserves—fully 8 percent of the area being designated as national parks. Proportionately it is among the very top nations in total area/preserve ratios. (By comparison, the United States has only 1.5 percent of its area so dedicated.)

In 1977, while receiving a much deserved international conservation award in Washington, D.C., then Costa Rican president Daniel Oduber attested that he believed that "when nations have shown little or no respect for the environment, and where the natural environment has been ruined or lost in an over-hasty and uncoordinated exploitation of Earth's resources, human relations inside these nations are also likely to be characterized by a lack of respect for individuals and for human rights."

How Much is "Adequate" Habitat?

Many tropical forest animals exist at very low densities and require large territorial ranges. The select fruit trees that form the base of their food chains are also often widely distributed in very low numbers. To ensure the survival of adequate gene pools of animal and plant species we must accept that huge tracts of protected land will be required.

Recent research gives us some rough estimates of minimum reserve sizes. It is often anticipated that areas surrounding preserves (and their buffer zones) will be disturbed or cleared, effectively creating "conservation islands," and the theory of island biogeography states that the number of species in each of these islands will fall, as the carrying capacity has been reduced, until it reaches a new equilibrium. Even here, questions arise over the merits of conserving an area with one massive preserve compared with the benefits of preserving an archipelago of "islands." The consensus, however, seems to favor the sound ecological concept of preserving entire biotic communities. Justifiable scientifically, logistically, and economically, it directs us to conserve whole working relationships; that is, ecologically dependent entities.

With this in mind, how can we, in planning Earth's tropical forest preserves, keep our species losses to a minimum? According to biologists Michael Soule and Bruce Wilcox at the University of California at San Diego, no large mammals have been known to evolve into new species on islands smaller in area than 232,000 square miles (600,800 sq km)—an order of magnitude larger than any existing national park. "Evolution is in trouble," Soule warns, adding that we can look forward to a "biological holocaust without precedent."

Ensuring a Minimum Breeding Pool

Field zoologists have verified the extensive ranges certain animals require in order to forage successfully. Estimates of the minimum populations required to ensure a viable breeding pool also indicate the size some preserves need to be. Different species, of course, vary widely. Certain butterflies, for instance, in order to collect enough amino acids from specific kinds of nectar, need in excess of 39 square miles (100 sq km). Hornbills, it appears, need 5,000 individuals to maintain population equilibrium, and this population requires an area of between 770 and 3,900 square miles (2,000 to 10,000 sq km). Tigers, on the other hand, need a breeding pool of only 400, but the area of forest necessary to support this group may be as large as 15,000 square miles (almost 40,000 sq km). When the tiger's hunting range is restricted by agriculturists, the great cat is known to prey on people and their livestock.

On the smaller scale, World Wide Fund For Nature's Minimum Critical Size of Ecosystems project outside Manaus, Brazil, illuminates certain specifics. Within local forest-clearing operations, natural forest plots of varying sizes were left intact, and have since been intensively cataloged and studied. Thus far, the results show that a 2.47-acre (1-ha) plot isolated in a large cleared area became severely sun-scorched on its periphery, and windblown and desiccated well into the interior, grossly affecting the forest. In one heavy storm the plot was virtually leveled as a consequence of the typically shallow-rooted structure of lowland wet forest.

A 25-acre (10-ha) "island" fared somewhat better, but was unable even to support a colony of army ants, which range over a 75-acre (30-ha) area.

A 250-acre (100-ha) area supported the army ants but not the ant-following birds, including woodcreepers (Dendrocolaptidae) for example, that depend on them for opportunistic feeding. As we would suspect, many bird species chose to fly out of this size "island." A mitigating positive factor in this example was the presence of a "corridor" of virgin forest running from the isolated plot to a more extensive area of undisturbed habitat. Conversely, when even narrow strips are cut across such corridors, the ant-followers disappear.

A 3.9-square-mile (10-sq-km or 1,000-ha) plot resulted in a more normal bird population, but larger predator and prey species such as tapir and jaguar were absent. The larger mammals are also responsible for creating water-holding "wallows," on which many smaller but no less crucial species are dependent.

On "islands" of nearer 40 square miles (100 sq km or 10,000 ha), certain species, such as capuchin monkeys (*Cebus* sp.), will still range far beyond the area, and Norman Myers suggests that parks of at least 10 times this size will be needed to ensure stable populations of such animals. A viable breeding population of 300 jaguars is not expected to reside in an area of less than 2,900 square miles (7,500 sq km) given their known breeding behavior (Terborgh 1992).

Plant species are somewhat more difficult to quantify. Oxford University botanist T. C. Whitmore, author of *Rain Forests of the Far East*, has estimated that in order to perpetuate many tree species, a reserve of significant genetic diversity would require at least 5,000 trees inhabiting an area of between 6.6 and 52 square miles (17 to 135 sq km). Whitmore concludes, "The prospect is frightening."

The "Island Effect"

By analyzing the species loss of oceanic islands separated from the mainland 10,000 years ago at the end of the ice age, we can estimate fairly accurately the

▲ *A viable breeding pool of tigers (Panthera tigris) requires a large area of forest, and as that habitat is encroached upon by man and his livestock, tigers and some other great cats may turn on them as prey. Udu, the infamous man-eating tigress of Tapak Tuan, Sumatra, was trapped just minutes before this picture was taken. She had killed and eaten three men, one of them just four hours earlier, and with her appetite firmly established she could not be rereleased. She now resides in a Sumatran zoo as an international megastar.*

UNDERSTANDING THE RAINFOREST BIOME

It has been said with some justification that we are currently burning our bridges before we can even cross them. The tropical forests represent the world's last great repository of plant and animal life – a resource of such promise for the good of mankind that its study and preservation is vital.

▼ **Detailed habitat studies**
We can conserve a habitat only if we understand it. Studies on Barro Colorado Island, Panama, measured the density and the biomass contribution of the main resident mammal species.

▲ **High-level scientists**
Canopy biologist Donald Perry pioneered many new techniques of access and movement. Julian Steyermark discovered 97 new species in 1988, and more than 2,200 in his lifetime.

RESIDENT MAMMALS	no/km²	kg/km²
CARNIVORES		
Felis pardalis (ocelot)	0.14	2
ANTEATERS		
Tamandua mexicana (Mexican anteater)	5	20
Cyclopes didactylus (fairy anteater)	37	13
INSECT-EATERS/OMNIVORES AND FRUIT AND INSECT EATERS		
Marmosa robinsoni (mouse opossum)	55	3
Dasypus novemcintus (nine-banded armadillo)	8	28
FRUIT AND SEED EATERS		
Sciurus granatensis (squirrel)	300	75
Heteromys anomalus (spiny pocket mouse)	67	5
Oryzomys sp. (rice rat)	434	22
Dasyprocta punctata (agouti)	46	92
Proechimys semispinosus (spiny rat)	350	105

RESIDENT MAMMALS	no/km²	kg/km²
FRUIT-EATERS/CARNIVORES AND FRUIT-EATERS/OMNIVORES		
Philander opossum (four-eyed opossum)	27	37
Didelphis marsupialis (opossum)	45	45
Cebus capucinus (cebus monkey)	16	42
Tayassu tajacu (peccary)	16	373
Nasua narica (coati mundi)	24	72
Eira barbara (tayra)	3	12
FRUIT-EATERS/BROWSERS		
Alouatta palliata (black howler monkey)	80	440
Agouti paca (paca)	26	208
BROWSERS		
Bradypus infuscatus (three-toed sloth)	123	393
Choloepus hoffmanii (two-toed sloth)	25	108
Tapirus terrestris (tapir)	0.53	139
Mazama americana (brocket deer)	2	30

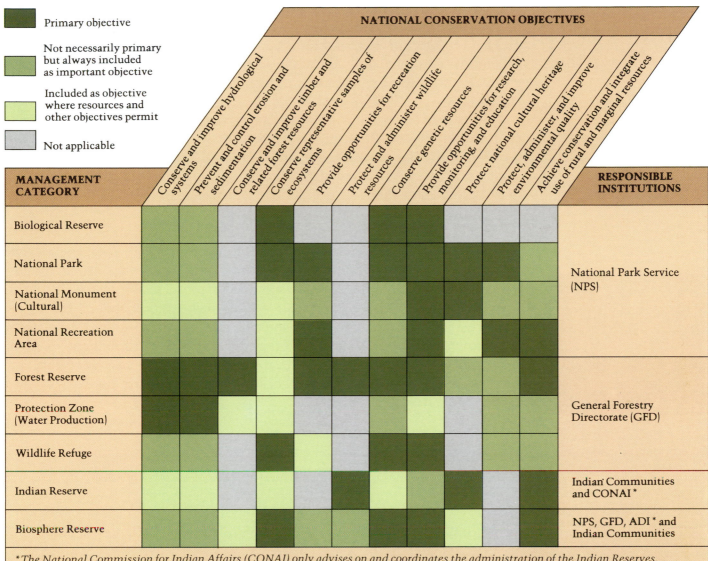

Legend:
- ■ Primary objective
- ■ Not necessarily primary but always included as important objective
- ■ Included as objective where resources and other objectives permit
- ■ Not applicable

NATIONAL CONSERVATION OBJECTIVES

National conservation objectives (column headers):
- Conserve and improve hydrological systems
- Prevent and control erosion and sedimentation
- Conserve and improve timber and related forest resources
- Conserve representative samples of ecosystems
- Provide opportunities for recreation
- Protect and administer wildlife resources
- Conserve genetic resources
- Provide opportunities for research, monitoring, and education
- Protect national cultural heritage
- Protect, administer, and improve environmental quality
- Achieve conservation and integrate use of rural and marginal resources

MANAGEMENT CATEGORY	RESPONSIBLE INSTITUTIONS
Biological Reserve	National Park Service (NPS)
National Park	National Park Service (NPS)
National Monument (Cultural)	National Park Service (NPS)
National Recreation Area	National Park Service (NPS)
Forest Reserve	General Forestry Directorate (GFD)
Protection Zone (Water Production)	General Forestry Directorate (GFD)
Wildlife Refuge	General Forestry Directorate (GFD)
Indian Reserve	Indian Communities and CONAI*
Biosphere Reserve	NPS, GFD, ADI* and Indian Communities

*The National Commission for Indian Affairs (CONAI) only advises on and coordinates the administration of the Indian Reserves.
*ADI: Agricultural Development Institute (lands and colonization)

▲ Conservation planning
National parks are often seen solely as strictly protected nature reserves, but with proper planning, other elements can often be incorporated, including human use, research, watershed management, and other national and global conservation objectives. The chart shows the categories of protected wild area used in Costa Rica.

▶ Minimum critical size
These 1-ha and 10-ha plots in Amazônia, surrounded by clear-cut areas and in some cases linked to virgin forest by corridors, form part of a Brazilian-American study of minimum effective reserve sizes carried out by WWF.

minimum "island" park size. A practical translation for conservation use tells us that if 90 percent of an extensive virgin forest area is disturbed, leaving 10 percent intact, we can expect to preserve no more than half the species in the island. Loss will be rapid in the initial period. If the area of preservation is increased tenfold, survival rate for species will double. These figures indicate that unless you desire to trade off, by protecting specific target species, it is far more advantageous to preserve one large area than to conserve two of half its size.

A real concern is the possibility that whatever the final amount of tropical forest biome we settle for, say 15 percent, will suffer from the inevitable erosion of invasive deforestation and be reduced in time. We can reasonably expect pressure to increase in proportion to the biome's diminishing size. It is far better that a 30 percent biome be whittled to 20 percent than a 15 percent biome be slashed to a meager 5 percent.

The World Conservation Monitoring Centre reports that 8 percent of the world's tropical moist forests, 9 percent of mangroves and 5 percent of tropical dry forests are under some form of protection. Together they cover roughly 240 million acres (97 million ha) in some 2,000 protected areas (Collins 1990). However, many of these are "paper parks," protected in theory, but not in practice, that is, inadequate patrol and enforcement of laws, or in some cases, government-sanctioned logging or other development within "park" borders. It should be further noted that most preserves are in mountainous regions, not species-rich lowland forests (Terborgh 1992) which justifiably demand a greater proportion of protection.

CHARISMATIC SPECIES AS CAMPAIGN LEADERS

In many specific instances, intensive fund-raising campaigns may be centered on well-known or appealing animals or even plants, while also keeping as a primary target the conservation of the habitat that supports these popular life-forms. In this way countless less charismatic, unrecognized, or even unknown species have greatly improved chances of survival. It will be this holistic approach that will keep the broadly intertwined ecological relationships intact.

Many of the most "spectacular" animals are at the top of the food chain and are less likely to suffer mass extinctions via the domino principle than many of the less visible species that receive a more subdued public support. Again, this "web of life" may be preserved only by extensive preserves, which include, ideally, entire watersheds.

Yet the situation is circuitous. Can the world afford to lose a spectacular animal such as, for example, the African mountain gorilla? Obviously, in order to ensure the survival of this endangered species, a very large part of its forest habitat, the Virunga Volcano Range must be preserved.

Many such gallant species exist and can be brought into the service of conservation to ultimately effect their own survival. Roxanne Kremer's Preservation of the Amazonian River Dolphin (PARD), a project of the International Society for the Preservation of the Tropical Rainforest (ISPTR), has brought awareness to the plight of the river dolphin (*Inia geoffrensis*) in parts of the Amazon and Orinoco river systems. This species is bright pink in color and so tame it can be called to a canoe quite easily. Sadly, this is one reason for the dolphins' precarious survival profile, as fishermen destroy them effortlessly for their sexual organs and eyes, which are sold as *macumba* (magical amulets) in

▲ *The gorilla is one of our closest relatives: we share 99 percent of our DNA with them and our blood is barely distinguishable. Genetically, gorillas are closer to humans than they are to chimpanzees. So remarkably palpable is their connection to humanity, that with awed compassion, the world watched a videotape of a three-year-old boy who had fallen 18 feet onto concrete in the gorilla exhibit of the Brookfield Zoo in Chicago. Binti, a seven-year-old female with a baby gorilla on her back, gently picked up the unconscious child, cradled him in her ample arms, and placed him at the door where keepers could retrieve him. The child survived without permanent injury. To many, the brutal killing of this superb creature is close to homicide—often for the sake of "trophy" heads and hands to be sold to undiscerning tourists.*

THE MOUNTAIN GORILLA PROJECT

Discovered only some 100 years ago, the mountain gorilla now has a population of about 600. Given the huge problems of aiding the recovery of a species whose numbers dropped as low as 239 in 1979, the Mountain Gorilla Project (MGP) is one of the most heroically successful conservation stories of recent years. Far from being a hostage to destiny, this charis-matic creature played a key role in its own campaign, its poster image firing widespread public support. Through Carl Akeley, George Schaller, Dian Fossey, and the MGP, the gorilla has helped preserve its own unique montane habitat, despite the nearby carnage of the Hutu/Tutsi massacres during the late 1990s, although it is still under threat.

◀ ▼ Home of the gorilla
The mountain vastness of the Virunga Volcano Range straddles the wild borders of the Democratic Republic of the Congo, Rwanda, and Uganda. Cutting the great-est swath through the highland home of Gorilla gorilla beringei *is the human population, using the land for agriculture, wood-cutting, and grazing livestock. By controlling rainwater runoff, the forests protect downslope farms.*

◀ ▲ Habitat pressures
Generally gentle and con-templative by nature, gorilla groups often gather at the forest's edge to stare in disbe-lief as trees are cleared to make way for fields. MGP rangers assist tourists and mount constant patrols against poachers who plague the gorillas, forcing them higher and higher into the mountains, where damp and cold conditions can often lead to pneumonia.

▶ Gorilla behavior
A fierce glare shows this silverback male perceives my camera as a threat. He beats his chest at me in a deafening display, and, not quite satisfied with his ef-forts to humble me, he shakes a bamboo plume full of rainwater—but douses himself instead.

▲ *Roxanne Kremer created a high level of Brazilian and Peruvian government awareness and widespread public support for her Preservation of the Amazonian River Dolphin project (PARD). Now, International Dolphin Day (June 26) is dedicated to this engaging and fearless creature.*

▲ *In a poignant letter written just a month before his murder, Chico Mendes wrote, "I wish no flowers after I die, for I know they would be taken from the forest. All I want is that my murder will serve to put an end to the impunity enjoyed by the criminals . . . who, since 1975, have killed more than fifty persons like me, rubber-tapper leaders dedicated to defend the Amazonian forest." Since his death, and largely due to it, his Rural Workers Union holds the highest influence in his town of Xapuri and millions of acres have been preserved for the rubber tappers and nut gatherers he defended.*

certain Latin American countries and as an item of minor export to France. The dolphins are also unintentionally caught and often drown in commercial fishing nets, an increasing threat to the entire riverine food chain.

Kremer has secured recognition in Brazil and Peru for this endearing dolphin, which now has an International Dolphin Dedication Day (June 26) in its honor and a safe haven in the River Dolphin Preserve at the mouth of the Yarapa River, a tributary of the Amazon, outside Iquitos, Peru. In this tightly knit scenario we see the enhanced potential for survival of an important species, the preservation of portions of its habitat, and a crucial realization by the governments and people of Brazil and Peru that the pink dolphin is attracting tourist and science revenues, both locally and internationally.

Multiple-Use Forestry for People

Tropical forest reserves can in many cases be put to multiple use as a much preferred alternative to destruction. In addition to providing gene pool perpetuation, watershed protection, tribal culture insulation, tourism, and educational uses which will result in enthusiasm for conservation, other less conventional uses may also be allowed. These may include minimal, noncommercial selective forestry and game cropping, and use by local people for fruit and other forest product gathering. Buffer zones of no disturbance may surround or be imbedded in these areas of light disturbance. In many areas the more the resident population is integrated into the forest reserve the more chance the forest will have for survival in the long run: far more so than under the protection of typically inadequate ranger patrols. This concept is recognized by, and central to, the Man and the Biosphere (MAB) Reserve System.

Toward the realization of those concepts, internationally acclaimed Francisco (Chico) Mendes, a rubber tapper, or *seringueiro,* led the heroic and successful demonstrations against cattle barons' attempts to annihilate the forest. As a direct legacy, the rubber tappers of the state of Acre regularly earn between U.S.$1,000–$1,500 annually plying the forest sustainably for rubber, fruits, nuts, and other nonwood forest products, earning more than do typical slash-and-burners. These activities now involve more than 100,000 households covering 39,000 square miles (100,000 sq km) of "extractive reserves," setting a global precedent and representing 10–20 percent of the regional primary sector's income, principally in the states of Acre, Amapá, Amazônia, Rondônia, and Pará (Homma 1992). Less than a century ago, rubber was collected by actually felling the tree in a wasteful, one-time latex harvest. Mendes and his *seringueiros* have tapped into much more than rubber. They have inscribed into history itself the peasant genius of a self-renewing lifestyle—one that perpetuates income as it does the forest resources from which people derive sustenance.

Several additional constructive directions yet untapped are the collection of copaiba oil (*Copaifera langsdorfii*) (see page 124), raw material for the production of vegetable leather which has a value three times that of rubber and is currently enjoying a popularity in the manufacturing of ecologically sensitive shoe production in the United States. Piacava, a nontree vegetable fiber is also taking a marked foothold, enhanced by its direct connection to the Brazilian rainforest conservation movement. The Institute of Amazon Studies conducted an investigation for the FAO in identifying more than 100 plants with potentially sustainable economic use, many for the burgeoning "green markets" with a value of almost U.S.$1 billion per year (IEA 1991).

Three days before Christmas 1988, Mendes was murdered by shotgun, one of a great many to die for the cause in Acre. While the cattle ranchers responsible have been imprisoned, Mendes's martyrdom has immeasurably strengthened the Brazilian people's conservation tenacity.

Former Brazilian minister of the environment Jose Lutzenberger considers Brazilians themselves to be outsiders when they enter the region with their development plans. "This talk of, 'We can do with our land exactly what we want' is not true," says Luzenberger. "If you set your house on fire it will threaten the homes of your neighbors."

◀ While the cattle baron power structure that killed Chico Mendes is still destroying vast tracts of forest, yielding a meager U.S.$47 per hectare for seven years at best, rubber tapping leaves the virgin forest unscathed, and yields U.S.$50 per hectare indefinitely.

▼ The gathering of Brazil nuts from virgin tropical forest accounts for 50 percent of household income in some areas. Attempts to establish plantations failed, however, because the trees' pollinator lives only in primary forest.

II STABILIZING THE MIGRANT CULTIVATOR

Some 800 million people in developing-world rural areas, the majority from tropical forest countries, are landless or nearly so, and jobless as well. Caught also between cultures, these unfortunates are at the mercy of nature and government. In recognizing the crucial and timely importance of sustainable development, there is a growing concentration on identifying and producing manageable and realistic agricultural alternatives to swidden agriculture. Policy makers should agree that this must be replaced with more frugal and efficient systems, given that the supply of fields for rotation is very limited and the loss of the tropical forest biome is, for a host of reasons, unacceptable.

THE FERTILE VARZEAS

It is known, for example, that the seasonally flooded "varzea" forests of the Amazon can sustain agriculture indefinitely without the use of expensive fertilizers, as supplies of rich silt and vegetation debris are delivered free of charge by the rivers every year without fail. Indeed, any reference to the seasons in the vicinity of the Amazon is a reference to high water or low, with a water-level difference at Manaus, Peru, of 49.5 feet (15 m) separating the two (Prance, et al. 1985). On my first trip to the Amazon, I looked up perplexed as to how alluvial flotsam was deposited that high in tree branches.

It now appears that varzeas are also significantly enriched by a high potential for nitrogen fixation, and some sites have recorded values as high as 176 pounds per acre annually (200 kg/ha/yr). Through two crops a year, rice yields of 11 tons per hectare are achieved on high varzea flooded once every decade or so, whereas outside Amazônia the yield on irrigated land is often only 3 to 4 tons. With abundant organic nutrients delivered free of charge, the varzeas can sustain agriculture as rich as any along the fertile Nile.

Pioneering tropical entomologist Terry Erwin has patterned a raised-bed garden on ancient Mayan techniques in a swamp forest in Tambopata, Peru. Known as the Amazon Gardening Project, the prototype bed, surrounded by a moat for drainage, is filled with the superrich swamp forest muck that retains its fertility. This soil is harvested at small cost to the forest, and the one-tenth of an acre (less than 1/25 of a hectare) garden is expected to feed four families over an extensive period. The Brazilian Kayapó Indians transport topsoil, along with leaf debris and its biological activity, from surrounding natural forest to their farm plots as nourishment and subsoil cover. Studies have shown that an acre and a half (1 ha) garden can be littered sustainably from a 12- to 20-acre (5–8-ha) area of primary forest (Wilkin 1987).

The earliest European explorers in Amazônia vividly reported a much more advanced and affluent culture (perhaps 1 million people) living along the varzeas than existed in the terra firme forests. The nutrients of the annual siltation fed a rich aquatic food chain which culminated in caimans, manatees, turtles (which in lieu of refrigeration were reportedly corralled for use when needed), as well as strikingly large and abundant fish. Farming

produced copious harvests. Two crops of maize were grown each year, a variety of cassava was developed that matured in six months to avoid inundation, and wild rice was harvested and fermented into wine. This rice and the profusion of other aquatic grasses attracted large flocks of water birds which further enriched the lives of the varzea occupants. Large numbers of turtle eggs were pressed into oil to preserve meats. Why such diverse productivity escapes the modern descendents of those people is exemplified by their persistent use of inappropriate crops such as standard cassava, whose roots rot with the slightest flooding.

With all this potential on the horizon, a word of caution is necessary. Because of the nutrients that support such rich fisheries, care must be taken to avoid the serious consequences of overexploitation of the varzea. The indigenous peoples have long understood what we have only recently learned: that approximately 75 percent of the commercial fish of the Amazon are dependent on fruits and seeds and other organic material which falls into the water from the forest at high-water periods, during which time even piranhas switch to a diet of rubber tree (*Hevea brasiliensis*) seeds. A great many tree species, in turn, are dependent on the fish for germination of their seed. For this reason, attuned Amazon residents who do cut wood leave the forest intact at the water's edge to protect these crucial relationships.

Fisheries are, in fact, the most important source of animal protein for Amazonians and make up 78 to 88 percent of riparian indigenous people's meals. But mismanagement of this resource is now outstripping the yield, which is currently very noticeably on the decline. For this reason, both the avoidance of overexploitation and the regulation of fishery activities are urgent priorities. Yet there are plans for neither. Smithsonian biologist Tom Lovejoy astutely points out that although rice culture in the varzea far exceeds fish production in weight, it does not do so in protein value. He suggests that

▨ Flooded area

‒ ‒ ‒ ‒ Limits of drainage basin

▲▲ *"Ribeirinhos" farm and collect the bounty of the floodplain. One tree alone, the açaí palm (Euterpe oleracea), if sustainably managed, can yield fruit worth U.S.$136 per hectare per year indefinitely. This can yield average households some U.S.$4,000 per year, four times the income of the average smallholder and cattle rancher.*

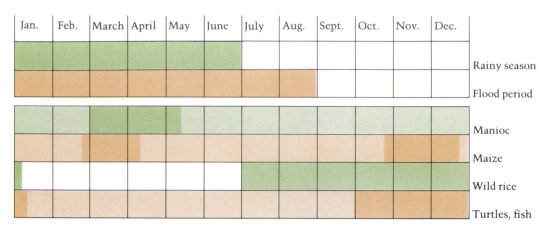

▶ The river's seasonal flow is the calendar for varzea farmers. High flood (May–July) is the period of scarcity when stored foods are relied on. As the flood recedes, wild rice plants root on the lakesides. The peak time for hunting, and for gathering forest foods, is during low water (October–December). Crops of rice, maize, and manioc are harvested before the waters rise again.

▲ ▶ The fertile varzeas can support 10 times the population of terra firme forests. Covering some 24,000 square miles (62,000 sq km), these alluvial zones can support villages of 2,500 people (Tapajos) compared with 300 (Omagua) in the terra firme. Silt-enhanced productivity is the key. Turtle ranching produces 440 times as much meat as upland cattle, while rice yields of 11 tons per hectare per year are excellent even by world standards.

provision be made to support rice and fishery production, and even fish culture, but that floodplain parks are an essential investment as well to protect the vital river community.

It is encouraging that the Brazilian government has proclaimed that 80 percent of the land bought for development in its Amazonian region will be left in its natural state.

THE ORCHARDS OF THE AMAZON

The floodplain produces 60,000 tons of fruit annually along the Amazon. These fruits include those of the prolific açaí palm (*Euterpe oleracea*), the mauritia palm (*Mauritia flexuosa*) (whose fruit contains three times the amount of vitamin A found in carrots and an amount of vitamin C equal to that found in oranges), the ever-popular sapucaia grande (*Pachylecythis egleri*) nuts, several species of passion fruit (*Passiflora* spp.) that tolerate flooding and are prime candidates for hybridizing to produce fruit of notable flavor for market, cannonball tree fruits (*Couropita guianaensis*) for livestock fodder, wild relatives of the soursop (*Annoa muricata*) which through crossbreeding could produce a delectably sweeter fruit, the enormous berries of the ginipap (*Tocoyena formosa*) for juice, ice cream, and a cheap fermented drink sold as *licor de jenipapo*, the sweet creamy bacuri fruit (*Rheedia brasilienses*), the hogplum (*Spondias purpurea*) for ice cream, drinks, and sherbet and whose inner bark is used for tea and to treat diarrhea. According to Amazonian biologist Michael Goulding it is abundantly clear that "from the standpoint of fruit-eating monkeys and fish, these floodplains are truly the orchards of the Amazon. Could they become so for humans?"

A New Hoof-Hold on the Amazon

The fragile, flooded forests cover only 2–3 percent of the Amazon Basin, yet are its most endangered habitat. This is primarily due to large-scale ranching of water buffalo, whose numbers now reach 800,000, and cattle, two breeds of livestock that are extremely destructive to this ecosystem. It is estimated that thousands of animal species (including invertebrates) have vanished from the floodplain forests and floating meadows in which the Amazon giant water lily (*Victoria amazonica*), the very signature plant of the Amazon River, is threatened as well. Sadly, this development has failed to relieve poverty—the average floodplain household earns less than U.S.$1,000 annually. We cannot lose sight of the fact that these disappearing floodplain forests are referred to as *fish forests* and *fish meadows* because they serve as the sustainable base for the region's extensive fisheries (Goulding, et al. 1996). This habitat is also the sustained font for an aquarium fish trade of U.S.$1 billion per year in the central Amazon Basin. So why not act on the obvious advantage of fish aquaculture in the very heart of these freshwater fish nurseries with the highly applauded, delicious, prolific—and native—tambaqui (*Colossoma macropomum*) instead of exotic *Tilapia* species. The remnants of these habitats have become precious indeed and in need of priority preservation.

Sustained Agriculture, the Elusive Goal— Farming to Simulate Nature

An innovative, yet obvious method of retaining soil fertility observes the natural and reproducible regeneration cycle which occurs when forest is disturbed or removed and applies it to our own agricultural practices.

A *sustained-yield agro-ecosystem* is designed to mimic instead of resist forest succession, by using plants useful to humans at each stage of the cycle. First to appear after a burn is the herb community, and so this plan utilizes food crops analogous to the naturally occurring herbs, such as pineapple (*Ananas comosus*), sugar cane (*Saccharum officinarum*), and beans (*Phaseolus* spp.). Year two brings pioneer trees naturally, and so the farmer is instructed to introduce cashew (*Anacardium occidentale*), bananas (*Musa* spp.), and papaya (*Carica papaya*) which could be productive for five to 10 years. Simultaneously, food and cash-crop tree species that correspond to primary forest trees are introduced. Such long-lived favorites as peach palm (*Bactris gasipaes*) are planted, from which not only fruit but also palm heart may be harvested on a sustained basis as the tree produces suckers when cut. This highly prolific native Amazon species provides one of the basic aboriginal staple foods.

SOIL CONSTRAINT	MILLION ACRES	MILLION HECTARES	% OF AMAZON
Nitrogen deficiency	1,080	437	90
Phosphorus deficiency	1,077	436	90
Aluminum toxicity	946	383	79
Potassium deficiency	934	378	78
Calcium deficiency	746	302	62
Sulfur deficiency	692	280	58
Magnesium deficiency	689	279	58
Zinc deficiency	578	234	48
Poor drainage and flooding hazard	287	116	24
Copper deficiency	279	113	23
High phosphorus fixation	190	77	16
Low cation exchange capacity	175	71	15
High erosion hazard	96	39	8
Steep slopes (>30%)	74	30	6
Laterization hazard if subsoil exposed	52	21	4
Shallow soils (<50 cm deep)	7.4	3	<1

▲ *Leached by tropical storms for eons, many of the red and yellow soils of the Amazon Basin were laid down 180 million years ago when the great southern continents first began drifting apart. Only 8 percent of the basin's soils are fertile—yet plots are assigned to shifted agriculturists indiscriminately.*

It remains productive from its eighth year to its 50th, with an annual crop of up to 150 pounds (68 kg) of versatile and nutritious fruit. Brazil nut (*Bertholletia excelsa*) and rosewood (*Aniba rosaeadora*) may also be planted, and when these become senile they may be felled and the process repeated as the fallow period would be sufficient to allow a natural return of fertility.

In addition, the following garden candidates were shown, in field trials in Panama by the Smithsonian Tropical Research Institute, to perform with high productivity in soils of low fertility: arrow root (*Maranta arundinacea*), tuber-bearing yam (*Dioscorea bulbifera*), Mexican yam bean (*Pachyrhizus erosus*), again the versatile peach palm (*Bactris gasipaes*), hardy banana clones (*Musa* spp.), a shade-tolerant, soil-covering vine (*Desmodium ovalifolium*), and leguminous shade trees (*Erythrina* spp. and *Gliricidia sepium*) for nitrogen capture.

Fertility is now secured and maintained without the need or high cost of chemical fertilizers, which often result in runoff into water sources, neutralizing the acid pH and creating favorable breeding conditions for the snail necessary for the life cycle for schistosomiasis.

No better target for rural farm credit could be envisioned. Creative aid toward agroforestry will be bankrolling success. Make no mistake, agroforestry is not just another color on the palette; it has the resounding potential to transform the habitat holocaust, caused mainly by shifted cultivators, into a steady state system, saving those masses from their unintentional migrations of destruction.

A *corridor system* formerly used in highly populated areas of Africa, employed 30- to 150-foot (9- to 46-m) strips cut through old-growth forest and planted with crops. Close proximity to the forest edge ensured leaf-litter enrichment and soil protection, and when the plot was abandoned, seeds and mycorrhizae quickly repopulated the cut. We should presume that biotic diversity was maintained at a level sufficient to prevent excessive competition from pests. This successful method of agriculture fell into disuse as soon as production of cash crops demanded continuous use of the land.

▶ *Simulating a natural forest succession after the initial clearance, this managed system of garden and field crops, pig forage, and forest species, replaces natural forest vegetation with analogous plantings of greater economic value. Incorporating a commercial tree species such as paraiso* (Melia azedarach) *would give an additional long-term cash return.*

Because agriculture must not be discouraged in the wet tropics, it is considered imperative that a significant proportion of migrant cultivation should be directed into areas of seasoned secondary forest, of which 2 billion acres (800 million ha) of fallow secondary growth exist globally.

Although there is need for much additional research in this area, it has been shown that shifting agriculture is not significantly less stable on secondary forest than on primary forest provided the fallow period is long enough. Tests in Amazônia suggest that 14–21 years fallow is sufficient to regenerate soil fertility. Conversely, return to short-fallow secondary growth is unproductive, and can permanently incapacitate the land.

It is ironic that while virgin tropical forest is being depleted by swidden agriculturists, there exists an astounding 591 million acres (239 million ha) of fallow or previously cut closed-canopy forest, much of this standing as mature secondary growth, ripe for agricultural use or reuse.

*▲ The incandescent coral tree (*Erythrina sp.) *seen here in the Central Valley of Costa Rica, probably inspired the intermixing of food crops and such nitrogen-fixing species. The tree is a deciduous legume, often used as a shade tree in coffee plantations, and its ability to fix nitrogen at up to 40 kilograms per hectare per year makes an invaluable contribution to sustained productivity.*

UNTAPPED POTENTIALS FOR AGRICULTURE

Bamboo culture in much of the tropics has been largely ignored, yet there is evidence that would recommend it strongly. Moso bamboo (*Phyllostachys edulis*), for instance, has long been a staff of agriculture in China, where 5 million acres (2 million ha) are planted. It is surprising then that it is extremely scarce outside China and Japan. The fastest-growing of the bamboos, it reaches 80 feet (24 m) in height and 7.5 inches (19 cm) in diameter. Its reputation as timber, pulp, and splitwood is second to none, as is the quality of its edible shoots. Among its greatest assets, however, is Moso's tolerance, perhaps almost preference, for very poor red clay soils, the curse of tropical forest agriculture. Further, it thrives on deforested mountain slopes, often regarded as wastelands and long discarded as sterile, where it prevents erosion, excludes weeds, and regenerates readily after clear-cutting.

▲ *Bamboos, the world's fastest-growing plants, are an excellent source of building material, pulp, and edible shoots, yet their cultivation is conspicuous by its rarity outside China and Japan.*

▲ *The babaçu palm (Orbignya martiana) is another multiple-use plant that thrives on poor soils. It has great potential as a plantation tree and as a shade tree in agroforestry mixed-planting systems.*

The remarkable babaçu palm (*Orbignya martiana*) is so versatile that its fruit yields oil (more per acre than any plant ever measured), feed and fertilizer cake, flour, charcoal, methyl alcohol, tar, and acetic acid. Some palms have yielded up to half a ton of fruits per year. It is noteworthy that its seeds can simply be strewn in degraded areas and they will sprout and grow so effectively that as they mature it is difficult to clear them, even with fire and machete! The huge fronds are harvested for an inexhaustible source of coal-like fuel. This palm's industrial potential appears unlimited, yet it is still all but unknown outside its wild range in Amazônia.

Intensifying Productivity

As yet we have seen no one single answer to the problem of extending the productivity of the slash-and-burner's plot. Research directed in this area, however, has been fruitful. The answers will no doubt lie in combinations of techniques tailored to the needs of specific locations. But one thing is certain: they will be far removed from the old regimen of corn and cassava.

Nitrogen depletion, we know, is one of the major constraints on sustained agriculture. It is no surprise then to find that nitrogen-fixing plants are a major feature in many productivity-enriching schemes. So generous are the amounts of nitrogen fixed from the air and made available to crops by certain legumes, that trials in Rwanda (*Project Agro-Pastoral de Nyabisindu*) using *Crotalaria* spp., *Tephrosia vogelii,* and *Cajanus cajanas* as a legume fallow, incorporated at 10 months, have increased maize yields more than four times compared to control plots with no addition of fertilizers.

It will be obvious to any home gardener that the addition of the legume crop mulch not only enriches the soil but also improves soil stability, water retention, absorption, and access to air. These are all high priorities, none of which can be acquired through use of chemical fertilizers.

It will be very difficult for those readers in the southeastern United States, and other areas afflicted by the fiercely aggressive kudzu vine (*Pueraria* spp.), to appreciate that a tropical variety is used as an effective ground-covering, nitrogen-fixing legume and intentionally planted with crops such as plantain (*Plantago* spp.). Additionally, it has been used successfully as forage for pigs and other livestock in tests conducted in Progresso, Panama.

Near the Brazilian Amazonian town of Tomé-Açu, researchers are studying the surprisingly successful sustained agriculture of a Japanese community, the Nissei Cooperative, which has farmed there for more than half a century. Seemingly, these people have succeeded under the adverse conditions that most commonly result in short-life, traditional slash-and-burn agriculture. Their highly intensive system first employs quick-growing rice, cotton, and beans, which are then integrated with moderate-lived perennial vines such as passion fruit (*Passiflora edulis*) and black pepper (*Piper nigrum*). These are then followed by trees planted for fruit and latex, and on the trees are grown epiphytes such as vanilla bean orchid (*Vanilla fragrans*). So intensively frugal is their methodology that the residue from the black pepper processing is applied to the garden as an insect control. More than any other single factor, this colony's attitude, attributing immeasurably high value to a given plot of land (as in their homeland, where it is the scarcest of commodities), has given rise to a highly productive, labor-intensive (70 man-days per hectare per year go to weeding alone) form of sustained agriculture. This form has succeeded in sustaining an income of U.S.$358 per acre (U.S.$885 per ha) or an average of U.S.$1,700 annually per year per family, equaling some U.S.$5 million per year for the community of some 280 families (Subler and Uhl 1990).

Most slash-and-burn cultivators, however, expect maximum returns for a minimum amount of effort, and so move on to greener pastures (virgin forest) as soon as more effort is required. This is not to say that the swidden agriculturist's life is an easy one, or that he is essentially slovenly. Quite the contrary: these people are among the world's hardest working. Indeed, an FAO study reveals that it takes an average of 86 man-days to fell and burn each hectare of climax forest. The gross waste of the biomass is simply inherent in swidden agriculture, the method of long-standing habit. It incorporates not a single modern agricultural principle or advantage. Slash-and-burn agriculture supports only a paltry 7 persons per square kilometer (0.39 sq mi). Compare this to successful areas of permanent cultivation such as the Tonkin Delta, which supports 354 times as many people per square kilometer without putting excessive pressure on the land.

Edible Giants and Miniatures

There is every reason to expect that as investigations continue into innovative crops to complement the impoverished selections available to swidden agriculturists, the developed world's limited selection of about 20 crops on which we depend will also expand.

From the Asian tropics comes the surprising giant wax gourd (*Benincasa hispida*), which holds great promise in upgrading tropical field production. It grows so fast (1 inch [2.5 cm] every three hours at peak) that four crops yearly can be achieved. When mature, the gourd weighs 77 pounds (35 kg) and measures

▲ *Biointensive gardening systems in the Philippines achieve high levels of sustained productivity on home plots of only 540 square feet (50 sq m). All debris is composted. Crop diversity and close planting helps to reduce the spread of weeds, and the roots of plants that have been removed are left in the ground to add humus.*

▲ *Kudzu (*Pueraria* spp.), a prolific weed outside the tropics, is used in tropical sustained agricultural tests as ground cover, to suppress other invasive plants to protect the soil, and as a source of nitrogen and nutritious animal fodder.*

more than 6.5 feet (2 m) long by more than a yard (1 m) in diameter. Its juicy pulp can be eaten at any stage of development, and this mammoth vegetable can be stored for a year, even in the humid tropics, thanks to its thick, protective skin.

Experiments show that giant kelp (*Macrocystis pyrifera*) may have growth rates of up to 3 feet (0.9 m) per day. Farmers use this alga as fodder for goats, sheep, and other stock, but palatable varieties can also be grown for human consumption as anyone fortunate enough to have sampled Japanese seaweed soup or seaweed-wrapped sushi can testify. It is also lauded nutritionally. *Principes*, the Journal of the International Palm Society, reports a recent hybrid Indonesian coconut palm (*Cocos nucifera*) that promises to quadruple nut production.

China has made other innovative and practical strides. Azolla (*Azolla* sp.), a floating aquatic fern, reacts symbiotically with a blue-green alga (*Anabaena azollae*) which resides in the fern's leaf cavity, where it fixes atmospheric nitrogen. The Chinese grow 3.5 million acres (1.4 million ha) of *Azolla*, which produce the annual equivalent of at least 100,000 tons of nitrogen fertilizer. The fern is then plowed into rice fields. By this method alone the Chinese have increased their rice yields by 158 percent!

When the conquistadores first came to Mexico, they found the Aztecs using a blue-green alga as their main source of protein. Fully 60 to 70 percent of its bulk is high-caliber protein, and it flourishes in saline, even alkaline, water, producing food in arid lands unsuitable for other agriculture. A mere 2.47 acres (1 ha) can yield 187 pounds (85 kg) of protein a day. Until recently the alga (*Spirulina platensis*) was apparently used in modern times only by villagers around Lake Chad in Africa.

Plant geneticists are working on a strain that will tolerate magnesium. *Spirulina* could then be grown in seawater, a development that could have a significant impact on world hunger. I have found great advocacy among nutritionists for supplementing the diets of sub-Saharan drought-famine victims with *Spirulina* where there was no cultural resistance to its consumption. The plant extract was also administered as a "vitamin" supplement with considerable success.

Of special note in this context is the winged bean (*Psophocarpus tetragonolobus*), whose beans, leaves, shoots, tendrils, and buds are among the world's richest sources of protein, amino acids, and vitamin A. The plant, therefore, has great potential to save the eyesight of multitudes of malnourished developing-world children. Furthermore, the bean's enlarged tuber is

▼ *A popular variation on the taungya method of cultivation uses coconut palms* (Cocos nucifera) *as shade trees and producers in their own right. For up to eight years, space permits the planting of annual or short-term perennial crops; from eight to 25 years the palm cover dominates to the exclusion of herb or shrub species; but from 25 years onward the high elevation of the canopy again allows understory species such as cocoa* (Theobroma cacao) *to grow.*

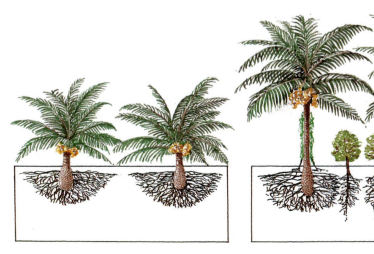

not only protein-rich and extremely tasty, but is also of higher food value than the common potato, sweet potato, or manioc.

Do As the Lacandon Do

An example of a semi-archaic people who engage in agriculture as well as hunting and gathering are the Lacandon Indians of the Mexican Chiapas Forest. On a single hectare they plant up to 80 food and raw material crops. In addition, they ply the nearby forest for as many as 100 varieties of wild fruit and other foods, 20 species of fish, six varieties of turtle, three types of frog, two species of crocodile, two kinds of crab, three types of crayfish, and two species of snail. And this is by no means all the (renewable) resources they exploit.

Known as *milpa* gardens, the Lacandons' 1.2-acre (0.5-ha) plots of intensely managed land reportedly produce a quarter metric ton of corn and an equal weight of root and tree crops annually. The rich plots last five to seven years (up to 300 percent longer than less intensive swidden plots) so that a single farmer may need only clear as little as 25 acres (10 ha) in his lifetime. In addition, as these diverse farm plots are left to fallow, the vegetation that takes over will contain many plants attractive to animals, thus creating an agriculturally based game farm of sorts which will continue to supplement the nearby farmer.

The very antithesis of the diverse Lacandon method of land use is the conversion of tropical forest to cattle pasture which, on a like-size plot to our milpa

▲ *Where cultivable land is scarce, as here in tropical China, there is a growing emphasis at community and government level on crop intensification, increased crop diversity, natural pest control, terracing, and other measures to improve land husbandry and maximize productivity.*

above, will produce less than 9 pounds (4 kg) of beef. Such enterprises are typified by a small labor force and large landholdings, displacing peasant farmers to wilderness areas and so perpetuating destructive deforestation practices.

Small landholdings yield far higher returns than larger farms, as farming families have all hands in the field maximizing production. This is especially so in the tropics. Even so, an unsponsored study covering 83 countries found that roughly 3 percent of landowners control 79 percent of the farmland. These inequities call for cutbacks in cattle-enterprise credit (a welcome development in Brazil) and an imposed ceiling on the size of landholdings.

MORE EFFICIENT ANIMAL HUSBANDRY

No agricultural application produces less sustenance per unit area than cattle grazing. A Cornell University study shows that a switch in emphasis from beef to chicken production would produce a 50 percent saving in energy. Further, if American beef production shifted from grain to grass feed, a saving of 135 million tons of grain a year valued at U.S.$20 billion could be realized; enough to feed the world's starving peoples and take pressure off the virgin tropical forests while simultaneously realizing a 50 percent energy saving. In addition, if 50 percent of our animal protein were supplemented by plant protein (as is widely advised for cardiovascular fitness) 50 percent in energy could be saved in its production as well. The use of tariffs to raise the price of imported beef is an obvious device at our disposal. As cattle ranching is unlikely to completely disappear from the Amazon scene, where it comprises 15 percent of smallholder land area and 30 percent of large, there is an environmental trade-off to switching from beef production to intensified dairy production, which relies on smaller herds and a more stable market. This has particular merit for water buffalo as its milk contains 8 percent fat, compared to 3 percent for zebu cattle—if water buffalo can indeed be forced out of sensitive aquatic habitats, a difficult task given its instinctive affinity for water.

Higher yields than those resulting from cattle grazing can also be realized by the use of multispecies forage, the food supply regime responsible for the high wildlife-carrying capacity of African savannas. In this uniquely

▶ The perilous decline of wild crocodile populations through hunting and habitat destruction gave birth to the concept of the crocodile farm. In the early 1960s, conservation laws and natural scarcity forced up the price of skins, making such farms commercially viable. Now, the farms produce meat and skins for sale, and many also breed rare species for return to the wild.

biologically sound regimen, nature is mimicked by incorporating pigs, chickens, ducks, fish, and domesticated native wildlife such as tapirs (*Tapirus* spp.), deer (*Cervinae*), crocodiles (*Crocodylus* spp.), banteng (*Bos banteng*), capybaras (*Hydrochoerus hydrochaeris*), and others. By taking advantage of the full spectrum of sustainable aquatic and terrestrial fodder and live feed, an increase in production of these delicacies can be achieved that will far outstrip its antithesis, the concentration on cattle and its rapidly depreciating food source.

Manure from the livestock will provide the fertilizer that is largely lacking in primitive agriculture, and this can be a major factor in increasing the life span of the farmer's plot many times over. Introduction of dry-season grasses can boost the life of the plot even further. An added bonus is that the domestication of forest animals can relieve the pressure of overhunting of these species in the wild.

In Panama, considerable success with green iguana (*Iguana iguana*) ranching provides a traditionally prized food and valuable skins for export. Iguanas are raised in a variety of trees that are also useful to the farmers, who harvest the fruit while the lizards eat the leaves. Early reproduction, the fast growth rate, and the iguana's tendency to remain around the release area commend this program. By cultivating a breeding stock, incubating the eggs, and protecting the hatchlings at their young, vulnerable stage before releasing them into the foraging area, iguanas can yield some 10 times as much meat as cattle on the same land area. It produces impressive results in undisturbed forest as well.

INTENSIFIED AGROFORESTRY— THE LINCHPIN OF SUSTAINED DEVELOPMENT

While the discipline of agroforestry has been studied in depth for only several decades, we may now realistically appraise the outstanding benefits that await the swidden agriculturist should he choose to intensify his production capacities and remain on his plot. This, against the very real and considerable losses he suffers annually in labor, produce, and fertility as he continues the rote habit of migrant cultivation.

While researching the comparative benefits of the new, integrated, agricultural strategy, I was greatly encouraged by the many researchers in diverse disciplines who contributed their data, as the comparative analysis (see chart pages 184–87) so clearly illuminates for decision makers the efficacy of sustained versus migrant cultivation/cattle production.

We are advised that as a migrant cultivator moves into 10- to 20-year fallow secondary forest with nonmotorized hand tools (steel axes, machetes, etc.) he will expend 50 man-days (400 man-hours) felling, preparing slash for torching, and burning 2.47 acres (1 ha). In primary forest the labor rises to 86 man-days, or 688 man-hours. The entire process, including planting and harvesting, will require 1,588 hours. This is no small expenditure of energy and is consistent for most grain-crop annuals, whether corn (*Zea mays*) or rice (*Oryza* spp.).

With even a most simplified agroforestry plot, one incorporating only corn and *Leucaena leucocephala* for its nitrogen-fixing capacities and fuelwood, corn production was 4,400 pounds (2,000 kg) per hectare. Corn production for the first year was the same for the slashed-and-burned plot,

The following measures would relieve the tropical forests of Brazil from significant pressures from cattle ranching. As they are either administrative or downsizing in public expenditures, they can be implemented at neutral costs or at a saving to the Brazilian government.

1. *Removing pasture establishment as an "improvement" (benfeitoria) for establishing land tenure claims.*
2. *Taxing pasture on an increasing scale as it degrades.*
3. *Taxing beef (from both cattle and water buffalo) over other livestock.*
4. *Tax relief when cattle or water buffalo are used for dairy production.*
5. *Increase taxes on land sale profits that fuel cattle pasture conversion.*
6. *Clarify and amend the interpretation of the present government decree regarding disengagement of pasture incentives and subsidies for all projects, notably including more than 300 Superintendency for the Development of Amazônia (SUDAM) projects already approved.*
7. *Instill tax incentives for agroforestry which will promote long-term occupation of land and discourage land speculation—the principal rationale for conversion of forest to pasture.*
8. *Scale down the road-building trend into remote Amazônia which results in arteries for forest conversion to cattle pasture and slash-and-burn agriculture.*

▲ *A major step toward sustained productivity can be achieved by planting* Leucaena leucocephala *in garden plots. This fast-growing tree produces huge amounts of fuelwood, pulpwood, timber, animal fodder from its foliage, and human food in the form of pods, young leaves, and seeds. At the same time it provides good soil erosion control, shade, and crop protection. Just as important, this legume is also a prodigious fixer of atmospheric nitrogen.*

but soil loss was 20 tons per hectare for the short-cycle shifting cultivation while it was only half that for year one on the nonintensive agroforestry plot. Year two sees production on the shifting plot drop to 2,700 pounds (1,225 kg) as soil loss increases to 25 tons per hectare per year, the last year it will marginally pay to farm the plot. But here the *Leucaena* kicks in for the agroforester: his soil loss is reduced to 2 tons per hectare per year while his plot is producing 3,400 pounds (1,542 kg) of corn. By year three the migrant is back to square one with some 1,588 man-hours of labor, cutting primary forest, while our agroforester has frugally gone to between 5 and 8 hectares of surrounding forest for renewable supplies of mulch, replacing the phosphorus and other essential nutrients his corn crop has removed. In addition, his *Leucaena* now produces 4,400 pounds (2,000 kg) of wood, cut 3 inches (8 cm) above the ground to induce further sprouting for fuelwood, and an additional 5,500 pounds (2,500 kg) of foliage for mulch, which will give a net return of 500 pounds (227 kg) of nitrogen for soil enrichment. At the same time, his soil loss is only 0.75 tons per hectare per year. He can maintain this production of corn and *Leucaena* into a 25-year horizon with labor dropping to 300 man-hours per year.

Organization for Tropical Studies president, dendrologist Gary Hartshorn, counsels that through new shoot growth, the prudent farmer can expect to continue to crop the original level of harvest of *Leucaena* indefinitely. Even greater efficiency, in terms of labor, soil loss, and production, is realized by *intensifying*, that is, by incorporating, in a simplified example, corn, papaya, and oranges, which produce into perhaps the 40th year, and laurel trees (*Cordia alliodora*) as a timber cash crop. A look at the chart on pages 184–87 shows labor dropping to 40 man-hours per year, as the high labor factor of weeding is now markedly minimized, soil loss is down to 0.3 tons per hectare per year as the mulch and crop protect the soil, and income increases to U.S.$2,690 per hectare, more than 13 times the migrant's best year. As a benchmark, cattle produce U.S.$47 per hectare per year. Pedro Sanchez, director general of the International Centre for Research in Agroforestry (ICRAF) states that such systems also play an important role in keeping carbon in the terrestrial ecosystem and out of the atmosphere. Primary forest sequesters 250 metric tons of carbon per hectare, while crops and pasture sequester only 60 metric tons. Yet agroforests only 10 years old sequester 160 metric tons, or two-thirds the amount of primary forest (ICRAF 1997). We now move to a facet of intensification that can inject a true measure of prosperity.

The Aquaculture Boom—the Ultimate Protein Source

Given human nature, attempts to change traditional food production systems to more intensified methods often meet with resistance. But if it can be demonstrated that a new plant or technique will provide a bounty of produce, especially with less physical effort, it is likely to take hold in peasant agriculture, especially if agricultural extension services are provided during the transition period. Families observe their uncles' successes and abundance of produce, and will be quick to copy any profitable innovation.

Aquaculture of fish is possibly the premier method we can employ to keep the "shifted cultivator" grounded on his plot. When first I reported on the extraordinary merits of fish farming in the first edition, the technology was still in its infancy, especially so in the developing tropics. I can now say it has grown enormously. To cite only the modest efforts of my organization, Africa Tomorrow, and CARE, we now see tens of thousands of villagers fed on results of aquaculture projects in the tropics, but the global picture is inspiring. (Minimal yet sufficient water supply is essential throughout the year.)

Aquaculture output, growing at 11 percent per year over the past decade, has become the fastest-growing sector of the world food economy. Climbing from 13 million tons of fish produced in 1990 to 31 million tons in 1998, fish farming is actually poised to overtake cattle ranching as a food source globally within a decade. (It presently accounts for 20 percent of all fish and shellfish production.) That figure will undoubtedly rise as the impact of overfishing and environmental damage to both oceans and freshwater are felt. Another advantage in aquaculture is that cattle require some 7 kilograms of grain, compared with only 2 kilograms for fish to add 1 kilogram of live weight. China, by far the world's leading producer, accounts for 57 percent of the world's farmed fish production, dominated by low-tech ponds; India is second, at 9 percent in 1994, and projections indicate that global production will double by 2010. This is particularly welcome as FAO statistics show that some 60 percent of the world's 200 commercial fish stocks are either virtually gone or severely depleted. Nearly 25 percent of all marine life caught yearly—30 million tons—is thrown back into the sea dead or dying, unmarketable, or a maimed by-product caught in choking-line or gill nets.

In what was then Zaire, during a tour of inspection of tilapia ponds instituted by the Peace Corps, parades were held honoring Loret Miller-Ruppe, the Corps' director. Cloth tilapia flags were flown on the streets signifying the people's enthusiasm for this new source of protein.

In China, the Philippines, India, and Togo, synergistic interactions have increased farm production markedly. There, swine and chicken enclosures are constructed directly over fish ponds so that animal wastes drop directly through a grated floor. In this intensified system, manure is also collected and placed in chambers where anaerobic fermentation produces methane gas which, in turn, is employed to heat buildings, produce light, and, of particular merit in the tropics, power refrigerators. The solid sludge that remains in the biogas reactor, as it is called, is used in the fields as fertilizer. The liquid residue (*caldo*) is used in the cultivation of a nitrogen-fixing alga that, in turn, produces a protein-rich feed for the swine and poultry—thus completing a highly efficient closed cycle of productivity.

Integrated Agroforestry and Aquaculture

The International Center for Aquaculture at Auburn University reports compelling results following more than five years of fish-culture projects in Rwanda, Jamaica, Panama, and Guatemala.

Ponds were hand dug with an average water area of 4 ares (1 are is 119,599 square yards, or 0.04 ha) in Rwanda and 2,200 square feet (204 sq m) in Guatemala. The smaller pond is more feasible for family construction: larger ponds are often communal in construction and operation, involving many families. The former required 53 man-days (eight-hour days), less than that required to fell and burn a hectare of forest. Clay soils serve excellently. In many cases, ponds can be glayed, a process promoting algal growth in water. This involves draining the pond and allowing the algae to seal the surface and dry in. Given the edge-effect of many smaller-sized ponds, leading to enriched crop planting on the

It is impossible to overstate the potential of fisheries combined with agriculture as a means of improving the diet and economic well-being of forest people, and of simultaneously stabilizing migrant populations and removing a major cause of deforestation. Carp fisheries in India ▲▲, like the tilapia farms of Panama ▲, can add U.S.$7,985 per hectare per year to family incomes.

SHARE OF GLOBAL AQUACULTURE PRODUCTION, 1994	
Country	Percent Share of Global Production
China	57
India	9
Japan	4
Indonesia	4
Thailand	3
United States	2
Philippines	2
Korea, Republic of	2
Other countries	17

levees, and proportionately superior tilapia production, the smaller size is the more logical family choice. Pond maintenance requires some 488 man-hours per year and involves putting in crop residues and manures, culling fish, etc. (For consistency, we extrapolate production figures for a 1-hectare pond.) Extension services—important to the program's success—supply seed fish, often the highly prolific and successful tilapia (*Tilapia* spp.), and expertise. One of the tilapia's preferred foods, aside from algae, is termites, an especially abundant commodity in the forest. Three nests a week of high-protein termites are fed to the fish, which also eat a great variety of vegetable matter. The fish usually prosper and multiply—as do the farmers. Especially significant is the strong tendency of peasants to remain on the land after investing their labor in pond construction, and after banking marketable reserves of fish protein. This, in turn, encourages the acceptance—even the pursuit—of more such intensive methods of farm plot cultivation and animal husbandry.

For Auburn, fish (*T. nilotica*) production was 1,760–2,200 pounds per acre per year (2,000–2,500 kg/ha/yr) and exceeded 3,500 pounds per acre per year (4,000 kg/ha/yr), on only moderately intensified ponds in Guatemala. Those incorporated only some 20 chickens over a 2,200-square-foot (200-sq-m) pond. Manure and chicken feed (animal and/or green) that subsequently fall into the pond increase production of plankton, which is the natural food of tilapia. (Yields in the range of 7,055–8,800 pounds per acre per year [8,000–10,000 kg/ha/yr] were reported in the Jamaica project when the fish were fed rice, wheat, or chicken meal. However, for our purposes we will keep with the easily affordable start-up pond scenario without extensive feeding, even though the more capital-intensive method has a premium return on investment.) It is an indication of the project's success that by the end of five years, Auburn reports 2,365 ponds were operating, serving more than 7,000 Rwandan families and producing 22 tons of marketable fish during that year. In addition, farmers were growing crops on pond levees, benefiting not only from pond moisture during the dry seasons but also by applying the enriching pond mud to planting beds, and so also increasing traditional crop yields.

Spread over 25 years (although ponds dug 50 years ago are still quite operable), the net present value of the return on the investment was 21,197 FRW (Rwandan monetary unit) (U.S.$258). The "average" farm family has an income of 55,441 FRW (U.S.$676), of which coffee, the universal crop, contributes 4,023 FRW (U.S.$49). While the net returns for fish were negative for the first two years, returns exceeded costs for years 3 to 25. In fact, the net benefit investment ratio was 17:1 (1:0 is considered acceptable). Chinese researchers are developing an inexpensive protein supplement based on yeast that substitutes for more than half the fishmeal in certain aquaculture feed preparations. The success of tilapia fish farming is increasingly applauded yet, as tilapia is an exotic species, its escape into wild habitat has caused havoc with many indigenous species. Every effort must be made to either prevent its escape or replace it with native species of similar merit such as the delicious tambaqui (*Colossoma macropomum*) of the Amazon Basin. With this caveat duly noted, a strain of tilapia has been bred that grows 60 percent faster with a higher survival rate than the common species.

We note that gross returns per acre are almost five times that for beans and almost twice that for rice production. Further, fish farming enjoys a harvest every 15 weeks and has no defined season, so harvests can be planned to coincide with periods of low crop productivity. In the grand plan to stabilize

agriculture and improve income/nutrition in the tropical developing world, fish in aquaculture admirably succeeds in injecting cheap, high-quality protein where the propensity did not previously exist. The price of fish is relatively high, yet compares favorably when measured against other protein sources; and while fish comprises 35 percent protein, beef comprises only 23 percent.

At this point we can readily appreciate the security and stability that eludes the migrant cultivator not presented with these alternatives. Should we now fine-tune such an operation and introduce pigs, goats, turtles, and so on, we see just how little there is to recommend the slash-and-burn methods of the migrant farmer.

A slightly different turn on agroforestry is the technique known as *alley cropping*, which offers a practical alternative to slash-and-burn. This method leaves rows of forest trees standing as hedgerows between rows of agricultural crops. The trees protect the soil from erosion and provide a rain of nutritious leaf litter which suppresses weeds, serves to lower soil temperature, reduces evaporation, provides fuelwood, and serves as supports for vine crops.

In addition, as trees along the hedgerow mature, they may be judiciously sold, allowing seedlings to develop and replace them. This all adds up to the

▲ *Quite unlike the illusory fertility of tropical forest soils, floodplains such as that of the Amazon sustain a large biomass of aquatic life, especially fish. This is the most important source of animal protein for local, rural, and urban populations. There is cause for concern, however, that deforestation, consequent silting of rivers, overfishing, and the building of dams are depleting this otherwise infinitely renewable food resource.*

TOWARD SUSTAINED PRODUCTIVITY

While sustained productivity is widely recognized as environmentally sound and desirable, this comparative chart demonstrates that there is every reason for the migrant cultivator to adopt these new technologies entirely on their own merit. Sustained extraction of rubber, nuts, fruit, and game can yield U.S.$1,000 per hectare per year without degrading the forest, while fish, turtle, and game farming can produce 20 times the income with only minimal disturbance. By contrast, cattle ranching in tropical forest regions yields a meager U.S.$47 per hectare per year. (See Appendix 3.)

TYPE OF AGRICULTURAL ACTIVITY Showing labor input (man-hours/ha/year), quantity, and value of produce (lbs/ha/year; U.S.$/ha/year), and soil loss (tons/ha/year).	YEAR 1	YEAR 2	YEAR 3	YEAR 4	YEAR 5	YEAR 6
SHORT-CYCLE SHIFTING CULTIVATION Growing corn only, on 1-ha plots cleared in primary forest.				Plot abandoned at end of year 2: cycle then		
Labor (man-hours/ha/yr) 688 hours to clear new plot every 2 years, plus 900 hours annual input of labor on planting, weeding, and harvesting.	1,588	900	1,588	900	1,588	900
Quantity of corn produced (lbs/ha/yr)	4,400	2,700	4,400	2,700	4,400	2,700
Value of corn produced (U.S.$/ha/yr)	200	123	200	123	200	123
Soil loss (tons/ha/yr)	20	25	20	25	20	25
NONINTENSIVE AGROFORESTRY Growing corn and *Leucaena* on 1-ha plot (using renewable natural fertilizer—manure, mulch, and slash).						
Total labor (man-hours/ha/yr)	1,650	700	500	400	300	300
Quantity of corn produced (lbs/ha/yr)	4,400	3,400	4,000	4,400	4,400	4,400
Value of corn produced (U.S.$/ha/yr)	200	155	182	200	200	200
Quantity of *Leucaena* produced (lbs/ha/yr). (From year 3 onward = 4,400 lb of wood for fuel, plus 5,500 lb of foliage for mulch.)	0	4,000	9,900	9,900	9,900	9,900
Net return of nitrogen to the soil (lbs/ha/yr)	0	1,000	1,500	1,500	1,500	1,500
Soil loss (tons/ha/yr)	10.0	2.0	0.75	0.70	0.60	0.40
PARTIALLY INTENSIFIED AGROFORESTRY Growing corn in year 1, papaya in years 1-3, and oranges in years 1-25+. Laurel trees (*Cordia alliodora*) utilized to best advantage with shade-tolerant perennials, for mulch, poles, fuelwood, and eventual sale for timber.						
Total labor for clearing (man-hours/ha/yr), Amortized over 5 years to conserve soil.	1,088	1,000	700	600	500	100
Value of laurel crop (U.S.$/ha/yr). Trimmings taken in years 6–12; mature trees cut for sale in years 18 onward.	0	0	0	0	0	100
Value of crops (U.S.$/ha/yr): Corn (year 1), papaya (years 2/3), oranges (years 3–25+)	150	1,000	1,000	270	330	465
Soil loss (tons/ha/yr)	1.00	0.40	0.30	0.29	0.25	0.20
CATTLE PASTURE On manually cleared 7 percent slopes in primary forest.						
Labor (man-hours/ha/yr)	928	50	50	50	50	50
Live-weight cattle production (kg/ha/yr)	50	50	50	43	37	16
Value of cattle production (U.S.$/ha/yr)	47	47	47	40	35	15
Soil loss (tons/ha/yr)	20	5	5	5	5	5

Multispecies agroforestry
Shifting cultivation requiring 1,588 man-hours per hectare per year yields only U.S.$200 in the best (first) year of its two-year cycle, and the price is a huge drop in soil fertility. Partially intensified agroforestry can yield U.S.$2,690 a year, with labor falling to only 40 man-hours per hectare per year and topsoil loss no greater than in the natural forest. When fish aquaculture is added, formerly migrant cultivators are already moving from mere subsistence toward comparative affluence—with no detrimental impact on the forest.

YEARS 7/8	YEARS 9/10	YEARS 11/12	YEARS 13/14	YEARS 15/16	YEARS 17/18	YEAR 19	YEAR 20	YEAR 21	YEAR 22	YEAR 23	YEAR 24	YEAR 25

repeated on new primary forest plot.

YEARS 7/8	YEARS 9/10	YEARS 11/12	YEARS 13/14	YEARS 15/16	YEARS 17/18	YEAR 19	YEAR 20	YEAR 21	YEAR 22	YEAR 23	YEAR 24	YEAR 25
1,588 / 900	1,588 / 900	1,588 / 900	1,588 / 900	1,588 / 900	1,588 / 900	1,588	900	1,588	900	1,588	900	1,588
4,400 / 2,700	4,400 / 2,700	4,400 / 2,700	4,400 / 2,700	4,400 / 2,700	4,400 / 2,700	4,400	2,700	4,400	2,700	4,400	2,700	4,400
200 / 123	200 / 123	200 / 123	200 / 123	200 / 123	200 / 123	200	123	200	123	200	123	200
20 / 25	20 / 25	20 / 25	20 / 25	20 / 25	20 / 25	20	25	20	25	20	25	20

YEARS 7/8	YEARS 9/10	YEARS 11/12	YEARS 13/14	YEARS 15/16	YEARS 17/18	YEAR 19	YEAR 20	YEAR 21	YEAR 22	YEAR 23	YEAR 24	YEAR 25
300	300	300	300	300	300	300	300	300	300	300	300	300
4,400	4,400	4,400	4,400	4,400	4,400	4,400	4,400	4,400	4,400	4,400	4,400	4,400
200	200	200	200	200	200	200	200	200	200	200	200	200
9,900	9,900	9,900	9,900	9,900	9,900	9,900	9,900	9,900	9,900	9,900	9,900	9,900
1,500	1,500	1,500	1,500	1,500	1,500	1,500	1,500	1,500	1,500	1,500	1,500	1,500
0.30	0.20	0.20	0.20	0.20	0.20	0.20	0.20	0.20	0.20	0.20	0.20	0.20

YEARS 7/8	YEARS 9/10	YEARS 11/12	YEARS 13/14	YEARS 15/16	YEARS 17/18	YEAR 19	YEAR 20	YEAR 21	YEAR 22	YEAR 23	YEAR 24	YEAR 25
90	80	70	60	50	40	40	40	40	40	40	40	40
400	700	900	0	0	1,000	1,200	1,300	1,400	1,500	1,600	1,700	1,700
780	990	990	990	990	990	990	990	990	990	990	990	990
0.15	0.12	0.10	0.09	0.08	0.07	0.05	0.04	0.03	0.03	0.03	0.03	0.03

Pasture abandoned as no longer productive and infested with toxic weeds.

TYPE OF AGRICULTURAL ACTIVITY Showing labor input (man-hours/ha/year), quantity, and value of produce (lbs/ha/year; $US/ha/year), and soil loss (tons/ha/year).	YEAR 1	YEAR 2	YEAR 3	YEAR 4	YEAR 5	YEAR 6

UNSUSTAINED LOGGING
One-time fee paid to colonist by logging company: no replanting undertaken.

	YEAR 1	YEAR 2	YEAR 3	YEAR 4	YEAR 5	YEAR 6
Value ($US/ha)	78					
Soil loss (tons/ha/yr)	5.0	1.0	0.5	0.1	0.05	0.03

TERRACED CULTIVATION
Growing corn on 40% slopes in primary forest on eastern Andean foothills.

	YEAR 1	YEAR 2	YEAR 3	YEAR 4	YEAR 5	YEAR 6
Labor (man-hours/ha/yr) 688 hours to clear forest cover, plus 500 to build terraces (year 1); then annual input of 800 hours cultivation labor and 30 hours terrace maintenance.	1,988	830	830	830	830	830
Value of corn produced ($US/ha/yr)	190	190	190	190	190	190
Soil loss (tons/ha/yr)	2.0	1.0	0.6	0.6	0.6	0.6

NONTERRACED CULTIVATION
Growing corn on 40% slopes in primary forest on eastern Andean foothills.

	YEAR 1	YEAR 2	YEAR 3	YEAR 4	YEAR 5	YEAR 6
Labor (man-hours/ha/yr) 688 hours to clear forest cover (year 1); plus 800 hours cultivation labor in years 1 and 2. Plot then abandoned.	1,488	800	Plot abandoned at end of year 2:			
Value of corn produced ($US/ha/yr)	170	80				
Soil loss (tons/ha/yr)	200	160	80	50	25	20

FISH AQUACULTURE (IN ASSOCIATION WITH AGROFORESTRY)
Area of pond is 4 ares (0.04 ha), but for ease of comparison production figures are given per hectare.

	YEAR 1	YEAR 2	YEAR 3	YEAR 4	YEAR 5	YEAR 6
Labor (man-hours) 500 hours to dig, prepare, and stock pond (year 1); then 488 hours annual labor input on pond maintenance, and feeding and harvesting the fish.	988	488	488	488	488	488
Quantity of fish produced (lbs/ha/yr)	1,144	2,200	4,500	5,500	7,000	8,800
Value of fish produced ($US/ha/yr)	0	0	4,082	4,990	6,350	7,985

SUSTAINED EXTRACTION FROM PRIMARY FOREST

		YEAR 1	YEAR 2	YEAR 3	YEAR 4	YEAR 5	YEAR 6
Fruits, nuts, etc.	Labor (man-hours/ha/yr)	560	560	560	560	560	560
	Value ($US/ha/yr)	650	650	650	650	650	650
Latex collection	Labor (man-hours/ha/yr)	63	63	63	63	63	63
	Value ($US/ha/yr)	50	50	50	50	50	50

BUSHMEAT EXTRACTION, FOREST ANIMAL FARMING

		YEAR 1	YEAR 2	YEAR 3	YEAR 4	YEAR 5	YEAR 6
Bushmeat collection	Labor (man-hours/ha/yr)	50	50	50	50	50	50
	Value ($US/ha/yr)	40	40	40	40	40	40
Wild crocodile skins	Labor (man-hours/yr)	220	220	220	220	220	220
	Value ($US/yr)	150	150	150	150	150	150
Capybara farming	Labor (man-hours/ha/yr)	500	500	500	500	500	500
	Value ($US/ha/yr)	0	560	560	560	560	560
Turtle ranching	Labor (man-hours) 500 hours to dig 4-are pond then annual input of 1,200 hours feeding, harvesting. For ease of comparison, all production figures are given per hectare.	1,700	1,200	1,200	1,200	1,200	1,200
	Value ($US/ha/yr)	0	0	600	1,000	1,200	1,400

YEARS 7/8	YEARS 9/10	YEARS 11/12	YEARS 13/14	YEARS 15/16	YEARS 17/18	YEAR 19	YEAR 20	YEAR 21	YEAR 22	YEAR 23	YEAR 24	YEAR 25
0.03	0.03	0.03	0.03	0.03	0.03	0.03	0.03	0.03	0.03	0.03	0.03	0.03
830	830	830	830	830	830	830	830	830	830	830	830	830
190	190	190	190	190	190	190	190	190	190	190	190	190
0.6	0.6	0.6	0.6	0.6	0.6	0.6	0.6	0.6	0.6	0.6	0.6	0.6

land may require 20-100 years fallow to regenerate adequate fertility.

YEARS 7/8	YEARS 9/10	YEARS 11/12	YEARS 13/14	YEARS 15/16	YEARS 17/18	YEAR 19	YEAR 20	YEAR 21	YEAR 22	YEAR 23	YEAR 24	YEAR 25
488	488	488	488	488	488	488	488	488	488	488	488	488
8,800	8,800	8,800	8,800	8,800	8,800	8,800	8,800	8,800	8,800	8,800	8,800	8,800
7,985	7,985	7,985	7,985	7,985	7,985	7,985	7,985	7,985	7,985	7,985	7,985	7,985
560	560	560	560	560	560	560	560	560	560	560	560	560
650	650	650	650	650	650	650	650	650	650	650	650	650
63	63	63	63	63	63	63	63	63	63	63	63	63
50	50	50	50	50	50	50	50	50	50	50	50	50
50	50	50	50	50	50	50	50	50	50	50	50	50
40	40	40	40	40	40	40	40	40	40	40	40	40
220	220	220	220	220	220	220	220	220	220	220	220	220
150	150	150	150	150	150	150	150	150	150	150	150	150
500	500	500	500	500	500	500	500	500	500	500	500	500
560	560	560	560	560	560	560	560	560	560	560	560	560
1,200	1,200	1,200	1,200	1,200	1,200	1,200	1,200	1,200	1,200	1,200	1,200	1,200
1,600	4,000	10,000	20,000	20,000	20,000	20,000	20,000	20,000	20,000	20,000	20,000	20,000

magic words "sustainable development," the ultimate goal in the tropical deforestation arena.

ENCOURAGING SUCCESS STORIES

- In India, due to the creation of the National Wasteland Development Board and reorganization of the Environment and Forestry Ministry, the annual rate of plantation increased to 4.4 million acres (1.8 million ha) and was almost 84 million acres (34 million ha) in total plantations by 2000, with some commendable emphasis on agroforestry (FAO 2000).
- The Republic of Korea is working toward filling every available niche with trees. Slogans such as "Love Trees, Love Your Country" are posted and 20 percent of the national land area is now planted with trees less than 20 years old. Village forestry associations have been established in almost every village. An esprit de corps has succeeded where an order to plant might have failed. Privately held, unproductive hillsides are either donated for use, or 10 percent of the profit, where formerly there was none, goes to the owner. The benefits of availability of wood and profit have boosted the average family's income by 15 percent, and all this money goes directly to the peasant, not to moneylenders, big landholders, or government officials. We can take an important lead from this success in noting that the government provides a 75 percent subsidy to encourage small-scale private forests (90 percent of plantations are on private land) and low, 3 percent interest loans with long repayment periods.
- Support for village woodlots, agroforestry schemes, and environmental rehabilitation has been provided by the World Bank, FAO, USAID, the U.S. State Department, the U.S. Congress, and the Canadian and Swedish governments under project titles such as Forests for Local Community Development.
- During the 1980s sub-Saharan drought, the Treepeople, a southern California conservation group, transported from the United States more than 6,000 appropriate species of fruit trees. In a community effort involving a host of African countries, the trees were planted successfully and are now producing fruit, to the sustenance and delight of their new owners.
- Over 3,500 improved wood stoves were built in Senegal, principally by women: 77 percent were still in use several years later.
- Uganda's logging residues, once wasted, are now converted into charcoal, and the resulting output of charcoal has risen from 200 to 63,700 tons per year.
- In Nigeria, maize production increased from 1,100 pounds (500 kg) to 4,410 pounds (2,000 kg) per 2.47 acres (1 ha) by mulching with nitrogen-fixing *Leucaena* tree leaves. Agroforestry programs in Senegal have increased millet and sorghum production from 1,100 to 2,200 pounds (500 to 1,000 kg) per 2.47 acres (1 ha) by using *Acacia albida* trees in fields.
- Village farmers in Gujarat, India, realizing the extra income to be generated by planting trees for pole production, increased seedling distributions from 17 million to an impressive 200 million plants per year.
- Another social forestry program in Uttar Pradesh, India, far exceeded the program's goals by planting degraded forest areas and farm forests with 8 million seedlings. In the process the scheme employed people for 17 million workdays—including 4 million days for women.

▲ *Private enterprise "bore fruit" in spectacular fashion in 1986 when the U.S. organization Treepeople acquired more than 6,000 surplus fruit trees that would otherwise have been incinerated by American growers and, with freight donated by Pan Am and Cameroon Air, airlifted the trees to Ethiopia, Kenya, Tanzania, and Cameroon. In addition to cropping many tons of fruit, the people of those areas have benefited from the many thousands of new trees propagated from cuttings from the original stock.*

- In parts of Nepal, family income quadrupled after manure sufficient for a second annual crop was amassed by use of increased fodder from planted grasses, and by tethering livestock. The scheme also produced an abundance of fuelwood from multipurpose tree planting.
- One of the most resourceful schemes to date has been established with great success by the Paper Industry Corporation of the Philippines, in conjunction with loans from the World Bank. Farmers rent, say, 25 acres (10 ha) of deforested land through a 75 percent loan; 20 acres (8 ha) are planted in pulp trees and 5 acres (2 ha) are used for food and livestock production. The farmer then receives the entire first year's food production. Trees are grown and sold to the pulp mill after 8 years, providing earnings to tenant farmers of U.S.$2,600 per 2.47 acres (1 ha), an enormous income for these people. While at the same time reducing deforestation considerably, the company can obtain 40 percent of its required pulpwood from the farmers, where previously the Philippines had imported U.S.$30 million worth of paper pulp annually.
- In order to preserve the forest and the chimpanzees of the Gombe National Park against increasing waves of human encroachment, the Jane Goodall Institute, with funding from the European Union, instituted a highly successful program of reforestation, agroforestry, and erosion control, as well as "micro-credit" for groups of women to start sustainable development projects in 27 villages.
- In order to tap into the commitment and energy of young people around the world, Jane Goodall developed the *Roots & Shoots* program: *Roots* creep underground everywhere, making firm foundations; *shoots*, though young and small, in their reach to the bright light break apart stone walls. The stones in this case are overpopulation, deforestation, erosion, desertification, poverty, hunger, pollution, cruelty, and warfare. As of 2001, more than 2,000 *Roots & Shoots* groups are at work in more than 40 countries.

Without minimizing the specter of ongoing forest recession, these stunning successes point perhaps to a ray of hope in the dark jungle of apathy that has dominated development/deforestation until now. As consumptive land use comes increasingly under scrutiny, intensified production methods become first more palatable, then profitable. As proof of this propensity, parks and preserves in tropical moist forest regions worldwide have increased from 2 percent in 1988 to 8 percent in 1999.

ARRESTING AND RECLAIMING ERODED LANDS

We have previously addressed the enormous problems resulting from erosion when tropical forests are removed. Gully erosion, one of the more formidable yet common forms, can remove topsoil immediately and etch a canyon 70 feet (21 m) deep in 50 years in steep, rainy regions such as Nepal.

Such a loss of fertility can be appreciated by looking at the geological history that preceded that 70-foot-deep sterile canyon. Fifty-one years before, a protective forest resided on that slope of·the Himalayas. The mountain range, through the pressures of plate tectonics, grows some 1.5 inches (4 cm) every 10 years. But even as they rise up, ice, frost, and water conspire to wear the mountains down. This natural process in turn serves to transform the parent rock (which contains dramatic ancient seabed fossils) into soil.

It takes, in fact, thousands of years to produce even 0.4 inches (1 cm) of precious soil from such weathering, a painfully slow process. Population pressures accompanied by overgrazing, crude farming, and wood abduction, none on a sustained yield, have resulted in the denuding of slopes at higher and higher elevations.

A manageable equation dictates a single cow or buffalo per person grazing up to four times as much land area as the family cultivates. Present realities, however, show the impact of animal grazing to be much greater—not as a result of greed, but of expediency. Population grows simultaneously with the elimination of fertile areas by the thief called *erosion*. The hungry move further upslope for more fuel, pasture, and garden space, perpetuating the tragedy of lethal flooding in geometric progression for those downslope, all the way from the mountains of Nepal to the plains of India.

As gargantuan as this morass appears it is now quite possible, with concerted and dedicated effort, to reverse the effects of such erosion and reclaim the land in an acceptable time span. Formerly, in Nepal, cost-prohibitive barbed wire was used to protect critical areas containing young trees which would otherwise have been grazed by cattle. Under the present program, people are allowed into the forest, *but not their stock;* the forest grasses are cut and carried back to the cattle as feed. Dung now stays at home where it is used to enrich the fields, increasing the harvest by up to 20 percent.

When the Nepalese-project people and their stock were forcibly kept out of the forest by foresters, the latter became the enemy of both. The compatible-use program, however, has indoctrinated the villagers into a positive, friendly, and productive attitude whereby they too have become

▼ *These meticulously maintained rice terraces in Bali show conservation land-use at its best. On unprotected mountain slopes, soil losses are as high as 300 tons per hectare per year where an acceptable loss rate would be 1 ton per hectare per year. With this system, soil loss is as low as 0.6 ton per hectare per year on 40° slopes, and the land has been in stable production for centuries.*

protectors of the land that feeds their stock. Moreover, an innovative refor-estation project has also been implemented using fast-growing pines to protect and build the soil, after which broad-leaved trees naturally take hold. Only 21 years after the pine planting, a very healthy mixed forest now stands. The villagers, who were the labor force in the planting, receive three-fourths of the wood the forest produces, a welcome source of income and fuelwood.

In the case of our 70-foot eroded canyon, and other areas like it, these were seeded with strong, aggressive grasses and appropriate trees with pugnacious root systems. Grazing was prohibited and the degraded area has become sta-bilized in a matter of years.

Finally, a planting method known as *tied ridging* has been established in the fields. Planting vegetables and other crops in a raised grid pattern prevents runoff, preserves the soil surface, and eliminates the necessity for applications of fertilizer.

While such documented progress in tropical developing-world agriculture and forestry exists, the results are often obscured by the litany of unchal-lenged problems in these arenas. Such projects offer infinitely fertile grounds for concerted International Development Bank investment.

Although prevailing conditions in tropical and temperate regions differ, it is interesting that the greater portion of eastern North American forests were removed during colonial settlement and subsequent periods of extensive farm-ing. It is encouraging that with the implementation of modern intensive methods, adopted in the United States since then, less land has been needed for cultivation, allowing for the present return of vast areas of natural for-est—and that despite large population increases!

▼ *Abused and eroded hill-sides can be healed and stabilized by terracing them and planting with nitrogen-fixing ground-cover species and multipurpose trees. Live-stock are excluded: fodder is taken to them in lower-eleva-tion fields and their manure is carried back to the ter-races. Once stable, the terraces are put to productive use by intercropping.*

III International Logging

Timber mining is a short-sighted strategy for unlike petroleum and minerals, forests need not be exhausted. They are a renewable resource and should be conserved for use in perpetuity.

MAHARAJ K. MUTHOO
DIRECTOR, FORESTRY
OPERATIONS SERVICE, FAO-
UNITED NATIONS

▼ *In Tobago, coconut palms* (Cocos nucifera) *produce nuts, copra, fiber from refuse, and fuelwood from senile trees. The trees benefit from cattle dung.*

As we have noted, the two main causes of tropical deforestation are archaic and wasteful forms of agriculture (including cattle production) and logging. Food must and will be grown in these difficult regions, and it is hoped that in the preceding pages we have shown that not only does a new direction appear both possible and feasible, but also that we have no option but to pursue these directions with the single-mindedness of those with their backs to the sea. With exactly the same determination we must also approach our alternatives to the present course of tropical timber extraction.

The "Faustian Bargain" in Forestry

The answer to the question, "Is obsolescence built into current tropical forestry management?" still rests on decisions that are yet to be made by international commercial operations. By direct effect, sustained commercial yield means sustaining corporate longevity as well as forest products well into the future, when demands for those materials will be ever more pressing. Current trends clearly indicate an avoidance of that coming reality, given that it is financially more expedient in the short term to concentrate on harvesting the "standing crop."

It is not difficult to recognize powerful economic disincentives at play here. Yet, as a function of self-preservation, the industry has a good many

reasons to close ranks on a common policy designed to sustain long-term yields. If that fails to evolve (a likely prospect), then given the grave global impacts precipitated by logging in the tropics, that fully 70 percent of slash-and-burn agriculture takes its ingress only by logging roads, the industry *must* be regulated by intergovernmental forum.

A common factor which propels such inequity and compounds deforestation is the view, especially among developing nations' resource administrators, is that standing forest has no value and is in fact an impediment to progress. This position fails to take into account the vast benefits and services that forests provide free of charge and *in perpetuity*. Only when watersheds are destroyed and the goods and services of the forest are removed in perpetuity can the "Faustian bargain" analogy be clearly perceived.

TIMBER CERTIFICATION

Consumers have made clear their desire to make their purchasing habits very much a part of the solution to deforestation—not a contributing cause. This can be seen, for example, in the popularity of the wildly successful Ben & Jerry's Rainforest Nut Crunch ice cream and many other health, beauty, and food products. To substantiate "green" claims of wood producers, Daniel Katz's Rainforest Alliance pioneered the now burgeoning wood certification movement in 1990 with its visionary "Smart Wood" program. The Forest Stewardship Council followed suit in 1993 with similar programs by which logging companies wishing to use their seal are accredited after passing muster under strict criteria of sustainability and low-impact practices. While these noble initiatives are still in their infancy, there is a growing consensus in the timber industry that the label of good environmental behavior is well worth the added price of production. Consumers have proven receptive to paying the small increase in market price for the privilege of good conscience—the concept being a beacon of light in the darkness of exploitation which rules the industry globally.

In 1996, slightly less than 3 percent of wood traded internationally was certified—double the 1994 volume (FAO 1996). As of 1998, only five industrial logging operations, aside from plantations, are certified in the tropics.

We would hope that ITTO, as an "OPEC-ization" of tropical hardwood, will facilitate moves toward these countries increasing the price of hardwood exports, for which they are currently being grossly underpaid. We could then perhaps look for an increase in foreign exchange and a decrease in exported timber.

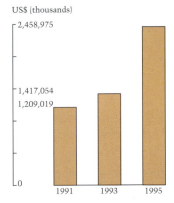

Thailand—increasing imports
of forest products

US$ (thousands)

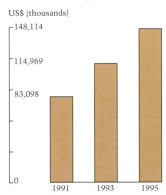

Costa Rica—increasing imports
of forest products

US$ (thousands)

▲ *The "Faustian bargain" in unsustainable logging is clear in these examples from Thailand and Costa Rica, which now must bear the prodigious economic burden of increasing imports of forest products. This, unfortunately, is a pattern that will increasingly affect tropical forest developing nations globally.*

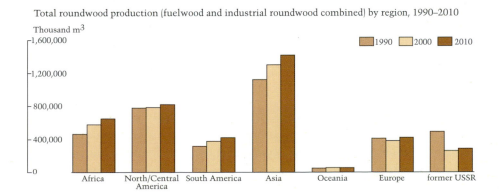

Total roundwood production (fuelwood and industrial roundwood combined) by region, 1990–2010

Thousand m³

◀ *As Asian forests are nearly depleted of accessible commercial timber, Asian logging companies are invading the Amazon to repeat the predaceous process.*

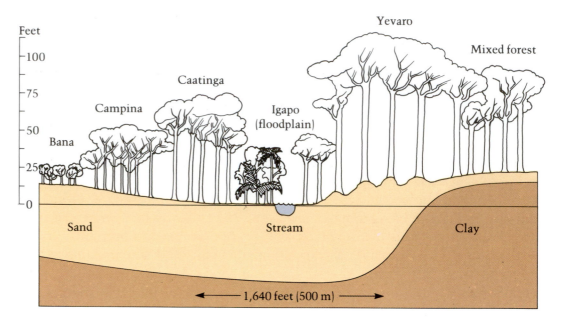

▲ *Amazônia's rainforests do not comprise a single homogenous type: widely differing formations are found according to the terrain and underlying soil. This example is from San Carlos de Rio Negro in the northern Amazon Basin. Exploitation of the forest should take account of such variation. Cultivation, for example, is impractical on nutrient-poor sand podzol soils where the usual forest type is the stunted* bana, campina, *or* caatinga. *These sand forests produce blackwater rivers as tannins from decaying vegetation pass easily through the sand. Forest management has more potential in the productive* yevaro, *while limited but nutrient-rich terra roxa soils have high potential in some areas.*

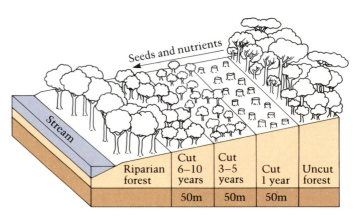

▶ *Strip cutting is one method by which valuable timber can be extracted sustainably, especially on undulating terrain. Mature forest left intact on the uphill side provides a source of seed for natural forest regeneration, while gravity feeds leaf litter and nutrients into the logged strip. Line planting of other useful tree species and crops may be integrated.*

While this arrangement would have an inflationary effect on fine furniture and hardwood paneling, the market adjustments and consumption patterns should not be traumatic.

TOWARD SUSTAINED TIMBER YIELDS

The Brundtland Commission has said that "sustainable development," the keystone environmental phrase of the 1990s, "is the means by which development is to meet the needs of the present without compromising the ability of future generations to meet their own needs." There is a growing consensus that as sustainable tropical forestry has yet to be proved and, says World Bank environmental officer Lee Talbot, "any such logging [outside of plantations] must be recognized as mining, not sustaining the basic forest resource."

It has long been an assumption of development that a standing forest is a wasted resource, one just waiting to be felled for conversion into timber, pulp, or agriculture. On the contrary, standing primary forests support infinitely more people over an eternal horizon of time. This is quite a boast, so let us illuminate the facets of sustainability at work. Mangrove forests are a particularly valuable timber and easily harvested as they exist, generally in mono-stands which exclude other species. If we compute values commonly overlooked in a mangrove ecosystem—which include fish, both marketable and consumed, erosion control, and forest products used locally—far and away the most profitable strategy is mangrove forest preservation, as it yielded U.S.$4,800 per hectare per year, compared to the one-time possible yield of U.S.$3,600 in timber. In Irian Jaya, the sustained local use of the area ensured U.S.$10 million annually, providing 70 percent of the local income and protecting broader-based fisheries worth U.S.$25 million per year in perpetuity (Fearnside and Ruitenbeek 1992).

As primary forests grow more remote and less economically rewarding, timber companies will be enticed to turn an eye to reworking areas cut some years ago and since grown over. Many quite valuable timber species exist in secondary forests. They are fast-growing and light, are part of a less perplexing species mix, and due to their light tolerance they exist in several stories. Of 240,000 acres (97,130 ha) of secondary forest in Puerto Rico, for example, one-fourth had the 100 pole-size trees per hectare of commercially useful species deemed essential for a viable logging venture. There are also certain advantages in cropping secondary forest as opposed to plantation forest. Although the former are not as productive, their exploitation involves neither high initial costs nor the downside risks of plantations, and there are far more than a hundred times the amount of ever-maturing regrowth areas lying idle.

While data to date on the natural regeneration of specific preferred industrial species from cropped forests is scant, there is evidence that natural cycles could produce reasonable returns. Experimental plots at Curua-Una in Brazil, the oldest such data available from the Amazon (1955), show that commercially valuable primary forest species, such as *Goupia glabra*, will regenerate naturally after harvesting to the extent that a perpetually sustained yield could be expected—or so we shall see.

MODERNIZING DEVELOPING WORLD FORESTRY PRACTICES

Procedures that have been suggested include severing the lianas that bind the crowns of desired trees to those of noncommercial species before felling. The significance of this is made apparent by realizing that the cumulative collateral mortality to all size classes by felling only the few commercial trees per hectare is on the order of 50 percent (Johns 1997). Logging damage could be reduced by at least 20 percent, and is easily worth the added cost of U.S.$2 per tree, which would amount to approximately 2 cents on each cubic meter of log exported. The selective liana cutting would also avoid the possible extinction of liana species threatened by the indiscriminate killing of all vines (as many as 2,000 per hectare) as is practiced in some overly "managed" forests.

Biologists hired by the corporations may work to salvage plant and animal specimens in an "operation rescue" as the logging or dam flooding proceeds. As well as saving individual specimens, such operations provide an opportunity for scientists to study endangered and unknown species for description and possible subsequent transplant. A few of the more scrupulous commercial collectors of rare plants engage in collecting only at logging sites, as these plants would be largely doomed at any rate. Levying fees for such lucrative collecting could well defray the expense of the biologists' salaries.

Helicopters can be employed to lift out tree boles as an alternative to the highly destructive hauling practices that obliterate a high percentage of noncommercial species en route. Although this will add considerable cost to the process of extraction, helicopters and balloons are used successfully by timber corporations in the northwest United States and Canada increasingly. This results in extremely low impact on nontarget trees and as destructive logging roads are no longer necessary, not only is there considerable saving on costly infrastructure, but the inflow of slash-and-burn agriculturists by road is negated.

Certain ecological practices are now followed quite routinely in the United States, such as keeping felling operations 650 feet (200 m) from bald eagle nests during the nesting season. Such restraint is not applied in the tropics for similarly endangered species. Environmental impact reports—the norm in developed nations—are rare exceptions in the tropics, and even when they are implemented the burden of proof is left to conservation interests.

Unutilized Forest Products

The forests contain myriad fruits, nuts, drugs, bamboos, barks, scents, perfumes, resins, gums, waxes, turpentine, latex, tannins, alkaloids, rattans, beeswax, palm fibers, and exotic plants for export, as well as fodder for cattle and other livestock—all of which is left largely unexploited. These products and many more could be salvaged during a logging operation, and in many cases could open up a vast cornucopia of forest wealth generally known as "minor forest products." The fact that U.S.$10 billion is now traded annually reveals the potential bounty in these still largely untapped resources, which would lessen the impact on undisturbed forest. Indeed, the main constituents of wood are lignin and cellulose, and both go virtually unused. Possible applications number in the thousands, from innovative plastic production (like those indestructible yellow screwdriver handles) to fertilizers to oil well drilling dispersals to synthetic textile manufacturing.

A single ton of tropical dry wood can yield 660 pounds (300 kg) of coal-like residue, 3.7 gallons (14 l) of methanol, 20 gallons (76 l) of wood oil and light tar, 3.2 gallons (12 l) of creosote oil, 66 pounds (30 kg) of pitch, 2 gallons (7.6 l) of esters, and 14 gallons (53 l) of acetic acid. Along with this, 4,944 cubic feet (140 cu m) of gas may be produced, which can then be used to power the equipment extracting these useful distillation products. It is estimated that in

▲ The considerable contribution of sustained forest food production is often overlooked in the evaluation of national production statistics.

▲ Business is brisk in the busy Lingala market in the Democratic Republic of the Congo, with numerous varieties of protein-rich beans for sale, all produced by sustainable methods.

▲ In areas of the Democratic Republic of the Congo where timber exploitation has not yet raped the soil, cultivation often takes advantage of forest fertility and shelter.

the tropical forest's yearly new growth alone, the available energy matches half the world's present consumption of energy of all forms combined.

K. F. S. King, former director of FAO's forestry department, described present forestry practices as "primitive, costly and wasteful." Norman Myers's analysis of tropical forests as "overexploited and underutilized" also typifies the current global response to the lack of thrift in logging practices.

Enforcement of International Responsibility

Gallup polls show that worldwide opinion is overwhelmingly in favor of seeing more done to conserve wildlife and threatened species, and although the world sees its species as a "global heritage" it has had great difficulty asserting this in the face of the concept of national sovereignty. Thus, conservative parities paid to developing countries can be effective and palatable door-openers to those nations wherein the bulk of Earth's species exist. This concept is not a new one, but it needs expansion.

In force today are several international trade agreements on endangered species, and their nesting, mating, and calving sites. They include special treaties offering protection for whales, sea turtles, migratory birds, and other species whose survival wholly depends on the real concept of "global heritage." The tropical rainforest could logically be accorded equal if not priority protection.

Such is the legacy of the seminal 1972 Stockholm Conference, as well as the Rio Earth Summit two decades later, guaranteeing sovereign rights yet not the right to "cause environmental damage to states beyond the limits of national jurisdiction." The late Paul W. Richards (1908–95), Emeritus Professor at the University College of North Wales, Bangor, and pioneering tropical forest botanist, viewed the conservation of the tropical forests as "beyond the unaided resources of the poorer developing countries, so it is important that the conservation of tropical forests should be treated as an international as well as a national responsibility."

Cross-regulation of the ITTO in field activities may be administered through the currently operating United Nations Commission on International Investment and Transnational Corporations. In this way, environmental muscle may be enhanced, and the logging industries be relieved of the impractical and unsatisfactory responsibility of policing themselves.

IV WOOD PRODUCTION FOR THE FUTURE

If you plan for one year, plant rice. If you plan for ten, plant trees. If you plan for one hundred years, educate mankind.

KUAN-TZU

For anyone alert enough to read it, the writing is on the wall. As a result of the expansion of the world economies, demand for forest products has increased several times; lumber use has tripled, paper use went up sixfold and fuel-wood use has soared—all since midcentury. The West African economy of Côte d'Ivoire flourished in the 1960s and 1970s, due significantly to timber exports. But as timber was not sustainably harvested, export earnings from forest products have plunged to virtually zero today. Nigeria, the Philippines, and Thailand, whose forests are now critically depleted and which were once considerable exporters of tropical hardwood, are now net importers of forest products. The Malaysian peninsula (arguably the most perniciously aggressive nation in the tropical forest timber industry, whose companies decimated once lushly forested Asian nations) is now looking to Latin America. Indeed, beginning in the mid-1980s, imports into tropical countries began to exceed the value of their exports by 30–50 percent. By 2000, only 10 tropical countries were net exporters (Brown 1998).

TIMBER SHORTAGES ON THE HORIZON

Timber exports in the early 1990s were worth U.S.$10 billion annually to tropical countries (up from U.S.$600 million annually in the early 1970s). Most production (20–30 percent) now originates in Indonesia, Malaysia, and Brazil. Japan remains the largest importer of timber by volume in the world and imports 80 percent of internationally traded wood chips. Demand for tropical timber is projected to increase over 1993 figures by a full 56 percent as early as 2010. Increasing shortage of tropical specialist hardwoods is currently evident due to increasing inaccessibility of remaining commercial species. As tropical forest nations can earn as much from timber as from cotton, twice that from rubber, and three times that of cocoa, overharvesting of timber is expected to produce a vital decrease in revenue, creating steep economic limitations on dependent nations. To many of those nations, the added economic imposition of being transformed from net exporters of timber to net importers will be prodigious.

Emerging patterns of increasing desperation are evident. The Secretary of Strategic Issues (SAE), the CIA of Brazil, reports with considerable acrimony on illegal logging by Asian companies. SAE claims Indonesian and Malaysian companies, most often controlled by ruling families at home, operate under fictitious names (i.e., Samling, Musa, Ribnon, Hiba, etc.) to hide their identity, are quietly buying up large sectors and, the report states, blatantly "invading Brazilian resources." Armed poachers are now commonly taking valued species in the moist tropics globally—30 to 40 forest guards are killed in gun battles yearly in Thailand alone.

TACKLING THE GREENHOUSE EFFECT

In view of the statement by atmospheric scientists in Toronto at the World Conference on the Changing Atmosphere that "humanity is conducting an

uncontrolled and globally pervasive experiment whose ultimate consequences could be second only to a global nuclear war," is our present course—"do nothing—attempt at a later date to adjust to projected global warming"—really the decision we want to commit to?

It is estimated that the world needs to cut its emissions of global warming gases by 50 to 70 percent, just to stabilize the level of gases in the atmosphere. Yet many believe that the energy battle will be hard fought and that humanity's key technology for doing something meaningful to retard and eventually reverse the greenhouse effect will be through forestry and forest conservation in the tropics!

By extrapolating recent research findings that in lowland rainforest there are an average of 206 (Richards 1996) trees per acre greater than 4 inches (10 cm) in diameter at breast height (DBH), we can now calculate the actual number of trees felled daily in the deforestation of the tropics—a body count, if you will. We presently lose 69 acres (28 ha) of tropical moist forest per minute—more than one per second! Perhaps nothing can better bring home the grim reality of human activities than the following figures. I was awed while multiplying trees per acre to find this represented 11,309 per minute, 678,568 per hour, and 16,285,623 trees per day felled! (And this may yet prove to be only half the true rate.)

Burning of tropical forests globally contributes 27 percent of total atmospheric carbon, or 2.0 (+ or – 0.8) gigatons (1.0 gigatons = 1 billion tons) per year. South American forests still take in 0.3 to 0.9 gigatons of carbon annually while

▲ *In the front line of what has been likened to "World War III"—the global struggle to retard the greenhouse effect—these Eucalyptus seedlings being prepared for planting in Brazil's Turmalina Reforestation Project will help absorb excess CO_2 while contributing to soil and forest conservation.*

AFFORESTATION SCENARIOS FOR A CARBON FOREST TO ACHIEVE A RANGE OF REDUCTIONS IN ANNUAL ATMOSPHERIC CARBON DIOXIDE INCREMENT OVER PERIODS OF 10, 20, 30, AND 50 YEARS					
Reduction in Annual CO_2 Increase	Total Planted Area (million ha)	Target Planting Rates (million ha/yr)			
		10 years	20 years	30 years	50 years
100%	600	60	30	20	12
50%	300	30	15	10	6
25%	150	15	8	5	3
10%	60	6	3	2	1

fossil fuel use contributes 5.5 gigatons annually. After accounting for the capacities of Earth's vegetation and oceans to absorb carbon, we are still left with a net flux into the atmosphere of approximately 3.3 gigatons of carbon per year due to human activities (Houghton 1999).

Approximately one-half of forested carbon is tropical; most of the balance is boreal. Without minimizing the gargantuan task at hand, yet recognizing the forest's capacity to absorb CO_2 from the atmosphere and store carbon (one-half a tree's mass is carbon), the 2,000 scientists of the Intergovernmental Panel on Climate Change (IPCC) have forwarded a proposal of planting 46,000 square miles (120,000 sq km) of trees each year for 20 years, creating a total of 930,000 square miles (2.4 million sq km) of carbon-absorbing biomass (Houghton, et al. 1990) which could sequester between 24 and 36 gigatons of carbon from the atmosphere over the next 50–100 years.

We can begin to perceive the tragic momentum at work by realizing the IPCC's 930,000 square miles (2.4 million sq km) represents reforestation of 122 billion trees, if we are to approximate tropical rainforest density—yet we decimate 6 billion annually in tropical forests alone. If we multiply that loss over the 20 years of the IPCC's heroic project, we come in with 120 billion lost trees—equal to the number of trees required for that project! Consider also that FAO estimates that of the roughly 350,000 square miles (900,000 sq km) projected to be converted to agriculture in developing nations by 2010, half (excluding China) are currently forested, representing a considerable loss in carbon storage capacity.

WILL HUMANITY BE UP TO THE TASK?

With Norman Myers's characteristic optimism, let us take the trees by the boughs here and expand on the IPCC plan of action. By using fast-growing trees for the tropics in a plantation setting we can generate 20 metric tons of additional wood per 2.47 acres per year (1 ha/yr). Because a tree's mass is one-half carbon, it absorbs 10 tons of carbon per year from the atmosphere for 30–40 years, its fastest growth period. Our tropical moist location will yield several times more wood than most temperate moist areas. The figures are admittedly roughcut, but also conservative, as in southern Brazil, the best varieties of eucalyptus plantations will perform three and a half times better than our example.

With this reckoning, in order to absorb 1 billion tons of carbon, a considerable accomplishment, we need to plant 386,000 sq mi (1 million sq km), an area one and a half times the size of Texas, a considerable task. But with the 3 million square miles (8 million sq km) of already deforested land in the moist tropics suitable for reforestation and in need of watershed restoration

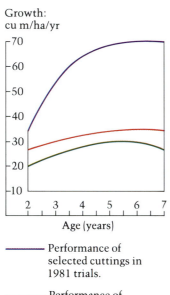

Growth:
cu m/ha/yr

Age (years)

—— Performance of selected cuttings in 1981 trials.

—— Performance of seedlings from South Africa and Zimbabwe, 1974–78.

—— Performance of seedlings from original Brazilian sources, 1967–73.

▲ *Brazilian paper company Aracruz Florestal increased its* Eucalyptus *plantation yields more than 250 percent by genetic improvement of its imported stock. It is easy to see how such fine-tuning methods could create future significant advances in plantation productivity. The FAO 1990 Tropical Forest Plantation Resources Assessment stated that due to genetic improvement, "Aracruz has yielded the world's highest mean annual increment of about 70m³/ha per year."*

(Houghton 1993; Myers 1996), this formula offers a win/win situation, especially so if one utilizes the gargantuan labor force available in those regions. If the land were provided free of charge, local people would gain immensely from reforestation. One hectare of plantation could be established and maintained for U.S.$400, landing us at 1 million square kilometers at U.S.$40 billion—or amortized more realistically, only U.S.$4 billion per year for 10 years (Myers 1992). When we compare the cost of action against the hidden future cost of inaction, I should expect such a trade-off to emerge as the peerless bargain of the 21st century.

Should we find additional justification necessary to exercise a seismic shift of thought and direction, India's losses in crops and damage due to Ganges River flooding caused by the denuding of the Himalayas is U.S.$1 billion per year. For global warming, the cost to the United States alone for irrigation and hydropower installations necessary is estimated by the U.S. Environmental Protection Agency at some U.S.$200 billion. Adding another U.S.$95 billion to safeguard only the eastern seaboard against sea level rise gives us an admittedly rough total of U.S.$295 billion, still far from the full skein of protection required. Now on the other side of the ledger, weigh the "opportunity costs," those of relieving most of the tropical forests of further exploitation. Call it a pay-out to tropical developing nations, but one that is necessary for the world's environmental security of some U.S.$20 billion per year (Myers 1992).

But consider just several valorous achievements. A gallant reforestation effort by CARE, Oxfam USA, Catholic Relief Services, and 200 other groups in Haiti, arguably the most completely deforested nation in the world, gathered a veritable army of 135,000 farmers who planted 85 million trees averaging 270 trees per smallholding—with not a thought to carbon sequestering.

In 1988, the American Forestry Association, during International Rainforest Week (October 9–16), announced its resolve to see 100 million trees planted in the United States by 1992. During a press conference on the program, in which I was a participant, urban afforestation was revealed to have additional significance to its role as a carbon absorber. As a shade provider for homes, and as a reducer of the city "heat-island" effect, even a minimal planting of trees can reduce the use of air conditioning, resulting in an average saving of 1,000 kilowatt-hours annually, which translates into a reduction of 1,000 pounds of carbon burned. Emerson wrote, "the creation of a thousand forests is in a single acorn." The millionth tree was planted on Arbor Day in 1993 in Hakalau Forest National Wildlife Refuge in Hawaii.

Richard A. Houghton, senior scientist at Woods Hole Research Center puts forward a resoundingly practical strategy of substituting wood energy for fossil fuel, at least for the interim period of adjustment to clean energy. In the many sectors (electricity production, manufacturing, etc.) where this would be feasible, plantations would provide the resource and while emissions would be similar to fossil fuel burning, regrowth of next year's wood supplies would absorb the carbon released by the current year's burning, creating an equilibrium.

Myers eloquently picks up the fallen colors on the deforested battlefield and empowers the troops when he refers to the task in front of us as "the most exhilarating we can envisage." He states that ours is the most privileged of all human generations to face this challenge and asks, "in the eyes of future generations, won't we have made ourselves giants of the human condition?"

▶ During the 1990s, the alarming trend of tropical nations such as Indonesia and Brazil to convert massive acreage (more than 1 million acres or 400,000 ha per year) of primary forest to commercial oil palm plantations certainly falls into the category of unrestrained development, and was the major cause of the cataclysmic fires of 1997–98. Sadly, the International Monetary Fund (IMF) and World Bank funding has lubricated the slippery slope of oil palm proliferation. While the deforestation/plantation ratio is less than 1:4, an improvement over that of a decade ago of 1:10, much of this reflects the global reckless trend of conversion of primary forest.

▲ The corridor system harvests timber in a line cut through old-growth forest. Here, near Pimenta Bueno in Brazil, mahogany, a highly prized commercial species, is replanted. Taking advantage of the canopy shade and leaf-litter nutrients, the new trees will be ready for cutting in about 30 years.

Hearken Myers's call to arms: "Those tropical forests are waiting to hear from us. Let's give them a message."

Fast Growers and New "Supertrees"

We can be encouraged by the species available to us from man-made forests. Pines and other conifers for softwoods, and eucalypts for hardwoods, make efficient and traditional starters. Their growth, though considered rapid in temperate regions, is dramatic in the moist tropics. There are, however, other tree species less known or largely unrecognized that possess an unparalleled pulp source potential. Some of these are pioneer species whose growth rates make even pines and eucalypts seem slow. It is to these in combination, depending on site-specific conditions, that our hopes turn for satiating the world's demand for wood produce. A tropical plantation of 193 square miles (500 sq km) produces more than 35 million cubic feet (1 million cu m) of marketable timber annually, 10 times the natural forest yield.

More important today than construction timber is the growing need for soft, pale timber used for its cellulose and fiber content. Some secondary-growth trees meet this criterion and many also grow in pure stands naturally. This is an important feature when considering species for plantation use, as species that grow dispersed in the wild often fall prey to insect and fungal attack when planted in dense monoculture stands. Seed availability is good, and seed germination is as high as 98 percent in some species.

For pulp production a small plant called *kenaf* (*Hybiscus sabdariffa*) yields up to 23 tons per hectare, as much as some fast-growing hardwoods and five to seven times as much pulp per hectare as pine trees. Koichiro Ueda of the University of Kyoto clocked moso bamboo (*Phyllostachys edulis*) at a phenomenal 47.6 inches (121 cm) in 24 hours. I calculated that world record for any plant to represent a speed of growth of 0.00003 miles per hour (0.00005 kmph) and duly entered it into the *Guinness Book of Records*. Among the fast-growing trees, *Albizzia falcata* grew 35 feet, 3 inches (10.7 m) in 13 months, *Paraserianthes falcataria* at 32.5 feet per year (9.9 m/yr), and *Eucalyptus deglupta* grew to 100 feet (30 m) in less than six years. These are clear examples of "plant your seedling and jump aside." The use of eucalyptus has become controversial in recent years, as it is known for its prodigious thirst and tendency to outcompete crops, especially in areas of moderate rainfall. However, eucalyptus plantations are very productive, allowing several successive crops to be harvested from the rapid growth of new shoots, while in suitable conditions fodder and certain palm crops can be planted between the rows. *Gmelina arborea*, one of the fastest-growing trees known, is from Asia, and plantations of this species have already been harvested in Brazil and elsewhere, where they perform well on the more fertile soils.

Our friend the *Cecropia*, from the American tropics, has also performed well in test plantations. This should be no surprise, as the trumpet tree, as it is known, is a secondary-growth tree that springs forth in forest clearings with a speed that can almost be seen. Its companion, the super-light wood balsa (*Ochroma lagopus*), known to every model airplane hobbyist, also a neotropical pioneer species, has grown 18 feet (5.5 m) per year in plantations.

Another fairly recent introduction, the *Leucaena*, has been hailed as the "tree that does everything." (This, unfortunately, includes escaping cultivation and, under certain conditions, establishing itself in the native flora.) A native of Mexico and Central America, in cultivation it is said to yield more wood than any other hardwood, and is an excellent fiber source, as well as being a strong and attractive lumber. Its vegetation is a delectable, high-protein animal feed, and its pods and young leaves are gaining favor as a human food source as well.

As a fast grower (growing out of reach of livestock within six months), it is economical as a fuelwood and has 70 percent of the heating value of fuel oil when turned into charcoal. As a nitrogen fixer it does sterling service in reforestation schemes, producing 1,100 to 1,500 pounds (roughly 500 to 700 kg) of nitrogen per kilogram per hectare per year—twice as much as a close competitor, *Acacia mearnsii*. In short, it is a "tree superstar."

Protracted yields from these and other candidates will relieve much of the burden now carried by the tropical rainforest, and their rapid growth

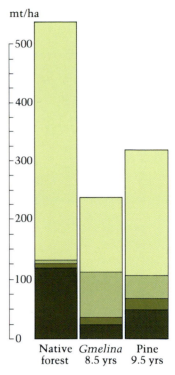

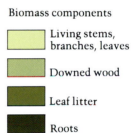

Biomass components

Living stems, branches, leaves

Downed wood

Leaf litter

Roots

▲ ◄ *Controversial in the 1970s and 1980s as it cleared 300,000 acres (120,000 ha) of primary forest, the ambitious Jari Project in the Brazilian Amazon should have been installed on seasoned secondary forest. Eucalyptus proved highly suitable for the site and on six-year cycles has produced an astounding five to six cycles so far. So efficient is the production that the area under management has been reduced to 167,000 acres (67,000 ha), yet is still sufficient to fill its 850-metric-ton-per-day pulp factory capacity. While logging of primary forest for commercial species produces only some 35 m³ per hectare on only a single harvest, Jarilandia's current yield is 30 m³ per hectare per year or 180 m³ per hectare on a six-year cycle. Radiantly productive sustainability at last!*

assures their volume intake of atmospheric carbon. However, it is good to bear in mind that ecologically these plantations are barren lands compared with natural forests, as they support little of their wildlife and basically none of their botanical diversity. Strong emphasis should be placed on the establishment of such plantations on mature secondary-growth areas, a commodity in long supply in the moist tropics, where 4.4 million acres (1.8 million ha) of plantation are added annually (FAO 2001).

To underscore the importance of individual endeavors, in Rwanda scattered trees planted by individuals collectively total half a million acres (200,000 ha), representing more than the country's combined remaining natural forests and all its state and communal plantations. Village planting programs have found most success within a structure highlighting personal ownership of each tree planted, rather than in regimens where rural people are employed simply as laborers. CARE's message to villagers is uncompromising: "This is your tree. If it dies it is your loss. If it survives you reap the benefits."

The FAO further reports that reforestation is not taking place in the main areas of current deforestation, a situation that could be remedied by making replanting programs a requirement of logging contracts. But what of the mode of operations of large-scale logging/planting operations on virgin forest?

PULP FACTS

It is formulated that current annual demand for tropical hardwood could be produced sustainably on just 69 million acres (28 million ha) of plantations (Grainger 1993), which is only five times the area logged annually in tropical moist forests. Plantations produce wood on short rotations of seven to 30 years (as compared to natural forests' cycles of 30 to 150 years) and their wood is of more uniform size and quality (FAO 1995).

Average commercial cuts per hectare in tropical moist forests are 45 cubic meters in Indonesia and 25 cubic meters in Côte d'Ivoire. A typical high-grade hardwood plantation could yield 225 cubic meters per hectare after 35 years; a typical teak plantation, 245 cubic meters after 60 years (Lanly 1981, Grainger 1988). Fast-growing pulp plantations produce 150 cubic meters per hectare of *Gmelina arborea* after only 10 years. Plantations in the moist tropics produce at two to four times the rate of temperate plantations (Price 1999).

Factoring in the massively destructive impact on tropical forests for iron and steel production such as Brazil's Grande Carajás Project, instead of cutting primary forest for energy to drive the process, fuel should be increasingly met by autonomous pig iron producers through reforestation with "supertrees."

PAPER RECYCLING—A NOTABLE ARENA OF PROGRESS

Where will we obtain raw materials for paper production, projected to double by 2010? So successful were the inroads made on recycling paper in the 1990s that paper companies in the United States now negotiate long-term contracts with local communities for their scrap paper. As a result, the new trend is to build paper mills near heavily populated centers rather than in heavily wooded areas. This means important strides toward sustainability, but also

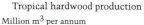

Tropical hardwood production
Million m³ per annum

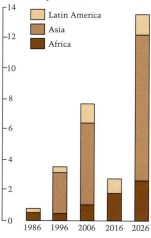

▲ *There is reason for hope in the growing trend towards tropical hardwood production from plantations, which hold promise of reducing pressure on wood stocks in natural tropical forests. Additionally, growing forests, such as plantations, absorb more atmospheric carbon than do steady-state forests of equal biomass.*

keeps massive amounts of paper from the regions' trash dumps and landfills, as well as removing the costs of collection and disposal, which are U.S.$590 million in the United States alone. The payoff is clearly worth the effort, as recovering the print run of a single issue of the Sunday edition of the *New York Times* would save some 86,000 trees.

I could not be more pleased to report that in 1997, the United States, due to participation by homeowners and municipalities, recovered 45 percent of paper and paperboard, an improvement from 29 percent in 1987. Yet there is scant participation by offices and businesses, the largest potential source of high-quality wastepaper, as well as uneven enforcement of laws mandating recycled content. This is especially troubling as paper accounts for 30–40 percent of landfill waste in the United States.

TAUNGYA—FAMILY-PROJECT REFORESTATION

Another reforestation scheme seems even more suited to socioeconomic conditions in the tropics. The traditional *taungya* plantation system requires industrious, land-hungry cultivators—people in long supply in the tropical developing world. Allotted an area of forest (in the past virgin, but now preferably old second growth) which is first cut, stumped, and torched, the

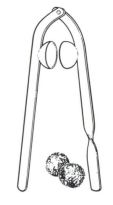

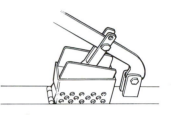

▲ *Surprisingly simple yet effective technology can be used in areas of fuelwood shortage to make optimum use of whatever combustible material is available. Lever-operated presses can convert sawdust, chaff, and other waste into fuel briquettes for domestic use, and can be made wherever there is basic metalworking skill.*

◀ *The equation "1 ton of charcoal = 212 cubic feet (6 cu m) of wood" shows how wasteful is the process of charcoal making. Some traditional methods waste up to 60 percent of the wood's energy value. Yet fully 80 percent of all wood removed from tropical forests is used for fuelwood or for conversion to charcoal.*

TACTICS	• Increase productivity of existing resources	• Create new resources	• Improve fuelwood distribution	• Improve conversion technologies	• Find substitutes for fuelwood
TECHNIQUES	• Introduce better management • Protect over-worked areas • Subri conversion technique • Utilize 'waste'	• Individual planting • Village woodlots • Strip plantations • Shelter belts • Block plantations	• Organize marketing cooperatives • Improve transport • Provide storage • Investigate import/export	• Improve charcoal production • Improve and disseminate wood stoves • Improve cooking habits	• Subsidize kerosene, bottled gas, coal • Investigate biogas • Investigate solar energy • Rural electrification

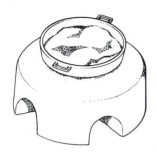

▲ *This baked-mud-and-sand fire enclosure, used in Senegal, can drastically reduce the energy waste of cooking on an open fire.*

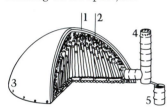

▲ *Simple technology like this earth kiln greatly improves charcoal-making efficiency. Sand (1) and straw (2) retain heat; air vents (3) promote even burning, and U.S.$75 worth of oil drums provide chimney (4) and tar trap (5).*

▲ *Uganda's logging waste, once discarded, now yields 63,000 tons per year of charcoal.*

farmer cultivates the plot for food crops for the family unit and for surplus which is sold for cash income. Plantation seedlings are introduced into the agricultural crop and are weeded for at least one year so that they are well established at the time the cultivator moves on to establish another plot.

Fuels for the Masses

Worldwatch Institute alerts us that one-half of all wood cut in the world is for firewood for cooking and heating, and that more than one-third of humanity still relies on wood for fuel. These vital needs are often ignored in public statistics but put awesome pressure on the world's vegetation. In some areas, such as Java, home gardens supply a fair share of family-firewood demands. More often, however, this is not the case, and until agroforestry becomes much more prevalent, this demand will remain a serious drain on standing forests. Further, escalating demand and resulting increases in market price for fuelwood, up 100 percent since the 1980s, has provided a strong motivation for farmers in many areas to shift from food crop to tree crop for cash incomes (FAO 1998).

An alternative to unrestrained wood depletion will be the dissemination of inexpensive but efficient wood-burning stoves to replace the wasteful open fires used by the bulk of the more than 2 billion people who rely on wood fuel. In the poorer countries, fuelwood provides more than 90 percent of the total energy consumption. So grave is the situation that in some areas people are cutting back on the use of vegetables that require cooking. Most primitive stoves use only 10 to 15 percent of the heat generated. Efficient stoves made mostly of mud can use 40 to 65 percent of the heat, and sell for only U.S.$5. The use of solar stoves in the tropics, where sun is the major commodity and is free, holds great promise. Although the stove cost would be in the U.S.$30 to U.S.$50 range, long-range savings would be spectacular.

As all activities involving meaningful quantities of wood must be analyzed, even India's cremation practices are significant. In a country where most deceased are, by religious dictum, consumed on funeral pyres, the amounts of wood consumed are remarkable. Foresters, and a private organization in Gujarat, are now trying to promote a process of cremation that reduces wood consumption from an average of 992 pounds (450 kg) to only 353 pounds (160 kg), a substantial saving for the family as well.

V THE FUNDING OF PROJECT RAINFOREST

Of the major problems facing the world today, global scientific opinion places tropical deforestation among the very highest priorities.

As environmental consultant Norman Myers states, "Our tools of economic analysis are far from able to apprehend, let alone comprehend, the entire range of values implicit in forests." Robert Castanza of the University of Maryland and his colleagues internationally synthesized more than 100 studies to compute the value that major ecosystems provide worldwide. That conservative figure is currently at least U.S.$16–54 trillion annually—and in perpetuity, which far exceeds the gross world product of U.S.$28 trillion (in 1995 dollars). But, as recent history has demonstrated, when the proceeds of forest exploitation go into private hands, ledgers not only go unbalanced, they are abandoned forthwith. While statistics are available, quantifying the area of new forests required to absorb the global excess of CO_2 (see page 200), the author is unaware of the budgeting of any public sector program, however preliminary, toward implementing preventive or corrective strategies.

An enormous span of opportunity exists for the World Bank to take positive action for both the global environment and its occupants. The bank is capable of producing the funding necessary to create the wings with which to fly in appropriate technologies for sustained development to the fields of peasant agriculturists. NGOs and developing nations "Peoples' Corps," with World Bank funding, can be these wings. Such programs can perhaps be molded after President Franklin D. Roosevelt's highly effective Civilian Conservation Corps (CCC) which created employment in the depression era, as well as healing large areas of degraded American environment.

It should be noted that the World Bank and other multinational development banks spearheading the funding of Project Climate Change Challenge, in the creation of areas for new forests to avert a bleak future due to continued global warming, should be viewed symbiotically as developmental in scope, as they will create much-needed employment for great numbers of developing-world citizens.

As the issues of tropical deforestation are essentially social and economic, remedies must not be divorced from the realities of farm-plot life extension, seedlings for woodlot planting, facilities for providing uncontaminated water, education on environmental protection and proper use of toxic chemicals, and provision of family planning services. It is out of those seeds that global habitat preservation will germinate, and it is likely that such approaches will prove far more economically expedient than encircling tropical forest parks or gorillas with armed guards. Yet, due to ever-mounting public concern, there is reason to believe that aid for tropical forestry may be entering its Cinderella years.

The Earth Summit of 1992 formulated that at least U.S.$30 billion would be necessary to enrich programs of sustainable development toward safeguarding tropical forests. World attention to the importance of tropical forests has raised foreign aid funding for that agenda from U.S.$400 million in 1985 to U.S.$1.3 billion in 1992.

FUELWOOD AND AGROFORESTRY Summary of needed investments, 2000–05	
AFRICA	**US$ mill**
Botswana	15
Burkina Faso	25
Burundi	20
Cape Verde	15
Chad	14
Ethiopia	45
Kenya	55
Lesotho	10
Madagascar	35
Malawi	24
Mali	35
Mauritania	16
Niger	20
Nigeria	55
Rwanda	35
Senegal	25
Somalia	15
Sudan	40
Tanzania	35
Uganda	15
ASIA	
Bangladesh	60
China	275
India	550
Nepal	35
Pakistan	45
Sri Lanka	35
LATIN AMERICA	
Bolivia	25
Brazil	440
Costa Rica	15
El Salvador	10
Haiti	15
Peru	25
Total (*32 countries*)	2,079

▲ *The Tropical Forestry Action Plan indicates that considerable investment will be required to move the developing countries toward self-sufficiency.*

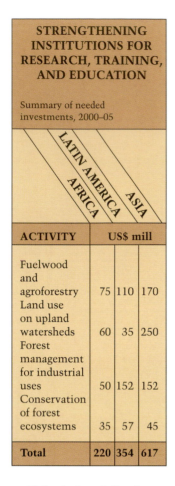

▲ *If the industrialized nations fail to invest in developing countries, short-term economic imperatives will inevitably result in continued massive global deforestation. Nowhere is investment more urgently needed than in strengthening national institutions.*

The Convention on Biological Diversity (CBD), resulting from the Earth Summit, has installed the admirable Global Environmental Facility (GEF) of the World Bank as its financial mechanism. The largest GEF funding sector is allocated to forest ecosystems, comprising 59 projects with an allocation of U.S.$381 million. This includes the 1999 allotment of U.S.$18 million to help create the 4-million-acre (1.6-million-ha) Central Suriname Nature Reserve, one of the world's largest tropical forest wilderness reserves, which was formerly targeted by Asian concerns for logging concessions. When cofinancing from national governments, international agencies, the private sector and environmental groups is added to GEF funds encompassing its mandate in the global environmental arenas of biodiversity loss, climate change, land and international waters degradation, and ozone depletion, the project portfolio is impressively valued at more than U.S.$7 billion.

Brent Blackwelder, president of Friends of the Earth, elucidates its "Green Scissors" program, which illuminates the often hidden fat and unnecessary government programs which were created at the environment's expense and at extreme costs to taxpayers. In its first several years, "Green Scissors" has saved more than U.S.$20 billion. It would not be difficult to envision astute NGOs of world nations emulating this cogent assault on government waste and redirecting funding toward fossil fuel cutbacks, clean energy, and forest conservation.

Further, an estimated U.S.$650 billion (Brown 1999) is clearly misused, even squandered, by governments globally on subsidies for environmentally destructive activities such as clear-cutting (i.e., selling whole trees in forests of public domain at a loss—for U.S.$2), overfishing, etc. In the United States, eliminating this pork would provide funds for positive environmental action or a tax refund of that amount equal to $2,000 per family of four.

It is more insightful than simplistic that governments tax jobs and investments too heavily—and tax resource depletion and pollution too lightly. By shifting only 15 percent of the global tax pie from payrolls and investments, to the taxing of destructive activities of the industries that perpetrate and perpetuate them, at least U.S.$1 trillion can be relegated to the coming environmental revolution.

An *ad valorem* tax of 0.1 percent on crude oil produced internationally would raise U.S.$450 million per year for such global emergency projects, and yet direct support for conventional energy sources is estimated at U.S.$200 billion worldwide, raising very little objection. Expand this tax to all goods traded internationally and the figure soars to U.S.$1 billion.

DEBT/DEFORESTATION DEBACLE—INTERNATIONAL LOGGING CARTELS AS PAWNBROKERS

At the annual meeting of the Organization for African Unity in 1987, 50 member states in requesting amnesty on U.S.$200 billion in debts stated that "the problem is not one of liquidity but of a complete inability to pay." Such debt, of course, serves to entrench environmental disaster by ensuring that southern nations step up their exploitation of tropical forests in their desperate attempts to stabilize their balance-of-payments situation.

The following example illustrates the all-too-common consequence of the developed world's export of "debt-as-lifestyle" to the eager recipients, the developing world nations. Brazil currently experiences a substantial net outflow of capital to multinational development agencies on the average of U.S.$650 million annually since 1992 to pay down accumulated debt with no new significant lending. This debt burden has attracted Malaysian timber corporations to finesse contracts to extract Brazil's Amazon hardwoods. This process is further lubricated by tighter controls and exhaustion of timber in Southeast Asia. Since Brazil's forests are not being exploited sustainably, what will be its options as the resource becomes increasingly depleted? Following this, in 1995, Belize, strapped with debt, sold logging rights to more than 2 million acres (812,000 ha) in its most pristine forest region, directly on the flyway of many U.S. nesting songbirds, to another Malaysian company.

So compelling is the link between debt and deforestation that it has been documented in certain instances that a U.S.$5 billion pay-down in debt was the result of 95–385 (occasionally more) square miles (250–1,000 sq km) of annual deforestation (Kahn and McDonald 1992; Gullison and Losos 1993). One would be hard pressed to find clearer scenarios of cause and effect than international debt and the pawning of national forests.

CONVERTING DEBT INTO HABITAT ASSETS

In July of 1987, a precedent-setting "debt for nature swap" was facilitated by Conservation International. It purchased U.S.$650,000 of Bolivia's debt at a discounted rate of U.S.$100,000 resulting in more than 3.7 million acres (1.5 million ha) adjacent to the Beni Biosphere Preserve receiving conservation status. By the end of 1992, 124 swaps were made globally by other NGOs, with a face value of U.S.$122 million, generating conservation funds of more than U.S.$75 million while costing only U.S.$23 million (Myers 1996). In 1998, the U.S. Tropical Forest Conservation Act was passed. It allows for multifaceted programs including reduction of debt owed the United States by tropical forest nations toward debt-for-nature swaps, and establishes investment treaties with the Inter-American Development Bank and World Bank to preserve or restore tropical forests. I am pleased to report that in September 1999, President Clinton announced that the United States would cancel 100 percent of

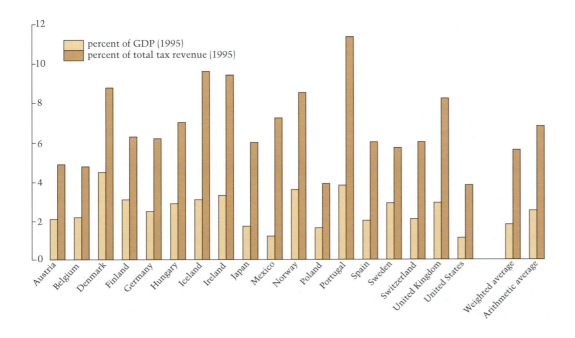

Environmental taxes will play an increasing role in the global economy.

the debt owed it by the world's poorest nations (not including International Monetary Fund or World Bank debt) on condition that the money be spent on basic human needs by these nations.

▲ Kenya's globally publicized sacrificial torching of U.S.$3 million worth of illegally held tusks hopefully signals the end of the international trade in African elephant ivory. In 1988, 1,600 elephants were killed in Africa every week; in 2000, only some 600,000 remain. An unusually united international outcry culminated in the species being placed on "Appendix I" of CITES—the Convention on International Trade in Endangered Species—and with that action, some 90 percent of the world market for elephant ivory was closed. This successful campaign gives some justification for optimism that the cause of species and habitat conservation is now gaining ground.

THE SPECTER OF THE WORLD TRADE ORGANIZATION

The trend toward global free trade applies very well to wretched exploitation as it does to trade. The wild card introduced by the General Agreement on Tariffs and Trade (GATT) has been embraced by members of the timber trade who fear the threat of timber nations' official bans and boycotts on wood products. In addition, the World Trade Organization (WTO) is presently lobbying logging industry groups to create a global agreement for free trade in forest products which, in effect, will outlaw environmental safeguards and trade controls as many corporations view them as barriers to trade. Safeguards that could be invalidated by WTO policies include import restrictions on forest products that carry invasive pests; certification on ecolabeling schemes and what could be interpreted as "unreasonably" high standards for forest management and production. If this trend is not governed judiciously, its capacity for environmental malignancy is unlimited.

So disillusioned are international citizenry and organizations, ranging from environmental to labor, of WTO's policies that massive rioting broke out at the Seattle WTO conference in December of 1999, requiring deployment of the National Guard.

SANITY IN GLOBAL PRIORITIES

The organizers of the Hague Appeal for Peace Conference of 1999 noted that "the past 99 years have seen more death, and more brutal death, from war, famine and other preventable causes than any other time span in history." Does this not challenge us to view our current concept of "military security" as something of an oxymoron? The cost of six U.S. stealth bombers is equal to the amount necessary to safeguard two-thirds of the Amazon rainforest.

The world's nuclear armament reserves now stand at more than 50,000 weapons, whose capability for destruction is equal to 1,300,000 bombs of Hiroshima magnitude (roughly 2.5 tons of TNT for every woman, man, and child on Earth). Few would deny that such stockpiles represent, in military jargon, an "overkill" of ludicrous proportions. Try comparing our spending on weapons with our investment in the environment. FAO's budget for forestry, the United Nation's lead role in that sector, was a mere 5 percent in 1975 and is now 3 percent. The world's weapons budget is more than U.S.$2.1 billion per day. A single B-2 bomber costs U.S.$1.5 billion, yet the United Nations Environment Program's budget is less than U.S.$40 million *a year*.

Costa Rica, while opting not to maintain an army, has in the trade-off 26 percent of its land under parks and reserves, one of the world's lowest illiteracy rates, most effective social programs, and excellent national health care. Immediately apparent to any visitor is that in place of soldiers bristling with automatic weapons are bright-faced children in freshly pressed uniforms going to and from school. The nation boasts a 93 percent literacy rate, and these same children look forward to a life expectancy of 75 years—a truly staggering contrast to the general perception of a developing country.

THINK GLOBALLY—ACT LOCALLY

It is argued that species are the "heritage of humanity," and that "in the United States twice as many people visit zoos and aquariums each year as attend baseball, football, hockey, and basketball games."

A Gallup poll shows that three-fourths of the people of both developed and developing countries want to see more effort and money expended in protecting wild species, and many feel a definite and instinctive responsibility for species in foreign lands "as part of humankind's common heritage." On the other hand, the exploiter views this common heritage more as a common property resource, up for grabs to the first comer. It is illuminating that a live animal or tree in the wild is common property; a dead one readily becomes private property.

Apparently, the inherent bond between humans and their biological inheritance is woven so deeply into their makeup that the intergovernmental organization comprising the drought-stricken states of the West African Sahelian Zone (CILSS) repeatedly listed wildlife conservation in its priorities for developmental projects and foreign aid. Thus far, such aid has not been forthcoming from the international community.

Concerned members of the public should be aware that they do have real and effective opportunities to express their anguish, sorrow, indignation, and even anger at species depletion, and to demand appropriate action on the part of their elected representatives.

▲ *The U.S.–Soviet Cooperative Initiative on Tropical Deforestation was declared "one of the few reasons for optimism on the tropical deforestation front" by the United Nations Environmental Program. During negotiations in Moscow (which included the author, head of the U.S. delegation, at right and Brent Blackwelder, president of Friends of the Earth, second from right), academician Vladimir Sokolov (at left), representing the Soviet Academy of Sciences, stated that in order to fund the program, the respective nations "should make the transfer from missiles to tropical forests." How splendidly fitting that as the 21st century dawns, the former president of Costa Rica, Oscar Arias, heads a commission of Nobel Peace Prize winners in the International Code of Conduct on Arms Transfers, leading the international community to, perhaps, a safer, saner place.*

If you can't do great things in a small way, do small things in a great way.

MOTHER TERESA

Renowned zoologist George Schaller, who is involved in the preservation of the endangered giant panda, among other species, crystallizes the gravity of the challenge when he states, "A failure to preserve the panda would be a serious moral blow to the human spirit, an indication that even an aroused consciousness, scientific wisdom, and dedication may not be enough to save humankind from ecological doom."

Yet humankind has met great challenges before and its course is not inexorably set and inflexible. If some part of the same energies spent in zealous exploitation are rechanneled into implementing enlightened conservation

ACTION PLAN FOR THE CONCERNED INDIVIDUAL

1. Letters and other communications from individuals and organizations to government representatives are the most direct and effective way of expressing your concern over the issues of tropical deforestation. Also write to the World Bank, USAID, United Nations agencies, and other international development bodies, demanding that their projects within the tropical forests are not environmentally destructive. It is interesting to note that in expressing your concern to legislators, one to five letters on an issue will generally elicit a form letter; five to 10 letters elicits a legislative assistant's response; more than 10 letters will most often compel the legislators themselves to respond personally. You should address your correspondence to:

President
The World Bank
1818 H Street NW
Washington, DC 20433
Tel. (202) 477-1234
Fax (202) 477-6391
Web: www.worldbank.org

Administrator
US Agency for International Development
1300 Pennsylvania Avenue NW
Washington, DC 20523
Tel. (202) 712-4810
Fax (202) 216-3524
Email: pinquires@usaid.gov
Web: www.info.usaid.gov

President
Inter-American Development Bank
1300 New York Avenue NW
Washington, DC 20577
Tel. (202) 623-1000
Fax (202) 623-3096
Web: www.iadb.org

Conversely, should you be fortunate enough to visit a tropical forest park or region in a foreign country, take the time to write to the minister of parks, the Forestry Department, the Department of Tourism, or the country's president, to say how impressed you were with the experience and urge the conservation of these resources. One such positive letter has more impact than several negative messages.

2. Lobby against your government's support, financial and otherwise, for certain short-sighted and highly destructive colonization schemes which move masses of ill-prepared people into tropical forest wilderness areas (e.g., Brazil into its Amazon Forest; Indonesia into New Guinea). On the positive side, implore that methods at our disposal be taught and implemented to sustain the tropical peasant farmer on his land (e.g., terracing of fields, agroforestry, tilapia fish farming, and other practical measures).

3. Be personally involved in efforts to ensure that timber extraction in the tropics proceeds through sustainable and environmentally sound harvesting methods (e.g., strip harvesting, reforestation of plantation species in cut areas, etc.). Ask fast-food chains whether or not they import beef raised in tropical forest pastures—patronize them accordingly.

4. Give your support to the following conservation organizations working in the tropical forests:

The International Society for the Preservation of the Tropical Rainforest
3931 Camino de la Cumbre
Sherman Oaks, CA 91423
(The author is president of this organization.)
Tel. (818) 788-2002
Fax (818) 990-3333
Email: forest@nwc.net
Web: www.isptr-pard.org

programs, constructive aid policies, and the linchpin around which lasting success will turn—sustainable agricultural and wood-producing practices—there is no reason why the tropical forests and the human species cannot coexist, each sustaining the other through the ages.

By so doing, we may still avert a descent into a maelstrom of irrevocable deforestation effects. While the historic opportunity to embrace that challenge is before us, we should be well aware that the decision is now fully ours: we must choose between temporary opulence and perpetuating life.

Cultural Survival
96 Mount Auburn Street
Cambridge, MA 02138
Tel. (617) 441-5400
Fax (617) 441-5417
Email: csinc@cs.org
Web: www.cs.org

Rainforest Action Network
221 Pine Street, Suite 500
San Francisco, CA 94104
Tel. (415) 398-4404
Web: www.ran.org

Friends of the Earth
1025 Vermont Avenue NW, 3rd Floor
Washington, DC 20005
Tel. (202) 783-7400
Fax (202) 783-0444
Email: foe@foe.org
Web: www.foe.org

The World Conservation Union (IUCN)
28 Rue Mauverney
1196 Gland
Switzerland
Tel. 41-22-999-00-01
Fax 41-22-999-00-02
Email: mail@hq.iucn.org
Web: www.iucn.org.

5. Continue to educate yourself and others around you about this wonderfully rich environment. Know that each of us is, in part, responsible for these forests becoming the Earth's first endangered habitat, and use conscience in modifying your behavior to prevent its extinction. Recycle paper and other forest products whenever possible; avoid adding to market pressures by being an abundant or unnecessary consumer of these products; refuse a paper bag when shopping whenever possible; and see that these practices are contagious. Address your town or city council to pass motions or legislation in town or city projects which prohibit the use of tropical hardwoods that are not sustainably produced (see page 239 for alternatives). Many cities, from small to large, have painlessly, even proudly, passed and adhered to this stipulation.

6. Gather data on tropical deforestation and conservation. As you accumulate knowledge on this "temple of flora," schedule talk programs and perhaps slide shows (see Educational Resources, Appendix I) at schools, clubs, and religious centers. As the media, as well as the public, are now increasingly primed on the issues, solicit press, television, and radio coverage. Schools at all levels should be encouraged to include such information in their curricula.

7. *Know that you personally can make a difference.* For those who feel that these issues loom large (indeed they do), and that any of your efforts would be meaningless, take with you forever the following: After the high tide produced by a storm on a Caribbean forest island, a multitude of starfish, still alive in the early morning before the sun would bake them, littered the beach. A tourist observed a native man walking briskly along the waterline among the stranded starfish picking one after another up and throwing the writhing creatures back into the sea. The tourist approached the native protesting, "Why are you doing this? There are so many starfish, you can't make a difference. What you're doing can't possibly matter." Our man, still focused on his mission of mercy, flipped another sea star back into the water and said, "It mattered to that one!"

6
REASON FOR HOPE

The greater danger for most of us is not that our aim is too high and we miss it, but that it is too low and we reach it.

MICHELANGELO

A new level of scientific exploration, as well as ecotourism, is now made possible with the canopy walkway, here at the Amazon Center for Environmental Education and Research (ACEER) in the Peruvian Amazon. The rainforest canopy, Earth's last frontier, is accessed safely by students as well as seasoned nature travelers who universally report the event as zenith, experience in their lives.

1 A GROWING PUBLIC AWARENESS

Nineteenth-century German explorer Theodor Koch-Grün-berg, during his final visit to the northeast Amazon, wrote: "The Indians of Rio Branco are close to their end. Those who escaped influenza, which killed entire [villages], are now being liquidated forever by balata gatherers, gold prospectors or diamond seekers. The few Indians who survive have been deprived of their rights and reduced to slavery. Their ingenuous happiness has gone, their solemn dances have ceased . . . the joyful playing of children on the sandy center of the village by moonlight has ended. Happy are those who died in time."

Man did not weave the web of life, he is merely a strand in it. Whatever he does to the web, he does to himself.

CHIEF SEALTH,
DUWAMISH INDIAN,
WHO BEFRIENDED
AMERICAN EXPLORERS
AND FOR WHOM THEY
NAMED THE CITY OF
SEATTLE – MID-19TH
CENTURY.

A REMOTE VIEW OF HISTORY

Play in your mind a time-lapse film of Earth viewed from space and let the last 10,000 years, the epoch of human civilization, be synchronized to pass at a rate of a millennium every minute. Of the 10 minutes, the first nine appear to be a still photograph. One thousand years ago, a minor encroachment begins of developing civilization into forests of Europe, China, and India. Two centuries ago (12 seconds to our film's end) parts of Europe and China go bare. The Industrial Revolution, seen at six seconds to the end, results in eastern North American forests receding to the ax, but otherwise little else has markedly changed globally.

Only in the last three seconds, after World War II, does deforestation begin to fester, then erupt, and now violently hemorrhage. This is humanity's global assault on the tropical rainforests where fires rage like a death fugue in wet, cloistered, closed canopy cathedrals where they never did before. We freeze-frame the final second and see that 54 percent of all tropical moist forests are gone and the remainder now covers only 6 percent of Earth's land surface, casting a dense penumbra over the planet's capacity for evolution. The reasons for this habitat holocaust are as follows: Only one-fifth is due to highly destructive logging, mostly in Southeast Asia; one-tenth to cattle ranching, mostly in Central America and Amazônia; one-seventh to road building, dam construction, commercial agriculture, and fuelwood gathering. But the formidable specter that looms over our satellite image is the slash-and-burn farmer, responsible for almost three-fifths of tropical moist forest removal (Myers 1992; FAO 1992).

The reasons for this become evident when we consider that 60 percent of the 1.2 billion people in the world who are in the grips of absolute poverty inhabit environmentally fragile biomes such as tropical moist forest regions, where sustainable livelihoods are not yet practiced and the landlessness of rural populations ranges from 15 to 34 percent. The numbers of dispossessed continue to grow even faster than population growth rates (Jazairy, et al. 1992), and if this remains unmitigated, these hapless, shifted cultivators could well number 1 billion in tropical forest lands by the year 2015. This represents by far the most massive movement of people in world history in so short a period of time—little more than 50 years—resulting in deforestation in the tropics as the largest land use conversion to have ever occurred in such a correspondingly short space of time (Myers 1994).

October 12, 1999, was dubbed "the day of the 6 billion" by the United Nations. We have now doubled the world's 1960 population, increased the size of the world economy over the same period by three and a half times, more than doubled the world production of grains, doubled production of fuelwood, and more than tripled production of paper. As we saw in Chapter 3, the connection between population increase and habitat loss, especially in tropical forests, is undeniable. By 2025, a global total of 8 billion souls is projected

(United Nations 1999), and a full 80 percent of these burgeoning numbers will be living in tropical forest nations; that is 6.4 billion people, more than the global population of today!

Since we now know that the main cause of tropical deforestation is migrant slash-and-burn agriculture, even though access is provided by roads built for logging, we can deduce the outcome with abundant clarity: Unless we muster the international political will and good governance to address the sustainable production of food for these billions so that they can remain stable on their plots, the remaining tropical moist forests will evaporate in a cloud of smoke within some 35 years.

A Course for Concerned Citizens

Paradoxically, we presently have ample justification to take heart. There is *reason for hope*, to recall Jane Goodall's vibrantly edifying phrase in the introduction to this book and title to her recent best-selling book, as there is now a palpable, ever-growing public concern for the fate of these forests and an acknowledgment of the hard science that informs us exactly what is at stake if we become complacent and lose these forests. This concern clearly includes, yet goes beyond the quid pro quo of medicines, food, and industrial materials these forests hold for us in their promise to enrich all our lives immeasurably and over millennia to come. I genuinely believe that humanity at large has, since the late 1960s when tropical deforestation first raised its head as the sleeper issue of the 20th century, come to find abhorrent the desecration of creation itself—the expunging of 137 species per day, or 50,000 per year. These losses can now be clearly discerned in vertebrate species, signaling a bellwether effect of human activities on habitat. The results include deeply declining tiger populations—only 3,000 to 5,000 remain, mostly in isolated groups too small to be effective breeding pools; all rhino species are approaching extinction, with only 40 to 60 Javan one-horned rhinos (*Rhinoceros sandaicus*) remaining, their breeding pool likewise compromised; and we can now say farewell to the golden toad (*Bufo periglenes*) of Costa Rica, the flamboyant ambassador to the environment. This bright orange, cherubic fellow with a gregarious mass mating rendezvous has not been seen since 1989; sadly, it has now been declared extinct. All these are but tips of icebergs. In response to recent global amphibian population implosions, the cause of which remains shrouded in mystery, Kenneth Dodd, research zoologist for the U.S. Department of the Interior, declared in 1998, "What we're seeing is a pervasive collapse in the biosphere." Bruce Babbitt, while U.S. Secretary of the Interior, noted that the calamity spotlighted "a landscape of extinction that goes all the way around the world."

There is reason for hope, however, even at the 11th hour. The technologies to sustain the agriculture of tropical forest peasantry (many of which were reviewed in Chapter 5) are at our disposal, should we choose to use them. Yet food production necessary to meet the rising demand, mainly from the developing countries, is likely to be in the region of 1.8 percent per year from now until 2010. Be forewarned: Unless we do employ technologies of sustained agriculture, an additional 222 million acres (90 million ha) will be brought into agricultural production in those 10 years in developing nations, a large proportion of which is now under forest cover (FAO 1997).

▲ *No bird elucidates the chromatic brilliance of the tropical rainforest more than the resplendent quetzal* (Pharomarcus mocinno) *of Central America. These trogon family members nest in tree holes in the deep forest. The emerald tail feathers of a male can be 3 feet long (0.91 m). This bird is robed in glittering, hairlike plumage, its breast a lustrous shade of crimson. [Talamanca Range, Costa Rica.]*

A Global Greenhouse

When global warming was reported a decade ago in this book's first edition, a degree of controversy existed within certain arenas of the scientific community as to its validity. Much has transpired in the decade since, and in bringing readers up to date, I must confess mixed emotions. I am saddened that global warming is now a mainstream scientific consensus—that it is indeed a tragic reality according to the more than 2,000 scientists of the Intergovernmental Panel on Climate Change. But I also find reason for hope. Perhaps humanity will now meaningfully defend itself against this insidious phenomenon, one whose mechanisms we understand today much more clearly than we did only a decade ago. It is probable that over the long term, no global disturbance to date will have a more profound effect on our well-being or on the state of our planet. While we have investigated the many aspects of global warming comprehensively in Chapters 4 and 5, recent developments deserve reporting.

Drunken Forests—the Hall of Mirrors

Alaska appears to be a harbinger of global futures. Trees growing there in permafrost are now often seen leaning in all directions, a phenomenon referred to as *drunken forests*. This is caused by the permafrost melting into swampy pits known as *thermokarsts*, which have spread 80 miles (129 km) northward in the last century in some places. These unstable foundations have wreaked havoc with buildings, roads, bridges, power lines, and telephone poles. Even the University of Alaska's headquarters for International Arctic Research, under construction in Fairbanks, had to be moved.

An estimated one-third to one-half of all Earth's plant communities, as well as the animals which depend on them, might be required to shift in response to morphing environmental conditions. However, a significant

▶ *Drunken forests*
As temperatures rise in the Arctic and sub-Arctic regions, the permafrost thaws for the first time—increasingly creating swampy bogs called thermokarsts. While frozen, the ground supported vast far northern boreal forests known as taiga. Sadly, the doomed trees now list drunkenly. Scientists warn that if the warming runs its course as predicted, thermokarsting will eventually be complete, moving the permafrost line farther north, a line that has already migrated a significant 80 miles (129 km) in the last century.

percentage of those communities will not be up to the task of moving with the required speed. The fossil record indicates that the maximum rate at which various plant species have migrated to more suitable areas is about 0.03 miles per year (0.04 km/yr) for the slowest, to 1.3 miles per year (2 km/yr) for the fastest. Yet—and this is the obstacle that vegetation of the near future must hurdle—projected temperatures in many parts of the world could require plant species to migrate at 1 to 3.5 miles per year (1.5 to 5.5 km/yr), or as much as 117 times faster than they are able. It is further projected that forests will not achieve this speed; rather, fast-growing, often non-native species—in other words, weeds—will (UNEP, WMO 1996).

Industry's Initial Reaction to Severe Weather Event Increase

Perhaps the first sector of the economy to be severely affected by climate change is the insurance industry, whose leaders are demonstrating considerable concern about the greenhouse effect. Warmer surface waters, particularly in the tropics and subtropics, release more heat into the atmosphere to drive storm systems. Because a hotter planet and hotter seas experience more evaporation and energy, many climate experts expect more extreme weather events, which mean more severe storms as well as droughts and fires. This has been evident over the past several decades. As a result, storms are projected to be more frequent, more intense, and more destructive.

Evidence suggests that wave heights produced by storms at sea are rising and that rogue waves of 80 or 90 feet (24 to 27 m) are becoming more common. The world record wave was measured at 112 feet (34 m). Wave heights off the coast of England have risen an average of 25 percent over the past several decades, which extrapolates to a 20 foot (6 m) increase in the highest waves over the next half-century (Junger 1997). A study by Travelers Group of Hartford, Connecticut, estimates that even a modest 0.9°F (0.5°C) increase in average global temperature by 2010 could produce an extension of 20 days in the hurricane season, a 33 percent jump in hurricane landfalls in the United States, an increase in storm severity, and an annual rise in U.S. catastrophic losses by 30 percent. Such revenue depletions would easily obliterate the U.S.$160 billion the insurance industry has in reserve for catastrophes.

Worldwide, weather-related insurance claims have climbed from U.S.$2 billion per year during the 1980s to U.S.$12 billion per year during the 1990s, resulting in rocketing insurance rates. In Florida, for example, premiums have increased by 72 percent since 1992. Consider that before 1987, there were no losses larger than U.S.$1 billion. Now losses in the tens of billions of dollars are common, with 1992's Hurricane Andrew alone producing losses on the order of U.S.$40 billion. It is estimated that a sea level rise of only 7.7 inches (20 cm)—a very likely scenario within the next 20 years—would erode sand barriers that protect U.S.$2 trillion worth of insured properties along the U.S. Atlantic and Gulf Coasts. The head of the Reinsurance Association of America stated that unless something is done to stabilize the climate, it could bankrupt the industry. Why not march in tandem with more than 70 of the world's largest insurers, who have signed the United Nations Environment Program (UNEP) initiative calling for governments to reduce greenhouse gas emissions 20 percent below 1990 levels?

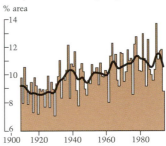

Proportion of the United States affected by extreme-event* precipitation

% area

*Precipitation exceeding 2 inches in 24 hours.

▲ *High latitude areas are tending to see more significant increases in rainfall, while precipitation has actually declined in many tropical areas.*

▲ *In this spectacular view captured 22,300 miles (35,900 km) high by the GOES-8 satellite, we see five storms parading across the North Atlantic Ocean in August 1995. From left to right are Tropical Storm Jerry, a tropical wave, Hurricane Iris, Hurricane Humberto, and what was to become Tropical Storm Karen. Tropical Storm Gil lurks in the Pacific. This is most unusual since an average of only nine tropical storms, including five hurricanes, form annually! Dubbed "the year of the hurricane," 1995 spawned 11 hurricanes, a record since the late 1800s.*

THE ATMOSPHERIC OUNCE OF PREVENTION

It is clearly urgent that we commit to the December 1997 Kyoto Protocol, (having failed to do so at the Hague in December 1999). It is far less stringent than the insurance industry's directive, which by 2012 would reduce greenhouse gas emissions to at least 5 percent below 1990 levels. To date the protocol has been ratified by only 32 of the 84 nations that signed it. While gaining significant signatories as of late, the United States, highest of any of the major industrial emitters, is still not among them. In addition, in March 1999, FAO defined the following mechanisms aimed at slowing CO_2 buildup: maintaining existing stocks of carbon in forests through forest protection, conservation, and sustainable harvesting; increasing the net uptake of CO_2 from the atmosphere by enlarging forest areas; substituting biomass energy from sustainably managed forests for fossil fuels; and substituting wood products for energy intensive alternative products (such as steel and concrete). Over the long term, 2.47 acres (1 ha) of Malaysian forest is estimated to provide more than U.S.$3,000 worth of carbon storage value (Panaytov and Ashton 1992).

This apparent value, especially under the current threat, could well bestir us to flex our conservation muscle for self-preservation and mount the global groundswell necessary to preserve these imperiled forests. How gloriously ironic it would be if runaway deforestation were combined with another simmering, yet sobering problem—the greenhouse effect—to foster a solution to both. In that solution, forest conservation and a concerted tree-planting campaign would take place principally in tropical forest nations, which would be richly compensated by the global community for their sacrifice and efforts. Even the guardedly optimistic can easily see the pieces fitting together. I find considerable inspiration in the world-record tree-hugger, Julia "Butterfly" Hill, who on December 10, 1997, climbed to the top of a 180-foot (55-m) redwood tree named Luna to protect the proposed felling of that tree and others in one of the few remaining magisterial old-growth forests in California. After more than two years, she descended Luna on December 18, 1999, having secured a preservation agreement with the logging company. As a sad footnote, in December 2000 a saboteur cut 60 percent through Luna's trunk, and it is not known if the great tree will survive, despite heroic efforts by arborists at bracing against wind-fall. In a tearful press conference, Hill stated that it will take more than a chainsaw to destroy Luna. "Although symbols can be attacked, what they stand for can never be destroyed."

◀ The author, during a tornado near Rolla, Kansas, while conducting a Global Warming/Severe Weather Events research project with the National Severe Storms Laboratory. Relatively small changes in global climate could produce large changes in the frequency of extreme weather events such as this tornado (McMichael, et al./ WHO 1996).

Daniel Schrag, director of the Laboratory for Geochemical Oceanography at Harvard University, states that his climate modeling foresees aberrations such as blistering heat waves, record low temperatures, and tornadoes where they do not normally occur. To accent that forecast, Barrow, Alaska, recorded its first thunderstorm!

It is expected that global warming will produce warmer, more moisture-laden air moving over the United States from warmer South Atlantic seas. This is a petri dish for hurricane culture. As this mass collides with the Arctic cold front, itself increasingly moist due to warmer Arctic seas, the scenario is just the prescription for violent tornadic events. The disastrous May 3, 1999, Oklahoma City killer tornado of F-5 caliber (the most destructive category) was recorded at 318 miles per hour, the highest wind speed ever documented on Earth!

Forest plantations in the developing regions, 1980 and 1995

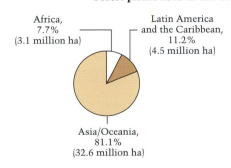

Africa, 7.7% (3.1 million ha)
Latin America and the Caribbean, 11.2% (4.5 million ha)
Asia/Oceania, 81.1% (32.6 million ha)

1980: total planted area = 40.2 million hectares

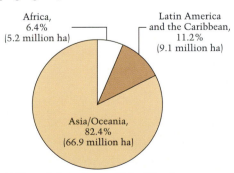

Africa, 6.4% (5.2 million ha)
Latin America and the Caribbean, 11.2% (9.1 million ha)
Asia/Oceania, 82.4% (66.9 million ha)

1995: total planted area = 81.2 million hectares

II INTERNATIONAL EFFORTS

RECENT INTERNATIONAL AGREEMENTS RELATED TO FORESTS

▶ *Earth pledge*

In this compelling highlight of the 1992 Earth Summit in Rio de Janeiro, Chief Raoni (with lip disc) of the Brazilian Kayapó tribe and other tribal leaders were admitted into the high security sector—with their weapons—at the behest of the International Society for the Preservation of the Tropical Rainforest. There they presented their plea to save their forest homelands from destruction to 114 heads of state—more than ever before gathered at one time, for any purpose. In signing the Earth Pledge, these globally renowned leaders of indigenous peoples' rights assert a new, sustainable direction for humanity's activities for the new millennium.

THE GLOBAL SUMMITS OF HUMANITY

Another reason for hope is the current internationalization of environmental/developmental/social issues. Notable among these were: the United Nations Conference on the Environment and Development (UNCED), or "Earth Summit," convened in Rio de Janeiro in 1992 and attended by 114 heads of state, which led to the 1997 Kyoto Protocol through the United Nations Framework Convention on Climate Change (FCCC); the Intergovernmental Panel on Forestry (IPF) in 1995, spawned by the United Nations Commission on Sustainable Development (CSD) in order to encourage international cooperation and consensus on key issues related to forests; the World Food Summit in Rome in 1996; and the landmark 1994 International Conference on Population and Development (ICPD) in Cairo.

At UNCED, two major texts on forests were adopted: "The Non-Legally Binding Authoritative Statement of Principles for a Global Consensus on the Management, Conservation and Sustainable Development of Forests" (otherwise known as the "Forest Principles") and Chapter 11 of Agenda 21 ("Controlling Deforestation"). Not surprisingly, the usual suspects—the foremost tropical logging nation of Malaysia leading the south and the United States leading the north—led the way to deflecting a legally binding agreement even as the European Community seemed poised to favor such action. Still, the agreements represent the very first international consensus on forests. The high-profile, substantive arenas of sovereignty over forests and compensation derived from their conservation by southern nations must be resolved with the wisdom of Solomon. When they are (Rio + 10 is scheduled for 2002), the current logjam can finally be diffused, resulting in a formidable call to action and a legally binding pact for the long-awaited preservation of tropical forests.

FUTURE FOREST PRODUCTS SECURITY?

The area of plantations has doubled in developing regions since 1980, and industrial wood production from farm forestry and agroforestry systems is

becoming increasingly important in several countries. There is reason to hope that this trend will encourage decreasing levels of timber harvesting in natural forests due to increasing environmental concerns (FAO 1997).

Further, possibly connected, reasons for hope are the significant increases in the recovery and recycling of paper, coinciding with restrictions placed on harvesting in North American national forests and some tropical Asian and South Pacific countries, and the growing green campaign for certification of sustainable wood production. Thailand, the Philippines, and peninsular Malaysia are among the nations that now have logging bans in force, even if they were prompted by runaway forest depletion. However, accessible commercial timber resources in most of tropical Asia are fast becoming exhausted, posing major challenges. As Asia's consumption of many industrial forest products already equals or exceeds that of Europe and deficits are now apparent, the resulting growing demand is projected to outstrip the potential supply for almost all products—leading to fast growth in imports. As a direct result, an invasion of Asian logging corporations into Amazônia is already a reality. (The term *invasion* is not mine—it is from Brazilian government agency reports on the crisis.)

In counterbalance, the recent fifth United Nations European Timber Trends Study considered the growing possibility of a "deep green" future, giving rise to growing demand for certified wood. A certified wood program would result in significant price increases and thus encourage use of substitute materials in place of wood, beginning perhaps in North America. This utopian prospect is not entirely impractical, for in the pulp and paper field, any shortages or restrictions to access to forest raw materials would tend to encourage greater reliance on nonwood fiber such as straw, bagasse from sugar cane waste, expired coconut trees, reeds, and bamboo—all available in huge and reliable quantities (several billion tons per year). China and India already avail themselves of these materials.

WILL WE ALLOW THE LAST OF THE RAINFOREST TRIBALS TO BECOME THE GHOSTS OF THE FOREST?

While the winds of change begin to waft through these forests, it would be negligent not to question whether positive change will come in time for the forest tribals. Be assured: When the last of the tenuous origins of our culture have been dispossessed, disenchanted, and deculturalized—when we have wrenched from the rainforest tribals even their religious beliefs, the genesis of which predates the Old Testament, "imposing our beliefs on others," in the words of His Holiness the Dalai Lama (1999)—it will be a mournful day for our species. It is a point from which to look back with wonder that we ever had both the rare fortune to coexist with these archetype people who still reside in the Garden of Eden and live much as they did in the time of Genesis, and a full realization of what they had to offer us—aside from their tribal lands.

The pendulum on the upswing allows some hope, at least in Latin America, where in the past decade Bolivia, Brazil, Colombia, Ecuador, and Venezuela have recognized, to one degree or another, the land rights of indigenous peoples who have inhabited and conserved their forests since arriving there millennia ago. In many cases demarcation of these lands proceeds, even if slowly. Much to my delight, the efforts of tribal peoples

Land dive
Heroic cultural richness passed on from generation to generation is elegantly exhibited in this land diving ceremony. The Small Nambus tribe (so named for their banana leaf penis wrapping) of Pentecost Island, New Hebrides, displaying their fearlessness and thankfulness to their creator for the yam harvest, construct a 110-foot (34 m) tower from tree trunks bound by vines. Volunteers of men and those coming of age climb the tower and attach to their ankles lengthy vines,

measured precisely to the height of the individual— even accounting for the amount of stretch in the vine due to the volume of rainfall that year. After prayer and elucidating his grievances with certain villagers, the diver sails forth on his harrowing journey to Earth—which, as proper form dictates, he hits with his head and

hands—just as the vines stretch and break his fall before he breaks his neck (which vividly differentiates this ancient practice from bungee-jumping inspired by these land divers). He is then congratulated and embraced with gusto by the villagers, who then continue to chant and dance for another diver.

themselves, supported by environmental and human rights organizations, have resulted in official recognition of indigenous homelands, which has in turn been directly responsible for saving more tropical forest than any other measure or movement in the arena of tropical forest conservation. For example, the Yąnomamö in Brazil and Venezuela, despite their problems with gold miners who brought homicide and rampant disease, peerlessly shepherd a forest area as vast as Uruguay, far larger than any other forest reserve in the world. The boundaries of the indigenous lands and extractive reserves are visible in satellite images; you can clearly see that there is someone down there defending the forest from the chainsaws and torches.

In view of this, I am pleased to report that in April 2001, Brazil decreed the demarcation of 14 tribal areas totaling 4,893,500 acres (1,980,500 ha), which together with other preserves totals 11.85 percent of Brazilian territory.

While the survival prognosis for Latin American tribes is precarious indeed, we can only work toward the day when Asian and African nations follow suit in evolving a more enlightened indigenous lands policy. There, tribals have minimal rights, as discussed in Chapter 4. The Pygmies of Central and West Africa, the most ancient of all forest dwellers, having inhabited their homeland for 40,000 years, hold no enforceable claims. This is compounded by the fact that governments in the tropics are universally unable to prevent commercial timber theft, even from protected or tribal lands, due to the grossly inadequate numbers of forest guards spread over immense tracts of forest. In the Democratic Republic of the Congo (Zaire), for example, a forest staff of 800 is responsible for protection of 390,000 square miles (1 million sq km) inhabited by 15 million people. This disparity is analogous to patrolling the state of New York with the police force of the small city of Rochester (Durning 1993).

OIL AND TROPICAL FORESTS—A SLIPPERY SLOPE

Over their 30 years of oil exploration and production, the majority of oil companies have left a resounding legacy of environmental destruction and misery for tribal people in the Ecuadorian, Peruvian, and Colombian Amazon, usurping their traditional homelands, civil rights, livelihoods, health, and safety. A classic case in point is the U'wa tribe of Colombian cloud forests. So coercive and unlawful has been their widely reported harassment that tribal spokesperson Roberto Afanador Cobara decried in an open letter to Occidental and Shell Oil Companies "the beating I received by hooded men in the night, demanding I sign an authorization agreement or die." In a global plea, 5,000 U'wa have vowed to leap to their deaths from a 1,400-foot (427-m) cliff atop a sacred mountain if Occidental drills for oil in their forest home. Such drilling would force them to choose a quick death or a slow one, as oil pollution of soil, streams, and rivers has always been inherent in tropical forest oil production.

In March 1999, three Americans, members of separate indigenous rights groups, were murdered by the Colombian paramilitary group FARC while visiting and advising the U'wa. Following this tragedy, demonstrators denounced Occidental at their headquarters in Los Angeles, prompting shareholders to direct Occidental to commission an independent risk analysis report on the profitability of the venture, including the potential decline of stock price likely to result from a mass suicide of U'wa Indians (Amazon Watch 1999). Given the high visibility of the tribe's global appeal, the government of Colombia legalized the U'wa People's Unified Reserve; yet it granted Occidental a license to drill for oil just outside the reserve, still within U'wa traditional territory, where it would greatly impact the livelihood of the tribe. In 2000, the Colombian military moved into U'wa territory and began forcibly evicting the tribals as Occidental was ushered in to begin drilling. During a peaceful blockage of Occidental, police attacked the U'wa, driving them into the river and killing three children and five adults. Demonstrations still rage internationally. Adding considerably to concerns is Colombian rebel groups' tactic of blowing up oil pipelines, polluting the nation's forests with more than 2 million tons of crude oil destroying 3,600 square miles (9,300 sq km) of forest and agricultural land and 1,625 miles (2,600 km) of river systems in the past decade.

In 1997, more than 60 indigenous, environmental, and human rights groups around the globe denounced Shell and Mobil's U.S.$2.7 billion gas project in an isolated Peruvian rainforest region. Undaunted, the Peruvian Indigenous Federation, COMARU, represented 13 affected Machiguenga communities and cited the National Engineering University's analysis of streams used by the tribes for drinking, bathing, and fishing. A full complement of tests found levels of hydrocarbons, cadmium, and mercury to exceed levels permitted under Peruvian law. These findings mirror Shell's highly contested toxic legacy on Ogoni lands in Nigeria, where pollutants saturate the delta of the Niger River, impoverishing the once fertile soil (Davis 1999).

Before Texaco came to Ecuador, our rivers, lakes and streams had many fish, our waters were clean and there was ample game in the forest. Now, our rivers are contaminated, the fish have disappeared, and the animals have gone away.

ARCELIANO ILLANEZ
FCUNAE (INDIGENOUS COMMUNITY ORGANIZATION)

The Shuar women will not die on their knees. We will die fighting until every last drop of blood is gone.

WOMAN OF THE SHUAR TRIBE
ECUADOR, 1999

III ASSESSING THE DAMAGE

▲ *Thicker than the author's waist, giant bamboo (Dendrocalamus giganteus) from Malaysia is actually a woody grass that grows to 100 feet (30 m). Bamboo, the fastest-growing plant in the world, has been clocked at 0.00003 mph (0.00005 kmph)—or 47.6 inches (121 cm) in 24 hours. Tolerant of poor soils and resprouting after harvesting, planted in deforested areas, bamboo has the potential to fill the world's future wood pulp needs.*

And our needs are great, indeed, for if each of the 6 billion humans inhabiting our planet consumed the natural resources and emitted carbon dioxide at the rate equal to the average American, European, or Australian, we would require at least another two Earths! So revealed the World Wildlife Fund Living Planet Report 2000, which concluded that the natural wealth of Earth's forest, freshwater, and marine ecosystems has declined by one-third since 1970. Further, the area required to produce the natural resources consumed and absorb the carbon dioxide emitted by humanity has doubled since 1961, and by 1996 was 30 percent larger than the area actually available.

"THE YEAR THE WORLD CAUGHT FIRE"

"More forests were burned around the world in 1997 than in any other year in recorded history," stated World Wide Fund for Nature (WWF) spokesperson Jean-Paul Jeanrenaud, head of the fund's forest program. "Nineteen ninety-seven will be remembered as the year the world caught fire," Jeanrenaud added, referring to the Asian, South American, Australian, Chinese, Russian, and European blazes. Then came the global crucible of fires of 1998.

It had been believed that tropical rainforests were simply too wet to burn. That belief has proved incorrect, meteorologists believe, by monumental droughts caused in part by land clearing, exacerbated by global warming, and fueled by an El Niño year. El Niño episodes, it should be noted, are increasing in frequency, possibly in response to greenhouse gas accumulation in the atmosphere (Trouberth and Hoar 1997). The episode that ended in 1995 lasted five years and eight months, making it a once-in-2,000-year event. In 1997 and 1998, the world watched in disbelief as fires of gargantuan proportions—conflagrations visible from space—roiled unabated through much of Southeast Asia, Mexico, and Brazil, in the last case torching more than 12,000 square miles (30,000 sq km), an area the size of Belgium. Studies now show that due to logging and drought, some 100,000 square miles (270,000 sq km) of Brazilian Amazônia are vulnerable to fire and that a considerably wider area is influenced than was previously reported. Furthermore, the area of Amazon forest affected by surface fires each year may be similar in scale to the area affected by deforestation, such as that caused by total forest clearing for pasture and agriculture (Nepstad, et al. 1999). Brazilians now speak of three seasons: the rainy, the dry, and the *queimadas*, or burnings.

The 1997–98 fires spawned an impenetrable blanket of smoke and suffocated much of Indonesia, Malaysia, Brunei, Singapore, the Philippines, and southern Thailand. In many regions, the Sun could not be seen for days at a time; the dense pall from fires deep in Mexico reached far north into the United States. The inferno on three continents killed hundreds and sickened tens of millions more.

The culprits in Asia were found to be palm oil, pulp, and rubber agribusiness owners who slashed and burned their extensive forest holdings, which burned out of control to incinerate more than 15,000 square miles (40,000 sq km) of primary forest. These recalled the very first such human-made tropical rainforest firestorms in 1983 in Borneo, which immolated some 19,000 square miles (50,000 sq km) and more than U.S.$5 billion in standing timber (Dudley 1988). Although droughts were recorded prior to the 1983 event, huge fires were unknown (Sayer and Whitmore 1990). Scientists believe that those fires still burn today in massive underground peat deposits. There is a growing consensus that the phenomenon of rainforest wildfires is the effect of desiccation caused by longer dry seasons and, in some cases, the occasional absence of a significant wet season, perhaps due to deforestation (Dickinson and Virji 1987). The fires that raged in Sabah, Malaysia, destroyed 5.6 times as much logged forest as primary forest. The increased combustibility of the disturbed forest was due to dehydration caused by opening the canopy and the fuel of slash (logging debris) remaining on the ground after logging (Johns 1997).

INROADS INTO AMAZÔNIA

The Brazilian Amazon, which encompasses two-thirds of the Amazon Basin, comprises 30 percent of the world's remaining tropical forests and is home to fully one-tenth the entire world's animal and plant species. Given this scope, it would be difficult to regard Brazil's forests as anything short of central to the evolutionary capacity of our planet yet they illustrate its vulnerability.

A 1999 study by Daniel Nepstad of the Woods Hole Research Center, his colleagues from NASA, and a variety of Brazilian institutes finally defined the hidden damage resulting from logging and fire in Brazilian Amazônia. Heretofore that assessment has either escaped analysis (such as in FAO studies, which report on complete deforestation due to agriculture and ranching) or have been wildly speculated upon, resulting in widely disparate figures. This problem is due to the inability of satellites to see selective logging and much of the fire damage as the canopy closes over those gaps in one to five years.

By interviewing saw mill operators and corroborating their testimonies in many instances with on-the-ground observations, the Nepstad study reveals that in the Brazilian Amazon, "logging crews severely damage 10,000 to 15,000 km² [3,900 to 5,800 square miles] on average of forest annually that are not included in deforestation mapping programmes." If fire damage (see page 226) is added, the Nepstad report calculates, present estimates capture less than half the forest area impoverished each year and even less during years of severe drought. At the very least, then, in 1994–95, some 16,000 square miles (42,000 sq km) were deforested and degraded. Account for damage from fires and the figure rises to 22,000 square miles (58,000 sq km), or 1.62 percent of Brazilian Amazônia. For 1995–96, a year of decidedly less total forest clearing, INPE gives the figure of 7,000 square miles (18,000 sq km) of completely deforested land; relying on the Nepstad report, this figure can now be doubled to include degraded regions, totaling 1.02 percent of remaining area.

While there is no way to accurately assess the impact of logging or fires for previous years, for comparison the total estimated deforested area of Brazilian Amazônia by 1975 was 12,000 square miles (30,000 sq km). By the end of 2000, the devastation had reached 227,000 square miles (589,000 sq km), or more than 14 percent of the total of Brazil's legal Amazon of 1.5 million square miles (4 million sq km) (INPE 2001). This is an area greater than the size of France and fully 12 percent of the entire Amazon Basin's forest cleared to date. Brazil's recent efforts to link Manaus, a major city on the Amazon River, to the southern Amazonian state of Rondônia by paving highway BR-319 have raised considerable concerns, as the road would open the region to slash-and-burn settlers. By 1996 the state of Rondônia was 83 percent deforested (INPE 2001). The new road raises the alarming prospect of actually *bisecting* the Amazon forest over the next decade by an expanding swath of deforestation and logging.

Globally, the area of tropical forests affected by logging is vast. Of the remaining tropical forests, 31 percent are officially allocated to timber production (Johns 1997). This is significantly more than the roughly 8 percent currently under some form of protection. And the volume of forest under timber production is not static, but growing, especially in the tropical Americas, driven by increased foreign investment in forestry (Bowles, et al. 1998) and the heightened demand for tropical hardwood products in both domestic and international markets (FAO 1993; Uhl, et al. 1997).

THE PLUNDERING OF AMAZÔNIA

Meanwhile, forest protection in Brazilian Amazônia is weak. In 1996 alone, the area of Amazonian forest under Asian logging company concessions quadrupled to more than 46,000 square miles (120,000 sq km). In a highly controversial move, Brazil announced in 1998 that it would grant timber leases in 39 national forests, opening an additional 3,900 square miles (10,000 sq km) to logging. Finding such easily available foreign ground just when their home governments are tightening environmental controls and law enforcement, roving international companies ply their trade in Amazônia like robber barons, virtually without restriction, creating wakes of destruction similar to those they left behind in Asia.

These companies are more than capable of taking economic advantage of Brazil. Wielding size, power, and liquid currency in compromised developing nations typically sets the stage for unequal transactions. For instance, Malaysian, Indonesian, and Chinese timber companies recently proposed investments in Suriname of U.S.$500 million, a sum essentially equal the country's gross national product; in the Solomon Islands, landowners were paid U.S.$2.70 per cubic meter of timber, which the logging company then resold for U.S.$350 per cubic meter. Brazilian authorities asserted in 1998 that four-fifths of logging in Brazil's Amazon holdings are illegal and unregulated due to the expanse of the frontier. To compound this, lack of law enforcement is legendary, collecting only 6 percent of fines imposed.

Those who track the future of Amazônia are vividly aware of an unsettling ebb and flow not unlike the incoming and outgoing of a great, tempestuous tide. In 1998, in a widely applauded decree, President Fernando Cardoso of Brazil committed to place an additional 97,000 square miles (250,000 sq km) of Brazilian Amazon forest under protection soon into the 21st century. This flow, a conservation commitment of the highest magnitude yet for Brazil, will more than triple the existing protected area to more than 10 percent of the total Brazilian Amazon Basin. Yet, in an ebb, so committed is that country to logging programs that President Cardoso's decree included provisions for some logging within the "protected zone." Another ebb occurred in 1999 when an IBAMA officer was murdered and another seriously injured. We saw flow in early 2000 when Brazil's IBAMA National Control Agency's chief Rodolpho Lobo stated that "a new stage begins in the control of deforestation" by the use of satellite monitoring to identify illegal deforestation. It is revealed that eight of 10 people involved in the largest amount of forest clearing are cattle breeders. Later in 2000, another ebb was marked when the Brazilian government proposed a law that would make it possible to increase from 20 to 50 percent the amount of forest a landowner may cut. The law did not pass, but its specter still looms large as it is regularly reintroduced.

Venezuela, a country known for its intact forests, is now considering opening up its Guiana Shield region, a uniquely picturesque tepuí mesa region of high species diversity, endemicity and tribal refuge south of the Orinoco, to gold, diamond, and timber development. This eventuality would be highly

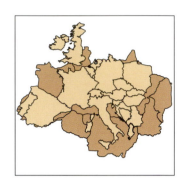

▲ *The gravity of deforestation in Amazônia is apparent considering that Brazil's portion of the Amazon Basin alone is some 75 percent larger than the cumulative land areas of all the countries of western Europe. To date, more than 14 percent of Brazilian Amazônia is deforested.*

disruptive to pristine tribal groups in the area; it also would encourage unlicensed exploitation, a nationwide problem that brings no additional tax revenues to the government. The conservation community is anxiously watching developments.

AIDS

It will no doubt surprise readers to see a connection between AIDS and tropical deforestation. AIDS was first identified in 1984, but the first confirmed case is of a Bantu man from what is now Congo, who died in 1959—first suggesting the tropical forest region of Africa as a source of the virus. There has been much speculation as to African primates' role in the evolution of the disease. On February 4, 1999, University of Alabama researcher Beatrice Hahn published in *Nature* the real case breaker in this important question for humanity.

Hahn's definitive DNA work now isolates the chimpanzee (*Pan troglodytes troglodytes*) as the source of the strain of simian immunovirus disease (SIV) that resulted in the global human immunovirus disease (HIV) pandemic. The likely scenario is as follows: During the colonial period in Central and West Africa, perhaps beginning in the 1940s, when HIV apparently first appeared (Hahn, pers. comm. 1999), forest clearing began in earnest, sending logging roads into primary forest. Slash-and-burn farming followed, as did bushmeat hunters, whose wild game hunting and trapping became more commercialized at that period due to the new ingress, according to Anthony L. Rose, director of the Institute for Conservation, Education and Development at Antioch University and a leading researcher of the consequences of bushmeat trade (pers. comm. 1999). This incursion gave hunters from the forest periphery the opportunity to dispatch a great many more chimpanzees. In addition, forest remnants caused by deforestation isolated small clusters of 12 to 15 chimps which were easily hunted down, reported Virginia Landau, a chimpanzee researcher for the Jane Goodall Institute (pers. comm. 1999).

When natives butchered the primates, they allowed abundant opportunity for a transfer of blood from primate to man (Desrosiers 1990). Especially relevant in this context is the finding that multiple exposures to infected chimpanzee blood far increase the chances of human infection. Interestingly, subsequent testing of blood samples taken from deep-forest Pygmies in the 1970s and 1980s (for other research purposes) showed no HIV (Rouziox, et al. 1986). This fact even further implicates an HIV-deforestation connection. Hahn's work finally confirmed that SIV then mutated into HIV-1 and the rest, unfortunately, is history.

As of this writing, the HIV infection rate in adults of many African nations is terrifyingly high: Botswana, 36 percent and Zimbabwe, 25 percent. Worldwide, 50 million have been infected, 16.3 million in 1999 alone; the AIDS conflagration continues to blaze out of control. Without AIDS, life expectancy in Botswana and Zimbabwe would be 70 years, but with AIDS it is expected to fall to 30—more like a medieval lifespan than a modern lifespan. (UNAIDS 2000). We now know that HIV-2, common in growing areas of Africa and Asia, was transmitted from the sooty mangabey (*Cercocebu torquatus*) from West Africa. Now that the genesis of HIV-1 has been revealed, it is doubtful that humanity could find a better rationale for a rigidly enforced ban on the taking of Central and West African primates—unless we wish to court the unknown wrath of HIV-4 and beyond.

IV A Call to Action

STABILIZING POPULATION

Consider the following:

1. There is not a single species on Earth that does not erode its quality of life with the exponential increase of its numbers. Ungulates overpopulate, overgraze, and fall prey to starvation and disease. Even cancer cells, if too "successful," perish by killing their host. It is arrogant to assume our species would fare any better than the other 1.75 million species thus far described by science that abide by one of the earliest observed biological principles, the balance of nature.

2. The problems clearly attributed to Earth's current population of more than 6 billion souls, which affect habitats as disparate as tropical forests, oceans, and the atmosphere, are increasing. What will be the state of the Earth, our own species, and others we share this planet with in 2050, when projected United Nations figures place world population at 8.9 billion? Global population is likely to increase as much in the next 50 years as it has in the past 50, with virtually the entire increase occurring in developing nations.

3. Food production will likely lag behind population growth. Factoring only minimal increases in nutrition, twice as much grain will be required. This will call for irrigation equal to 20 Nile Rivers—with water presently in short supply! Meanwhile, the advances of the "green revolution" of the 1950s and 1960s, which required costly input of fertilizer, pesticides, and machinery, have leveled or even reverted to previous production levels in many areas.

OPTIONS TO A MALTHUSIAN FUTURE

The developed world is projected to achieve a zero population growth soon into the new millennium, assuring its food-secure status. What strategies can we undertake in developing nations so that they too may be vouchsafed entry into this cloistered realm?

1. Remove social and physical barriers to women's use of family planning services, as one-third of population increase will be due to unwanted pregnancies.

2. Persuade developing-world governments—with sensitivity, for cultural proclivities are often staunchly defended—to remove the restricted access to contraceptives by women.

3. Provide aid to nations where geographical access to contraceptives is limited by budget. For example, in sub-Saharan Africa, it can take more than two hours to reach a contraceptive provider.

4. Inform both husband and wife about the advantages and methods of contraceptives so as to remove the husband's objections, as in

Projected world population by 2050
(three scenarios projected by the UN)

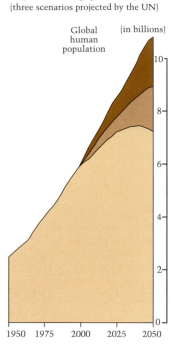

Global human population (in billions)

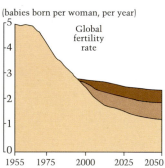

(babies born per woman, per year)

Global fertility rate

▲ *The United Nations expects world population to reach somewhere between 7.3 billion and 10.7 billion by 2050. The exact number depends on how far fertility rates fall in the meantime.*

POPULATION DENSITY AND GROWTH IN TROPICAL CLOSED BROADLEAVED FOREST DOMAINS		
	Population Density 1990	Annual Population Growth 1981–90
	Inhabitants per km²	% per annum
Rainforest Domain	41	2.2
Moist Hill/Mountain Domain	56	2.6
Moist Forest Domain	55	2.4

many countries women need their husbands' approval for contraception.

5. Reduce infant mortality, giving parents for whom children are a matter of family survival the confidence to produce fewer children.

6. Institute credit for microenterprises that include women, emulating programs such as those Grameen Bank has pioneered, in order to provide economic security for women. This will provide a living that does not require habitat conversion.

7. Commit to the 1994 Cairo Accord on Population and Development by funding its U.S.$17 billion-a-year budget for its 20-year program.

Should the task seem too daunting, consider the following reasons for hope:

1. Due to spirited international efforts, the world's population growth has slowly but steadily dropped from its zenith of an average of 6.2 children per family in the 1950s to less than 3 today. It is projected to fall to 2.1 by 2045 (United Nations 1999).

2. The Dominican Republic's fertility rate has halved in the past two decades.

3. Mexico, the world's leading population explosion example, has cut its growth in half in the past 25 years. The average woman there now has 2.7 children, versus 6.7 in 1970 (Schrader 1996).

THE CONSERVATION CONCESSION

Establishing a forest preservation strategy for the 21st century, Conservation International (CI) proposes the world's first "conservation concession" in Guyana. This new market mechanism is similar to a logging concession, but

▼ *Dick Rice at Conservation International spearheads a movement to conserve tropical forests that have undergone only light timber harvest. Such a strategy would appear to be highly justified, as these images reveal. At left is a clear-cut on Vancouver Island, British Columbia, in which the entire forest logged is destroyed. At right is the Chiquitas Dry Forest of Bolivia in which only one species, mahogany (Swietenia macrophylla), has been extracted. The canopy gaps (not apparent in this image) heal within five years, interior damage becoming less apparent over time. At a negotiated bargain price, a huge expanse of such forest was recently added to Bolivia's Noel Kempff Mercado National Park.*

in this case it rewards a developing forest nation for its unique advantage—large areas of intact primary forest. Concession fees equal to those paid for the right to log the tract are paid to the country's foresting commission to ensure the forest is placed in preservation status, to be maintained in its pristine state for the length of the concession (in this case, at least 40 years), after which an option for renewal may be exercised.

In addition, economic development is stimulated by the concession holder's investment in constructive development projects in an amount equal to or greater than the foregone economic value that would have resulted from logging. In this way, creative conservation can at once compensate forest nations for the environmental services they provide to the world and provide an alternative to logging as well as meaningful economic progress and the maintenance of pristine forest habitats—in the Guyanan example, 1 million acres (405,000 ha)—fluently demonstrating to the world that conservation pays abundant dividends.

REASON TO ACT

In his best-selling book, *Ethics for the New Millennium*, His Holiness the Dalai Lama eloquently reasons that it is essential for humankind to cultivate universal responsibility for the global environment. After all, "when two families share a single water source, ensuring that it is not polluted benefits both." As environmental decay worsens, and with no handy escape route at our disposal, we must deal with these formidable obstacles. His Holiness goes on to reason, however, that

> if we have the capacity to destroy the earth, so, too, do we have the capacity to protect it. . . . Moreover, the fact that air we breathe, the water we drink, the forests and oceans which sustain millions of different life forms, and the climatic patterns which govern our weather systems all transcend national boundaries is a source of hope. It means that no country, no matter either how rich and powerful or how poor and weak it may be, can afford not to take action in respect to this issue.

At any one time, a cacophony of voices denying the need for change can be heard saying: "We have always cut forests"; "global warming is not a legitimate phenomenon"; "the ice caps are not melting"; "our planet can support any number of our species without dire consequence to us, other species, or the environment." They are difficult at times to drown out, but if we are to err, let us do so on the side of caution.

In the end, one voice matters most: yours. Evaluate for yourself the scientific validities and probabilities of the many interconnected issues involved. If you find what you read in this revised edition and vast selection of existing data compelling, then respond robustly and act on your convictions. Now is the time! It is probable that never before has more been at stake and never again will we have the opportunity to effect change on these grave issues.

Imagine a future when the time-lapse satellite film reveals forests spreading out in a glorious blooming, reoccupying their former range—indicating a blossoming of human wisdom as well. If that spark of hope within you has been ignited and reached a critical mass, then remember: "If not you, who? If not now, when?"

▲ *The electrifying incandescence of the morpho butterfly* (Morpho peleides), *blinking on and off against the verdant green screen of the rainforest, seems to permanently "emboss" itself on one's temporal lobe. No one who has seen this morphing spectacle will ever forget it. [Costa Rica.]*

CONCLUSION

It is among humanity's most curious anomalies that we would herald the confirmation of a simple, single-celled organism in the great void of space as the most profound and triumphant of our legacies. Yet how casually, even callously, we are able to proceed with the consummate dismantling of the celebration of creation itself on our own planet.

At the present rate of exploitation, the tropical rainforest, Earth's first endangered habitat of global consequence, will be virtually extinct around the middle of the new millennium. This grim actuality looms within our lifetime! It is no wonder that the scientific community has named the impending loss of the tropical rainforest "the act our descendants will least forgive us for."

As I pen this conclusion to the revised edition, approximately 50,000 species per year, 137 per day, and six per hour pass into extinction. The dinosaurs may finally have failed, but in the grand scheme of things this was of no great consequence, as mammals replaced them as the dominant life-forms. Today, however, a consensus of biological scientists believe our Earth systems are not flexible enough to fill such evolutionary gaps again—and as those gaps become increasingly large they form an abyss upon whose edge we are perched. Are we survivors? As Lewis Thomas put it, "The survival of the fittest does not mean those fit to kill, it means those fitting in best with the rest of life."

Will humanity use enlightened technology to keep its numbers within bounds, or blindly increase them, causing pernicious environmental decay? Will *Homo sapiens,* a single species on a planet we share with a multitude of other species, endorse appetites and directions so preferential as to exclude the great balance of creation on Earth? Ironically, those elements we dislike and fear most—disease, vermin, and famine—are in fact the ones that thrive in the destruction we wreak. This may be the epitaph of a species which became so successful that it may have already purchased a one-way ticket for the train bound for extinction.

We would do well to try, difficult as it may be, to keep our own existence on Earth in perspective. For illustrative purposes, should we condense the some 4 billion years of the existence of life on Earth into a single calendar year, humans came on the scene only during the latter part of the last day of that year! If we appear a rash and perhaps arrogant species, our impulses are not all poorly founded. Our desire to taste and consume the resources of our planet date back to a time when such assets were thought to be infinite. Only recently have we come to realize that the land that holds the greatest biomass on Earth, the tropical rainforest, cannot sustain a large human population dependent on conventional agriculture. We are also learning, not without making painful mistakes, that these fragile forests cannot continue to be a convenience to temperate regions as the cornucopia of low-cost materials, harvested by boom-town methods that are simply no longer applicable. We now understand that, judiciously preserved, this yielding womb can issue forth from its reservoir a neverending plethora of goods, medicines, and food, while at the same time regulating Earth's systems and climate as it was meant to do—at no cost and in perpetuity.

If a man takes no thought about what is distant, he will find sorrow near at hand.

CONFUCIUS

How wonderful it is that nobody need wait a single moment before starting to improve the world.

ANNE FRANK

More than 2,000 respected scientists comprising the Intergovernmental Panel on Climate Change (IPCC) point to melting polar ice caps, retreating glaciers, rising sea levels, flooded cities, salted water supplies, more frequent and violent storms, diminished food production, and famine. All this chaos mimics the plot of a 1950s science fiction movie. But how will it play out? In the Saturday matinee of that era, the world was on the brink of doom, but the day was finally won. Empowered by the triumph of humanity over its own errant forces, we filed out of the Main Street Theater into the bright, sunlit Saturday afternoon.

Humanity is very much on that brink now, as voiced by the IPCC. The panel soberly asks two essential questions: Will governments globally commit to meaningful, enforceable efforts to reduce fossil fuel emissions? And will the developing nations likewise commit to preservation of their forests, despite their understandable concerns over sovereignty? While these are unimpeachable ideals, at the time of this writing neither has transpired. National leaders are still reticent, acting as though we will have no more children—as if this were the last generation. I, like you, would love to walk out of this deadly debacle into the bright afternoon sun. When you and I do enough to convince our leaders—to act on humanity's behalf, exercise their statesmanship, leave a righteous legacy, seize this rarest of opportunities to preserve these wondrous forests for our children and theirs, then we may yet enjoy that light of day with light heart. But, alas, not before.

There will never be a better time for a new environmental ethic to dawn. As environmental philosopher Aldo Leopold wrote, "A land ethic changes the role of *Homo sapiens* from conqueror of the land community, to plain member and citizen of it. It implies respect for his fellow members, and also esteem for the community as such." This ethic demands an understanding of the consequences of our activities, along with a respect for life that will allow other species to coexist with us in their natural, preordained state in spite of the temptations of economic expediency.

We now know that conservation on a global scale cannot afford to divorce itself from socioeconomic imperatives, which themselves do not exist in a vacuum. Given no viable alternatives, the ever-growing land-starved, yet blameless masses will home in on the opulent tropical forests and obliterate them far more effectively and permanently than any armaments, logging equipment, or botanical defoliants yet devised!

But let us look at the other side of the coin. Thanks to agroforestry and aquacultural technologies, sustained timber extraction methods, population stabilization programs, equitable distribution of fertile farmland, relief from the staggering debt that fuels deforestation in developing nations, revisions of archaic and destructive import-export policies, and constructive, hands-on aid principles, we can, in fact, relieve the intolerable pressure currently focused on the tropical forests. And unless these golden keys are used to open the door, famine unlike any we have seen will decimate these masses as the last of the tropical forests are finally slashed and burned.

I urge those who perceive this issue as a moral responsibility to refer to the previous chapter for viable solutions as well as direction on how to respond personally. Nothing has a more profound influence on policy makers than concerned citizens asserting their well-founded opinions in personal communications. This principle is succinctly expressed by Edmund Burke, who wrote, "No man makes a greater mistake than he who does nothing because he can do only a little."

▶ *Employing a stylistic embroidery of the rich resources of his environment, this New Guinea Stone Age man of the forest adorns himself in mud, flowers, feathers, and shells as both an artistic statement and to frighten enemies in neighboring tribes, who routinely practiced cannibalism when the image was taken in 1971. Intense eye contact, as exhibited here, imparts a dialogue on an island where at least 1,000 dialects are spoken and verbal communication between tribes is minimal.*

The Zen-like challenge, "If the success or failure of this planet, and of human beings, depended on how I am and what I do, how would I be? What would I do?" is answered by the ancient Chinese proverb, "If we do not change our course, we will end up where we are going!"

Aldo Leopold describes a tinker who does not fully comprehend the pocket watch he attempts to fix, but saves all the gears for the day when he does understand its mechanisms. Should we reduce and squander our diversity today, we will reduce in as great a measure the alternatives and options available to our children and grandchildren. If, however, like Leopold's tinker, we save all the gears of our biological mechanism, we ensure the full spectrum of possibilities for the immediate as well as the far distant future. We do not opt to burn the Rembrandt, the pinnacle of creation itself, for a moment's warmth.

In closing this revised edition, I choose rather to believe that the spark of humanity is inherently worthy, intelligent, and resilient enough to embrace an enlightened alternative that will maximize our potential and preserve our dignity while protecting the fellow creatures with whom we share this miracle called life, whether or not many of them can be of direct benefit to us. Let us now open those opulent vaults of opportunity and release not a rivulet, but a riptide of transformation—a genuine metamorphosis—and once again allow our planet, a veritable temple of flora, to flower.

◀ *The intelligent eyes of this Indonesian silver langur (Presbytis cristata) seem to search our souls for some understanding of humanity. Is this elegant primate, one of perhaps a million species that may vanish into extinction, imploring us to carefully reconsider the annihilation of global tropical rainforests, the sanctuary of biodiversity?*

APPENDIX 1   EDUCATIONAL RESOURCES

STUDENT AND TEACHER AIDS

- *Resources for Teachers and Students*

A six-page listing of curricula, teaching aids, resource guides, and books on tropical rainforests and deforestation. Available from: Rainforest Action Network, 221 Pine Street, Suite 500, San Francisco, CA 94104. Phone: (415) 398-4404, Website: www.ran.org/ran/info_center/factsheets/16a.html

- *Rainforest Researchers/Cultural Debates* companion CD-ROMs.

These challenging programs team students in a collaborative effort with Harvard researchers and, funded by the National Science Foundation, produce a compelling, top-notch classroom experience on both cutting-edge research and rainforest tribal issues. Available from: Tom Snyder Productions, 80 Coolidge Hill Road, Watertown, MA 02472. Phone: (800) 342-0236, Fax: (888) 877-3295, Website and Email: www.tomsnyder.com

- *Environmental Education Resource Guide*

A booklet listing a plethora of educational curricula materials, films, magazines and newsletters. Available from: Friends of the Earth, 1025 Vermont Ave. NW, 3rd Floor, Washington, DC 20005. Phone: (202) 783-7400, Fax: (202) 783-0444, Website: www.foe.org

- *Rain Forest: Lessons Towards a Global Understanding* by Ilene Miller and Laurie Agopian.

An in-depth, multidisciplinary thematic study of life in rainforests. Insightful lessons, projects, and experiments on reproducible pages designed to keep students' attention and enthusiasm. Elementary through high school. Available from: Teacher Created Materials, Inc., 6421 Industry Way, Westminster, CA 92683, Phone: (714) 891-7895, Fax: (714) 892-0283, Website: www.teachercreated.com

- *Vanishing Rainforests Education Kit*

Brings the wonders of the rainforest into the lives of students; includes a video. Grades 2–6. Available from: World Wildlife Fund, 1250 24 Street NW, Washington, DC 20037. Phone: (202) 293-4800, Fax (202) 293-9211, Website: www.wwfus.org, Email: wwf.org

- *Listing of Rainforest Curricula Teaching Kits and Activity Guides.*

Selections described are useful, low cost, or free—or may be rented (four at a time for $5 postage and handling fee). Available from: Center for Environmental Education, 400 Columbus Avenue, Valhalla, NY 10595. Phone: (914) 747-8200, Fax: (914) 747-8299, Email: cee@teachgreen.org

- *Tropical Tribune*

A quarterly newspaper format of enthusiastic reporting by students on the range of rainforest issues, natural history, and reviews on publications. A rare forum by which your students can have the empowering experience of having an article published in the Tropical Tribune. Its founder, Harold Beedle, is the preeminent middle school tropical rainforest educator. Available from: J. C. McKenna Middle School, 307 S. First Street, Evansville, WI 53536. Phone: (608) 882-4780, Fax: (608) 882-5744, Email: devils@inwave.com

RAINFOREST FILM LIST

- **Rainforest Audiovisuals.**

This nine-page listing of rainforest-related films and their sources is available from The Rainforest Action Network.

- **The Decade of Destruction.**

An award-winning (best instructional film, NAAEE) comprehensive, six-part (The Rainforest, The Development Road, The Colonists, The Indians, The Rubber Tappers, The Politicians—10–19 minutes each) video by Adrian Cowell documenting the complex factors at work in the ongoing destruction of the Amazon and its effect on tribal peoples and the environment leading many to declare it "the century's worst environmental disaster." Coswell's Banking on Disaster is a distillation of some of the material in this series. Available with study guide from Bullfrog Films.

- **Blowpipes and Bulldozers.**

This 78-minute video documents the heartfelt tragedy of the Penan Tribe of Sarawak, Borneo, who after 40,000 years of living at one with the forest are now being logged out of existence. Their resistance has led to worldwide attention to their plight. Available from Bullfrog Films.

- **In the Ashes of the Forest Parts 1 and 2.** (55 min. and 57 min.)

This highly rated (***** Video Rating Guide for Libraries) documentary follows the compelling saga of Chico and Renato and a never-previously-filmed Indian tribe, the Uru Eu Wau Wau, who kidnap Chico's seven-year-old son in retaliation for cutting down forest to grow crops. The crops fail due to poor soil and the search for the little boy reveals the despair of slash-and-burn farming in Eden. Available from Bullfrog Films.

- **Mountains of Gold.** (54 min.)

Brazil has one of the world's largest untapped gold reserves and 70 percent of its production is mined by freelance prospectors, or *garimpeiros*, who create havoc in the forest environment and with tribal groups. This now looms as the sleeper issue of the 21st century as lethal disease brought in by the miners decimates the tribal groups. (**** Video Rating Guide for Libraries.) Available from Bullfrog Films.

- **Killing for Land.** (51 min.)

Nearly 24 million Brazilian small farmers have lost their land while almost half of Brazil's arable land is now owned by 1 percent of the population. The dispossessed have migrated to the Amazon, where large companies with absentee landlords hire gunmen to frighten the squatters off. (**** Video Rating Guide for Libraries.) Available from Bullfrog Films.

- **The Killing of Chico Mendes.** (55 min.)

In this film we learn about the homicide of Chico Mendes on December 22, 1988, as he is martyred for trying to preserve the rainforest for the sustained collection of rubber, Brazil nuts, and other nontimber forest products. Mendes formed the Seringueiros (rubber tappers) Union, which resulted in large areas of forest preserved as extractive reserves. International outcry over his death resulted in the incarceration of the cattle barons who took his life. (**** Video Rating Guide for Libraries.) Available from Bullfrog Films.

- **Arrows Against the Wind.** (52 min.)

An emotionally moving documentary of the Irian Jayan, Dani, and Asmat tribes and how the Indonesian government rendered them expendable. Available from Bullfrog Films.

- **Gorilla.** (60 min.)

This National Geographic Society film is an engaging and informative look at humanity's closest relative, the mountain gorilla of Central Africa. Discovered only 100 years ago, fewer than 600 remain. Available from video stores.

- **Jungle Pharmacy.** (53 min.)

Produced by Better World Society, the film brings together dedicated scientists, physicians, and environmentalists with forest shamans illuminating the untapped wealth of medicinal benefit (25 percent of all prescription drugs are derived from rainforest plants) we lose to deforestation. Available from The Cinema Guild.

- **Keepers of the Forest.** (28 min.)

The Lacandon Maya of Chiapas, Mexico, understand that migrant cultivation leads to the loss of the rare forest resource. In this award-winning film, they demonstrate their intensive sustainable methods of farming that are just now becoming understood by modern agricultural scientists. Available from Documentary Projects.

- **The Monk, the Trees, and the Concrete Jungle.** (26 min.)

Portrays deforestation and the trade in endangered species with a focus on Latin America. Available from Bullfrog Films.

- **The Emerald Forest.** (90 min.)

Major motion picture release, this fictionalized account, based on fact, of the effect of a dam project on an Amazon tribe. Available from local video rental stores.

- **Kings of the Jungle.** (51 min.)

The stirring account of the famed Villa-Boas brothers as they retrace their first contact with a number of uncontacted tribes for development purposes going back to the 1940s until they realized what sorrow development had on the forest and those tribes. Available from Bullfrog Films.

- **People and the Rainforests Slide Show.** (15 min.)

A panorama of the world's primeval tribes, who now only exist in the insulation of the tropical forests—both rapidly diminishing resources. Available from Cultural Survival.

- **Songbird Story.** (15 min.) (ages 6–11.)

In an animated film, two children dream they fly along the flyway of migratory songbirds and discover to their dismay that the Latin American wintering rainforests are being cut down and that there is little time to save the birds from extinction. Available from Bullfrog Films.

- **Yąnomamö: Keepers of the Flame.** (58 min.)

A first contact by an expedition of journalists, anthropologists, and physicians into the Venezuelan rainforest to the village of Ashidowa-teri of the compelling Yąnomamö tribe, never before contacted by the outside world. Available from The Video Project.

- **You Can't Grow Home Again.** (58 min.) (ages 8–14.)

Produced by the Children's Television Workshop as an introduction to the life science of the rainforest, its biodiversity, and its function as a steady-state system in the control of global warming. Highly informative. Includes a study and activity guide. Available from The Video Project.

- **Rainforest Action Network Slide Show.** (80 slides or option of 39.)

Addressing the issues of rainforest ecology, destruction and grassroots solutions, this powerful slide set is tailored for individuals and local groups interested in doing something about this problem by establishing their own Rainforest Action Groups (RAGS). Available from RAN.

- **The Last of the Hiding Tribes.** (3 part series, 51 min. each.)

Another superb Adrian Cowell film tells that 1,000 years ago, most of the human race consisted of hunter-gatherer tribes. At the close of the 20th century, only a handful of uncontacted tribes remained—a poignant reminder of how very rich and varied our species once was and what a rare and treasured resource the last of the primeval tribes are. Available from Bullfrog Films.

- **A Naturalist in the Rainforest: A Portrait of Alexander Skutch.** (54 min.)

A world-famous naturalist makes his home in the Costa Rican rainforest and describes the biology of this unique habitat. This inspiring man was the genesis of a thousand naturalists transformed from students who read of his life's example. Available from Bullfrog Films.

Bullfrog Films
P.O. Box 149
Oley, PA 19547
Phone: (800) 543-3764
Fax: (610) 370-1978
Website: www.bullfrogfilms.com

The Cinema Guild
1697 Broadway, Suite 506
New York, NY 10019
Phone: (800) 723-5522
Website: www.cinemaguild.com

Documentary Projects
5209 Manila Avenue
Oakland, CA 94618
Phone: (510) 595-5306
Fax: (510) 595-5307

Cultural Survival
96 Mt. Auburn Street
Cambridge, MA 02138
Phone: (617) 441-5400
Website: www.cs.org

The Video Project
5332 College Avenue
Oakland, CA 94618
Phone: (800) 475-2638
Website: www.videoproject.org

Rainforest Action Network (RAN)
221 Pine Street, Suite 500
San Francisco, CA 94104
Phone: (415) 398-4404
Website: www.ran.org

APPENDIX 2   TROPICAL TIMBERS AND DOMESTIC ALTERNATIVES

The international trade in tropical timbers is a growing threat to the future of all tropical forests. A number of countries that once maintained lush forests have depleted them to the point where they must now import wood. Commercial logging in the tropics as it is practiced today cannot provide long-term ecological or economic sustainability. However, there is much potential for sustainable timber harvesting in temperate forests.

It is encouraging to note that timber importers as well as fine woodworkers in furniture and musical instruments, for example, are increasingly catering to consumer demand in supplying "green" (sustainably) produced tropical woods and products. In fact, as a result of the United Kingdom's Ecological Trading Company's early efforts at locating verifi-

ably sustainably produced tropical timber, the very concept of timber certification was born.

The demand for tropical timber continues to rise because it is generally less expensive and also because of its unique qualities. Low costs for tropical timbers are a result of several factors, including lower wages for workers in producer countries, government subsidies and trade policies that keep timber prices low, and forestry policies that encourage short-term financial returns and damaging, low-cost harvesting methods. Temperate alternatives to tropical hardwoods are available that are comparable in beauty, workability, and durability.

The following information comprises lists of tropical hardwoods to avoid and alternative domestic timbers.

TROPICAL TIMBERS TO AVOID

Common name	Scientific Name	Origin
Apitong	*Dipterocarpus* spp.	Malaysia, Thailand, Philippines
Banak	*Virola* spp.	Central and South America
Bocote	*Cordia elaeagnoides*	Central and South America
Bubinga	*Guibourrtia demeusii*	West Africa
Cocobolo	*Dalbergia retusa*	
	D. hypoleuca	Central America
Cordia	*Cordia* spp.	Central and South America
Ebony, African	*Diospyros* spp.	Africa
Ebony, Macassar	*Diospyros celebica*	East Indies
Goncalo alves	*Astronium fraxinfolium*	Brazil, northern South America
Greenheart	*Ocotea rowdioea*	Central America
Iroko	*Chlorophora excelsa*	West Coast of Africa
Jelutang	*Dyera costulata*	Malaysia, Brunei
Koa	*Acacia koa*	Hawaii
Lauan	*Shorea* spp.	Philippines
Mahogany, Honduran	*Swietenia macrophylla*	Central and northern South America
Mahogany, Philippines	*Shorea* spp.	Philippines
Meranti	*Shorea* spp.	Malaysia
Andaman Padauk	*Pterocarpus dalbergioides*	Andaman Islands
African Padauk	*Pterocarpus soyauxii*	Central and west tropical Africa
Purpleheart	*Peltogyne* spp.	Central and northern South America
Ramin	*Gonystylus* spp.	Indonesia, Malaysia
Rosewood, Honduran	*Dalbergia stevensonii*	Central America
Satinwood	*Chloroxylon swietenia*	India, Sri Lanka
Teak	*Tectona grandis*	Indigenous to India, Burma, Thailand, Indo-China, and Java. Planted in East and West Africa and West Indies
Virola	*Dialyanthera otoba &* *gordonifolia*	Central America and Venezuela
Wenge	*Milletia laurentii*	The Democratic Republic of the Congo
Zebrawood	*Microberlinia brazzavillensis*	Gabon, Cameroon, and West Africa

NORTH AMERICAN ALTERNATIVE TIMBERS

Common Name	Scientific Name
Ash	*Fraxinus americana*
Basswood	*Tilia americana*
Beech	*Fagus grandifolia*
Birch	*Betula papyrifera*
Butternut	*Juglans cinera*
Cherry	*Prunus serotina*
Cottonwood	*Poplus* spp.
Cypress	*Taxodium distichum*
Douglas Fir	*Pseudotsuga menziesii*
Elm	*Ulmus* spp.
Black Gum	*Nyssa sylvatica*
Red Gum	*Liquidamber styraciflua*
Hackberry	*Celtis laevigata*
Western Hemlock	*Tsuga heterophylla*
Hickory	*Hicoria* spp.
Sugar Maple	*Acer saccharum*
Soft Maple	*Acer* spp.
Red Oak	*Quercus* spp.
White Oak	*Quercus* spp.
Pecan	*Hicoria* spp.
Ponderosa Pine	*Pinus ponderosa*
Yellow Southern Pine	*Pinus* spp.
Yellow Poplar	*Liriodendron tulipiferia*
Sitka Spruce	*Picea sitchensis*
Sycamore	*Platanus occidentalis*
Black Walnut	*Juglans nigra*

APPENDIX 3 TOWARD SUSTAINED PRODUCTIVITY

Explanatory notes to chart on pages 184–187

A great many variables have been brought together within the framework of this synthesis. As such, figures for man-hours, production, and soil loss are not precise for all conditions and locales, but are designed to fall within acceptable ranges. While the author draws on hard data for initial and final years, for some examples the figures were extended by extrapolation, in concurrence with researchers in the field.

SHORT CYCLE SHIFTING CULTIVATION

Production and soil loss (Pimentel 1989; El-Swaify 1990; Bainbridge 1990: all pers. comm.). Slopes of 7% used here. Acceptable level of topsoil loss is less than 1 ton, but perhaps 0.5 tons/ha/yr (Lal 1988). Soil loss of 20 to 25 tons/ha/yr not unusual in Amazon Basin oxisols (El Swaify, pers. comm. 1990). Figures for manual clearing, no tillage, were 0.4 t/ha/yr. Crawler tractor/tree pusher—conventional tillage—produced 19.6 t/ha/yr in African scenario (Lal 1981). Loss of topsoil on 7% slope in primary rainforest (Ivory Coast) was 0.03 t/ha/yr, but on bare ground loss was 138 t/ha/yr (UNESCO 1978). Slopes of 20% (Peru) produce 26 t/ha/yr soil loss on bare ground, but 4.6 t/ha/yr under annual cropping, while with alley cropping on 15% slopes, soil loss was 1.2 t/ha/yr and under forest cover the loss was 0.7 t/ha/yr (Alegre 1989). The prescription for intensified agriculture makes allowance for copious mulch until crop species provide soil cover.

NONINTENSIVE AGROFORESTRY

All above references. Corn/Leucaena production is representative of best-case scenario of adequate selection for soil fertility (7% of Amazon Basin) and conscientious soil mulching. Leucaena production (Pimental and Hartshorn 1989; Lal 1990; all pers. comm.). Labor for Leucaena trimming estimated at 36 man-hrs/ha year 2 and 48 hrs/ha at years 8–25 (Lal, pers. comm. 1990). Tree component must be appropriate to site, i.e. Leucaena is not acceptable for highly acid soils (El Swaify, pers. comm. 1990). An increase in maize yield of about 1.4 t/ha/yr was observed in association with hedgerows of Leucaena, with or without fertilizer (Watson and Laquihon 1985). Shading, root competition, and immobilization by mulch are among factors reducing maize yields in alley cropping treatments, especially in vicinity of trees, compared to nonfertilized controls where subsoil is extremely low in nutrients and cations (Szott 1987). Leucaena hedgerows are, however, a positive factor in erosion control (Lal 1989).

PARTIALLY INTENSIFIED AGROFORESTRY

Corn, papaya, and orange agroforest figures are from Chanchamayo, Peru (Villachica *et al.* 1990). Annual incomes vary quite widely according to market availability. Corn price is based on 22 lbs per U.S.$1.00 (U.S.$0.04545 per lb). Direct costs of production are variable. Figures given are gross. Figure of U.S.$653/ha/yr for 25-year-old fruit tree swidden plot allowed to fallow. Labor perhaps 40 hrs/ha/yr. This $ figure represents close access to market geared to produce (Tamshiyacu Village/Iquitos Market). This also represents plots converted from 6–7 year old secondary plots which are far from returning to maximum fertility (Padoch, DeJong, and Unruii 1985). Start-up labor estimated at 20% more for mixed agroforest than short cycle shifting cultivation (Buol, pers. comm. 1990); labor estimates (Bainbridge and Gleissman, both pers. comm. 1990). Labor for clearing intensified agroforestry plot spread over 5-year period to conserve soil (Nair, pers. comm. 1990). The literature and experience in agroforestry is less than complete. Laurel tree's (*Cordia alliodora*) self-pruning and narrow crown recommends it strongly as timber species in agroforestry. Years 6 to 12 increasingly yield U.S.$100–900/ha/yr in trimmings. At harvest, around 18–25 years, 150 trees/ha can be 18″-20″ DBH (diameter at breast height); and market value, where such quality wood is scarce, can be U.S.$100–$150 per tree (Budowski and Borel, both pers. comm. 1990). While perennials and fruit-tree crops may possibly be sustained and increased over a 25-year period without inputs, annuals, including grains, will require inputs for sustained or increased yields. The payback—in increased produce to costs—can, however, be amply rewarding (see text) (Sanchez 1982; Lal, pers. comm. 1990). Inputs of nutrient need not be purchased, but gleaned sustainably in the form of litter from surrounding forest as in the Kayapó system (Hecht 1989; Gleissman, pers. comm. 1990). A 1-ha garden can be littered from a 5–8-ha area of primary forest (Wilkin 1987). Areas of high rainfall in S. China have carried out productive sustainable agriculture for some 4,000 years without nonrenewable inputs—using green, animal, and human manures only (Gleissman, pers. comm. 1990). Maturing agroforestry plots are a consistent and often growing source of wild animal products not reflected in the analysis.

CATTLE PASTURE

Soil loss rough estimates for land/cattle speculator less likely to mitigate poor pasture practices on 7% slope (Sanchez, Buol, and Bainbridge, all pers. comm. 1990).

Root-rake/tree pusher used in clearing land reduced labor to 192 man-hrs/ha but increased soil loss from a potential low of 0.4 t/ha/yr in manual clearing to 19.6 t/ha/yr in year 1 (Lal 1981). For Amazon Basin oxisols, soil loss can be 20 t/ha/yr for manual clearing and considerably higher for machine clearing where the potential for gully erosion is now a factor to consider, especially in overgrazed situations (El Swaify, pers. comm. 1990).

Year 1–928 hrs estimated to manually fell, burn and establish pasture per ha (Buol and Gleissman, both pers. comm. 1990). Cattle pasture requires 50 man-hrs/ha/yr for maintenance, once established (Nations, pers. comm. 1990).

TERRACED AND NONTERRACED CULTIVATION

Eastern Andean slopes of 40% used here. Terraced fields here are manured (green, animal, or human) (Winterholder, pers. comm. 1990). Andean terraces on even eastern slopes date back some 1500 years and have been producing sustainably for several hundred years with minimal soil loss (streams and rivulets run clear below terraces after rain storms), (Treacy 1989; Denevan 1990, pers. comm.). Slopes from 7% to 40% of equal length increase soil loss 10 times. Terraces reduce erosion some 100 times, and fallow may not be necessary (El Swaify, pers. comm. 1990). Unterraced 49% slopes in Burundi eroded 150 t/ha/yr under corn (Roose 1988).

Value of produce for western slopes (Treacy 1989). Rough estimated yields for eastern Andean slopes for terraced and nonterraced fields (Sanchez, 1990, and pers. comm. 1990). Maintenance of terraces estimated at 6% of construction labor, which is some 500 hrs (Buol and Bainbridge, both pers. comm. 1990). U.S.$650/ha in wages to construct terraces (Hooper and El-Swaify 1988). Cost of bench terracing U.S.$175 per ha but doubled return of yams in nonterraced field (Sheng 1989). Hillside ditches, however, reduced erosion by 80% and were 25% the cost of bench terracing (Sheng 1988). On slopes of 40% in Trinidad terraced pineapple field soil loss was 0.4 t/ha/yr (Gumbs *et al.* 1985). Soil loss on nonterraced land can reach 286 t/ha/yr and more on 70% slope of 164 ft (50 m) length. Unterraced fields of Huri Thung Choa, Thailand, required a period of 20–100 years fallow after only several years of cultivation (Hurni 1985).

FISH AQUACULTURE (IN ASSOCIATION WITH AGROFORESTRY)

See text (Moss, Moehl, Pompa and Frobish 1990, and pers. comm. 1990). Price based on U.S.$2.00 per kg, 1988. Small ponds, 26 by 33 ft, can produce an annual income of U.S.$600 (Barrau and Djati 1985). Note that in years 1 and 2, although fish are being produced, there is at this stage no cash return to the farmer.

SUSTAINED EXTRACTION FROM PRIMARY FOREST

Research was conducted on white sand forest formation. Richer soils and forests can be expected to produce even richer harvests (Peters, Gentry, and Mendelsohn 1989).

BUSHMEAT EXTRACTION AND FOREST ANIMAL FARMING

Bushmeat, crocodilian skins, turtle, and capybara ranching (Nations and Coello Hinojos 1989; Bailey pers. comm. 1989). Not known if harvest of 2 crocodilians/ha/yr is sustainable.

BIBLIOGRAPHY

Any book on a subject as vast as the tropical rainforests of the world and sustainable development within these regions must draw on the work of many other authors, in many disciplines and in many lands. To list them all would be impossible, yet even this selected bibliography runs to several hundred entries. Therefore, to assist the reader we have listed the various publications under a number of thematic headings. References are listed in alphabetic order of main author, under the following headings:

Amazônia
Botany
Cattle production
Climate and the
　greenhouse effect
Conservation

Deforestation
Forest resources
Fuelwood
Historical perspective
Plantation forestry
Population
Public health
Sustainable agriculture
Sustainable and
　unsustainable logging
Traditional cultures
Tropical forests—general
Zoology

AMAZÔNIA

Amazonia. Edited by Ghillean Prance and Thomas E. Lovejoy. Pergamon Press, 1985.

Amazonian Rain Forests. Edited by Jordan, C. F., Springer-Verlag, 1987.

Anderson, Anthony B., ed. *Alternatives to Deforestation: Steps Toward Sustainable Use of the Amazon Rain Forest.* Columbia University Press, 1990.

Goodland, R. J. A. and H. S. Irwin. *Amazon Jungle: Green Hell to Red Desert.* Elsevier Scientific Pub. Co., 1975.

Goulding, Michael, Nigel J. H. Smith and Denis J. Mahar. *Floods of Fortune, Ecology and Economy Along the Amazon.* Columbia University Press, 1996.

Hecht, Susanna and Alexander Cockburn. *The Fate of the Forest—Developers, Destroyers, and Defenders of the Amazon.* Verso, 1989.

Lisansky, J. *Migrants to Amazônia: Spontaneous Colonization in the Brazilian Frontier.* Westview Press, 1990.

BOTANY

Graf, Alfred Byrd. *Exotic Plant Manual.* Roehrs Co., 1970.

Halle, F. and R. A. A. Oldeman. *An Essay of the Architecture and Dynamics of Growth of Tropical Trees.* Penerbit University, Malaya, Kuala Lumpur, Malaysia, Pub., 1975.

Hartshorn, Gary S. *Tree Falls and Tropical Forest Dynamics.* Cambridge University Press 26–30 April 1976.

Holdridge, L. R. *Life Zone Ecology.* Tropical Science Center, San Jose, Costa Rica.

Janzen, Daniel H. *Costa Rican Natural History.* University of Chicago Press, 1983.

Jordan, Carl F. *Nutrient Cycling in Tropical Forest Ecosystems.* John Wiley & Sons, 1985.

Mathias, Mildred E. and Lincoln Constance. *Flora of Peru.* Field Museum of Natural History, 1962.

Meijer, Willem. "Saving the World's Largest Flower." *National Geographic,* Vol. 168, No. 1 (July 1985.)

Menninger, Edwin A. *Flowering Trees of the World.* Hearthside Press, Inc., 1962.

——*Flowering Vines of the World.* Hearthside Press, Inc., 1970.

Newman, Arnold C. "Euterpe at Iguassu Falls, Brazil." *Principes,* Journal of the Palm Society, Vol. 16, No. 2 (April 1972.)

Ray, Thomas S., Jr., "Slow-Motion World of Plant 'Behavior' Visible in Rain Forest." *Smithsonian* (March 1979.)

Richards, P. W. *The Tropical Rain Forest: An Ecological Study.* 2nd Edition, Cambridge University Press, 1996.

Schultes, Richard E. *Plants of the Gods: Their Sacred Healing and Hallucinogenic Powers.* Healing Art Press, 1992.

—— and Robert F. Raffauf. *The Healing Forest: Medicinal and Toxic Plants.* Dioscorides Press, 1990.

CATTLE PRODUCTION

Byron, N. and M. Ruiz Perez. "What Future for the Tropical Moist Forests 25 Years Hence?" *Commonwealth Forestry Review,* Vol. 75, No. 2 (1996.)

Fearnside, P. M. "The Effects of Cattle Pasture Fertility in the Brazilian Amazon: Consequences for Production Sustainability." *Tropical Ecology,* Vol. 21, 1980.

"The Hamburger Connection." Tropical Wildlands Conservation: The World Bank's Progress with Emphasis on Amazonia. The Ecological Society of America 73rd Annual Meeting, Davis, California. (17 August 1988.)

Hecht, S. B. "Cattle Ranching in the Eastern Amazon: Environmental and Social Implications." In *The Dilemma of Amazonian Development.* Edited by E. F. Moran. Westview, 1983.

Myers, Norman. "The Anatomy of Environmental Action: The Case of Tropical Deforestation." In *The International Politics of the Environment.* Edited by A. Hurrell and B. Kingsbury. Clarendon Press, 1992.

CHILDREN

Berger, Melvin and Gilda. *Life in the Rainforest.* Ideals Children's Books, 1994.

Cherry, Lynne. *The Great Kapok Tree.* Harcourt Brace, 1990.

Earth Works Group. *Fifty Simple Things You Can Do to Save the Earth.* Andrews and McMeel, 1989.

Goodman, Billy. *A Kid's Guide to How to Save the Planet.* Avon/Camelot, 1990.

Lewington, Anna. *What Do We Know about the Amazonian Indians?* Simon and Schuster, 1993.

Silver, Donald. *Why Save the Rain Forest?* Julian Messner, 1993.

CLIMATE AND THE GREENHOUSE EFFECT

Houghton, J. T. et al. *Climate Change 1995: The Science of*

Climate Change. Working Group I of the IPCC. Cambridge University Press, 1996.

Houghton, Richard A. "The Annual Net Flux of Carbon to the Atmosphere from Changes in Land Use 1850–1900." *Tellus,* Vol. 51, No. 2 (April 1999.)

——"The Role of the World's Forests in Global Warming." In *World Forests for the Future: Their Use and Conservation.* Edited by K. Ramakrishna and G. M. Woodwell. Yale University Press, 1993.

——"Tropical Deforestation and Atmospheric Carbon Dioxide." In *Tropical Forests and Climate.* Edited by Norman Myers. Kluwer Academic Publishers, 1992.

—— and J. L. Hackler. "Emissions of Carbon from Forestry and Land-Use Change in Tropical Asia." In *Global Change Biology* (1999) Vol. 5, Blackwell Science Ltd., (1999.)

—— and George M. Woodwell. "Global Climate Change." *Scientific American,* Vol. 260, No. 4 (April 1989.)

Myers, Norman. *Deforestation Rates in Tropical Forests and Their Climatic Implications.* Friends of the Earth, 1989.

Myers, Norman, ed. *Tropical Forests and Climate.* Kluwer Academic Publishers, 1992.

—— and T. J. Goreau. "Tropical Forests and the Greenhouse Effect: A Management Response." In *Tropical Forests and Climate.* Edited by Norman Myers. Kluwer Academic Publishers, 1992.

Woodwell, G. M. et al. "Biotic Feedbacks in the Warming of the Earth." *Climate Change,* Vol. 40, No. 3/4 (December 1998.)

Woodwell, G. M. and F. T. Mackenzie. *Biotic Feedbacks in the Global Climatic System: Will the Warming Feed the Warming?* Oxford University Press, 1995.

CONSERVATION

Atkins, E. G., ed. *Vanishing Eden: The Plight of the Tropical Rainforest.* Barrons, 1991.

Brown, Lester R. *State of the World 1999.* W. W. Norton & Co., 1999.

Brown, S. and A. E. Lugo. "Rehabilitation of Tropical Lands: A Key to Sustaining Development." *Restoration Ecology,* Vol. 2, No. 2 (1994.)

Drafts Agenda 21, Rio Declaration: Forest Principles. United Nations, 1992.

Durning, A. T. *Saving the Forests: What Will it Take?* Worldwatch Institute, 1993.

Ehrlich, Paul R. and Anne H. *Extinction: The Causes and Consequences of the Disappearance of Species.* Ballantine Books, 1983.

—— *Machinery of Nature.* Simon & Schuster, 1987.

—— "The Value of Biodiversity." *Ambio,* Vol. 21, No. 3 (May 1992.)

Fragile Lands of Latin America. Edited by J. O. Browder. Westview Press, 1989.

Goldman, Patti, et al. *Our Forests at Risk: The World Trade Organization's Threat to Forest Protection.* Earthjustice Legal Defense Fund, 1999.

Head, Suzanne and Robert Heinzman. *Lessons of the Rainforests.* Sierra Club Books, 1990.

Humboldt, Alexander Von. *View of Nature: Or Contemplations on the Sublime Phenomena of Creation.* Henry G. Bohn, 1850.

The Last Rainforests: A World Conservation Atlas. Edited by Mark Collins, Oxford University Press, 1990.

Leopold, Aldo. *A Sand County Almanac.* Oxford University Press, 1968.

—— "The Once and Future Land Ethic." *Wilderness,* Vol. 48, No. 168 (Spring 1985.)

Lindsey, Hal. *The Late Great Planet Earth.* Zondervan Pub., 1981.

Love, Sam. *Environmental Action Earth Tool Kit.* Pocket Books, 1971.

Martin, Esmond Bradley. "The World Ivory Trade." *Swara,* Vol. 6, No. 4 (July/August 1983.)

Mathias, Mildred E. *The Importance of Diversity.* Special Publication No. 1, Pacific Division, American Association for the Advancement of Science, San Francisco, CA (7 August 1978.)

McNeely, Jeffrey et al. *Conserving the World's Biological Diversity.* ICUN, WRI, CI, WWF-US, World Bank, 1990.

Mendes, Chico. *Fight for the Forest.* Latin American Bureau, 1989.

Michener, James A. "Where did the Animals Go?" *Reader's Digest* (June 1976.)

Mittermeier, Russell A. and C. G. Mittermeier. *Megadiversity.* CEMEX, 1997.

Myers, Norman. *The Sinking Ark.* Pergamon Press, 1979.

—— "The World's Forests: Need for a Policy Appraisal." *Science,* Vol. 268 (1995.)

—— "The World's Forests: Problems and Potentials." *Environmental Conservation,* Vol. 23, No. 2 (1996.)

—— *Gaia: An Atlas of Planet Earth.* Doubleday, 1984.

—— "The End of the Lines." *Natural History,* Vol. 94, No. 2 (February 1985.)

Newman, Arnold C. "The Vanishing Jungle." *Treasure Chest,* Vol. 5 (11 November 1975.)

Pasquier, Roger F. "Whose Birds are They?" *The Nature Conservancy News,* Vol. 32, No. 4 (July/August 1982.)

Raven, Peter H. "The Destruction of the Tropics." *Frontiers* (July 1976.)

—— "Tropical Rain Forests: A Global Responsibility." *Natural History,* Vol. 90, No. 2 (February 1981.)

—— "The Urgency of Tropical Conservation." *The Nature Conservancy News,* Vol. 35, No. 1 (January 1986.)

—— and Joel Cracraft. "Seeing the World as It Really Is: Global Stability and Environmental Change." In *The Living Planet in Crisis.* Edited by Joel Cracraft and Francesca T. Grifo. Columbia, University Press, 1999.

Resor, J. P. "Debt-for-Nature Swaps: A Decade of Experi-

ence and New Directions for the Future." *Unasylva,* Vol. 48, No. 188 (1997.)

Richards, Paul W. "Tropical Rain Forest." *Scientific American* (December 1973.)

—— "The Tropical Rain Forest." *Scientific American,* Vol. 229, No. 6 (December 1977.)

Sayer, J.A. and T. C. Whitmore. "Tropical Moist Forests: Destruction and Species Extinction." *Biological Conservation,* Vol. 55, No. 2 (1991.)

Tropical Deforestation and Species Extinction. Edited by T. C. Whitmore and J. A. Sayer. Chapman and Hall, 1992.

Wilson, E. O. *The Diversity of Life.* W. W. Norton & Co., 1992.

Wolf, Arol. "Arnold Newman—Rain Forest Naturalist." *Ecolibrium Interviews* (1984.)

Woodwell, G. M. "Forests: What in the World Are They For?" In *World Forests for the Future: Their Use and Conservation.* Edited by K. Ramakrishna and G. M. Woodwell. Yale University Press, 1993.

DEFORESTATION

Abrams, E. M. et al. "The Role of Deforestation in the Collapse of the Late Classic Copan Maya State." In *Tropical Deforestation: The Human Dimension.* Edited by Leslie E. Sponsel et al. Columbia University Press, 1996.

American Forests Magazine, Vol. 94, Nos. 11, 12 (November/December 1988.)

Bankrolling Disasters: International Development Banks and the Global Environment. Sierra Club, 1986.

Colchester, M. "The Indonesian Transmigration Programme: Migrants to Disaster." In *Forest Resources: Crisis and Management.* Edited by V. Shiva et al. Natraj Publishers, 1992.

Ellenbroek, A. "Rainforests of the Guyana Shield: Evergreen or Forever Gone?" *BOS Nieuwsletter,* Vol. 15, No. 2 (1996.)

Fearnside, P. M. "Transmigration in Indonesia: Lessons from its

Environmental and Social Impacts." *Environmental Management*, Vol. 21, No. 4 (1997.)

Ferwerda, W. "The Serrania de la Macarena in Danger: Territorial Conflicts and Conservation in the Most Western Part of the Guyana Shield." *BOS Nieuwsletter*, Vol. 15, No. 2 (1996.)

Grainger, A. *Controlling Tropical Deforestation*. Earthscan, 1993.

Gullison, R. E. and E. C. Losos. "The Role of Foreign Debt in Deforestation in Latin America." *Conservation Biology*, Vol. 7 (1993.)

McCully, Patrick. *Silenced Rivers: The Ecology and Politics of Large Dams*. Zed Press, 1996.

Nepstad, Daniel C. et al. "Large-Scale Impoverishment of Amazonian Forests by Logging and Fire." *Nature*, Vol. 398, No. 6727 (April 1999.)

Newman, Arnold and Brent Blackwelder. "Tropical Deforestation: Global Consequences and Alternatives." *Znanie Science and Humanities Yearbook—The Future of Science and Our Planet*, 1989.

FOREST RESOURCES

Clusener-Godt, M. and I. Sachs, eds. *Extractivism in the Brazilian Amazon: Perspectives on Regional Development*. UNESCO, 1994.

Counsell, S. and T. Rice, eds. *The Rainforest Harvest: Sustainable Strategies for Saving the Tropical Forests*. Friends of the Earth, 1992.

Donovan, R. Z. and M. Dunne. *Smart Wood Bibliography on Forest Certification*. Rainforest Alliance, 1995.

Fearnside, Philip and H. J. Ruitenbeek. *Mangrove Management: An Economic Analysis of Management Options with a Focus on Bintuni Bay, Irian Jaya*. Environmental Management Development in Indonesia Project, 1992.

Forest Resources Assessment 1990: Global Synthesis. FAO Forestry Paper no. 124 (1995.)

Gentry, A. "Tropical Forest Biodiversity and the Potential for New Medicinal Plants." In *Human Medicinal Agents from Plants*. Edited by A. D. Kinghorn and M. F. Balandrin. American Chemical Society, 1993.

Ginu, C. "The Experience of the Alto Jurua Extractive Reserve with Vegetal Leather: Engaging Forest Product Markets for the Survival of Ecosystems and Cultures." In *Local Heritage in the Changing Tropics: Innovative Strategies for Natural Resource Management and Control*. Edited by G. Dicum. Yale University, 1995.

Harcourt, C. S. and J. A. Sayer, eds. *The Conservation Atlas of Tropical Forests: The Americas*. Simon and Schuster, 1996.

Hladik, C. M. et al, eds. *Tropical Forests, People and Food: Biocultural Interactions and Applications to Development*. UNESCO/Parthenon, 1993.

Kreig, Margaret. *Green Medicine: A Search for Plants that Heal*. Rand, 1964.

Lampietti, J. and J. A. Dixon. *To See the Forest for the Trees: A Guide to Non-Timber Forest Benefits*. World Bank, 1995.

Mendelsohn, Robert and Michael J. Balick. "The Value of Undiscovered Pharmaceuticals in Tropical Forests." *Economic Botany*, Vol. 49 (1995.)

Peters, Charles M., et al. "Valuation of an Amazonian Rainforest." *Nature*, Vol. 339 (29 June 1989.)

Plotkin, Mark and Lisa Famolare. *Sustainable Harvest and Marketing of Rain Forest Products*. Island Press, 1992.

State of the World's Forests, 1997. FAO, 1997.

FUELWOOD

Firewood Crops: Shrub and Tree Species for Energy Production. National Academy Press, 1983.

Leach, G. and R. Mearns. "Beyond the Woodfuel Crisis." In *The Earthscan Reader in Tropical*

Forestry. Edited by S. Rietbergen. Earthscan, 1993.

Mangium and Other Acacias of the Humid Tropics. National Academy Press, 1983.

HISTORICAL PERSPECTIVE

Darwin, Charles. *The Voyage of the Beagle*. Doubleday & Co., 1879.

Thoreau, Henry David. *Walden and Civil Disobedience*. Harper & Row, 1965.

PLANTATION FORESTRY

Dato, Dr. Abdul Razak Mohd Ali. "Plantations—The Key to Malaysia's Timber Needs." *Asian Timber*, Vol. 16, No. 6 (1997.)

Fu-geng Qui. "*Phyllostachys pubescens* in China." *Journal of the American Bamboo Society*, Vol. 3, No. 3 (August 1982.)

Jordan, C. F. et al, eds. *Taungya: Forest Plantations with Agriculture in Southeast Asia*. CAB International, 1992.

McNabb, Kenneth L. and Lineu H. Wodouski. *Multiple Rotation Yields for Intensively Managed Plantations in the Amazon Basin*. Kluwer Academic Publishers, 1999.

Vietmeyer, Noel. "The Tree that Does Everything." *International Wildlife* (September/October 1983.)

POPULATION

Bilsborrow, R. and D. Hogan, eds. *Population and Deforestation in the Humid Tropics*. Oxford University Press, 1994.

Ending Hunger—An Idea Whose Time Has Come. The Hunger Project. Praeger, 1985.

Ehrlich, Paul R. *The Population Bomb*. Ballantine, 1968.

Fearnside, P. M. "Deforestation in Brazilian Amazônia: The Effect of Population and Land Tenure." *Ambio*, Vol. 22, No. 8 (1993.)

Griffin, Michael. "Madagascar's High Fertility Rate Leads to Chronic Poverty." *Popline* (April 1988.)

Myers, Norman. "Population and Biodiversity." In *Population: The Complex Reality*. Edited

by F. Graham-Smith. The Royal Society, 1994.

———— "Tropical Deforestation: Population, Poverty and Biodiversity." In *The Economics and Ecology and Biodiversity Decline: The Forces Driving Global Change*. Edited by T. M. Swanson. Cambridge University Press, 1995.

Thomas, Lewis. "Are We Fit to Fit In?" *Sierra* (March/April 1982.)

PUBLIC HEALTH

Abisudjak, B. and R. Kotanegara. "Transmigration and Vector-borne Diseases in Indonesia." In *Demography and Vector-borne Diseases*. Edited by M. W. Service. CRC Press, 1989.

Coimbra, C. E. A. "Human Factors in the Epidemiology of Malaria in the Brazilian Amazon." *Human Organization*. Vol. 47 (1988.)

Cook, G. C. ed. *Manson's Tropical Diseases*. W. B. Saunders & Co., 1996.

Forattini, O. P. "Chagas' Disease and Human Behaviour." In *Demography and Vector-borne Disease*. Edited by M. W. Service, CRC Press, 1989.

Gao, F., E. Bailes and B. H. Hahn. "Origin of HIV-1 in the chimpanzee *Pan troglodytes troglodytes*." *Nature*, Vol. 397, No. 6718 (February 4, 1999.)

Garrett, Laurie. *The Coming Plague: Newly Emerging Diseases in a World Out of Balance*. Penguin Books, 1994.

Walsh, J. F., D. H. Molyneux and M. H. Birley. "Deforestation: Effects on Vector-borne Disease." *Parasitology*, Vol. 106 (1993.)

SUSTAINABLE AGRICULTURE

Agroforestry Systems in the Tropics. Edited by P. K. R. Nair. Kluwer Academic Publishers, 1989.

Burby, Liza N. *World Hunger*. Lucent Books, 1995.

Clusener-Godt, M. and I. Sachs. *Brazilian Perspectives on Sustainable Development of the Amazon Region*. UNESCO/Parthenon, 1995.

Cooperatively Managed Panamanian Rural Fish Ponds—The Integrated Approach. Auburn University, 1986.

Current, D., E. Lutz and S. Scherr, eds. *Costs, Benefits, and Farmer Adoption of Agroforestry: Project Experience in Central America and the Caribbean.* World Bank, 1995.

The Development of Commercial Farming of Tilapia in Jamaica, 1979–1983. Auburn University, October 1984.

Fragile Lands of Latin America—Strategies for Sustainable Development. Edited by John O. Browder. Westview Press, 1989.

Newman, Arnold. "On the Road from 'Earth Summit Brazil': Can We Deflect Tropical Deforestation and its Consequences?" In *Sustainable Agriculture Solutions: The Action Report of the Sustainable Agriculture Initiative.* Novello Press Ltd., 1999.

Ngandu, M. S. and S. H. Kolison Jr. "Zaire." In *Sustainable Agriculture and Environment in the Humid Tropics.* Committee on Sustainable Agriculture and Environment in the Humid Tropics. National Academy Press, 1993.

Nicholaides, J. J., with D. E. Bandy, et al. "Agricultural Alternatives for the Amazon Basin." *Bioscience,* Vol. 35, No. 5 (May 1985.)

Padoch, Christine, et al. "Amazonian Agroforestry: A Market-Oriented System in Peru." *Agroforestry Systems* 3: W. Junk Publishers, 1985.

——— and Wil de Jong. "Production and Profit in Agroforestry: An Example from the Peruvian Amazon." In *Fragile Lands of Latin America—Strategies for Sustainable Development.* Edited by John O. Browder. Westview Press, 1989.

Peters, William J. and Neuenschwander, Leon F. *Slash and Burn—Farming in the Third World Forest.* University of Idaho Press, 1988.

"Rwanda National Fish Culture Project." Auburn University (July 1989.)

Soil Erosion and Conservation. Edited by S. A. El-Swaify et al. Soil Conservation Society of America, 1985.

The State of World Fisheries and Aquaculture, 1996. FAO, 1997.

Sustainable Agricultural Systems. Edited by Clive A. Edwards et al. Soil and Water Conservation Society, 1990.

Sustainable Agriculture and the Environment in the Humid Tropics. Committee on Sustainable Agriculture and Environment in the Humid Tropics. National Academy Press, 1993.

Tull, Kenneth and Michael Sands. *Experiences in Success: Case Studies in Growing Enough Food Through Regenerative Agriculture.* Rodale Institute, 1987.

SUSTAINABLE AND UNSUSTAINABLE LOGGING

Benavides, M. and M. Pariona. "The Yanesha Forestry Cooperative and Community-Based Management in the Central Peruvian Forest." In *Case Studies of Community-Based Forestry Enterprises in the Americas, Symposium, Madison, Feb. 3–4, 1995.* University of Wisconsin-Madison, 1995.

Bruenig, E. F. *Conservation and Management of Tropical Rainforests: An Integrated Approach to Sustainability.* CAB International, 1996.

——— "Sustainable Natural Forest Management: Where do We Stand?" *Asian Timber,* Vol. 16, No. 2 (1997.)

Callister, D. J. *Illegal Tropical Timber Trade: Asia-Pacific.* TRAFFIC Oceania, 1992.

Coto, Z. and S. Manan. "Sustainable Forest Management and Eco-Labeling of Forest Products in Indonesia." In *Timber Certification: Implications for Tropical Forest Management.* Edited by J. O'Hara et al. Yale University, 1994.

Dudley, N., J.-P. Jenrenaud and F. Sullivan. *Bad Harvest: The Timber Trade and the Degradation of Global Forests.* Earthscan, 1995.

The Final Cut: Illegal Logging in Indonesia's Orangutan Parks. Environmental Investigation Agency, Telapak Indonesia, 1999.

Goodland, R. et al. "Tropical Moist Forest Management: The Urgent Transition to Sustainability." In *The Price of Forests: Proceedings of a Seminar on the Economics of Sustainable Use of Forest Resources.* Edited by A. Agarwal. Centre for Science and Environment, 1992.

Hartshorn, G. S. "Ecological Basis for Sustainable Development in Tropical Forests." *Annual Review of Ecology and Systematics,* Vol. 26 (1995.)

Heaton, K. *Perspectives on Certification from the Smart Wood Certification Program.* Rainforest Alliance, 1994.

ITTO Guidelines on the Conservation of Biological Diversity in Tropical Production Forests. ITTO, 1993.

Johns, A. G. *Timber Production and Biodiversity Conservation in Tropical Rainforests.* Cambridge University Press, 1997.

Johnson, N. and B. Cabarle. *Surviving the Cut: Natural Forest Management in the Humid Tropics.* WRI, 1993.

Upton, C. and S. Bass. *The Forest Certification Handbook.* Earthscan, 1995.

Wakker, E. "Mitsubishi's Unsustainable Timber Trade: Sarawak." In *Restoration of Tropical Forest Ecosystems; Proceedings of a Symposium, Oct. 7–10, 1991.* Edited by H. Lieth and M. Lohmann, Kluwer, 1993.

Wilkie, D. S. "Logging in the Congo: Implications for Indigenous Foragers and Farmers." In *Tropical Deforestation: The Human Dimension.* Edited by Leslie E. Sponsel et al. Columbia University Press, 1996.

TRADITIONAL CULTURES

Babbitt, B. "Gold Rush Brings Cultural Clash to Amazon Region." *Forum for Applied Research and Public Policy,* Vol. 7, No. 4 (1992.)

Biocca, E. *Yanoáma: The Story of Helens Valero, a Girl Kidnapped by Amazonian Indians.* Kodansha Globe, 1996.

Bodley, J. "Indigenous Peoples and Development." In *The Earthscan Reader in Tropical Forestry.* Edited by S. Rietbergen. Earthscan, 1993.

Centeno, J. C. "Deforestation—Out of Control in Venezuela." *Global Biodiversity,* Vol. 5, No. 4 (1996.)

Cook, C. D. "The Divided Island of New Guinea: People, Development and Deforestation." In *Tropical Deforestation: The Human Dimension.* Edited by Leslie E. Sponsel et al. Columbia University Press, 1996.

Durbin, J. C. and J. A. Ralambo. "The Role of Local People in the Successful Maintenance of Protected Areas in Madagascar." *Environmental Conservation.* Vol. 21, No. 2 (1994.)

Fernandes, W. "Power and Powerlessness: Development Projects and the Displacement of Tribals." *Social Action,* Vol. 41, No. 3 (1991.)

Lamb, Bruce F. *Wizard of the Upper Amazon: The Story of Manuel Cordova-Rios.* Houghton Mifflin Co., 1974.

Monbiot, G. *Mahogany Is Murder: Mahogany Extraction from Indian Reserves in Brazil.* Friends of the Earth, 1992.

Posey, D. A. "Indigenous Knowledge, Biodiversity, and International Rights: Learning about Forests from the Kayapo Indians of the Brazilian Amazon." *Commonwealth Forestry Review,* Vol. 76, No. 1 (1997.)

"Resource and Sanctuary: Indigenous Peoples, Ancestral Rights, and the Forests of the Americas." Edited by D. B. Bray and D. Irvine. *Cultural Survival Quarterly,* Vol. 17, No. 1 (1993.)

Schultes, Richard E. *Vine of the Soul: Medicine Men, Their Plants and Rituals in the Colombian Amazônia.* Synergetic Press, 1992.

Schwartzman, S. "The Panara: Indigenous Territory and Environmental Protection in the Amazon." In *Local Heritage in the Changing Tropics: Innovative Strategies for Natural Resource Management and Control.* Edited by G. Dicum. Yale University, 1995.

Soltani, Atossa and Tracey Osborne. *Arteries for Global Trade, Consequences for Amazônia.* Amazon Watch (April 1997.)

Stewart, Kilton. *Pygmies and Dream Giants.* Harper Colophon Books, 1975.

Tierney, P. *Darkness in El Dorado: How Scientists and Journalists Devastated the Amazon.* W. W. Norton and Co., 2000.

TROPICAL FORESTS— GENERAL

Boza, Mario A. with collaboration of Alexander Bonilla. *The National Parks of Costa Rica.* Instituto de la Caza Fotografica y Ciencias de la Naturaleza (INCAFO), 1978.

Emsley, Michael. *Rain Forests and Cloud Forests.* Harry N. Abrams, 1979.

Forsyth, Adrian and Ken Miyata. *Tropical Nature—Life and Death in the Rain Forests of Central and South America.* Charles Scribner's Sons, 1984.

Jacobs, M. *The Tropical Rain Forest, A First Encounter.* Springer-Verlag, 1988.

Jungles. Edited by Edward S. Ayensu. Crown Publishers, 1980.

Kricher, John C. *A Neotropical Companion: An Introduction to the Animals, Plants and Ecosystems of the New World Tropics.* Princeton University Press, 1989.

Matthiessen, Peter. *The Cloud Forest.* Viking Press, 1961.

McDade, Lucinda, et al, eds. *La Selva: Ecology and Natural History of a Neotropical Rain Forest.* University of Chicago Press, 1994.

Myers, Norman. *The Primary Source.* W. W. Norton & Co., 1992.

—— *Tropical Rainforests.* Routledge, 1992.

Newman, Arnold. *The Lungs of our Planet: The Tropical Rain Forest: Earth's First Endangered Habitat.* MIR Publishers, 1989.

—— *Tropical Rainforest: A World Survey of our Most Valuable and Endangered Habitat with a Blueprint for its Survival.* Facts on File, 1990.

Perry, Donald. "An Arboreal Naturalist Explores the Rain Forest's Mysterious Canopy." *Smithsonian* (June 1980.)

—— *Life Above the Jungle Floor.* Simon and Schuster, Inc., 1986.

Richards, Paul W. *The Life of the Jungle.* McGraw-Hill, 1970.

—— *Tropical Forests and Woodlands: An Overview.* Agro-Ecosystems, 1977.

Sanderson, Ivan T. *Green Silence, The Story of the Making of a Naturalist.* David McKay Co. Inc., 1924.

—— *Ivan Sanderson's Book of Great Jungles.* Julian Messner Pub., 1965.

Skutch, Alexander F. *A Naturalist in Costa Rica.* University of Florida Press, 1971.

—— *A Bird Watcher's Adventures in Tropical America,* University of Texas Press, 1977.

Terborgh, John. *Diversity and the Tropical Rain Forest.* Scientific American Library, 1992.

Whitmore, T. C. *Tropical Rain Forests of the Far East.* Clarendon Press, Oxford University, 1975.

—— *An Introduction to Tropical Rain Forests.* Clarendon Press, 1990.

ZOOLOGY

Buchsbaum, Ralph and Lovus T. Milne. *The Lower Animals: Living Invertebrates of the World.* Doubleday & Co. Inc., 1967.

Caras, Roger A. *Dangerous to Man.* Chilton Books, 1964.

Cochran, Doris M. *Living Amphibians of the World.* Doubleday & Co., 1961.

Crocodiles: An Action Plan for their Conservation. IUCN Publications, 1992.

Crocodiles and Alligators. Edited by Charles A. Ross. Facts on File, 1989.

Denis, Armand. *Cats of the World.* Houghton Mifflin Co., 1964.

Ditmars, Raymond L. *Snakes of the World.* Macmillan & Co., 1952.

Emmons, Louise H. and François Feer. *Neotropical Rainforest Mammals: a Field Guide.* University of Chicago Press, 1990.

Fossey, Dian. "Making Friends with Mountain Gorillas." *National Geographic,* Vol. 137, No. 1 (January 1970.)

—— "More Years with Mountain Gorillas." *National Geographic,* Vol. 140, No. 4 (October 1971.)

Galdikas-Brindamour, Biruté. "Orangutans, Indonesia's 'People of the Forest.'" *National Geographic,* Vol. 148, No. 4 (October 1975.)

—— *Reflections of Eden: My Years with the Orangutans of Borneo.* Little, Brown, 1995.

Gilliard, E. Thomas. *Living Birds of the World.* Doubleday & Co. Inc., 1958.

Goodall, Jane. *The Chimpanzee: The Living Link between 'Man' and 'Beast': The Third Edinburgh Medal Address.* Edinburg University Press, 1992.

—— *Reason for Hope: A Spiritual Journey.* Warner Books, 1999. Sound recording.

Gore, Rick. "A Bad Time to be a Crocodile." *National Geographic,* Vol. 153, No. 1 (January 1978.)

Haltenorth, Theodor and Helmut Diller. *Mammals of Africa Including Madagascar.* Collins, 1980. Reprint 1996.

Hogue, Charles L. *The Armies of the Ant.* World Publishing, 1972.

—— *Latin American Insects and Entomology.* University of California Press, 1993.

Jane Goodall: My Life with the Chimpanzees. Produced by National Geographic Society and Judith Dwan Hallet. Columbia TriStar Home Video, 1995. Video recording.

Klots, Alexander B. and Elsie B. *Living Insects of the World.* Doubleday & Co., 1967.

Kursh, Harry. *Cobras in his Garden.* Harvey House Inc., 1965.

Newman, Arnold C. "An Incident on the Rio Claro." *A Bulletin of the International Palm Society,* 1977.

Poisonous Snakes of the World. Dept. of Navy, Office of the Chief of Naval Operations, Office of Naval Intelligence (June 1962.)

Pope, Clifford H. *The Giant Snakes.* Alfred A. Knopf, 1969.

Primate Conservation: The Journal of the IUCN/Scc Primate Specialist Group No. 18. Edited by Russell A. Mittermeier. 1998.

Pritchard, Peter C. H. *Encyclopedia of Turtles.* T. H. F. Publishers, Inc., 1967.

Sanderson, Ivan T. *Living Mammals of the World.* Doubleday & Co., 1955.

Schaller, George B. *The Mountain Gorilla.* University of Chicago Press, 1976.

—— *The Year of the Gorilla.* University of Chicago Press, 1964.

—— and Peter Gransden Crawshaw Jr. "Movement Patterns of Jaguar." *Biotropica,* Vol. 12, No. 3 (September 1980.)

Schmidt, Karl P. and Robert F. Inger. *Living Reptiles of the World.* Doubleday & Co. Inc., 1957.

Thomas, Lewis. *The Lives of a Cell.* Bantam Books, 1975.

Veit, Peter G. "Gorilla Society." *Natural History* (March 1982.)

Wilson, Edward O. "Clockwork Lives of the Amazonian Leafcutter Army." *Smithsonian* (October 1984.)

Wilson, E. O. and B. Hölldobler. *The Ants.* Harvard University Press, 1990.

INDEX

Note: Page numbers in *italic* refer to illustrations.

Baker, James 128
balata 124
Bali *154–155, 190*
balsa 45–46
bamboo 6, 202, *226*
   culture 173, *174*
   moso 173, 202
   zone *23*
bamboo rats 63
banana 53, *54*, 171
Bangladesh
   electrification projects 105
   flooding *131*, 136
   fuelwood shortage 100
   population and forest area *107*
banteng 120
Bantu *31*, 142
banyon 16
barking deer 65
basilisk lizard 6
bats 6
   and flight 58
   pollination by 47, 49
   vampire 32
Bauhinia species 20, *20*
bean 171, *172*
   winged 121, 149, 176–177
bear 65
beetles *18*, 25–26, 48
beke tree 53
Belize 209
Bell's frog *64*
Benincasa hispida 149, 175–176
Bertholletia excelsa 48, 172
Beston, Henry 28
betel nut palm 66
Bhutan 100
"Big Bang" flowering 16, 52, *52*
bilharziasis (schistosomiasis) 145
biophilia 159
birds 60–61, 71. *See also specific
      birds*
   area necessary to support populations
      of 161
   defensive adaptations 58
   ground 65
   migratory 113, 115
   pollination by 47, *49*
   seed dispersal 20
birds of paradise 58, *60*
biting midge 31–32
blackfly 118, 144
black mamba *31*
black pepper 175
black water rivers 39
Blackwelder, Brent 208, *211*
blindness, river 144, *144*
blood python *30*
blue fairy flycatcher *4–5*

blue-green alga 176
boa 11, 29, *30*
boat-billed heron 65
Boiga dendrophila 30
Bolivia
   cocaine production 86
   conservation 159
   debt 209
   forested acres *13*
   hydroelectric power 104
   indigenous policy 223
   logging *231*
bombardier beetle 25, *25*
Borneo 3, *25*, 38, 119
Bos species 123
   B. banteng 119, 120
botfly, human 144, *144*
Bothrops atrox 30–31
Brachinus species 25, *25*
Brachyplatystoma filamentosum 27
Bradypus tridactylus 18
Branco, Castello 82–83
Brazil
   agriculture 168, 175, 179
   animals *27*
   Atlantic rainforest 21, 52, 54, 94, 95
   cattle ranching 82–83, 87, *91*, *91*, 179
   colonization (resettlement) 83–85
   conservation 166–167, 170, 228
   debt 208–209
   deforestation 88–89, 228
   diseases 141, 142, 143, 144
   food export 92
   forest areas *13*
   Grande Carajás Project 103, 204
   hydroelectric power 104, *104*
   indigenous policy 146–147, 149, 223,
      224
   logging 94, 95, 96, 97, 195, 198,
      227–229
   mining 103
   Nissei Cooperative 175
   plantations 124, *202*
   plants *16*, 124
   population and forest area *106*
   reforestation *199*, *202*, *203*
   Rio Cuieiras *34*
   road-building 83–85, *97*, 98, 141
   wildfires 226
"Brazil in Action" plan *83*, *97*, 98
Brazil nut 48, *167*, 172
breeding pools 160–161, 164
bromeliads 11, 16, 17, 20, *55*
Browne, S. G. 144–145
Brugia malayi 142
Brundtland, Gro Harlem 140
Brundtland Commission 194
Brundtland Report 156
Buceros rhinoceros 60

Bucerotidae 11
bucket orchid *49*
Buddha 74
buffalo 23, 171, 178
Bufo
   B. paracnemis 8
   B. periglenes 112, *160*, 217
bungee jumping *224*
Burkilliodendron album 93
Burmese python *30*
Burroughs, John 38
buruli ulcer *141*, 144–145
bush babies 59
bushmeat *186–187*
butterflies *4–5*, 58, 65, 161, *232*
buttresses 3, 6, *9*, *10*, 38, *39*

C

Cabral, Pedro Alvares 146
Cacicus cela 61
cacique *61*
cactus 16
caiman 27
Calamus species 11, 20
calanolide A 119
Calvin, Melvin 124
Cambodia 138
Cameroon 78, *94*, *107*
Canada *131*
cancer drugs 119
candiru 27, *27*
canes and fibers 111, 121
cannonball tree fruits 171
canopy
   animals of *4–5*, 16, *18*, 59–62
   "Big Bang" flowering 16, 52, *52*
   description 3, 15–17
   epiphytes 16–17
   light absorption/penetration 2–3, 6, *6*
capoten 112
Cappiburro 27, *27*
capybara *14*, *18*
capybara farms *186–187*
carbon 39, *125*, 126–127, *128*
   afforestation and 199–200, *200*
carbon dioxide (CO_2) 127, 221
carbon monoxide 128–129
Cardoso, Fernando 228
CARE 201, 204
Carex species *23*
Caribbean forests 10, *15*, 77, *77*
Carica papaya 171
carnivores, role of 56–57
carnivorous plants 17
carp *181*
carrion flies 49
Carvocar costaricense 17

debt and deforestation 208–209
debt-for-nature swaps 209–210
Decapoda 63
deciduous forest (monsoon forest) 14
decomposition 39
deer
  barking 65
  Pere David's 158
  red brocket *14*
deforestation rates and areas x–xi, *76,*
    76–77, 89, 96
Democratic Republic of the Congo
    (Zaire)
  agriculture *196*
  aquaculture 181, *182*
  forested area 10, *13*
  gorillas *165*
  indigenous policy 224–225
  Ituri Forest Region *13*, 31, *31*
  population and forest area *107*
Dendroaspis
  D. jamesoni 5
  D. polylepis 31
Dendrobates species *19*, *64*
Dendrocalamus giganteus 226
Dendrohyrax species 23, 62
Dermatobia hominis 144
Desmodium ovalifolium 172
Desmodus rotundus 32
Desmoncus 11
Dicksonia species *21*
dieffenbachia 20
Digitalis species 119
Dinia subapicalis 63
Dinoponera species 31
Dioscorea species 66, 119, *119*, 172
Dioscreophyllum cumminsii 120
diosgenin 119
Dioum, Baba 154
diseases
  change in distribution as a result of
      climate change 132–133, *134*
  deforestation and 140–145
  incidence of, in rainforests 33
  resettlement and 147
diversity, biological x, 6–7, 110–116,
    112
Dodd, Kenneth 217
dolphin 63, 164, 166, *166*
Dominican Republic *92*
Dorylinea 31
Dorylus species 31
dracaena 20
driver ant 31
drugs
  from animals 112, 119
  cocaine and heroin production 85–86
  from plants 117–119, 149
drunken forests *218*, 218–219

Dryobalanops aromatica 16
duiker 23
dung, as fuel source 102, *102*
durian *53*
Durio species *53*
Dynastes hercules 18
Dysoxylum angustifolium 67–68

E

eagles *5*, 57
Earthrise *vi*
earthstar *42*
Earth Summit. *See* United Nations
    Conference on the Environment
    and Development (UNCED)
Echinosorex gymnurus 63
ecotourism *214–215*
Ectatomma species *47*
Ecuador
  indigenous policy 223
  montane forest 24
  population and forest area *106*
  poverty 92
  species extinction 93
Ehrlich, Paul and Anne 113, 116
Einstein, Albert 2
Elaeis guineensis 116
Elaphurus davidianus 158
electric eel 27
Electrophorus electricus 27
elephant 23
  African 53, 63, 158, *210*
  Asian 63, 73
elephantiasis *141*, 142
elephant shrew *4–5*
Elephas maximus 73
elfin woodland *22*, 24
El Niño 226
El Salvador *92*
El Yunque Mountain (Puerto Rico) *15*
emerald tree boa *19*, *30*
emergent trees 3, *4–5*
endangered and threatened species
  growing public awareness 217
  international agreements 197
  numbers of 115–116
  preserving (*See* forest preservation)
endemism 112, 160
Ensifera ensifera 49
epená 149
Epidendrum ciliare 58
epiphylls 17
epiphytes 16–17, *54*, *55*, 71
Epipremnum 11
Erannornis longicauda 4–5
Erica arborea 23
erosion

dam construction and 104
  deforestation and 79, 136–138, *138*
  reclamation 189–191
Erwin, Terry 168
Erythrina species *16*, *173*
Erythroxylum coca 86
essential oils 111, 121
Ethiopia 106
Eucalyptus 199, 200, 203, *203*
Eudocimus ruber 65
euglossine bee 48, *49*
Eunectes marinus 27–28
Euterpe oleracea 169, *170*
Eutoxeres aquila 49
evolutionary capacity 11, 227
extinction 113–116. *See also* forest
    preservation
  diversity and 113
  of forest people and culture 146–147,
    149, 152–153
  growing public awareness 217
  and human population growth 105,
    116
  rate of xi, 116
  stemming the tide of 156–159
Extinction (Ehrlich and Ehrlich) 113,
    116

F

FAO (Food and Agriculture
    Organization of the United
    Nations) 77, 91, 93, 200, 204, 221
false gavial 11
Felis
  F. aurata 4–5, 57
  F. pardalis 19, 57
  F. tigrina 63
fer-de-lance 30–31
ferns 16, *21*
fibers 111, 121
Ficus species 7
  F. benghalensis 16
fireflies 25–26
fires 226. *See also* slash-and-burn
    agriculture
fish. *See also* aquaculture
  Amazon 35, 169–170, *183*
  aquarium 171
Flint, Oliver 35
floodplain agriculture (varzeas)
    168–171
floods 136–137
flowers, pollination of 16, 47–52
flying and gliding animals 58–59
flying fox 58
Food and Agriculture Organization of
    the United Nations (FAO) 77, 91,
    93, 200, 204, 221

Credits

Abbreviations are as follows: b=bottom; c=center; t=top; l=left; r=right.

ARTWORK REFERENCE SOURCES

6: Jenik & Rejmanek, unpublished material. 12: Main map after FAO, supplemented from Whitmore, Mori, et al. and other sources; histograms (bl) Trewartha, *An Introduction to Climate*. 13t: FAO and Newman; 13c: FAO and Newman; 13b: after *Times Concise Atlas*. 10–11: After J. D. Phillips, in *Oceanus*, 1973–74. 14: After John Terborgh, *Diversity and the Tropical Rain Forest*, 1992, modified by Newman. 20: After Bodley & Benson, in *Biotropica*, 1980. 22: Newman. 23t: Mitchell Beazley, *Atlas of World Wildlife*; 23b: Flenley 1979. 25: J. A. Miller, *Science News*, 1979. 27: After J. R. Norman, *A History of Fishes*, 1975. 40t: After Diamond et al., *Save the Birds*, 1987; and Colinvaux, *Introduction to Ecology*, 1973; 40b: after *Jungles*, 1980 (ed. E. S. Ayensu), supplemented by Newman. 41t: After Diamond et al.; 41c: after Salah; 41b: after Jackson & Raw, 1973, as reproduced in Carl F. Jordan, *Nutrient Cycling in Tropical Forest Ecosystems*, 1985. 56: Colinvaux, *Introduction to Ecology*, 1973. 68: *Atas. Soc. Biol.* 11, Rio de Janeiro. 72: Composite after W. W. Benson, Schimper, and others. 73: Newman. 76: After World Resources Institute, *The Last Frontier Forests*, 1997. 77: Forest Resources Assessment System (FORIS) and Newman. 79: After *Amazonian Rain Forest: Ecosystem Disturbance and Recovery* (C. F. Jordan, ed.), Springer Verlag, 1987. 81: Outlaw and Engelman, *Forest Futures: Population Action International*, 1999. 86: After *National Geographic Magazine*. 87: Toledo-Serrão, 1982. 88: Woods Hole Oceanographic Institution. 89: Map after Amazon Watch, 1999; graph from Newman. 96: After FAO *State of the World*, 1997. 97t: Newman; 97b: *New York Times*, February 19, 1989. 98: FAO Forestry Paper #128, 1995. 99: Dudley et al., *Bad Harvest*, 1995. 101: FAO. *Forestry for Development*; *Wood for Energy*; and *State of the World's Forests 1997*. 103: FAO, *State of the World 1998*. 104: *World Rivers Review*, Sept./Oct. 1988. 105t: Newman; 105b: after Burby, *World Hunger*, 1995. 106–107: Main chart after Outlaw and Engelman, *Forest Futures: Population Action International*, 1999; bar graph (107br) after *Reporter*, based on data from American Paper Institute, EPA, and ZPG. 110: After *National Geographic*, February 1999. 112: IUCN. 113: IUCN. 116t: Edward O. Wilson, *National Geographic*, February 1999; 116b: National Audubon Society and Global Stewardship Initiative, *Storm, Population and Habitat in the New Millennium*, 1998. 117: After Wagner & Wolff, 1977. 122: *Contributions from the University of Wisconsin Herbarium*, No. 7. 124: World Resources Institute, *World Resources 1998–99*. 125t: R. A. Houghton, in *World Forests for the Future*, 1993; 125b: R. A. Houghton et al., in *Tellus*, April 1999. 127: R. A. Houghton, 1993. 128t: UNEP/WMO, *Common Questions About Climate Change 1996*; 128b Houghton, 1993. 130c: *Newsweek*, July 1988; 130b: after *Time*, Aug. 9, 1999. 131t: *Newsweek*, July 1988; 131cl: graph after NOAA; 131cr: maps *Newsweek*, July 1988; 131b: Bangladesh map after *Woods Hole Notes* 18, 2, Woods Hole Oceanographic Institution, Dec. 1986; Florida map after *Winds: Earth's Endangered Atmosphere*, The Atlanta Journal-Constitution, July 1989; Netherlands map after Jelgersma, S. in *The Impacts of a Future Rise in Sea Level on the European Coastal Lowlands*, Vol. H, European Workshop on Interrelated Bioclimatic and Land Use Changes, Noordwykerhout, Netherlands, October 1987. 132: After Chris Doake, British Antarctic Survey. 134: From *World Resources 1998–99*. 137: FAO. 160: UNESCO, *Man and the Biosphere Program*. 162: After Eisenberg. 163: From *Managing Protected Areas in the Tropics*. 169:

Based on FAO-UNESCO, *Soil Map of South America* 1971. 170: After *Jungles* 1980 (E. S. Ayensu, ed.), modified by Newman. 171: Nicholaides et al., 1983. 172: After Bishop, 1979. 176: After Nair, 1979. 182: From *World Resources 1998–99*. 184–187: See Appendix 3 on page 241. 193t: Newman; 193c: Newman; 193b: FAO, *State of the World's Forests 1997*. 194: C. F. Jordan, *Soils of the Amazon Rainforest*. 200t: From Grainger, *Controlling Tropical Deforestation*, 1993; 200b: FAO, based on dos Santos, *A evolucao de pesquisa florestal na Aracruz Florestal*, unpublished manuscript, 1983. 203: After C. E. Russell, *Nutrient Cycling and Productivity of Native and Plantation Forests at Jari Florestal, Pará, Brazil*. Ph.D. dissertation, 1983. 204: After Grainger, *Controlling Tropical Deforestation*, 1993. 205: FAO, *Wood for Energy*. 206: FAO, *Wood for Energy*. 207: FAO and Newman. 208; FAO, updated by J. P. Lanly, FAO, in pers. comm., 1990. 209: OECD, *Service Development Agenda 2000*. 219: EPA, 1999. 221: FAO, *State of the World's Forests 1997*. 222: FAO, *State of the World's Forests 1997*. 228: INPE, 2000. 230: United Nations, 2000. 231: Newman.

ARTISTS

Amy Botello 14; Facts On File, Inc. 12, 13t, 13c, 76, 77, 81, 89, 96, 97t, 98, 99, 101t, 101br, 103, 105, 106–107, 110, 116, 124, 127, 128, 130, 131cl, 132, 134, 162, 165, 182, 193, 200t, 204, 207, 208, 209, 219, 221, 222, 228, 230, 231; Hardlines 6, 13b, 10–11, 20, 22, 23cl, 23b, 33, 41bl, 56, 79, 83, 86, 87, 88, 97b, 101c, 101bl, 104, 112, 113, 115, 117, 125, 131t, 131cr, 131b, 137, 138, 160, 163, 169, 170, 171, 172, 184–187, 194, 200l, 203, 205, 206; Alan Male/Linden Artists 4–5, 18–19, 25, 27, 29, 40, 41t, 68, 70, 144t; Ministry of Health, Mexico 144c; Joyce Tuhill/Linden Artists 7, 23r, 49, 53, 67, 72, 73, 111, 119, 122, 174, 176, 180.

PHOTOGRAPHERS

African Wildlife Foundation/Mt. Gorilla Project 165cr; Yann Arthus-Bertrand vii; Robert C. Bailey 67; Erwin and Peggy Baver/Bruce Coleman Ltd. 60–61b; Susan Becker 188; R. Bierregaard/WWF 163; Brent Blackwelder 211; James P. Blair/National Geographic Society 92; Bruce Coleman Ltd. 191; Arthur Butler/Oxford Scientific Films 192; Collaart/Frank Spooner Pictures viii; Dr. J. A. L. Cooke/Oxford Scientific Films 177; Steve Curry/Magnum Photos 137; A. J. Deane/Bruce Coleman Ltd. 60bc; Hans D. Dossenbach 17; Mark Edwards 202b; FAO 93, 96, 101, 145, 158, 174, 206; Michael Fogden/Bruce Coleman Ltd. i, 57l; Michael Freeman xii–1, 80b; Peter Frey 91, 104, 202t; Foote, Cone and Belding 154–155; Robin B. Foster 231br; Francis Halle 16b; Garry Hartshorn 203; George Holton/Photo Researchers Inc. 190; Globo/Rio de Janeiro 222; Julian Gonsalves/I.V. Domingo 185; Louise Gubb/J. B. Pictures Ltd. 210; Richard House/The Hutchinson Library 95br; Hugh Hunter, Jr. 214–215; Hugh Iltis 122; John F. Kessel, M.D. 141c; Roxanne Kremer 166t; Frans Lanting/Minden Pictures 74–75, 90; Aldo Brando Leon/Oxford Scientific Films 136; John Lever 28; David Lomax/Robert Harding 86; Luiz Claudio Marigo iv–v, 21, 52, 54b, 55, 57r, 60cl, 61t, 59l, 80t, 94bl, 95t, 95bl, 167, 199; Luiz Claudio Marigo/Bruce Coleman Ltd. 59r; Luiz C. Marigo/Peter Arnold, Inc. 34; Loren McIntyre 16t, 30t, 46, 84, 88t, 130l, 135; Wayne M. Meyers, M.D. 141l; Sean Morris/Oxford Scientific Films 139l; Brian Moser/The Hutchinson Library 86b; Dr. Don Moss 181; Darlyne Murawski/Peter Arnold, Inc. 42l; NASA vi, 88b, 89; NASA/GSFC 78t; Arnold Newman ii, ix, 2, 3, 8–9, 11, 15, 20, 24b, 22, 26, 27, 29, 30c, 30b, 31, 36–37, 38, 39, 41, 42r, 43, 45, 49, 50, 51, 54tl, 54tr, 58, 60tl, 60tr, 63, 64tl, 64tc, 64b, 69, 70, 72, 79, 86c, 94br, 102, 108–109, 114, 117, 118, 119t, 119b, 120, 139r, 144, 146, 147, 148, 149, 150, 151, 152, 153, 157, 159, 160, 161, 165cl, 165b,

CAPTIONS TO PHOTOGRAPHS IN FRONT MATTER

Half-title page (page i)

In a superb example of protective adaptation, this leaf-mimicking katydid from the Ecuadorean forest displays leaf veins, chewed leaf margins, patchy discoloration, and even fungus holes—a cunning camouflage engineered to perfection by the insect's inherited genetic code.

Verso of half-title page and title page (pages ii–iii)

The stunning beauty of an 8-foot (2.4-m)-long inflorescence of the rainforest heliconia (H. stilesii) lights the gloom of the forest in the Osa Peninsula of Costa Rica.

Copyright page and contents page (pages iv–v)

The little-known and highly endangered Atlantic rainforest of southeastern Brazil in dominated here by the imposing grace of giant tree ferns (Dicksonia selldwiana).

page viii

This expansive view over the rainforest canopy in Amazonia shows the dense mass of foliage, which can block as much as 99.6 percent of the Sun's light from reaching the herb layer far below.

page ix

From luxuriant forest to barren Moonscape: the effects of tropical deforestation are devastating, tragic, and permanent. Nothing will ever grow again in this manmade desert in Quintana-Roo, Mexico.